Film and the Holocaust

Film and the Holocaust

New Perspectives on Dramas, Documentaries, and Experimental Films

Aaron Kerner

continuum

2011

The Continuum International Publishing Group
80 Maiden Lane, New York, NY 10038
The Tower Building, 11 York Road, London SE1 7NX

www.continuumbooks.com

Library of Congress Cataloging-in-Publication Data

Kerner, Aaron.
   Film and the Holocaust / by Aaron Kerner.
     p. cm.
   Includes bibliographical references and index.
   ISBN-13: 978-1-4411-2418-0 (pbk. : alk. paper)
   ISBN-10: 1-4411-2418-7 (pbk. : alk. paper)
   ISBN-13: 978-1-4411-7092-7 (hardcover : alk. paper)
   ISBN-10: 1-4411-7092-8 (hardcover : alk. paper)
   1. Holocaust, Jewish (1939–1945),
   in motion pictures. I. Title.

PN1995.9.H53K47 2011
791.43'58405318—dc22   2011003535

ISBN: HB: 978-1-4411-7092-7
      PB: 978-1-4411-2418-0

Typeset by Pindar

Contents

Acknowledgements

There are many people that I would like to acknowledge. This book was made possible with the generous support of a number of institutions — and more specifically the individuals that work in them: Judy Janec, Director of Library and Archives Holocaust Center of Northern California; Tina Minh, at the USC Shoah Foundation Institute; and Edyta Chowaniec, chief audio-visual archivist at the Auschwitz-Birkenau Memorial and Museum.

There are a couple of filmmakers that have been quite generous with me sharing their work, and providing me with supporting material. Elida Schogt generously (and very promptly) supplied me with reviews of her trilogy of films — *Silent Song* (2001), *The Walnut Tree* (2000), and *Zyklon Portrait* (1999). Abraham Ravett — who made *Everything's For You* (1989), and *The March* (1999) — was also very generous. Nina Koocher kindly provided me with a DVD of her 2007 film *How Much to Remember: One Family's Conversation with History*.

Likewise, some of my fellow researchers have been quite generous as well. I would like to especially thank Joshua Hirsch.

I would also like to thank Griselda Pollock and Max Silverman for inviting me to their seminar series, "Concentrationary Imaginaries: The Politics of Representation," at the University of Leeds. This presentation was instrumental in developing the ideas found in exploitation and horror chapters in this book. Griselda, you continue to be an inspiration to me, and I only hope to be as productive and engaged as you are. I would also like to thank Francesco Ventrella for organizing my trip, and even helping to spring me from detention, after being detained by British Customs Agents at Gatwick.

A number of my colleagues have also been instrumental in shaping the book — Julian Hoxter, Randy Rutsky, Tarek Elhaik, and Bill Nichols. Julian was especially helpful in bouncing ideas off of.

I am *deeply* indebted to Chi-Hui Yang who read an early version of the book and helped to shape it.

To my family: I thank you for your patience. Ariel, Daddy can come out to play now. "And now, let the wild rumpus start!"

Chapter One

Introduction

INTRODUCTION

As a broad survey of Holocaust films this book aims to introduce readers not only to the established canon but also to films that do not share the notoriety that Charles Chaplin's 1940 comedy *The Great Dictator* or Steven Spielberg's 1993 film *Schindler's List* enjoy. Whether it is more obscure experimental works or foreign films that never entered wide circulation in the English-speaking world, this book is not an end point, but rather an entry into a broader investigation of Holocaust films. In addition to the films themselves, the book also aims to introduce the reader to some of the scholarship and critical literature that engages with the complexities of representing the Holocaust.

The Holocaust is *not* subject to question here; rather what is subject to question is *how* to represent it, or even more accurately *how* it has been represented. The point is not to police representations of the Holocaust, nor is it to function as a perspective guide on how a Holocaust film *should be made*, but instead to document the strategies that filmmakers utilize when representing it. What rhetorical strategies are available to artists and filmmakers? In surveying different rhetorical strategies we will discover that with each approach a different set of theoretical or ethical concerns is evoked. The knee-jerk assumption that the Holocaust should be represented "as it really was," maintains a strong hold on the popular imagination, and implicitly informs a lot of the critical literature, but the present book takes issue with this problematic assumption. With a circumscribed representational strategy we have perhaps unnecessarily hamstrung filmmakers, as Terrence Des Pres suggests: "We guard the future by bondage to the past. This seems a noble posture, reassuring, but perhaps also debilitating."[1]

Regardless of how fastidious, or not, a film might be, the popular imagination weighs heavily on the tradition of representing the Holocaust, and it's the conservative doctrine of verisimilitude that rules the day. Quite critical of the conventional wisdom surrounding Holocaust representations, Des Pres observes

[handwritten margin note: not-prescriptive entry point but DESCRIPTIVE]

that there are three basic commandments that govern its representations:

1. The Holocaust shall be represented, in its totality, as a unique event, as a special case and kingdom of its own, above or below or apart from history.
2. Representations of the Holocaust shall be as accurate and faithful as possible to the facts and conditions of the event, without change or manipulation for any reason — artistic reasons included.
3. The Holocaust shall be approached as a solemn or even a sacred event, with a seriousness admitting no response that might obscure its enormity or dishonor its dead.[2]

While rarely stated in such explicitly codified terms, these tenets breed what Millicent Marcus has dubbed, "Holocaust fundamentalism."[3] Imre Kertész, a Hungarian Jew and Holocaust survivor, concurs, "A Holocaust conformism has arisen, along with a Holocaust sentimentalism, a Holocaust canon, and a system of Holocaust taboos together with the ceremonial discourse that goes with it; Holocaust products for Holocaust consumers have been developed."[4] These general governing principles have shaped the critical body of Holocaust film research, defining the standard cadre of films that consistently attract the attention of scholars, while quickly dismissing, or omitting altogether, films that are brazenly crass, or do not conform to the principles of verisimilitude. How then might we profit from other narrative strategies? What alternatives are there to the realist imperative? And rather than simply wag an indignant finger at the more dubious representations of the Holocaust, what might we learn from the more exploitative strategies? This is one feature that sets the present book apart from many of the other books on the subject; there is no intention to "recoup" films that are frankly offensive; however, it is critical to understand *how* the Holocaust is represented, even when the narrative strategies are dubious.

WHAT IS A HOLOCAUST FILM?

The term "Holocaust" originates from Greek, meaning "A sacrifice wholly consumed by fire; a whole burnt offering."[5] The first known use of the term in association with the destruction of European Jewry appears in 1942. The theological connotations of the term are troubling for some, not to mention that the genocidal act can be summed up (and perhaps even conjured away) in a single term. "Calling the Holocaust a burnt offering is a sacrilege, a profanation of God and man," Bruno Bettleheim argues.

> To call these most wretched victims of a murderous delusion, of destructive drives run rampant, martyrs or a burnt offering is a distortion invented for our comfort, small as it may be . . . it robs them of the last recognition which could be theirs, denies them the last dignity we could accord them: to face and accept what their death was all about, not embellishing it for the small psychological relief this may give us.[6]

Indeed, naming it, and in turn by implicitly situating victims as sacrificial offerings, might be all too easy (for us). Because of the problematic nature of the term some prefer the Hebrew "Shoah," but this term too has similar connotations.

Claude Lanzmann, director of one of the single most important documentaries made about the Holocaust, *Shoah* (1985), struggled for years to come up with a title for his nine-and-a-half-hour film. Deeply troubled by the connotations of the word "Holocaust," he sought to avoid it. Effectively at the last minute, he decided to title his film *Shoah*, as he recounts, "The word *shoah* imposed itself on me at the end since, not knowing Hebrew, I did not understand its meaning, which was another way of not naming it." . . . 'Shoah' was a signifier without a signified, a brief, opaque utterance, an impenetrable word, as unsmashable as an atomic nucleus."[7]

Nevertheless, despite these reservations, in the English-speaking world, and certainly in other parts of the world, "the Holocaust" has come to signify the systematic destruction of European Jewry at the hands of the Nazi regime. Although well-established, especially in the wake of the publicity of the Adolf Eichmann trial held between April 11 and December 15, 1961, the 1978 NBC miniseries *Holocaust*, directed by Marvin Chomsky, helped to further solidify the term's common usage in Europe and North America. (The NBC miniseries and its impact are discussed in the following chapter.)

While I recognize that the Holocaust, that is to say the historical event, is specific to a particular time and place, and is a uniquely Jewish event, for the purposes of the present book a "Holocaust film" encompasses a broader spectrum.[8] Additionally, within the scope of systematic extermination other "undesirables" were targeted for liquidation as well, including gypsies, homosexuals, and Jehovah's Witnesses. A "Holocaust film" *is not* the event; it is a re-presentation of the event, and fidelity as such is always already a problematic enterprise. Furthermore, understanding that Nazism, or fascism more generally, and the Holocaust are in fact two separate subjects, I nevertheless find it next to impossible to pry one from the other. How can one speak of the horrors of the Holocaust without in some way positioning it in a social, political, economic, and cultural operation that made the industrialization of murder possible? In fact most surveys of "Holocaust films" — whether it's Annette Insdorf's *Indelible Shadows*, or Ilan Avisar's *Screening the Holocaust* — reveal that scholars have consistently looked beyond the specificity of the historical event when writing about Holocaust films. For example, Luchino Visconti's 1969 *The Damned* has more to do with the rise of fascism than it does with the Holocaust, or for that matter, a film like Steven Spielberg's 1993 dramatic narrative *Schindler's List*, which now stands for better or for worse as something of a gold-standard for mainstream (Hollywood) narrative Holocaust films, is more about Oskar Schindler, a Gentile, than it is about the Jews that he saved.

Appreciating the difference between the historical event, and the subsequent representations that derive from it, a "Holocaust film" exhibits a number of different characteristics. Representations of Jews might materialize explicitly, implicitly, or even be altogether omitted from a Holocaust film. Alain Resnais's 1955 landmark documentary *Night and Fog*, for example, does not focus on Jewish victims; instead it takes a more universal approach, and in fact only references Jewish victims once, along with images of deportees wearing the Star of David.[9] Resnais has certainly been taken to task for universalizing suffering, effacing the differences between Holocaust victims, but the point here is not to register moral fidelity — as if it is necessary to tally points for representing Jewish suffering — rather the point remains to gauge the filmmaker's rhetorical strategy. Within the confines of this book a Holocaust film, then, by precedent and by definition need not exclusively focus on Jewish suffering.

One of the major thematic tropes of a Holocaust film is the representation of victims and perpetrators. While Holocaust victims, and especially Jewish victims, have traditionally been feminized, the perpetrator — like the monster in slasher films — is frequently attributed with almost superhuman strength (or god-like powers). Recent trends in narrative film have broken with the more diminutive Jewish character — Edward Zwick's 2008 film *Defiance*, or Quentin Tarantino's 2009 film *Inglourious Basterds* are examples of this — nevertheless the Jew-as-feminized-victim is one of the most common tropes in Holocaust films.

Operating in a system of institutionalized cruelty, perpetrators are given to a sadistic pretension; and this general constellation of characters favors Manichaeist plots. A number of filmmakers utilize sadism as a character trope, but it materializes in many different ways. Sometimes simply manifesting as naked cruelty, and in the colloquial sense of the term characters seemingly derive pleasure from the pain and humiliation of others, such as those depictions found in exploitation cinema. There are, however, more cerebral forms of sadism that draw on its more clinical manifestation — a radical application of reason ungoverned by ethics — which is precisely what is found in Pier Paolo Pasolini's 1975 film *Salò, or the 120 Days of Sodom*. There are still other examples of sadism, those films that willfully conflate sex and violence — Liliana Cavani's 1974 film, *The Night Porter*, for example.

Content is of course important, but it should not come at the expense of neglecting form. The form that a Holocaust film takes dramatically shapes the perception of content. The historicist Hayden White reminds us that form inherently alters content; the discourse of history itself is a "manipulation" of content insofar as events are transfigured into the written form. His work challenges our preconceived notions about historicism, and "narrativizing" a historical event like the Holocaust. White observes that we all too quickly surrender to conventional thinking about representing historical events, "that a serious theme — such as mass murder or genocide — demands a noble genre — such as epic or tragedy — for its proper representation."[10] It is no accident given Western culture's predilection for these "noble genres" when depicting historical events of such magnitude that films made outside the parameters of conventional dramatic cinema, or documentary, are met with deep suspicion.

BOUNDARIES: ETHICS AND PROHIBITIONS

No sooner had Roberto Benigni's 1997 comedy *Life Is Beautiful* been released than were heard the shrill cries from some critics screaming blasphemy.[11] On the grounds that it crossed some ethical boundary by daring to represent the Holocaust in the form of a fanciful comedy, its lack of historical fidelity, and despite (or perhaps because of) the critical accolades bestowed upon the film and its filmmaker, a number of critics lined up to vociferously decry the film. Never mind the fact that by its very definition comedy is exaggeration (read: distortion), and that the film is framed as a fanciful recollection of a childhood memory, critics like David Denby nevertheless felt compelled to rail against it. Reflecting on *Life Is Beautiful*, Hilene Flanzbaum observes that, "It has become too easy a response, and a form of intellectual chic, to look disdainfully at popular representations of the Holocaust." Flanzbaum continues, "Let's all agree right now that no artistic representation of the Holocaust will ever sufficiently depict the horrors of that event — and move on to more explicit and meaningful discussion."[12] Despite the fact that it is abundantly obvious that a *re*-presentation of the Holocaust comes after the fact, and is always already an imperfect narrative construct, some stubbornly still demand that representations adhere to the principles of verisimilitude.

The stringent parameters of "permissible" representational form continue to evolve. There appears to have been, for example, comparatively little criticism of the Jewish Nazi hunters in Quentin Tarantino's 2009 revenge fantasy *Inglourious Basterds*. That's not to say that the film received praise from every corner, again Denby's *New Yorker* review finds Tarantino's film morally suspect. The ethics of representational boundaries and prohibitions have been shaped over time by figures like Holocaust survivors Bruno Bettelheim and Elie Wiesel.[13] The general anxiety about representations of the Holocaust resonates in Theodor Adorno's often-cited proclamation that, "To write poetry after Auschwitz is barbaric."[14] And despite the fact that later he would revise his position, in fact reversing his position altogether, saying that suffering "has as much right to expression as a tortured man has to scream; hence it may have been wrong to say that after Auschwitz you could no longer write poems,"[15] the conservative opposition to poetic strategies, and by extension all artistic representation of the Holocaust, weighs heavily on popular and critical assumptions leading to the insistent demand that the Holocaust be represented, "as it really was." In addition to Adorno's reversal there is also some irony in the fact that Adorno himself, along with his colleague Max Horkheimer, co-authored *Dialectic of Enlightenment*, which includes a discussion of the Marquis de Sade's *Justine*, which they read as a prophetic allegory of modern totalitarianism (discussed in Chapter 6, "Sadism and Sexual Deviance," and Chapter 9, "Body Genres III: The Horror Genre and the Holocaust"). So even while Adorno articulates the conservative perspective regarding representational boundaries for the Holocaust — condemning the use of the poetic form — at the same time, he "makes sense" of the Holocaust in the literary arts, through the poetic, the allegorical form.

The resistance to artistic treatments of the Holocaust, including approaching the Holocaust through the allegorical mode, is the result of a complex confluence of multiple historical trajectories, including the cultural and historical time in which the Holocaust is set, and the historical attitudes about narrative forms. By contrast a comparative study of the Japanese response to atomic attacks against Hiroshima and Nagasaki reveals a plethora of allegorical and poetic accounts, owing of course to the fact that the Japanese were not subject to the same historical prejudices.[16] Appreciating the history of narrative forms is important in contextualizing the motivation for the realist imperative when representing the Holocaust.

Whether we are discussing a documentary, or narrative feature films, these representational forms are always already constructs; there is no clear window onto the past, historical events are rather shaped and grafted onto the scaffolding of respective narrative forms. There are built-in limits to what any one narrative form has the capacity to communicate. While a fictional feature film might be constrained by the general principles of verisimilitude, and have a limited capacity to represent what we might designate as the "unspeakable" horror of the Holocaust, experimental cinema might be better suited to representing the "unrepresentable." Elida Schogt's 1999 experimental film *Zyklon Portrait*, which is discussed in Chapter 14, does not represent any specific event; rather, its abstract form evokes feelings of the abject — the unrepresentable suffering of Holocaust victims. "That the unspeakable is an inevitable product, or aspect, of language is axiomatic," Naomi Mandel observes.

> As language is a human enterprise, the inhuman — in the form of radical evil, infinite good, absolute beauty, or the utter alterity of the divine — poses a specific challenge to the potential of human conceptualization and hence to language. When we say that what the Nazis did to the Jews is unspeakable, we are implicitly identifying this action as "inhuman" and hence as inaccessible to human understanding, external to the speech communities that form human cultures.[17]

But, as Mandel posits, there is something amiss here, because as much as we prefer to imagine otherwise, the Nazis' genocidal program was all too human. Placing the Holocaust outside language, what Mandel terms "the rhetoric of the unspeakable," makes it easier for us, and facilitates an effacement of complicity under the ethical pretense "of refusing to further wrong the victims by misrepresenting their suffering through necessarily reductive conceptual and interpretive frameworks." Mandel continues, "This 'ethical position' reflects a certain self-congratulatory morality by which, under the guise of not wronging the victims, contemporary culture maintains its position as safely distant, conceptually and ethically, from this 'unspeakable' event."[18] And it's precisely for these reasons that I prefer to speak about the Holocaust (and its representations) in the present tense, rather than consigning it to the safety of the distant past.

Limiting representations of the Holocaust to specific narrative forms (e.g., tragedy, documentary), and to specific content, might well be detrimental to the larger moral implications of the historical event. Naomi Mandel concurs, warning against the localization of the Holocaust, and specifically limiting it within the frame of "Auschwitz," which she argues gives

> the horror a specific location and a name, the horror is localized, abstracted, and isolated, as if the Holocaust is (merely) what occurred at the camps. But the fact remains that family members, friends, neighbors, coworkers, students, teachers, employers, employees, religious leaders, municipal and government officials, real and imagined allies were all potential betrayers or murderers, and it is this dissolution of an entire network of human relations, not just the killing, that constitutes the Holocaust.[19]

By limiting the Holocaust to a specific location fixes it in time and space, and places a buffer in between us and an event that necessarily demanded a network of ordinary functionaries to make it possible.

Holocaust films evoke many strategies to erect buffers between the historical event and the spectator. Documentaries generally posit the subject of the Holocaust as an object of study, mediated through the discursive practice of the clinical gaze — containing the horror of the Holocaust by representing it as a survey of "objective" historical facts, or approaching Holocaust sites as an archeological enterprise. Narrative films, whether comedies, serious docudramas, or exploitation films, typically shield the spectator from any sense of responsibility by aligning identification with the victim of Nazi persecution, in narratives that neatly and clearly divide the diegetic world into blocs of "good" and "evil."

There are of course other considerations to take into account when assessing representations of the Holocaust, namely, the ethical boundaries of what is right and wrong, what is offensive and what is respectful. The actual ethical threshold is undoubtedly subjective, and to a degree relative to context. The parade of naked Holocaust victims in archival footage in a documentary is not necessarily read as offensive — insofar as it is representing a historical fact — while on the other hand Steven Spielberg's gas chamber/shower scene in his 1993 film *Schindler's List* has been roundly criticized for the fetishistic and sadistic portrayal of the naked (female) victim. There is legitimate concern here about preserving the dignity of Holocaust victims, but it would be a mistake to too quickly dismiss a film on the basis that it is offensive. The Holocaust itself is offensive, it is profoundly disturbing, and challenges our basic belief in humanity. As Günter Grass says regarding Auschwitz, "Finally we know ourselves."[20]

Alvin Rosenfeld insists that, "All such efforts at 'adapting' the Holocaust are bound to fail — artistically, for reasons of conceptual distortion, and morally, for misusing the suffering of others."[21] Indeed there is something profoundly disturbing about profiting from the suffering of Holocaust victims, but there is little point in assigning "ownership" to the Holocaust. Like other commentators Rosenfeld not only demands that Holocaust films (and literature) conform to the principle of verisimilitude, but also questions who can legitimately represent it. "There is something shockingly ambiguous about the jealous way in which survivors insist on their exclusive rights to the Holocaust as intellectual property," Imre Kertész notes, "as though they'd come into possession of some great and unique secret; as though they were protecting some unheard-of treasure from decay and (especially) from willful damage. Only *they* are able to guard it from decay, through the strength of their memory."[22] As Kertész suggests, making the Holocaust exclusive property is not only dubious but also short-sighted if the intention is to preserve a *vital* memory. Critics and scholars routinely police the boundaries of acceptable representations, and Hilene Flanzbaum concurs, saying that because, "they feel a moral compulsion to preserve the memory of the geno-cide in its most authentic form, many critics position themselves as 'caretakers,' observing an etiquette that, in this writer's view, is based on conventions that have outlived their usefulness."[23]

THE STRUCTURE OF THE BOOK

This book is a general survey of Holocaust films; I make no claim, however, that it is exhaustive. The subject is vast, one might even say boundless, and the films that represent the Holocaust — whether explicitly, implicitly, or in some cursory fashion — continue to expand. While paying deference to the established canon of Holocaust films, this book includes studies of films that have routinely been overlooked, specifically, Naziploitation films, horror films that utilize the Holocaust as a backdrop, and experimental films. The book is roughly divided in half: the first half of the book focuses on narrative films, while the latter half surveys non-narrative (i.e., documentary and experimental) films. The nar-rative film chapters are partitioned according to genres (e.g., comedy, horror, melodrama), or thematic tropes (e.g., sadism, resistance and defiance). The respective non-narrative film chapters, on the other hand, are divided generally along the lines of form — for instance, the poetic documentary, the expository documentary, or experimental films that utilize found footage. The introduc-tion to each chapter to one degree or another outlines some of the theoretical concerns, and/or the ethical challenges of representing the Holocaust detailed in the chapter's subject.

The realist imperative is the subject of the following chapter. Whether we are addressing documentaries or narrative fiction film there is an insurmountable fissure between the assembled material that manifests on-screen and the event itself. The point is not to open the Pandora's box of relativism, or to retreat into what Mandel terms "the rhetoric of the unspeakable," but rather to interrogate the narrative forms that are purportedly more "realistic." Drawing from Roland Barthes's conception of the "reality effect," the following chapter illustrates how films organize material to appear to represent reality, but instead only signify it. For example, Wanda Jakubowska's 1947 narrative film *The Last Stage* (also sometimes given as *The Last Stop*), filmed at Auschwitz shortly after the war, and made by a Holocaust survivor, trades heavily in the principles of verisimilitude, but is a *re*-presentation all the same. The second chapter also discusses at length Alfréd Radok's 1950 film *Distant Journey* (sometimes translated as *The Long Journey*), which freely mixes fact and fiction. The startling juxtaposition of forms and content invites the spectator to create associative links between the "real" footage and the fictional diegesis, and in so doing unsettles the illusion verisimilitude. Beyond the scope of the second chapter, interrogating the principles of verisimilitude is an implicit theme that runs throughout the book.

The third chapter focuses on conventional narrative strategies. The intention of the chapter is not to crown the most significant Holocaust narrative feature film but rather to survey some of the rhetorical strategies and motifs that are found in narrative films. For many narrative films the subject is not so much the Holocaust per se, but instead it serves as the site of dramatic conflict, where the Holocaust is a mere narrative excuse to witness a character's transformation. Whether it's Oskar Schindler in Steven Spielberg's 1993 film *Schindler's List*, Michael Berg in Stephen Daldry's 2008 film *The Reader*, or Stingo in Alan J. Pakula's 1982 film *Sophie's Choice*, the Holocaust is the impetus for the transformation of — specifically in the examples listed here — male characters that also happen to be Gentiles. While male protagonists undergo a positive transformation, the eroticization of the (Jewish female) Holocaust victim plays on our voyeuristic fantasies, and is on occasion amplified with the trope of the peephole, transforming the Holocaust into a spectacle. The figure of the Nazi, who reigns over the ghoulish spectacle, is commonly depicted as monstrous, an agent of absolute evil, who threatens to corrupt humanity, and this is precisely what Bryan Singer's 1998 film *Apt Pupil* depicts, which I discuss at length at the conclusion of the chapter.

Working against the trope, Jew-as-victim, the fourth chapter surveys films that dramatize acts of resistance or defiance, which manifests in multiple ways. A number of Eastern European films, in particular, represent the heroism of resistance fighters. More recently, American productions have portrayed Jewish resistance fighters, including Tim Blake Nelson's 2001 film *The Grey Zone*, and Edward Zwick's 2008 film *Defiance*. In addition to physical forms of resistance, there are a number of films that represent political defiance — Frank Beyer's 1963 film *Naked Among Wolves* for example — or still yet other forms of transcendental defiance, including Roman Polanski's 2002 film *The Pianist*, and the work of Zbynek Brynych specifically *Transport From Paradise* (1962). From William A. Graham's 1996 *The Man Who Captured Eichmann*, to Quentin Tarantino's 2009 film *Inglourious Basterds* the Nazi hunter film is also a fairly common trope of resistance and defiance films.

The fifth chapter, "Holocaust Comedies?", surveys films that take the Holocaust as a laughing matter. Without question there are serious ethical implications to consider when treating the Holocaust in the comedic genre. Not least of the concerns is that the comedic form inherently exaggerates, which poses problems for those critics and scholars that insist upon verisimilitude. Even prior to America's involvement in the war, comedic films like Charles Chaplin's 1940 comedy *The*

Great Dictator mobilized as a defense, or employed laughter as an aggressive act of ridicule, against the Nazi regime. Disney cartoons often adapted Chaplinesque routines to satirize the regime as well. In the late 1990s three Holocaust comedies were released — Roberto Benigni's 1997 film *Life Is Beautiful*, Radu Mihaileanu's 1998 comedic fantasy *Train of Life*, and Peter Kassovitz's 1999 remake of Frank Beyer's 1975 *Jakob the Liar* — all premised on perpetuating fantasies, or lies, within the narrative diegesis to protect a character, or community of characters, from the harsh realities of the Holocaust.

The casting of Nazis as sadists is a common trope of Holocaust films, and is the subject of the sixth chapter. There is, however, a number of different ways in which the trope has been utilized — in some cases quite tawdry and in others with a more nuanced appreciation, recognizing the philosophical tradition from which it originates. In its more tawdry guise, a colloquial form of sadism is equated with fascism (or Nazism more specifically), and is a manifestation of a character's "sickness," which all too conveniently "explains" the Holocaust away as the product of a deranged mind. Luchino Visconti's 1969 film *The Damned* is an example of this. The most sophisticated representation of sadism is Pier Paolo Pasolini's 1975 film, *Salò, or the 120 Days of Sodom*, which is an adaptation of the Marquis De Sade's novel, set in fascist Italy. Pasolini was very familiar with the philosophical basis for sadism and presents sadism in its clinical form — the strict application of reason, unchecked by ethics. While the film is just about the most fastidious narrative Holocaust film ever made, it is nevertheless graphic, and one of the most difficult films to sit through.

Chapters 7, 8 and 9 are framed according to the principles of the body genres, as outlined by film theorist Linda Williams. Pornography, horror, and melodrama represent the body genres. Each of these genres elicits a physiological response in the spectator: with melodrama spectators are brought to tears; the horror genre startles us, making us jump from our seats, gasp, cringe, or avert our eyes at the sight of gore; and the objective of pornography is the sexual arousal of the viewer. Chapter 7 surveys Holocaust melodramas, which rely on a couple of common tropes: tortured and torturing mothers, the fracture of the familial unit, and characters that are too late. As for this last trait, we might think of Sarah Jane in Douglas Sirk's 1959 melodrama *Imitation of Life* when she arrives *after* her mother dies; sprawled across her mother's casket Sarah Jane cries, "Mama! Mama!" It is in that instant, the moment of being *too late*, where the spectator is overwhelmed with emotions and is typically brought to tears. Alan J. Pakula's 1982 film *Sophie's Choice* exhibits all the key characteristics of the melodramatic genre, and is among the films discussed in the chapter.

Exploitation films, and specifically Naziploitation films, tend to mix graphic violence and sexuality; while the gore present in these films intends to "gross out" a spectator, the sexualized spectacle of tortured female bodies endeavors to titillate. The eighth chapter surveys Naziploitation films — most notably Don Edmonds's 1975 film *Ilsa: She-Wolf of the SS* — and posits that these films potentially reveal a certain "truth" in Holocaust films: that the spectacle of violence innate to the subject satisfies a morbid curiosity with death. There are also examples of unadulterated pornographic films that exploit the Holocaust as a narrative backdrop. Here, typically camp internees are either subject to the all-powerful male Nazi officer who rules the camp with impunity and has an insatiable sexual appetite, or a male officer that is impotent and commands internees to perform sexual acts. Bill Nichols observes that while eroticized cinema satisfies the spectator's desire to see, the documentary tends to satisfy the spectator's desire to know.[24] Usually shrouded behind the respectable guise of conveying historical information, exploitation cinema and pornography make the erotics of epistephilia in conventional narrative and documentary films manifest.

There are relatively few Holocaust films that are figured within the horror genre. However, recently there have been a few films where the Holocaust has materialized explicitly and implicitly. For example, David S. Goyer's 2009 film *The Unborn* makes explicit reference to the Holocaust, and the figure of Doctor Josef Mengele. Eli Roth's *Hostel* (2005), and *Hostel: Part II* (2007), on the other hand, makes implicit references to the Holocaust in the *mise en scène*, and the general trope of clinical sadism. Roth's films in particular are set within the sub-genre of torture porn (as dubbed by film critic David Edelstein), and can be placed in a genealogy of Holocaust-related films, including Roberto Rossellini's 1945 film *Rome, Open City*, and John Schlesinger's 1976 film *Marathon Man*.

The subsequent four chapters, Chapters 10 through 13, feature a survey of documentary films. These chapters are divided according to documentary modes as established by Bill Nichols: the expository, observational, interactive, and poetic modes. Holocaust documentaries that employ the expository mode are the subject of the tenth chapter; the expository conveys information, or posits an argument, and directly addresses the spectator through titles, and/or voiceover. The governing rhetorical principle of the expository mode is persuasion, and the editing strategy favors "rhetorical continuity more than spatial or temporal continuity."[25] Laurence Jarvik's 1982 documentary *Who Shall Live and Who Shall Die?*, the six-episode 2005 KCET/BBC series *Auschwitz: Inside the Nazi State*, Malcolm Clarke and Stuart Sender's 2002 documentary *Prisoner of Paradise*, and the 1985 *Memory of the Camps*, created under the supervision of British media magnate Sidney Bernstein, are among some of the films discussed in the chapter.

Documentaries perpetuate the problematic assumption that they somehow offer a transparent window onto the past by adopting modes that veil their construction, fostering the illusion that narratives "tell themselves," as if they emerge organically from the screen. And when documentaries incorporate witnesses into their narrative — manifesting in the form of testimony — the presumption is that the documentary provides the spectator with unassailable admittance to what "really happened." Testimony is a significant feature of the Holocaust documentary, typically appearing in documentaries that adopt the interactive mode, and is the subject of the eleventh chapter. In the canon of Holocaust films *Shoah* is the most significant, Claude Lanzmann's nine-and-a-half-hour 1985 documentary, which is constructed almost entirely from testimonial accounts, and is discussed at length in this chapter. In addition, the eleventh chapter discusses the practice of archiving and using video databanks — like the Shoah Foundation — that have amassed tens of thousands of hours of Holocaust testimonies.

Personal Holocaust documentaries — the subject of the twelfth chapter — are usually about discovery of one kind or another, and tend to use the observational mode. Implementing strategies that we commonly characterize as direct cinema, or cinéma vérité, an observational documentary unobtrusively records an individual, or a group, as they embark on a voyage of discovery — a survivor might return to the concentration camp where they were incarcerated, the child of a survivor might retrace their parent's Holocaust experience. By their very nature, because they are usually recording events as they happen, observational documentaries are usually situated in the present tense, which sets them apart from conventional documentaries that employ the expository mode that as a general rule addresses its subject in the past tense. While discoveries in an observational documentary might pertain to matters of history, and thus inherently in the past, the revelation is always made in the present. The cinéma vérité strategy that characterizes the observational mode potentially invites a voyeuristic gaze, as we are allowed to surreptitiously peer into a private world. Peter Morley's 1979 film *Kitty: Return to Auschwitz*, Steve Brand's 1984 film *Kaddish*, Manfred Kirchheimer's 1986 film *We Were So Beloved*, and Irene Lilienheim Angelico and Abby Jack Neidik's 1985 film *Dark Lullabies* are among some of the films discussed in this chapter.

Poetic documentaries are works that exhibit poetic elements emphasizing the aesthetics of the film, be it in the form of rhythm, tone, composition or any combination of these. The thirteenth chapter features a survey of documentaries that employ the poetic mode. In these films there is frequently a predisposition for visual analogies or metaphoric imagery, and rhetorical cohesion potentially gives way to radical juxtapositions, or (sometimes quite loose) associative imagery, ideas, or themes. Errol Morris masterfully constructs visual analogies and metaphors in his cutaways; this is beautifully displayed in his 1999 documentary *Mr. Death: The Rise and Fall of Fred A. Leuchter, Jr.* Alongside Lanzmann's *Shoah*, Alain Resnais's 1955 *Night and Fog* is also a significant documentary and exhibits poetic elements in its commentary and the cinematography which is so indicative of Resnais's work.

The last two chapters focus on experimental films that in some fashion negotiate the Holocaust. Chapter 14 discusses the ways in which memory is encoded in experimental films. The succeeding chapter features films that utilize found footage, or are associated with the practice of assemblage; these films do not constitute a style as such, but rather are grouped together according to a technique, where filmmakers collect and edit together material to fashion something entirely new. Experimental film, or avant-garde cinema as we sometimes refer to it, is generally concerned with what narrative and documentary film disavow. Inherent to the tradition of experimental filmmaking, these films press up against the boundaries of representation, and potentially forfeit narrative in favor of aesthetic and formal pursuits. The subject of experimental films tends to be that which resists conforming to the conventions of linear narrative practices (including documentary). In some cases, experimental filmmakers attempt to render what we commonly refer to as "unrepresentable," in others, experimental filmmakers might avail themselves of the form in order to represent something profoundly personal. Abraham Ravett's films *The March* (1999) and *Everything's For You* (1989) negotiate the fragility of memory itself. *Silence*, an animated documentary by Orly Yadin and Sylvie Bringas (1998), shares many of these characteristics.

In the case of Péter Forgács, memory is also reworked. His *Private Hungary*, a 12-film series (1988–97), reworks amateur film and home movies from the era prior to the Second World War, through those turbulent years, and beyond. Forgács's films — specifically *Free Fall* (1997), and *The Maelstrom: A Family Chronicle* (1997) — are among the most significant experimental works produced about the Holocaust, and yet have not garnered nearly enough critical and scholarly attention as they deserve. In addition to Forgács's work, this final chapter also considers, among other things, Hans-Jürgen Syberberg's 1977 seven-and-a-half-hour theatrical epic *Hitler: A Film From Germany*, and Elida Schogt's short 2001 film *Silent Song*.

By no means comprehensive, the present survey endeavors to function as an entry point into the study of Holocaust films. While many readers might be familiar with the established canon of Holocaust films, the book strives to shed new light on the subject, and to interrogate entrenched criteria on which Holocaust films are commonly assessed.

Chapter Two

The Realistic Imperative

THE PRINCIPLE OF VERISIMILITUDE

Authenticity is a red herring. Narratives, whether we are speaking of conventional fictional film or documentary, are always already a construct. Historical events can only be *re*-presented; there is no transparent window through which we might render the past. This is not to say that "realistic" representations cannot, or should not, be made, but rather that authenticity, whatever that might be, or look like, should not be the criterion on which we predicate our assessments. In speaking about the authenticity of Steven Spielberg's 1993 film *Schindler's List*, Imre Kertész, a Hungarian Jew, asks,

> Why should I, as a Holocaust survivor and as one in possession of a broader experience of terror, be pleased when more and more people see these experiences reproduced on the big screen — and falsified at that? It is obvious that the American Spielberg, who incidentally wasn't even born until after the war, has and can have no idea of the authentic reality of a Nazi concentration camp. Why, then, does he struggle so hard to make his representation of a world he does not know *seem* authentic in every detail?[1]

Kertész is not simply claiming that Spielberg got the details wrong, or that his vision of the Holocaust is not authentic enough, but more importantly that his error is the pretense of authenticity.

"Contemporary Holocaust etiquette stipulates verisimilitude and a commitment to exposing each scrap of the grim reality so that audiences can fully comprehend the horrors of the Holocaust," Kertész observes. "Yet the attitudes of survivors and the dissension between them and the critics reveal that this attachment to verisimilitude is futile and hopelessly misguided."[2] The authentic,

15

nevertheless, is the criterion on which many of the most important contributions to the study of Holocaust films are based. *Screening the Holocaust: Cinema's Images of the Unimaginable*, Ilan Avisar's survey of Holocaust films, measures films — whether implicitly, or explicitly — according to their verisimilitude, as does Annette Insdorf in her much-lauded book *Indelible Shadows: Film and the Holocaust*. In her introduction, for example, Insdorf states that: "My point of departure is therefore the growing body of cinematic work — primarily fiction — that illuminates, distorts, confronts, or reduces the Holocaust. Rather than prove a thesis, I wish to explore the degree to which these films manifest artistic as well as moral integrity."[3] Although Insdorf plainly states that she has no agenda as such — no thesis to prove — in fact throughout the book the author incessantly measures films against historical fidelity; in short, her methodology, although disavowed, is governed by this "realist imperative," which is perhaps what she means by "moral integrity." Even though Insdorf qualifies this position during an interview in the documentary *Imaginary Witness: Hollywood and the Holocaust* (Daniel Anker, 2004), acknowledging that fidelity to the historical event is always elusive, saying,

> Of all art forms, film is the one that gives the greatest illusion of authenticity, of truth. A motion picture takes a viewer inside where real people are supposedly doing real things. We assume that there is a certain verisimilitude, a certain authenticity, but there is always some degree of manipulation, some degree of distortion.

Nevertheless, in her book, time after time she employs the "authentic" as the primary criterion on which to access Holocaust films.

In the closing paragraph of Insdorf's introduction the author states her agenda in more explicit terms:

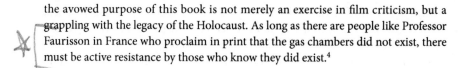

> the avowed purpose of this book is not merely an exercise in film criticism, but a grappling with the legacy of the Holocaust. As long as there are people like Professor Faurisson in France who proclaim in print that the gas chambers did not exist, there must be active resistance by those who know they did exist.[4]

Insdorf's motivation for using the "authentic" as the primary yardstick to judge representations of the Holocaust becomes abundantly clear here; the realist imperative is a product of fear where the lack of fidelity might in some fashion embolden or otherwise lend fodder to the agenda of historical revisionists or Holocaust deniers.[5] The importance of Insdorf's book to film studies and the all-too-important task of analyzing representations of the Holocaust go without saying, but what I wish to call the reader's attention to is the degree to which the realist imperative governs both our artistic practices when creating representations of the Holocaust *and* our critical criterion when accessing these representations.[6]

The discourse of reality itself, insofar as it is presented in conventional narrative modes — narrative fiction, documentary, historical discourse — masks the editorial process, presenting a narrative that has the look and feel of an "organic" linear trajectory, which in its very form signifies "reality"; this is what Roland Barthes calls the "reality effect."[7] In his essay, "The Reality Effect," Barthes discusses how "the realist speech act," for example in history, engenders the verisimilitude of an event, where "details are reputed to *denote* the real directly, all that they do — without saying so — is signify it."[8] The point here is not to argue that there is "no reality," but rather appreciating the difference between the event itself and how that event is "translated" into narrative form. What we might colloquially characterize as a "realistic film" is a narrative conceit, achieved through the conventions of narrative cinema that signify reality, which is quite different from accessing the event. Whether it is the Hollywood invisible style, which masks the construction of a narrative film with editing techniques (e.g., match on action), cinematographic conventions (e.g., hand-held camera), or the replication of period photography (e.g., grainy black and white footage), what "realistic" narrative films convey in addition to their content is a form that merely connotes reality.

Documentaries are no different than narrative film in this respect. The reality effect is also engendered in the evacuation of the subject from the documentary form; typically in documentaries there is no "I," but rather an invisible but omnipresent hand that governs the trajectory. Paradoxically, then, the documentary filmmaker is everywhere, and simultaneously nowhere at all; rarely, if ever, does the documentary filmmaker appear in the narrative in the form of the "first person," or revealing themselves and laying bare the constitutive process, the very assembly of the documentary itself. Even, for example, when we see or hear a documentary filmmaker pose questions to an interviewee, the overall governance of the narrative (e.g., editing, narrative construction) remains veiled behind the narrative conceit of realism. There certainly are exceptions to this, as in the case of personal documentaries, or experimental films, like the work of Abraham Ravett who not only makes himself part of the content of his films but is also present insofar as the medium of film itself and its crafting is made visible (Ravett's work is discussed at some length in Chapter 14).

What is so fascinating about the covertly shot material in Claude Lanzmann's epic 1985 documentary *Shoah* is that revealing the craft, effectively breaking the "forth wall," nevertheless encourages a "fetishistic disavowal," "I know, but . . .," rather than heightening an awareness of the film's artifice. Lanzmann secretly records the former SS Unterstürmfuhrer at Treblinka, Franz Suchomel, and Lanzmann includes shots of the Volkswagen van that clandestinely records the interview. The fetishistic disavowal is doubled in this case, because we are intended to say here: "I realize that the *Shoah* narrative is a construct, *but* I believe that the 'real' Suchomel is being revealed here." Despite what the surreptitiously recorded material reveals, the evacuation of the documentary filmmaker's subjective presence in *Shoah*, even despite his physical presence in the scene, connotes "objectivity," "reality," and denies the documentary filmmaker's editorial hand. Again as Barthes notes, "On the level of discourse, objectivity — or lack of signs of the 'speaker' — thus appears as a special form of image-repertoire, the product of what we might call the referential illusion, since here the historian claims to let the referent speak for itself."[9] Traditionally, the documentary film-maker has been viewed as a humble conduit, through which unmediated facts are conveyed, the connotations being that it is not the filmmaker who speaks but the event itself that speaks through the film. But just the opposite is true; it is not Suchomel that speaks, but it is Lanzmann that speaks Suchomel. This is the nature of the reality effect, and it is quite seductive, imagining that we are given unfettered access to the event itself via the referents that appear on-screen.

The reality effect functions in part because of the small details — and even those details that might register as imperfections, or mistakes — whether it is the grainy picture in the Suchomel interview, or the motion of a hand-held camera, these details signify reality. In narrative fiction film the details that material-ize, especially from within the *mise en scène*, tend to accrue as a charge of the authentic, and when the details are taken together amount to a reality quotient. Whether it's Sophie's measured walk in the thick mud of the concentration camp, for instance, in Alan Pakula's 1982 film *Sophie's Choice*, or the location shooting in Leszek Wosiewicz's 1989 film *Kornblumenblau* in the main camp at Auschwitz, or the precious utensils and bowls strapped to some of the internees' belts, the mud and puddles, the makeshift cigarette passed among the characters, and the menagerie of spoken languages in Wanda Jakubowska's 1947 narrative film *The Last Stage* (or *The Last Stop*), none of these details is "reality" as such; instead, they only signify it.

THE REALITY EFFECT IN THE LAST STAGE

The Last Stage trades heavily in the currency of realism. In view of that, let us use this film as an example of how the "reality effect" works. Shot on location at Auschwitz-Birkenau only two years after the war, Jakubowska reconstructs the concentration camp experience with a high degree of verisimilitude. The film is loaded with poignant details owing to the fact that Jakubowska, who directed and co-wrote the film, was an internee at Auschwitz, as was her co-writer Gerda Schneider. Many of the actors and extras in the film (of which there are an extraordinary number) had little trouble "understanding" or coming to terms with their character, because many were also concentration camp survivors. Jakubowska was actively engaged with the Communist Left and, during the war, with the Polish resistance, which ultimately resulted in her arrest in 1942. First imprisoned in Warsaw, Jakubowska would eventually be sent to Auschwitz; by her own account these years were the most formative for her as a person and artistically.[10] Indeed Jakubowska's intimate knowledge (along with her co-writer) materializes in the countless nuances of the film, and undoubtedly contributes to the overall feeling of realism. Jakubowska and Schneider conceived the film while at Auschwitz, compiling stories that they gathered from other women in the camp.[11]

In fact the "realistic" qualities of *The Last Stage* are so potent that Béla Balázs felt uneasy about the film's placement within the conventional genres of drama or tragedy: "The sizzlingly hot, vivid memories of the Auschwitz women's death camp and gas chamber did not fit into the well-rounded, well-formed shapes of previously known cinematic genres."[12] Rather, Balázs places *The Last Stage* somewhere between documentary and drama — the docudrama. Hanno Loewy succinctly characterizes Balázs's regard for the docudrama, which he sees inaugurating with Jakubowska's film: "A genre in that the events in a way begin to represent themselves, to speak through their metonymic traces."[13] In other words, *The Last Stage* is charged with the "metonymic traces" of the Holocaust, a metonym being a tangible referent that links itself — through proximity, or physical contact — to the actual event. These metonymic traces have affinities with what Barthes characterizes as "details" in his discussion of the reality effect. And it is the metonymic traces located in the film that strikes Balázs with unease, because to situate the film within the fictional genres of tragedy or drama is to effectively disparage its "authenticity," or maybe it's not that the film's authenticity is in question to Balázs's mind, but perhaps the Holocaust itself. Because *The Last Stage* harbors metonymic traces of the Holocaust other filmmakers have drawn from it, as Loewy notes, "From George Stevens' *The Diary of Anne Frank* to films like the German/Yugoslavian 1966 co-production *Witness from Hell* some directors even used clips from *The Last Stop* to authenticate their own visions, as others did with newsreel material or photographs."[14] And its "realistic" quality has in fact led to its incorporation into documentary films, including Alain Resnais's classic 1955 documentary *Night and Fog*. When considering the reality effect the confusion becomes clear; there is frequently a conflation between the realistic re-presentation *and* the event itself. Taking a nuanced approach, and appreciating how the reality effect functions, afford us the capacity to measure representations according to their form.

So despite all of its accumulated details, there is still something of a conceit in the realistic feeling of *The Last Stage*, for cloaked behind the veneer of extraordinary details and the compelling cohesive narrative structure there is an agenda. The film does not have a central character as such, but instead features an international collective: the nurse and committed Communist, Anna; the Russian doctor, Eugenia; and the Polish Jew, Marta, who works as a camp translator. And as Ewa Mazierska succinctly observes, "Apart from being individuals, Eugenia, Anna and Marta serve as symbols of the main enemies of fascism — Jewry, Communism and the East — in a way which conforms to the socialist realistic ideology."[15] And true to the Communist internationalist platform in the narrative the collective is given priority over the individual, and so there is no surprise when at various points during the film each of our individual heroines sacrifices herself for the greater good of the struggle against fascism. Such a narrative strategy stands in stark contrast with typical Hollywood fare, which rarely allows for its protagonist to die (with the exception of tragedies — e.g., *Sophie's Choice*), and more often than not features only one primary character rather than a collective (e.g., Schindler in *Schindler's List*).

We cannot take for granted all the (artistic) embellishments that film allows. Despite its overall "realistic" sensibility, the lighting code of *The Last Stage* has certain affinities with 1940s Hollywood melodrama; this is especially true of the interior shots where the lighting is more controlled. In general, the female internees, especially when seen inside their barracks, tend to be lit from above, and have an angelic quality. This is in stark contrast to the Nazis, who are depicted with a rather flat lighting code, and situates them as empty, lifeless, and ghost-like (fig. 2.1). When one of the women gives birth, for example, light emanates from the newborn (fig. 2.2). The connotations of the lighting code are far from "realistic," but it helps to convey the story with emotion.

Figure 2.1

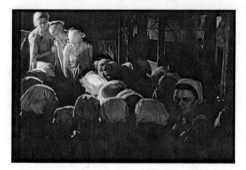

Figure 2.2

The political message in *The Last Stage* is not inherently "bad" or detrimental to the narrative, although some certainly argue that it is — indeed the political *is* the message, "only together we can defeat fascism, alone we die" — but rather what this illustrates, despite all of its overwhelming feeling of "reality," are the ways in which a narrative is governed, that there is *no clear portal* onto reality. A narrative *is* artifice, and always rendered after the fact. And a narrative is *constructed* not according to how things really were necessarily, but according to the social, cultural, and political context in which it is made. As a consequence films from the Eastern bloc tend to emphasize resistance narratives that typically efface religious, social, and national differences for the better good of all, tending towards what we might call a socialist perspective. This is not to say that films from the Western bloc are any *less* ideological, but that they are governed by a different set of values (e.g., rugged American individualism); is Edward Zwick's 2008 film *Defiance* — a fictionalized account of the Bielski brothers — little more than a Western, cowboys and Indians set in a European landscape? Furthermore, with respect to *The Last Stage*, there is no intention of negating the experience of international solidarity in the concentration camp. Instead, the narrative of international solidarity is premised on an editorial choice: Jakubowska and Schneider selected stories and assembled them in a way that is reflective of the collective experience; it is not *the* story of the Holocaust, it is *a* story of the Holocaust.

The overarching plot is premised on the historical account of Mala Zimetbaum, which is discussed at length in Chapter 11, who escaped with another internee at Auschwitz. But when recaptured Zimetbaum made a defiant last stand on the gallows, striking an SS man, and slitting her own wrist before she could be killed. The reality effect — the cumulative result of nuanced details in *mise en scène*, coherent linear narrative, and stories from first-hand witnesses — such as it materializes in *The Last Stage* leads us to believe that the narrative is "whole," "unified," or perhaps even exhaustive. As a committed artist, informed by the practice of socialist realism, and the strategy "first formulated by Andrei A. Zhdanov in 1934 . . . that [demanded] artists be 'engineers of human souls,'"[16] there is little doubt that Jakubowska would be the first to admit that the film is not *the* Holocaust, but a *representation* of it, a *reconstruction* of it, in order to locate meaning where otherwise there is nothing but senseless suffering.[17]

BETWEEN FACT AND FICTION

Non-fiction films are also narrative constructs, and trade heavily on their assumed privileged access to the authentic. While it is true that a documentary might record an event as it happens, or incorporate archival footage, the question remains as to how that material is subsequently used. Form always changes content. Composition, editing, narrative framing/context mediates the ways in which audio/visual material is received. Alfréd Radok's 1950 film *Distant Journey* (or *The Long Journey*) freely mixes fiction and non-fiction, editing together archival material along with what effectively amounts to — when stripped down to its most basic elements — a conventional love story. *Distant Journey* invites the spectator to interrogate the play between non-fiction and fiction.

Radok comes to filmmaking from theater, and *Distant Journey* is his first feature film, as well as being the first film in Czechoslovakia to deal with the Holocaust. Its initial release was extremely limited, and it was "banned for forty years, Czech audiences were only able to see the film again when it was screened on television on 6 May 1991."[18] The Jewess Hana Kaufmannová, a young professional, a doctor, marries Antonin Bures (Hana uses his informal name Toník) a Gentile; he too is a doctor. This inter-married relationship reflects Radok's own experience, as his father was half-Jewish, and his mother was a Gentile; the Radok family celebrated both Christian and Jewish religious holidays.[19] And perhaps also attributable to Radok's own personal experience, during the course of the film, Hana never hides her Jewishness, her husband never asks her to convert, and the signifiers of Jewishness dot the *mise en scène*; the relationship between the two lovers is an ideal microcosm of mutual respect, where Jew and Gentile co-exist, and more than that, affirm the respective values of each tradition.[20]

The opening credits begin with shadows cast upon a brick wall, countless people file past, moving right to left across the screen, and in the context of the film we (correctly) take it to be a deportation. This is immediately juxtaposed to archival material of fascist troops marching in unison in the opposite direction, left to right. Two separate actions — deportation and military mobilization — contrast against each other (fig. 2.3; fig. 2.4). In addition, there is an immediate contrast between the real historical world (archival material), and simulation (fictional diegesis). The shadows cast against the brick wall summon to mind Plato's Allegory of the Cave, and so from the very beginning of the film the stage is set for the interplay between simulation and the real. "Radok filmed some of the apparently documentary shots himself and *Distant Journey* is therefore a mixture of real documentary work and intentional mystification. This is linked to Radok's idea of the ideal film as an 'artistic report', a multidimensional structure in which different points of view can be compared."[21] And this comparative strategy appreciates the artifice of constructing a narrative, and candidly rejects the pretense of verisimilitude.

Figure 2.3

Figure 2.4

Distant Journey draws on Leni Riefenstahl's 1935 film *Triumph of the Will*, with specific intent. While many documentaries simply harvest clips of Nazi pageantry from Riefenstahl's film, Radok uses it to establish an ideological/ historical context in which the fictional film unfolds. In a clip from *Triumph of the Will* Rudolf Hess exalts his dictum, "The Party is Hitler! Hitler is Germany, just as Germany is Hitler! Sieg Heil! Sieg Heil! Sieg Heil!" A male voiceover, which retrospectively we attribute to Bures, from the fictional diegesis comments on the material selected from *Triumph of the Will*; Bures intones, "And Germany is Hitler." Followed shortly thereafter he continues, "All we want is the truth about Germany." The fictional world and the historical world come together in the meeting of visual (historical) and audio commentary (fictional); layering one on top of the other. Radok inserts into this sequence a bewildering shot of Terezín (what the Germans called Theresienstadt), a macabre procession of deportees going into the camp, and internees carrying coffins out of the camp (fig. 2.5), but it is situated with the voiceover commentary, "We are gradually moving towards truth. Political campaigning is a creative modern art, which depicts a new, strong, proud and happy life." The truth of the Nazi utopia spells misery for European Jewry, and the regime's tyrannical rule. And Terezín is exemplary of the cruel truth of Nazi policies, hidden behind the veneer of order; and this, as Bures continues his commentary, "can convince the international public. Wherever we look, new order is being built," which cuts to a panning shot surveying the vast expanse of Auschwitz-Birkenau. "National social justice is the basis of our state," which cuts from *Triumph of the Will* to a shot of a guillotine (fig. 2.6), and then a machine gun firing squad. "A nation which neglects the purity of its race will perish," cuts between members of the Hitler Youth in *Triumph of the Will* to a shot with a fence painted (in Czech) with the words, "Jews out!" (fig. 2.7). And from here the fictional world literally emerges from within the documentary world, a frame-with-frame increases in size until it fills the on-screen space, and supplants the documentary world (fig. 2.8).

Figure 2.5

Figure 2.6

Figure 2.7

Figure 2.8

Quite different from other Eastern European films (e.g., *The Last Stage*), where Jewish identity is typically effaced, or subsumed under the banner of anti-fascist resistance, in this case Jewish identity is central to the narrative. The latter half of the film is set in Terezín itself, and despite the Nazis' efforts to beautify the town-camp Radok reveals what lies beneath the façade: ramshackle dwellings that exude dust and filth, where everything and everybody are just clinging by their fingernails for dear life. Radok's father died in cell #3 in the Little Fortress, a detention facility in Terezín for political prisoners. While filming, though, Radok "avoided the Little Fortress, setting the film in other areas."[22] Radok's 90-year-old grandfather also died in Terezín. On the paternal side of his family many people were claimed by the Holocaust. The Holocaust and the experience of the war were omnipresent for Radok; he too was imprisoned. "The film was made only three years after the destruction of his own family and, as many witnesses have testified, filming on actual locations at Terezín was very difficult and painful for him."[23] Although shot on location, Radok takes great liberties in representing the town-camp, bringing to it a stylized aesthetic, what many have called expressionistic. Radok's theatrical background materializes in the expressionistic set design, particularly in interior shots of the blocks. His depiction of Terezín is a macabre and frightening version of an M. C. Escher illustration — stairs, doorways, and the multiplication of levels — families sleeping on top of one another.

There is no effort to represent Terezín as it really was, but rather to render the feeling of it: a grotesque nightmare, a world thrown into chaos, life was precarious, and the threat of deportation — which meant almost certain death in an Auschwitz gas chamber — hung overhead like the Sword of Damocles. In the contrast between the nightmarish fictional diegesis and the non-fictional material, Jiri Cieslar adds, Radok "thus juxtaposes the broader political history with the smaller personal history."[24]

The expressionistic style in the fictional *mise en scène* articulates real feelings, which are profoundly personal, rather than a historical reality. The art historian and critic Robert Hughes discusses the use and the limits of expressionism in the wake of the Holocaust, in the episode "The View from the Edge" from his documentary series *The Shock of the New*: "any distortion of the human body that an artist might make after 1945 was going to have to bear comparison with what the Nazis had done to bodies. And very few expressionist paintings could stand this strain. Here photography was enough, anything else would seem gratuitous."[25] (fig. 2.9) But it is precisely because of the photographic evidence that is so familiar to us now, and that Radok in fact uses (e.g., liberation footage from Bergen-Belsen), that the *mise en scène*, and bodies in the fictionalized diegesis are turned on their heads, distorted, set askew. Why surrender to the pretense of (documentary) realism, when the horror that Radok aims to document is nightmarish?

Figure 2.9

A strong proponent of realism, André Bazin, surprisingly, finds Radok's artistry befitting the subject; with *Distant Journey* Radok illustrates that, in Bazin's words, "the most questionable traits of expressionism paradoxically regain a profound justification."[26] To Bazin's mind the nightmarish reality that Radok exhibits necessitates the forays into aesthetic embellishment. "Out of internal and in a certain way metaphysical fidelity to the universe of the concentrationary ghetto, the film, unwittingly, no doubt, evokes the world of Kafka, and, more strangely, that of de Sade."[27] When for instance Hana is fired from her position because she is Jewish — in accordance to the newly adopted anti-Jewish laws — the individual that executes the ordinance is frankly ugly, his face covered in pockmarked scars (perhaps from the First World War?). Here is a literalization of the "ugly face" of fascism, the character part Kafkaesque bureaucratic functionary, and part sadistic libertine.

Many of the acts of naked violence in the fictional diegesis of the film take place off-screen. In the melancholic march of Jews out of Terezín to an awaiting train transport to the East, when a Jewess protests she is pulled out of line by gun-toting German guards who drag her into a dark doorway where she disappears into the black void; her screams are the only thing that remain. When Professor Reiter receives his notification for "relocation" to Terezín he commits suicide by jumping from his apartment window. The jump and its aftermath never materialize on-screen; we are simply left with an open window, curtains gently blowing in the wind (fig. 2.10), which is immediately juxtaposed to documentary material of Nazi festoons (fig. 2.11), and the pageantry of the regime.[28] The black void that swallows the female internee, and the open window, points to an absence in the visual record, but at the same time, the juxtaposition between the fictional diegesis and the documentary footage places these "visual absences" in the proper context of the history of the Nazi regime. This absence is also evident in Holocaust archives, for the most part there is no visual record of the mechanics of death, so much of it happened "off-screen," which leads to the perennial dilemma in documentary representations of the Holocaust. Given the fact that atrocities of the Holocaust happened "off-screen," what then comes to fill in the gaps in the visual record? How do documentaries negotiate this absence? In *Shoah* Lanzmann effectively leaves the fissures in place; conventional expository documentaries rely on archival material (e.g., liberation footage); and here in this case *Distant Journey* fills this void with the imagination, a dark grotesque poetic exchange between fiction and non-fiction, between nightmare and reality.

Figure 2.10

Figure 2.11

AUTHENTICATING PERSONALITIES

Although accused by some of distorting the reality of Terezín by rendering certain elements as surreal, others give Radok's *Distant Journey* some license precisely because of his personal relationship to the Holocaust. Whether an artist/filmmaker has firsthand knowledge of the Holocaust, or is a child of a survivor, personalities are sometimes mobilized to authenticate a Holocaust film. Roman Polanski was a child in the Krakow Ghetto, and this became something of a marketing point for his 2002 film *The Pianist*. Unlike the Hollywood propensity for narratives that appeal to the discourse of realism, *The Pianist*, as Michael Stevenson indicates, "does have a clear sense of documentary drama, but with a striking sense of controlled artifice."[29] In the simplest of terms, shots of Warsaw ablaze give way to a campy *Gojira* (Godzilla) aesthetic, pointing to the constructedness of the film and Polanski's narrative. Polanski though, as a survivor of the Krakow Ghetto, and hiding out posing as a Catholic child during the remainder of the war following the liquidation of the ghetto, presumably (but perhaps erroneously) stamps everything with the mark of the "authentic." Polanski himself emphasizes the authenticity of the film, a good deal of which is drawn from his own experiences and recollections from that time. "Being a Holocaust survivor gave Polanski a creditability to embark on this subject which no Polish director had enjoyed since Wanda Jakubowska. This 'authentic' aspect of the film was seized upon by the Polish press."[30] For all the harping upon the supposed authenticity of the film, the filmmaker is keenly aware that the narrative is filtered through historical distance, and the artifice of the medium he loves: cinema.

Individual experiences allow for a degree of license. In 1965 Jurek Becker drafted a screenplay for *Jakob the Liar*; however, the East German censors believed that the script was "too focused on Jewish suffering and too flippant about the Soviet contribution to the liberation of Germany."[31] Becker subsequently rewrote the script as a novel, which enjoyed success in both East and West Germany. Nearly a decade following Becker's first aborted screenplay, Frank Beyer adapted the novel along with Becker into a film, which was released in 1975. Beyer also made *Naked Among Wolves* (1963). More than two decades following Beyer's film

Jacob the Liar, Peter Kassovitz in 1999 remade the film (as *Jakob the Liar*) with an all-star Hollywood cast, including Robin Williams who plays the leading role (both versions are discussed in the comedy chapter). There are distinct similarities between the two films, but the endings are substantively different. Becker's novel and screenplay are based on personal experiences; he was interned in the Lodz ghetto and eventually deported along with his mother to Ravensbrück and then the Sachsenhausen concentration camp where his mother died. His father was deported to Auschwitz and managed to survive. Polish-born, Becker and his father settled in Eastern Berlin following the war.[32] Becker's personal experience afforded him, and by extension Beyer as well, the license to create a comedy based on a Jewish character that lies. Judging from the generally negative reviews, though, it appears as if Kassovitz was not afforded the same luxuries.

Like Radok's *Distant Journey*, Zbynek Brynych's 1962 film *Transport from Paradise* is shot on location at Terezín. Holocaust survivor and author Arnost Lustig wrote the script; his autobiographical account was also adapted for the Jan Nemec 1964 film *Diamonds of the Night*. All these films exhibit high degrees of verisimilitude; however, all these films introduce surrealistic elements as well. *Distant Journey* vacillates between reality and fiction, and utilizes "un-naturalistic" theatrical staging in Terezín. Nemec's *Diamond of the Night* includes shots that might be read as dreams, fantasies, or hallucination. Less overt, Brynych's *Transport from Paradise* includes elements in the *mise en scène* that are "out of place," but add to the dreamy atmosphere. Analogous to Becker's authority in *Jacob the Liar*, Lustig's authoritative hand endorses the surrealistic digressions in *Transport from Paradise* and *Diamonds of the Night*.

"Trivializing" is frequently just another way to say, "inauthentic." The 1978 NBC miniseries *Holocaust*, directed by Marvin Chomsky, is easy to dismiss as a tawdry dramatization of the Holocaust. In the *New York Times* Elie Wiesel characterized the miniseries as "untrue, offensive, [and] cheap."[33] For all its faults, though, and there are many, the NBC miniseries marks a critical turning point in the representation of the Holocaust, and is responsible for disseminating widespread knowledge of the event, if filtered through the lens of televised mediocrity. The miniseries also aired in Europe, and is largely credited with changing attitudes in West Germany, promoting public discussion about Germany's Holocaust responsibility, and prompting changes to the school curriculum reflecting this new introspection. In the United States, half the population, 120 million people, viewed the series, and following its broadcast President Jimmy Carter formed a presidential commission on the Holocaust to determine an appropriate way for the United States to commemorate the Holocaust. The end result of the commission materialized many years later with the construction of the US Holocaust Memorial Museum in Washington DC.[34] This institution is one of the most significant sites of research in advancing the study of the Holocaust and, more than that, is committed to showcasing history in a continuum, rather than cementing the Holocaust in a point in the distant past. For all its lackluster qualities, the NBC miniseries has perhaps had more material effect than all the representations of the Holocaust combined.[35]

As Ilan Avisar observes, *Holocaust* whitewashes the true horrors of the experience, and Hollywood's "treatment of the horrors on the screen has always been evasive or pussyfooting." He continues,

> But the popularization of the historical material into a sort of soap opera for prime-time American television is liable to diminish the horrors of the actual atrocities and to present a bland drama that fails to provoke a sustained aesthetic reaction corresponding to the extremity of the authentic human sufferings.[36]

Authenticity is not necessarily the issue, though; abstraction is inherent to the narrative process, as discussed earlier. What is at stake, however, and Avisar cites screenwriter Paddy Chayefsky to make the point, is that "Trivialization is television."[37] Finally, the problem is not that "Hollywood films do not merely trivialize history, but project images and attitudes that distort it and violate its incontrovertible moral lessons."[38]

Not that filmmaking is completely immune, but television is especially susceptible to market pressures in the way that the Holocaust is represented. Originally a 1959 teleplay for CBS's dramatic series *Playhouse 90*, Stanley Kramer's 1961 film *Judgment at Nuremberg* is a clear example of where "commerce clearly got in the way of authenticity," Annette Insdorf determines, and she continues to elaborate, "the sponsor of the show, the American Gas Association, objected to the use of the word 'gas' in reference to the concentration camp death chambers."[39] Insdorf accepts that there is little difference between an American teleplay and a cinematic narrative; the primary difference between the two is the form of the narratives, where televised dramas need to accommodate for commercial interruptions. Insdorf also cites the same interview with Chayefsky that Avisar does, but at greater length. Chayefsky reveals the true difference between a teleplay and cinema:

> NBC wanted to do *The War Against the Jews*. That's before they did *Holocaust*. I said the subject was simply too painful for me to write about. But if I had agreed to do it for television, I'd have had to make a soap opera of the whole thing. You'd have to get high emotional moments, regularly, because you have these damn ten-minute intervals all the time. You can never really accumulate the power; you have to capsulize a lot of emotion, and you have to overdramatize things. In fact, the words critics used on *Holocaust* was "trivialize," and in a sense that was an unfair criticism, even though accurate. Trivialization *is* television.[40]

And this seems to get to the heart of the difference between the two formats. Not only does the innately commercial enterprise of television necessitate an unseemly relationship between consumer culture and the solemnity of a Holocaust narrative, but there is also a problem in television form that obliges the discrete atomization of the narrative to accommodate for commercial interruptions. The authentic by most accounts presumes a narrative whole, continuity, and the very format of television narrative works against this principle.

Lanzmann is highly critical of the NBC miniseries. The melodramatic form of the narrative is deeply disturbing to the documentary filmmaker, who sees the genre flattening out the history of the Holocaust as a backdrop for what could ostensibly be just any other family drama. "In *Holocaust*," Lanzmann writes, "people await death gravely and with dignity, as good form prescribes." He continues later to say:

> In real life, things were different. After years of ghetto confinement, terror, humiliation, and hunger, the people who lined up in rows of five were driven by whips and bludgeons and knocked against each other as they entered the death chambers; they had neither the leisure nor the composure to die nobly. To show what really happened would have been unendurable. At the least, it would have precluded conscience-salving "identification." However, the film is a work of fiction. And in this instance, because the reality defies the resources of any fiction, *Holocaust* perpetrates a lie, a moral crime; it assassinates memory.[41]

Lanzmann believes that *Holocaust*, or trivializing narratives in general, assassinate memory because they come to function as "false memories"; that they stand as inauthentic memories. Lanzmann very well might be correct, but one of the central questions of the present book is not whether a film is authentic or not, which in any event presupposes that the film in some way impugns the reality of the event, but rather *how* the narrative is constructed to encourage the spectator to take it as a "false memory." What is at stake here is not necessarily *what* a film does, but *how* it does it.

Chapter Three

The Holocaust as Dramatic Spectacle

no values

no!

INTRODUCTION: CHARACTERS AND SPECTACLE

Rather than attempting to ascertain what film or films are the most significant, this chapter instead surveys a number of films that utilize the Holocaust as a dramatic spectacle. Quality as such is not at issue here; rather, the intended purpose of the survey is to illustrate *how* some of these films work (or don't as the case might be), irrespective of whether or not a film is presumed to be "good." Effectively, this chapter is less a survey of the best Holocaust narrative films than a survey of rhetorical strategies and motifs that are utilized when applying conventional narrative tactics to the Holocaust.

Holocaust films, like most films, adhere to the general principles of dramatic structure where a protagonist negotiates a conflict, and is subsequently compelled to undergo a transformation. The primary character in Steven Spielberg's 1993 blockbuster film *Schindler's List* is not a Jew but the profiteering Gentile, Oskar Schindler, who evolves from a self-centered womanizer to a self-sacrificing savior. In Gillo Pontecorvo's 1959 film *Kapò*, the primary female character undergoes multiple transformations; she begins as an ordinary bourgeois cultured Jewess, Edith, but upon entering the camp assumes the identity of a common criminal, Nicole. In her newly assumed identity she assumes the position of kapo (supervisor or functionary). Like Schindler, Nicole is only concerned for herself and brutally exercises her privileged position within the camp to ensure her own welfare. After meeting and falling in love with a Russian POW, though, she has a change of heart, reassumes her real identity, and sacrifices herself for the greater good.

self-serving

In *Schindler's List*, the conflict — strictly in the dramatic sense, not the moral sense — is between the SS and Schindler, or more specifically between Schindler and Amon Goeth, who has to be cajoled, bribed, and tricked so that

Schindler might achieve his immediate goal of becoming wealthy. Goeth is the narrative obstacle, the conflict, that has to be overcome. Contrary to common wisdom, Jewish survival is not the *narrative aim* of *Schindler's List*; it is rather an incidental artifact of Schindler's transformative accession as savior. In *Kapò* it is the concentration camp — and the system that governs it — that represents the narrative conflict. Edith becomes Nicole because the concentrationary universe demands it; in the end, though, humanity prevails, and in order for this to come to fruition Nicole needs to become Edith again, which ultimately necessitates a selfless act. Given the principles of conventional narrative cinema — conflict and character transformation — the Holocaust in many cases only serves as a backdrop or narrative alibi for dramatic conflict and/or a test of a character's fortitude that fosters his or her transformation.

Holocaust films that employ the conventional narrative form frequently draw on the Jew-as-victim motif, a subject that Judith Doneson extensively examines. As victim, Jewish characters lack agency, and narratives get played *through* or *around* them, as opposed to *by* them. Films that upend this motif are addressed at greater length in the following chapter. In the late 70s Doneson published a critical essay greatly enhancing our understanding of Holocaust films, "The Jew as a Female Figure in the Holocaust Film." She continued this work in other publications on the subject. *Schindler's List* is exemplary of this, where the Jew is depicted, as Doneson argues, "as a weak character, somewhat feminine," and needing the protection of "a strong Christian gentile." And in this coupling between Jew and Gentile there emerges something that resembles "a male-female relationship."[1] As the saying goes: "Behind every great man, there's a woman." And the relationship that develops between Oskar Schindler and Itzhak Stern is effectively a male-female romance; Stern is to all intents and purposes a "woman," relatively soft in demeanor and speech, the consummate domestic running the show behind the scenes, allowing Schindler to don the guise of the successful and philandering businessman. In one of the most explicit examples of this, the dutiful Stern hastily rushes Schindler off to an appointment with an SS officer to grease the palm of his government business associate, plying the SS officer with gifts (fig. 3.1). It is not until the end of the war is in sight that the couple consummates their relationship. Schindler laments, "Some day, this is all going to end, you know. I was going to say we'll have a drink then." The long chased Stern finally returns Schindler's affection; a tear running down his cheek, he shakes his head, "I think I better have it now."[2] (fig. 3.2)

Figure 3.1

Figure 3.2

Schindler's List throughout remains comfortably within the realm of dramatic realism. At the climax of the film, however, it takes a turn towards melodrama. One of the key tropes of the melodrama (discussed in Chapter 7) is being "too late." Whether it is delayed recognition, or circumstances that impede a character's ability to intervene in some fashion, pathos derives from the powerlessness to change things, and while this is true of the character(s) on screen, it is also true of the spectator that shares in the sensibility of "if only . . ."[3] Assembled outside the factory Schindler's Jews present him with a letter, "trying to explain things in case you are captured," Rabbi Menasha Lewartow says. "Every worker has signed it." Stern then presents Schindler with a gift, a ring fashioned from the gold fillings of one of the Jewish laborers. Schindler examines the ring, noting its inscription, and Stern explains, "It is Hebrew, from the Talmud. It says, 'Whoever saves one life, saves the world entire.'" Overwhelmed by the gesture, Schindler is flummoxed and clumsily drops the ring, but quickly recovers it, and places it on his left ring-finger (indeed, Schindler is not committed to his wife, who stands beside him, but to Stern and his private army of cheap labor) (fig. 3.3).

Figure 3.3

The melodramatic apex comes when Schindler *belatedly* recognizes that "I could have got more out." Clinching Stern's hand firmly, he says, "I could have got more. I don't know. If I just . . ." Schindler surveys his material possessions, listing them and quantifying how many more people he could have saved with each respective item (fig. 3.4). The melodrama not only materializes in the tears that are shed by Schindler, and perhaps the spectator too, but that those tears are the realization of being too late. "If I had just," "I could have," these refrains are variations on the melodramatic trope of "if only." And more than this, what the character Oskar Schindler realizes too late is who he is — strictly speaking within the realm of the dramatic diegesis, not the real historical man, which is a different story altogether. Schindler evolves into the Gentile savior, but it is too late by the time the character recognizes his own transformation. *Schindler's List* in this respect has nothing to do with Jewish survival, and instead the Holocaust functions as a mere backdrop for the transformation of a Gentile character.[4]

Figure 3.4

The taint of evil is a fairly common theme as well, and is present in films like *Kapò*, and Bryan Singer's 1998 film *Apt Pupil*, which is discussed at length in the latter part of this chapter. A related theme, selling your soul to the devil, is a theme that runs through many of István Szabó's films. It also appears elsewhere, for instance, Luchino Visconti's 1969 film *The Damned*. The Faustian theme explicitly materializes in Szabó's *Mephisto* (1981), of course, as well as *Taking Sides* (2001), and *Sunshine* (1999). The last film most explicitly depicts the Hungarian Jewish experience. The title is a direct translation of the family surname Sonnenschein, who over three successive generations shed their Jewish identity, including changing the family name to Sors and converting, in exchange for access to civil participation, state recognition and power. During the Second World War Adam Sors, a proud Hungarian Olympic gold medalist, and his son Ivan are sent to a Hungarian labor camp, and in one of the most harrowing depictions of torture, Adam is beaten to death for refusing to acknowledge his Jewish identity. A Hungarian guard repeatedly asks, "Who are you?" Adam continually espouses his national credentials, but never admits to being Jewish. Each response enrages the guard and brings increasingly more sever blows. Ordered to strip, Adam is bound and beaten before he is finally hung from a tree and hosed down with water until his body is fully encased in ice (fig. 3.5).[5] In the postwar Stalinist era, Ivan, who witnessed his father's torture and death, is recruited to join the police services and is all too eager to do the State's bidding: to exercise revenge on fascists and enemies of communism. Ivan resolves the narrative conflict by accepting his family's Jewish heritage, and changing his surname back to Sonnenschein.

Figure 3.5

voyeurism [handwritten]

In addition to being dramatic fodder, some filmmakers in an effort to represent the orgy of violence render the event as spectacle. Some resist the temptation of transforming human suffering into a voyeuristic spectacle, while others — consciously or not — turn suffering into entertainment. The spectacle in this sense is generally in keeping with Guy Debord's application of it, where in the simplest of terms the spectacle amounts to a manifestation of the commodity in a dematerialized form. A Holocaust film circulating in the economy of the spectacle is not engaged with critical ideas — a meditation on the human condition, history, and the like — but rather a commodity to be bought and sold, placed in relation to other commodities, where there is effectively no difference between *Schindler's List* and Spielberg's *Jurassic Park* released in the same year (1993). The Holocaust as spectacle is the twentieth century's Grand Guignol *par excellence*.

Relative to one's critical perspective, the filmmaker Bryan Singer might be accused of rendering the Holocaust as spectacle, or conversely of being a creative force that is helping us to rethink narrative possibilities.[6] He has returned to the subject (or at least brushed up against it) a number of times: *Apt Pupil* (1998), *X-Men* (2000), and *Valkyrie* (2008). While Singer certainly has his share of detractors who argue that he has trivialized the Holocaust, there are others who locate a new potential for narrativizing the event. The opening scene of *X-Men* for instance begins in a concentration camp, in Poland, 1944. When an adolescent boy is separated from his parents, who are sent to the gas chamber, he resists; the gate that divides the family begins to buckle as the youngster's mutant powers materialize — a magnetic force field, and hence the character's name, Magneto. Based on the original comic book series by Jack Kirby and Stan Lee, both American Jews, the *X-Men* and some of their other comic books helped to negotiate the "feelings of Jewish anxiety," that more than likely "fed the imagination," Helena Frenkil Schlam observes, "but in America it also seemed natural to imagine a solution — the existence of all-powerful protectors for the vulnerable in society."[7] In the tradition of the Golem, the mutants (and other comic book superheroes) are figured as protectors of the community.[8]

Experimental filmmaker Hans-Jürgen Syberberg posits that (commercial) cinema itself is fascism, and his 1977 seven-and-a-half-hour theatrical epic

Hitler: A Film From Germany (discussed in Chapter 15) equates the Nazis' love of pageantry with the Hollywood culture industry, and the manufacture of cinematic spectacles. Other filmmakers have posited similar theses, even those of the popular or commercial variety, as Thomas Elsaesser notes, "Bob Fosse's *Cabaret* (1972) or Mel Brooks' *The Producers* (1968) . . . also made much of the affinity between fascism and show business, underlining this 'aesthetization' of politics . . ." Elsaesser continues by asking,

> Doesn't *Cabaret*'s spectacle of putting-on-a-show, or *The Producers*'s song-and-dance routines, and especially its parodies of goose-stepping Nazis in a production number called "Springtime for Hitler," make light of the obscenity of a regime that put on the mask of entertainment and glamour, so as to hide the energy it put into destruction, terror, and contempt for human life?[9]

Indeed the ethics of representing the Holocaust are a paramount concern, but for better or for worse the Holocaust has entered the realm of our shared visual culture.

Some filmmakers simply skirt or "work around" the most troubling aspects of representing the Holocaust, namely the gas chambers. But as Libby Saxton suggests, "To avoid the gas chambers is arguably to avoid the Holocaust. Yet the vast majority of films dealing with the extermination assert in one way or another that it is neither appropriate nor legitimate to represent what happened inside the gas chambers directly."[10] As Saxton observes, there are some exceptions to this general prohibition, including Leszek Wosiewicz's 1989 film *Kornblumenblau*, which owing to its critical perspective — arguably — gives it license to go where most films do not dare. There are others that have crossed this threshold, such as Mark Herman's 2008 film *The Boy in the Striped Pyjamas*, Tim Blake Nelson's 2001 film *The Grey Zone*, as well as *Apt Pupil* and *Schindler's List*. This chapter focuses on the ways in which the Holocaust has been treated in conventional dramatic narratives, surveying various narrative tropes such as the taint of evil and the peephole.

THE HOLOCAUST AS SPECTACLE

One of the most provocative tropes in Holocaust films is the peephole, or alternatively a window, which opens onto a site of sadistic violence — be it physical abuse, sexual assault, or the gas chamber. Some filmmakers utilize the device cautiously, or from a critical perspective (Pasolini in *Salò*, or Wosiewicz in *Kornblumenblau*), while others utilize it seemingly with a reckless disregard (Spielberg in *Schindler's List*), and still others explicitly exploit the capacity of the device to heighten voyeuristic qualities of a scene (Tinto Brass's 1976 film *Salon Kitty*, or Don Edmonds's 1975 film *Ilsa: She-Wolf of the SS*). The peephole at the gas chamber door embodies the potential to elicit scopophilic pleasure derived from the pleasure in human suffering. At least three scholars have dedicated critical attention to this specific motif in Holocaust films: Caroline Joan Picart and David Frank in their co-authored book, *Frames of Evil: The Holocaust As Horror in American Film*, and Libby Saxton in her book, *Haunted Images: Film, Ethics, Testimony and the Holocaust*.

"The architectural term for a peep-hole or secret opening for spying is a 'judas hole,'" Saxton observes.

> The reference to Judas Iscariot, the disciple who betrayed Christ with a kiss, links the spyhole to an act of violence disguised as an embrace, bringing notions of treachery and deception into play. Spyholes impede frank exchanges and face-to-face encounters, disrupting viewing relations between self and other in ways that arouse moral suspicion.[11]

The peephole raises moral suspicion within the narrative diegesis, and without. The peephole engenders an innate power dynamic within the narrative diegesis: those characters that avail themselves of the peephole constitute subjects that look, as opposed to those that are subjected to the gaze. Outside the narrative diegesis, the peephole device invites the spectator to take victims as the subject of a sadistic and eroticized gaze. The peephole motif nonetheless can at once be used as a critical device calling attention to the spectacle of violence, or, on the other hand, a seamless way to integrate it into the narrative without disrupting the diegesis, analogous to the ways in which the showgirls, strippers, or other "incidental" displays of the female form materialize in mainstream narrative film without impeding narrative progression.[12] The danger of utilizing the peephole device is that it harbors the potential — despite our own vigilance — to elicit (perverse) pleasure from the spectacle of violence, where "punishments" are exacted on-screen; this is what some have called the Nazi gaze, or the perpetrator's gaze.

There are some explicit examples of this in exploitation films. In *Ilsa: She-Wolf of the SS*, for instance, the title character is the female commandant of Medical Camp 9, where she conducts medical experiments on internees. One of Ilsa's pet projects is to determine that a woman's pain threshold is higher than a man's, thus proving that women can serve in military combat. Among the many gruesome experiments that Ilsa conducts on female internees is an experiment in rapid decompression (a medical experiment in fact conducted by Nazi doctors). A buxom female internee is bound inside a compression chamber. Watching through the portal in the compression chamber door, Ilsa commands her assistant to reduce the pressure dramatically, causing the female subject to writhe in agony as she hemorrhages, spitting up comic-book-red blood from her mouth (fig. 3.6). Within traditional paradigms of power, women are not granted the "right" to look, and when women do look, it is ascribed as exceptional and seemingly more perverse.[13] There could hardly be a more explicit illustration of the sadistic gaze as illustrated in *Ilsa*, which so closely corresponds to feminist film theory, where "pleasure" derives from the control, subjugation, and punishment of the female form.

Figure 3.6

In Tinto Brass's 1976 film *Salon Kitty*, Aryan women destined to service Nazi officers are subjected to tests to determine their fortitude; the women are compelled to negotiate "deviations" in sexuality. Each female subject is locked in a cell, and Helmut Wallenberg, the SS officer overseeing the operation, examines the reaction of each subject to her respective test (e.g., sex with a midget, a lesbian encounter, sex with an amputee). Analogous to the compression chamber scene in *Ilsa*, Wallenberg spies on each test-subject through a small portal in the cell-room door (fig. 3.7). Exploitation filmmakers are generally unapologetic smut peddlers, and while we might be quick to dismiss films from the genre, they nevertheless deserve our critical attention precisely because they potentially illustrate the naked truth of more "legitimate" films like *Schindler's List* that disguise the fetishistic and sadistic gaze in narrative conceit and slick cinematic craftsmanship; exploitation films are discussed at length in Chapter 8.

[margin annotation: disguise or reveal / Sadistic smut]

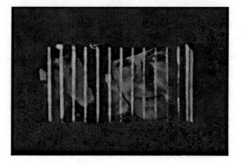

Figure 3.7

The peephole for Picart and Frank evokes the viewing position more commonly associated with horror films. Whether it's *Ilsa: She-Wolf of the SS*, *Salon Kitty*, or more conventional fare, like *Apt Pupil*, or *Schindler's List*, the spectator views some form of violence

through a peephole, in which the victims, in their nakedness, are utterly vulnerable and sexualized. The audience is separated from murder itself but is able to gaze at the victims. The peephole creates a clear demarcation between the space of murder (the shower stall in the movies) and the position the viewer takes behind the peephole.[14]

[margin annotation: demarcation b/n viewer and viewed]

Even if the perspective shifts between inside and outside the gas chamber — as it does for example in the gas chamber/shower scene in *Schindler's List* — the privileged, and ultimately omnipotent, position granted the spectator invites us to take pleasure in the mobility between spaces, victim and perpetrator, and all the while exorcising sadistic mastery over the victims. Picart and Frank argue, however, that the pleasure we ascertain rests on a clear division between exterior viewing positions and interior diegetic space, "This demarcation [behind the peephole] places the agents and site of murder safely outside the ostensible moral province of the audience but keeps the spectacle within their field of vision." And by partitioning the agents and site of murder as separate from the spectator facilitates the "guilty pleasure" of watching what "is portrayed as radically other and yet alluring or aesthetically fascinating."[15] Picart and Frank finally conclude that the strategy of demarcating spatial fields and agents of evil as alien to the spectator corresponds to what is "at the core of the classic horror frame."[16]

The Holocaust itself, and the concentration camp, do not take up much screen time in Sidney Lumet's 1964 film *The Pawnbroker.* Nonetheless, their significance to the overall narrative cannot be understated. When the Holocaust explicitly enters the narrative diegesis it materializes as subjective flashbacks attributed to the principal character, Holocaust survivor Sol Nazerman, who runs a New York City pawnshop. The customers that bring in various personal items to hock trigger flashbacks, recalling Nazerman's family and their internment in a concentration camp. To begin the flashbacks are lightning quick, but they increase in duration, and we learn progressively more about the curmudgeonly Nazerman. When a woman propositions herself for an extra 20 dollars in the backroom of the pawnshop, she takes off her clothes and demands, "Look. Look." The woman's demand to look, and her naked body, trigger flashbacks, cutting between the customer (fig 3.8) and a woman (fig. 3.9), Nazerman's wife, who was conscripted into the camp brothel servicing SS men.[17]

Figure 3.8

In the longest flashback in the film an SS man drags Nazerman by the scruff of his collar to see where his wife is interned. At the brothel door Nazerman's head is shoved through a pane of glass (fig. 3.10). The violence of looking is made literal here. The pawnshop customer's continued salacious demand, "Look," corresponds

Figure 3.9

to the SS man's order to "Look!" when forcing Nazerman to survey the brothel: two SS men wash down a female internee, other naked female internees wait to service German officers in their respective stalls, until finally in the last stall Nazerman sees his wife. His field of vision is partially obstructed, however, when an SS man steps into Nazerman's line of sight, presumably to avail himself of Nazerman's wife (fig. 3.11). In this flashback there is at least a doubling of victimization. Not only are the female subjects treated as fetish objects as well as subjugated by forcing them into sexual slavery but also Nazerman is made to occupy the Nazi gaze, obligating him to objectify his own wife. The spectator, through Nazerman's subjective perspective, is obliged to also occupy the perpetrator's gaze.

Figure 3.10

Figure 3.11

Tim Blake Nelson's 2001 film *The Grey Zone*, also discussed in the succeeding chapter, dramatizes the Sonderkommando uprising in Auschwitz-Birkenau, and complicates the line between victim and perpetrator. Nelson never utilizes the peephole device, but rather takes us right into the gas chamber itself, and is quite explicit in its depiction of the entire industrialized process of killing. Those films that do venture into this territory typically utilize the peephole as the device to gain entry into the gas chamber, Nelson, on the other hand, uses the Sonderkommando, through narrative and cinematic craft, to carry us across the threshold into the center of hell on Earth. The Sonderkommando were typically Jewish internees conscripted to do the dirtiest of work in the industrialization of death — coaxing deportees into the "showers," sorting through their belongings, cutting their hair, clearing away the dead bodies following the gassing, and finally the disposal of corpses. Aligning our gaze with the Sonderkommando complicates the clear distinction between the perpetrator's gaze and the victim's gaze. Through establishing shots and subjective perspectives, *The Grey Zone*, without the slightest hesitation or sensationalism, takes us into the aftermath of a gassing, (fig. 3.12) and to the gaping mouth of raging ovens (fig. 3.13). A small group of men in the Sonderkommando manage to save an adolescent girl who miraculously survives a gassing, and through her subjective flashback, however brief, we actually witness the gas chamber in operation (fig. 3.14). Relative to *Schindler's List*, Nelson attempts to treat the industrialization of death as dramatized fact as opposed to spectacle, de-emphasizing the fetishistic and sadistic viewing position with a matter-of-fact shooting strategy; even electing to remove shots that were deemed "too much," as discussed in the deleted scenes commentary of the DVD release. Regardless, for some the matter-of-fact tone in no way mitigates Nelson's trespass.

Figure 3.12

Figure 3.13

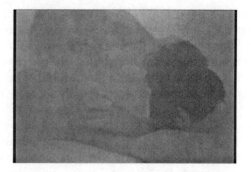

Figure 3.14

While the dialogue in *The Grey Zone* is overly verbose, its shooting palette is comparatively modest; by comparison *Schindler's List* clearly turns suffering into spectacle. When the Plaszow concentration camp is scheduled to be shut down, and all the internees are due to be transported to Auschwitz, Schindler negotiates a deal with Goeth, and buys 1,100 Jews. Due to an error in paperwork, however, the women on Schindler's list are transported to Auschwitz-Birkenau. When the women arrive in the camp they are processed, their hair is cut, and they are ordered to disrobe and enter the shower. The sequence invites the sadistic and fetishistic gaze of the spectator. The women are humiliated: subject to maltreatment and the barking orders of camp guards, scissors quickly shear long hair short, all standard operating procedure in the camp, but here it is transformed into spectacle. Lines of women get undressed; now the humiliated female body is transformed into fetish object (fig. 3.15). Having heard the rumors of the showers in the concentration camp, the petrified women are herded into the shower room. The hand-held camera follows the women right through the entrance and into the shower room (fig. 3.16), guards all the time commanding, "Schneller!" Naked and wracked by fear, the women gaze upward at the showerheads. The subsequent cut positions us outside the shower room where female guards shut the doors (fig. 3.17), followed by the camera moving straight in to the peephole; bringing the voyeuristic sensibility of the scene to a fever pitch (fig. 3.18). The next cut places us back inside the shower room, where the lights go out for a moment, causing the women to shriek in terror, before the lights inexplicably come back on. Stricken with fear, imaging that these are their very last moments, the women tremble and cry with dread (fig. 3.19). When water emerges from the showerheads (fig. 3.20) the women let out a mix of tears and laughter as an expression of relief. Given what we know (and the women on-screen certainly know it too) of the infamy of showers in Auschwitz, Spielberg creates a Hitchcockian sense of suspense. We know, or we think we know, what is about to happen, and the sequence builds up to this final moment; surely the Marquis de Sade would marvel at Spielberg's narrative craft — mixing humiliation, sex (fetishistic treatment of female bodies), and death (the threat of stepping into what we/they believe to be a gas chamber) into a single scenario.

Figure 3.15

Figure 3.16

Figure 3.17

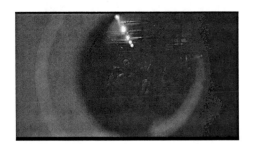

Figure 3.18

Figure 3.19

Figure 3.20

Spielberg's shower scene is not entirely out of touch with Hitchcock's shower scene in his 1960 film *Psycho*, which is also preceded with the sadistic perpetrator, Norman Bates, spying through a peephole shortly before he murders Marion Crane (fig. 3.21). Based on historical knowledge we might give Spielberg a "pass" on his shower scene if it were not for another scene that invites the sadistic and fetishistic gaze of the spectator. The shower scene has some merit in its however flawed attempt to render historical reality. The framing, editing, composition, and treatment of the female body, on the other hand, establishes a clear pattern that is not predicated on historical referents but rather on cinematic motifs that transform suffering into spectacle.[18]

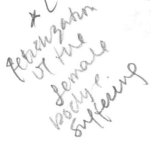

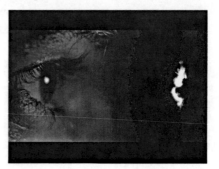

Figure 3.21

Despite his vigilance Goeth finds himself hopelessly attracted to his domestic

servant, a handpicked Jewess, Helen Hirsch. One evening Goeth descends into
the basement where Helen resides and happens upon her while she is bathing.
This scene is cross-cut between two other spatial fields, a marriage in the concentration camp, and with Schindler at a nightclub. The voice of a female singer
on stage and the diegetic music carry from the nightclub into the basement,
fostering an associative link between these two spaces. Helen is petrified at the
sight of Goeth, and she stands utterly paralyzed half-naked and dripping wet,
"So . . . this is where you come to hide from me," Goeth says, pacing back and
forth in the cellar. Goeth continues holding a one-sided conversation as Helen
remains silent and scared stiff. The aroused commandant, speaking to himself,
begins to justify his attraction and desire to have Helen. "Is this the face of a
rat? Are these the eyes of a rat? Hath not a Jew eyes?" Goeth caresses Helen's
hair (fig. 3.22), which is immediately cross-cut with the nightclub performer
caressing Schindler (fig. 3.23). "I feel for you, Helen," Goeth admits as he runs
his hand down her body, now caressing her breast. The nightclub performer leans
in to kiss Schindler (fig. 3.24), just as Goeth leans in to kiss Helen (fig. 3.25).
But Goeth breaks off his advance, "No, I don't think so. You're a Jewish bitch.
You nearly talked me into it, Helen, didn't you?" This is immediately followed
in quick succession to cuts between the three spatial fields, all marked by sharp
acoustic beats: (1) the breaking of glass under the groom's foot concluding the
wedding ceremony (fig. 3.26); (2) Goeth slaps Helen across the face, sending her
flying across the basement (fig. 3.27); and 3) the nightclub breaking into applause
(fig. 3.28). Spielberg cuts between these three spatial fields, as Goeth's assault
becomes increasingly more violent.

Figure 3.22

Figure 3.23

Figure 3.24

Figure 3.25

Figure 3.26

Figure 3.27

Figure 3.28

The use of L-cuts — where audio from one shot overlaps into another — the cutting between the different spatial fields, mixes together, very much like the shower scene, violence and sexuality. "The audience," Sara Horowitz concurs with these sentiments, "participates in Goeth's erotic gaze. Like Goeth, the viewer is meant to desire Helen's body, visually sexualized by the wet clothing. As Goeth's desire resolves in a physical beating, the audience participates in a voyeurism which encompasses both sex and brutality, with the victimized Jewish woman as its object."[19] The shots of the marriage to a lesser extent — however, the connotations of sexuality are certainly evident — but the nightclub shots most distinctly, confirm a *pattern* in Spielberg's film that conflates sexuality and violence. The seductive nightclub performer, who is not particularly sexualized, but is nonetheless on exhibition, in her sultry embrace of Schindler engages the fetishistic gaze, which through the editing, carries through to Goeth's caressing, fondling, gawking, and finally beating of Helen. The spectacle of the nightclub performance meets the spectacle of violence in the eroticized encounter between Goeth and Helen, and the climax of the scene displaces the hydraulics of orgasm — ejaculation — with Helen's blood. Thinly cloaked behind narrative diegesis and cinematic craftsmanship (cinematography, lighting, editing) *Schindler's List* proves to have more in common with *Ilsa: She-Wolf of the SS* than we might have first assumed.

While the spectacle of mixing sexuality and violence is deeply troubling in *Schindler's List*, the spectacle of clearing the ghetto is perhaps more productive. In the evening hours, when the operation is just mopping up, German soldiers search house to house looking for Jews that have secreted themselves away. As Jews emerge from their hiding places — literally coming out of the woodwork — the Germans ambush them. As the sharp acoustic bursts and lightning flashes of automatic weapons puncture the darkness of the desolate ghetto, a German SS man hammers out Bach on a piano, striking the keys with commanding force (fig. 3.29). Two SS men stand at the entrance of the flat where their compatriot is playing this beautiful piece of music; one says to the other, "What is this? Is this Bach?" The other shakes his head and insists, "No." The first SS man posits again, "Is this Bach?" The other SS man says, "No, Mozart." Still unsure and unconvinced the first SS man asks, "Mozart?" (fig. 3.30) [20] Setting Bach to the liquidation of the ghetto establishes a dialectical conflict between civilization

violence as climax [handwritten marginalia]

and destruction, between beauty and ugliness, between art and barbarity; the contrast is as sharp as the chiaroscuro lighting scheme that pervades the film. This spectacle of radical contrasts, without ever being didactic, allows for a subtle critique to quietly emerge from the bravado of violence: there is an abject lining to culture, that human progress is shadowed by the specter of human barbarity. That Germany can produce on the one hand the unsurpassed beauty of Bach's "concerto in D minor," and the Holocaust on the other hand, is a testament to the profound contradictions in the human condition. The spectacle of the scene allows for the tension between human progress and human barbarity to materialize without heavy-handed moralizing.

Figure 3.29

Figure 3.30

Classical music is also an important feature of Leszek Wosiewicz's 1989 film *Kornblumenblau.* The ending of the film is nothing short of a circus sideshow, somewhere between Peter Brook's 1967 film *Marat/Sade* and *Monty Python.* At the conclusion of the film, which cuts between the circus sideshow and one of the most graphic and "realistic" depictions of the gas chamber (which is discussed shortly), Wosiewicz reminds us in an epigraph, citing Montaigne, that we should never confuse "the mask and semblance for the real essence." An over-the-top per-formance of Beethoven's "Ninth Symphony" is played with a full orchestra (made up of camp internees), a choral group, and a troupe of male and female ballerinas — the male dancers are dressed in outfits that resemble the internee's standard issue garb (although the stripes run horizontally instead of vertically), while the women are dressed in black hats, leotards, and tutus modeled after the uniforms of the SS women (fig. 3.31). Camp internees also pull in a float of a Nordic god donning a Viking helmet with the SS emblem (fig. 3.32). This is cut with documentary footage of a German parade exhibiting similar romantic iconography, pointing to Germany's efforts to reclaim its pagan tradition during the Nazi era. The performance, however, is interrupted by an air raid. This of course is a complete fabrication — as if the circus atmosphere wasn't enough — as Auschwitz was never bombed. Nevertheless, explosions go off all around the performance, Germans scatter, running for their lives, as do some internees, while others cheer on the Allied bombers. Wyczynski, the principal character, and some of his fellow musicians begin to play the French national anthem, "La Marseillaise."[21]

Figure 3.31

Figure 3.32

The spectacle of sex and death is evident in *Kornblumenblau*, but it is wholly different from that of *Schindler's List*. Whereas the latter film places the spectator in the position of the perpetrator, and is obliged to "re-victimize" the tormented victims on-screen — via the sadistic nature of the gaze — in Wosiewicz's film, on the other hand, we are positioned in the place of the internee. No less voyeuristic, though, Wyczynski secretes himself in a storeroom. Peering out a window as he eats a raw onion, as if it were an apple, he watches the public hanging of internees. Treated like a sporting match, chairs are set up so that camp officials and their wives (or girlfriends) might watch the public hanging. The autumn wind kicks up a bit, hiking up the red skirt of one of the women. The framing of Wyczynski gets tighter, almost to the point of being an extreme close-up as he hurriedly, bite after bite, eats his onion (fig. 3.33). One of the internees on the gallows — there are a handful to be executed — shouts, "I shit on you and your whores! Kiss my ass! We shall win anyway! Fuck your whores!" The women grimace at the internee's protest, as the trapdoor opens beneath him. The noose tightens around the internee's neck; however, the trapdoor fails to open completely and a fellow internee — a kapo executing the public hanging — jumps on the poor soul; his weight is finally enough to break the man's neck. Watching this from the storeroom Wyczynski sheds tears, but is it the spectacle of death, the onion, or both that is the source of this tearful expression? Having seen enough, the women get up from their chairs and begin to walk away; one of the officers gropes the woman in the red skirt, grabbing her ass as she lets out a flirtatious laugh (fig. 3.34).

Figure 3.33

Figure 3.34

Unlike in *Schindler's List*, the victims are not compliant sheep. Nor in fact are they naked humiliated women petrified by the thought of being dispatched in the gas chamber. The framing — medium close-ups for the most part — and the subject of the executions are not easily given to the erotic gaze. The female company that the SS men keep, however, is sexualized to one degree or another. The framing of the woman in the red skirt, for instance, is classically fetishistic — framing and editing that cuts her body into bits and pieces: the white slip underneath the scarlet skirt, legs, feet, and ass. While the Germans on-screen make a spectacle of death, the film spectators via Wyczynski's subjective view make a spectacle of the Germans. Wyczynski assumes the voyeuristic perspective, alone in the darkened storeroom; he secretly watches the events through a window.[22] On the one hand, the voyeuristic gaze that the spectator inhabits — treating the perpetrators as fetish — intends to destabilize viewing positions, but at the same time it implicates the Nazi viewing position as one that eroticizes violence and suffering. Which is precisely what Spielberg did in *Schindler's List*, isn't it? This precise point is reinforced in the closing moments of the film, with one of the most explicit representations of the gas chamber in cinema. Set to the music of Beethoven's "Ninth Symphony," naked deportees — men, women, and children — file into the gas chamber in the main camp at Auschwitz. Wyczynski, working in the Sonderkommando, ushers the victims into the gas chamber and closes the steel door behind them. An SS man turns a valve and introduces the deadly gas into the hermetic room. Corresponding to the earlier scene — where Wyczynski watches the hanging of fellow internees — the SS man watches as the gas takes its toll and casually eats an apple, reminiscent of Wyczynski eating an onion. Viewed through a window, creating a frame-within-the-frame, the SS man watches, perhaps bemused, as the naked bodies writhe and scream in anguish. The writhing mass is so violent that bodies become almost indistinguishable from one another, bordering on a complete abstraction of human form. The glow cast on the SS man's face from the window looking into the gas chamber is reminiscent of the illumination of a television or movie screen, thus emphasizing the spectacle of the violent event. This does, in fact, share certain tropes with Spielberg's gas chamber/shower scene. And just like Spielberg, the camera moves between different vectors — a shot from inside the gas chamber, and outside, from the perpetrator's perspective, and the victims'. When it's finally over, Wyczynski and his Sonderkommando colleague put on gas masks and open the steel door. Dead naked bodies are stacked one on top of the other, floor to ceiling (fig. 3.35). Isolated outside the context of the climatic sequence, and the film in general, some might find this scene as a violation of the taboo against representing the gas chamber, but the context of the circus-like performance establishes a distanciation, insisting upon a critical evaluation of the representation, the nature of representing the gas chamber, and our position as spectators.[23] In addition, like the opening montage of the film, which includes self-referential nods to the cinematic apparatus and past films on similar subjects, the same pattern emerges here with the closing moments. Unquestionably for some, Wosiewicz crosses a threshold, and no distancing device, no self-referential critique will absolve him for including such a scene.[24]

"crossing" a line

Figure 3.35

At the climax of Pier Paolo Pasolini's 1975 film *Salò, or the 120 Days of Sodom,* the libertines (the sadists) take turns watching the final orgy of violence unfold in their villa courtyard. (This film is discussed at length in Chapter 6.) A Mackintosh chair perched on a platform gives the libertines a "balcony seat" to the spectacle below. As if at an opera, the libertines use small binoculars to view the event, as if at the theater or a sporting match. Pasolini frequently gives us subjective shots through the binoculars (fig. 3.36). At one point one of the libertines, the Duke, even turns the binoculars wrong-way around, suddenly "distancing" our perspective (fig. 3.37). The self-conscious alignment of the spectator's gaze with the libertines' in this way generates a critique of the sadistic voyeuristic gaze, for which the filmmaker is also complicit. This categorical self-awareness about the power and fascination of looking at the spectacle of violence is what sets *Salò* apart from other Holocaust films.

Figure 3.36

Figure 3.37

"NORMALITY IS THREATENED BY THE MONSTER"[25]

Bryan Singer's 1998 film *Apt Pupil*, adapted from the Stephen King novella of the same name, exchanges the standard monster for an aging Nazi. Todd Bowden, a high school student, gets deep (maybe too deep) into a research project on the Holocaust; during his research he discovers that his mild-mannered neighbor, Arthur Denker, isn't who he says he is; rather, he's Kurt Dussander, a Nazi war criminal, accused of conducting medical experiments in the camp — including testing human subjects in a decompression chamber. Rather than turning in his neighbor to the authorities, Todd cuts a deal with the former Nazi: "I wanna hear about it," the ambitious high schooler insists. "Everything they're afraid to show us in school. You were there. You did those things. No one can tell it better than you can. That's all I want. Then I'll leave you alone." Thus, he blackmails the Nazi into becoming a history teacher like none other, with Todd the ever apt pupil.

The film is something akin to an adolescent "after-school-movie" where, as reviewer Stuart Klawans observes,

> a kid . . . messes with the Forces of Evil . . . [and] toys with a power that might just as well emanate from an Egyptian amulet, or a book of spells or a mad ventriloquist's dummy unearthed from an Indian burial mound by a red-eyed dog named Fausto. But such contrivances have worn thin, and so [the film] uses the Holocaust to kick off its plot.[26]

Although sometimes characterized as a horror film, *Apt Pupil* is pretty anemic, and is bound to disappoint hardened fans of the horror genre, and is more in keeping with a dramatic thriller. Singer says of his film, "It is creepy. But it's also an intriguing premise: A boy plays with a monster and gets eaten. It is a true horror story." Not only is the story truly horrific, as Singer says, according to him it is a "gripping examination of the contagiousness of evil . . . 'done with the emotions, not the supernatural.'"[27] Within the narrative of the film, indeed, the eager youngster is "eaten up" with the details of the camp: "Once they were in the chamber, how long did it take? Like a minute, five minutes?" Dussander balks, "Gott, no. The prussic acid took about 15 minutes. But the monoxide," as he pours himself a drink, "could take an hour, sometimes more." Ever interested in the raw biological facts of mass extermination, the youngster persists, "What happened to them? I mean, exactly." "It was a mess," Dussander responds. "They would lose control of their bodies. They vomited, urinated and defecated themselves. Even though the gas came in from the vents in the ceiling they would climb on top of each other desperately reaching for fresh air that wasn't there. They died in a mountain of themselves." Todd asks, "What about the children?" Quickly Dussander responds, "On the bottom." "Did anyone ever survive it?" Todd asks, and the education continues like this for weeks on end.

Whereas exploitation films like *Ilsa: She-Wolf of the SS* projects male anxieties about the Women's Liberation movement onto the Holocaust narrative, in *Apt Pupil* latent homophobia is grafted onto the Holocaust, where evil is equated with homoeroticism.[28] Indeed, throughout the first half of the film, a strange romantic relationship simmers between the two men — Dussander recounts his stories by firelight as his young pupil is sprawled across a couch. And certainly there is no innovation here, as discussed in the later chapters that address sadism, numerous films adopt this motif, where the Nazis' criminality is "explained away" as a form of illness, typically accompanied by some manifestation of "sexual perversion," including homosexuality. *Apt Pupil* is comfortably situated then in a lineage of films from Visconti's *The Damned* to the proliferation of Naziploitation films (discussed in Chapter 8) that arrive at the tawdry conclusion: fascism and genocide are the product of "sickness." All of these films rely on a Manichean economy, in keeping with Picart and Frank's argument,

> of a series of binary dichotomies: normal versus monstrous, heterosexual versus homosexual, healthy versus sick. Yet this attempt to create easy dichotomies unveils hidden tensions, because the line between victim (feminized) and victimizer (masculinized) is a thin one, as revealed in the reversal of power that bind Todd and Dussander and vice versa.[29]

As if bringing home some sexy new lingerie for his partner, Todd buys a Nazi uniform for Dussander and insists that he put it on; the elderly man protests, insisting that he's suffered enough indignities but, unrelenting, Todd unleashes on him, "What you've suffered with me is nothing compared to what the Israelis would do to you. You forget that, and I'll admit that's my fault. But don't ever forget the file I have on you. I tried to do things the nice way, but you don't want it. So, fine. We'll do this the hard way. You'll put this on because I wanna see you in it. Now move!" This finally cuts to Dussander descending his stairway, only his jackboots within frame at first then we see him in his full regalia. Todd is elated at the sight; he studies him, and eventually calls Dussander to "Attention!" Snidely, Dussander complies and steps into position. "March!" Todd insists, as Dussander stands immobilized and somewhat dumbfounded, "Do it. I'm serious." Dussander begins tentatively marching in place, but then Todd demands, "Stop fucking around! March!" Todd continues, "That's it. March." Then barking orders: "Face right! Face right! March!" Dussander, beginning to get winded, steps up his pace, as Todd — almost with orgasmic excitation — watches on. Dussander then gives the Nazi salute to his young pupil (fig. 3.38). As Dussander works himself up to a fevered pitch, continuing to march, Todd exclaims, "Stop!" Winded and sitting at the kitchen table, Dussander admonishes, "Boy, be careful. You play with fire." Although the specter of Nazism is the "contagion" that Dussander refers to in his cautionary statement, it is clearly filtered through the lens of a perverse eroticism.[30]

Figure 3.38

Continuing to conflate Nazism with perverse sexuality, Dussander explains to Todd that, "it never goes away. Not for you." This statement is echoed later in the film through the use of a sonic flashback, when Todd, distraught by a sudden self-awareness, is confronted with a graffiti-swastika painted on the underpass. The "it" is slightly ambiguous, because the implication here is that the fascination with death, or the intoxicating power associated with the Nazi experience, "never goes away." And the suggestion is that Dussander knows that Todd has caught the bug, his fascination with the details of mass murder has crossed over into something more dubious. And while these suggestions are the intended connotations of Dussander's admonition, the subtext is that the homoerotic feelings that Todd harbors will never go away. Here the film conflates homosexual desire with Nazism. And, finally, at the conclusion of the film the "it" morphs into yet another sexual perversion: pedophile, a stain that *never* goes away.

Despite the sexual tension that runs below the surface, both characters — Todd and Dussander — are viewed as impotent. Cross-cut between a high school party, and a leisurely evening in Dussander's backyard patio, we see the ineptitude of both characters. At the party Todd's female companion tries to perform oral sex on him, but he cannot achieve an erection, and his companion even laughingly questions, "Maybe you just don't like girls?" Dussander, on the other hand, attempts to kill a cat by shoving it into his oven (reminiscent of his days in the concentration camp?), but he cannot even manage this; Dussander earns nothing but a nasty cat scratch, and laughs off his own incompetence. The impotence of these men, though, is yet another sign of "sickness," embodying the typical characteristics of the cinematic Nazi. While Dussander is a Nazi, Todd is clearly becoming one, evident in his inability to achieve an erection. Imagine a young high school boy, with a more than willing sexual partner; indeed, he must be "sick."

Todd does begin to feel uneasy about his relationship with Dussander, or perhaps more accurately the Nazi taint that's infecting him, which begins to take its toll, haunted by visions and nightmares. The shower scene is pivotal in Todd's character development. To begin with Todd views himself on the side of "good," and "innocence," and thus identifies with the victims of the Holocaust, but as his relationship develops with Dussander his identification turns towards the perpetrators of the Holocaust. After a game of basketball, Todd and his classmates return to the locker-room to take a shower. In the shower the high school students exchange typical high school banter as Todd, under the steaming blast of water, rubs his face. As he lowers his hands, though, the color palette shifts from warm yellow to a sickly blue-green, and as the camera pans left an elderly man stands where once one of Todd's classmates did; in fact, the shower is now filled with haggard and emaciated men (fig. 3.39) The pleasant warm steam of the high school shower suddenly connotes something rather menacing: the gas-filled chambers that the Nazis disguised as showers. Todd's position is somewhat unclear, while placed among the victims, plied over the scene is a voice — speaking German — barking orders, echoing Todd's commands shouted at Dussander earlier. Furthermore, Todd's vision is not totally unfamiliar, it is similar to an earlier nightmare — matching the blue-green color palette of the shower scene — where Todd peeks through the peephole in a gas-chamber door; (fig. 3.40) in a radical shift of positions — from victim to perpetrator, through a

turning to the side of perpetrator

series of very quick takes — Todd once inside the gas chamber (and gasping for air) is suddenly on the outside looking in as men are gassed.

Figure 3.39

Figure 3.40

As the shift in Todd's character takes hold, the relationship between pupil and teacher also begins to transform as well. Dussander, at once in an attempt to ensure Todd's continued company — he grows increasingly enamored with him — and at the same time to protect his own interests, places a 12-page document in a safety deposit box, or so he says, detailing the nearly year-long relationship between the two. Todd's knowledge of Dussander's crimes in this case suddenly becomes a liability, rather than an asset, having never gone to the authorities, not to mention the unmistakable sexual tension that permeates their relationship. Once Dussander turns the tables and blackmails Todd, the old man proposes a toast to their meeting, and pours his young companion a drink. Todd says, "I think you should fuck yourself." To which Dussander returns, "Oh, my dear boy. Don't you see? We are fucking each other." Todd grimaces as he drinks to Dussander's toast.

Homoeroticism also manifests in the interactions between Dussander and Archie, a local homeless man. Following Dussander home one evening, Archie gets himself invited into the elderly man's home: "Just like the boy," suggesting that Archie believes that Dussander (and Todd) might be of the homosexual persuasion. It's not immediately evident, but it becomes clear that Archie is an experienced gay hustler; this becomes apparent in some of his drunken dialogue later, and more specifically his colorful sweater and a scarf, which he waives about, coding him as gay. As the two men drink, Dussander plays Wagner, to which Picart and Frank remark, "The use of Wagner, of course, alludes not only to Nazism but also to the *Liebestod* (love-death motif) and emphasizes more strongly the implication of a sadistic homoeroticism between Dussander and Archie."[31]

While seemingly disavowing his own latent homosexual desire, Dussander apparently views Archie as a "legitimate" target for elimination precisely because he is coded as queer, and by killing Archie, Dussander might "regain" his sense of masculinity, which is tightly wrapped up with his former identity as an SS officer. Archie is seen as effeminate, queer, and sexually promiscuous — offering his services to Dussander. Furthermore, Archie, like the Gypsies, is a transient, and thus from Dussander's perspective of no consequence, justifying his murder.

Wielding his phallic dagger, Dussander stabs the hapless vagrant in the back; however, as with killing the cat, Dussander is incapable of finishing the job. Pushing Archie down into the basement, he calls Todd and deceives him into "finishing" the job by locking him in the basement with Archie, who is severely wounded, but certainly not dead. Dussander urgently calls Todd, and says after hanging up the phone, "Now we'll see what you're made of." Despite Archie's pleas for help, which turn to robust self-defense, Todd bludgeons the man to death with a shovel. This is no easy task, as Archie does not go quietly into the night, but instead the murderous act requires well-targeted blows, and not just one but several over a protracted period of time. This binds Todd and Dussander together. While this situates the characters as partners in crime, like one lover coming to the aid of another and covering up for it too, it also stakes a claim to lost masculinity.

Todd's guidance counselor at school, Edward French with a Freddie-Mercury-mustache, also makes what could be construed as homosexual advances towards the promising youth. After Todd's grades slip, French calls the wayward student into his office. As it turns out, though, Dussander, who poses as Todd's grandfather, prompted the meeting. French makes a deal with Todd, that if he can get "As" on his final, French will persuade his teachers to base their grades on his final, and disregard Todd's poor mid-term scores. The meeting ends with French explaining that he's just gone through a vicious divorce and he's ready to help Todd at any time.

At the conclusion of the film, French, after discovering that Todd (and Dussander) has not been truthful with him, confronts the recent high school graduate at home. French threatens to speak to Todd's parents — the ramification of which would be catastrophic for the youngster, the whole pack of lies would likely come crumbling down — but Todd does not take such threats idly and retaliates,

> Does it ever work? I really want to know, does it ever work, or am I the first one? Cause if I'm the first, I'm flattered really, but somehow I can't believe that . . . not after fixing my grades, and then giving me your home phone number, and then you come out here when my parents aren't home?

At first French is flabbergasted and doesn't seem to fully realize what Todd is saying. Todd continues, "I mean you've got some balls! Is this why your wife left you? You really must have wanted to shake my hand . . . or something else?" French interrupts, "Now wait a minute, what are you . . . You're gonna tell people I . . . I did something to you, Todd?" But the apt pupil doesn't relent, "The things that I'm going to say, they'll never go away, not for you. Think of your job . . . think of your son." The Nazi taint is evident here, as sexual aberration is something that will "never go away."

Apt Pupil conflates homosexuality, pedophilia, and sexual perversion with fascism, a theme that gets played out elsewhere, including Bernardo Bertolucci's 1970 film *The Conformist*, and Luchino Visconti's 1969 film *The Damned*, both of which conflate pedophilia and Nazism. *Apt Pupil* uses "the recurring representation of sexual 'abnormality' . . . as a series of codes meant to signal Todd's descent into Nazism, as well as a recurring pattern" found in cinematic representations of the Holocaust. Picart and Frank argue that King's novella "establishes Dussander as a homoerotic surrogate and as a monster because he threatens heterosexual masculinity,"[32] and this equally applies to the film. For it is Dussander that is the obstacle in Todd's path towards normality (heteronormative relations), but ultimately it is the monster that prevails.

Chapter Four

Defiance and Resistance

"We are what we've always been . . . victims."[1]

INTRODUCTION

There are many different types of resistance and defiance, and this chapter surveys the ways in which they have been represented. While some succeed in representing Jewish agency, a number of films rely on the standard convention of representing the Jew-as-victim. Defiance and resistance come in many forms, though not all manifest in visible forms of physical conflict, and nor do all forms of resistance or defiance end with the virtuous prevailing. Both the Warsaw Ghetto Uprising (April 19 through May 16, 1943) and the Warsaw Uprising (August through October 1944) were in military terms, ostensibly, failures; both insurgency campaigns were brutally crushed by the Germans, leading to a systematized retaliatory operation to level the city of Warsaw. Other much smaller scale forms of resistance also took place. Bruno Bettelheim, for instance, relays an artful encounter where a convoy of naked prisoners was being marched into the gas chamber. "Somehow, the SS officer, who had been in charge, had learned that one of the female prisoners had been a dancer. He ordered her to dance for him. She acquiesced and in doing so came close enough to him first to grab his pistol and then to shoot and kill him with his own pistol."[2] Despite the fact that the dancer was immediately shot and killed, her gesture of resistance butts up against the conventional representation of the concentration camp internee as nothing more than a hapless victim.

In Holocaust films, Jews in particular are frequently depicted as the quintessential victim, as if lambs compliantly marching to the slaughter. This portrayal of Jewish victimhood is designed to elicit the spectator's sympathy, and this further defines the perpetrators as the embodiment of unadulterated evil. This constellation of characters serves the spectator's ego, because the spectator's identification is most often aligned with the one character (or cast of characters) that does resist, or the character that tries to save the hapless Jews. This Manichean arrangement positions the protagonist, with whom we identify, against the very forces of evil, and the Jew is rendered as the mere foil that drives the good versus evil plot.

In her critical essay, "The Jew as a Female Figure in the Holocaust Film," Judith Doneson outlines the Jew-as-victim motif, which was introduced in the previous chapter. Over and over again, a Gentile character has to come to the rescue of hapless Jews. Michel Mitrani's 1974 film *Black Thursday* depicts the event of July 16, 1942, the first round-up of Jews in Paris. The primary character of the film, Paul, a Gentile, vehemently tries to persuade the Jews that danger lies just over the horizon. Although the film's aim might be to condemn the French police's role in the deportation of Jews, "it is much more successful in its condemnation of the Jews for not having been clever enough to resist their arrest."[3] Doneson, who wrote extensively about the Jew-as-victim throughout her career, says that "the passive non-resistant Jew" has "become the stereotype of the Jewish response to the Holocaust."[4]

In detailing the Jew-as-victim trope, Doneson observes that frequently the male protagonist — a Gentile — falls in love with a Jewess, and subsequently attempts to save her, and sometimes her family, but typically fails. "He is aroused to acts of goodness as a result of his love for the sexy, mysterious Jewess. Yet, conversely, the average viewer sees him as a hero moved by Christian altruism, while the Jew, the victim, continues to symbolize the weak female." But the innate weakness of the Jewish character as it is depicted in these films conspires against love — be it romantic love, lust, or Christian charity. "The Jewess, inspired by either loyalty or hindered because of an inability to wander from her roots, always returns to her people and their fate during the Holocaust."[5] Doneson identifies this motif in numerous films — including Konrad Wolf's 1959 film *Stars*, Carlo Lizzani's 1961 film *Gold of Rome*, Louis Malle's 1974 film *Lacombe Lucien*, Jiří Weiss's *Sweet Light in a Dark Room* released in 1960, and *Kapò* the year before, directed by Gillo Pontecorvo — all of these films correspond to Doneson's observation that the Jew is rendered as a feminine victim. And even when Jewish men appear in Holocaust films, they are frequently emasculated and figured as "incapable of acting alone without the help of the Christian, the male partner, as his protector."[6]

Even when our emotional identification is aligned with the Holocaust victim, or when we are encouraged to identify with Holocaust characters through subjective shots, aligning our gaze with a character's, these forms of identification are generally speaking governed by a degree of inertia. This happens in at least two ways: first, subjective perspectives are contained within the boundary of a ghetto or a concentration camp (sometimes interrupted with flashbacks or dreams, taking us beyond these physical boundaries); and, second, where emotional identification is conditioned by a nearly paralyzing melancholia preventing altogether or throwing up an almost insurmountable obstacle to a character's transformation — read: "moving on." For example, in the first instance where a character is physically confined, in Roman Polanski's 2002 film *The Pianist* the principal character watches as a passive bystander through the window of his various hiding places as others physically confront the Germans. And as for this latter trope, a character while physically unconstrained might find themselves in a prison without walls, emotionally trapped; films like Sidney Lumet's 1964 film *The Pawnbroker*, Alan J. Pakula's 1982 film *Sophie's Choice*, and André Ernotte's 1976 film *High Street* exemplify this.

The Pawnbroker, for instance, depicts its primary character, Sol Nazerman, almost utterly devoid of empathy, unable to act, emotionally void, and finally when his apprentice is killed he is left voiceless, uttering his silent scream in the closing moments of the film. The protagonist is haunted by repressed memories that return as ghostly flashbacks. In addition to the editing pattern that insinuates Nazerman's subjective state and traumatic experience, the *mise en scène* reinforces his emotional confinement; adopting a common trope of film noir lighting shadows cast by the pawnbroker's security cage externalize his emotional captivity. Arthur Hiller's 1975 film *The Man in the Glass Booth* makes literal what the lighting scheme in *The Pawnboker* connotes. "The man in the glass booth is like the pawnbroker of Sidney Lumet's film, encased both literally and figuratively. Goldman (whose flashbacks are aural, where Nazerman's are visual) is isolated by his memories, branded by what he has seen and been."[7] Goldman, like Nazerman, is enslaved by his traumatic memories.

In *Sophie's Choice*, Sophie's abusive boyfriend, Nathan Landau, on the surface of it might appear "hyper-masculine," but the fits of rage that he is prone to are more in keeping with hysteria than of a testosterone-fueled rage. Born in the United States, and having never served in the military due to mental illness, one of his symptoms manifests in an obsession with Nazi war criminals and the Holocaust. Sophie acts as a conduit through which Nathan can connect with his overly obsessive fascination with "victimhood," which is tangled up in his compulsion to "know." The couple's suicide at the conclusion of the film, a complete emotional retreat into victimhood, is yet another variation on the weak and feminine Jew. The couple's resignation to victimization in death defies the dramatic imperative for characters to change, and because the characters from start to finish remain virtually unchanged they succumb to their own boundless self-pity. Alberto in Vittorio De Sica's 1970 film *The Garden of the Finzi-Continis* is coded as homosexual. A dandy and a virtual shut-in, the young Jewish man falls ill and dies, as though his body simply yields — in advance — to the coming tragedy about to beset Italian Jews.[8]

Doneson suggests that a survey of Holocaust films reveals that the vast majority conform to the conventions of feminizing Jewish characters, in contradistinction to their Gentile counterparts, "irrespective of country of origin," and one might assume from these cinematic conventions that, because Jews are constantly being saved by Gentile characters, "goodness infiltrated Europe during this evil era."[9] While Doneson's thesis remains largely unassailable, the films discussed in this chapter attempt to counter the image of the Jew as the archetype of victimhood.[10]

AGENCY: ESCAPEES, PARTISANS, AND RESISTANCE MOVEMENTS

Aleksander Ford's 1948 film *Border Street* adopts many of the strategies and motifs of Italian neo-realism — the incorporation of newsreel footage, set in an urban environment, and a focus on children that are forced to negotiate the injustices of their time. Of the films that depict the Polish resistance, *Border Street* is one of the few that features Jewish characters, who for example in Andrzej Wajda's films are relegated to the background, quite literally in fact in *A Generation* (1955) where in the background the Jewish Ghetto burns during the uprising, seen as a plume of smoke. In *Border Street* Jewish children find solidarity with anti-fascist Poles, and are pit against Hitler youth. The relative harmony of Warsaw (despite the anti-Semitism) erodes with the eventual German invasion and occupation, putting increasing pressure on Jewish families until they are forced from their homes, sequestered behind the Ghetto walls, and finally building to the climatic uprising. The sewers running underneath the city function as a network allowing resistance members (or smugglers) to move between the divided quarters of the city. The sewer scenes reappear in amazing form in Wajda's 1957 film *Kanal*. Wajda was Ford's protégé, the latter taught at and was appointed the director of Film Polski in 1945, but he never felt at ease in Communist Poland; Stalin even denounced him for presenting "a Jewish instead of a class hero."[11] Nevertheless, it was in the Soviet Union that Ford developed as a filmmaker, spending "the war years in the Soviet Union as the chief of the Polish army's film unit,"[12] and developing his realist aesthetic.

Wajda's war trilogy — *A Generation* (1955), *Kanal* (1957), and *Ashes and Diamonds* (1958) — chronicles the Polish resistance following the Nazi invasion on September 1, 1939. These films drew on Wajda's own wartime experiences. Born in 1926, Wajda joined the right wing militia, Armia Krajowa, the Home Army. His father was an officer in the Polish military and was among the thousands massacred by the Soviet Army in the Katyn Forest; this is the subject of one of his most recent films, simply entitled *Katyn* (2007).

The trilogy does not explicitly reference or deal with the targeted effort to ostracize, ghettoize, deport, and exterminate the Jewish population (many of whom were fellow Poles), but Wajda was not entirely indifferent to the plight of his Jewish brethren either. Stuart Liebman wonders how much the implicit reference to the Warsaw Ghetto Uprising in *A Generation* has to do with Jerzy Lipman, his cinematographer; Lipman also shot *Kanal*.[13] The relationship between Poles and Jews is nevertheless ambivalent, and quite different from his predecessor and advisor Ford, where the solidarity between Jews and Poles is more evident in *Border Street*. *Kanal* shares much in common with *Border Street*, where in both cases the resistance retreats to the network of sewers beneath the streets of Warsaw. While *Border Street* features the sewers as a link between the city beyond the enclosed walls of the Warsaw Ghetto, a clandestine system where goods and munitions are brought into the Ghetto to support the Jewish uprising, in *Kanal* retreating into the sewers is a last ditch effort mounted by the Polish resistance to escape the German onslaught. The events depicted in *Kanal* are premised on Jerzy Stawinski, the screenwriter's own experiences.

Kanal, again like *Border Street*, share affinities with the Italian Neo-Realist films, especially *Germany Year Zero* (Roberto Rossellini, 1948), set in the ruins of Berlin. Despite its somber tone, in a colloquial sense there is something existential about *Kanal*: in the face of imminent annihilation the younger characters zealously embrace the most passionate parts of life. Sexuality is a prominent feature of the first part of the film; all the characters recognize the grave state of affairs and, despite this, during a lull in the fighting some seize the moment and fully embrace carnal pleasures. Walking in on a post-coital moment, one character says to two lovers in bed, "You'd better get up; this isn't the time . . ." To which the male partner in bed responds, "To the contrary, it's just the time." The following scene is undeniably and unabashedly sexy, even by contemporary standards. But, of course, such existential moments are not expected to last, and our lovers are abruptly interrupted by a German attack. *Kanal* is less about the lives of individual characters, though, and more about life itself. *Kanal* indeed is an amazing piece of cinema, but none of the films in Wajda's war trilogy is a Jewish film as such; as Annette Insdorf observes regarding Wajda films, "the Jews and the self-centered characters die, paving the way for the Communist order."[14]

Jan Nemec's 1964 *Diamonds of the Night* is a riveting film about survival. Adapted from Arnost Lustig's autobiographical book *Darkness Casts No Shadows*,[15] Lustig by sheer luck escaped his train transport when it was bombed. He also wrote the script for Zbynek Brynych's 1962 film *Transport from Paradise*. Amazing in its artistry, *Diamonds of the Night* relies very little on dialogue and uses cinematographic virtuosity to follow two escapees from a train bound, no doubt, for a concentration camp.

The film's camerawork is performative, as the viewer experiences the dizzying whirl of trees and brush, as the camera follows, or assumes the perspective, of our characters running for their lives. Here the cinematography *performs the narrative*, rather than simply *documenting* what is happening. The cinematography *is* the experience of running for one's life, rather than merely recording the act of running; it doesn't *show* running, it *is* running. There is absolutely no need for expository dialogue, or any other conventional communicative cues. This would be redundant and in all probability far less effective in conveying the escapee narrative. In fact, there is no need for language at all (save perhaps shouts of "Halt!" in the background), for the audio/visual experience of running "speaks volumes." We don't need an explanation for what is unfolding, because we can feel it in the kinetics of the film. We share something of the experience of running through the forest: the aural experience of cracking twigs and dried leaves underfoot, the frenetic visual experience of dodging branches, of darting looks while the body is in physical motion.

This is what sets *Diamonds of the Night* apart from so many other films — the virulent agency (especially at the beginning of the film) attributed to our protagonists. They are not passive victims having things *done to them*;

activity vs. passivity

rather they are characters in the physical act of resistance and are not only *shown to be doing*, but rather are *doing* as embodied in the cinematography.[16] This performative element — this dynamism —is not evident in many other Holocaust films. While the two protagonists are eventually captured, it is rare to see this sort of potency given to Holocaust victims. The protagonists escape physical confinement; as they flee the cattle-car destined for a concentration camp, the spatial field opens up to the characters, which is also relatively unusual in a Holocaust film. The performative cinematography, the sparse audio dialogue, contributes to the film's verisimilitude; however, Nemec adds surrealistic elements to disabuse its audience from reading the film as "realistic."

The spectator's emotional identification with the characters is complicated, though, by one of the character's fantasies. Hungry, one of the male characters enters a farmhouse to steal some food. When a woman confronts him, he attacks her, but it is unclear whether or not he imagines assaulting the woman or if he does in fact brutally assault her. The spectator might very well sympathize with the character's plight, and perhaps even accept (but not forgive) what seems like senseless violence, but we do not pity the characters. Pity is typically reserved for characters that are robbed of agency.

In their review of the film, Stuart Liebman and Leonard Quart observe that, "If the film was distinguished only by Nemec's exquisite editing and vertiginous tracking, it would risk estheticizing the horrors it depicts, caring more about creating richly textured images than about evoking the fear and anguish of the victims of arbitrary power." But there is far more to this film than an aesthetic exercise, and Liebman and Quart agree, because "Nemec . . . has created a trenchant, unsentimental fable, made richer by the poignancy and ambiguity of the ending."[17] When the pair is eventually captured by a band of locals, it is unclear if they are executed or not.

Liebman and Quart, reviewing a handful of Czech films — including Zbynek Brynych's 1962 film *Transport from Paradise*, and his 1965 film *The Fifth Horsemen Is Fear* — conclude that,

> The most abstract and formally imaginative of the three, *Diamonds of the Night*, is clearly the strongest of the films, and the one that gets closest (if not ever close enough) to the heart of the Holocaust's anguish. That is not to say that the Holocaust is best treated in a fabulistic or oblique manner rather than in more concrete and accessible or in more coolly distanced and formalistic ways. Perhaps the most one can conclude is that a few films, like *Diamonds of the Night*, manage to evoke in ways that are not always easy to define, one small element of the Holocaust's horror.[18]

Diamonds of the Night owes a debt not so much to figures like Brynych or Alfréd Radok, but instead to Luis Buñuel.[19] Nemec's film points beyond the realm of narrative cinema as a representational strategy and paves the way for experimental filmmakers and video artists when attempting to represent the Holocaust.

Tim Blake Nelson's 2001 film *The Grey Zone* depicts the heroic action of the Sonderkommando at Auschwitz II-Birkenau, where the men with the assistance from other conspirators destroyed Crematorium IV by blowing it up on October 7, 1944. The title of the film, and its basic elements, are taken from Primo Levi's essay, "The Gray Zone," published in *The Drowned and the Saved*. The film in turn is based on Nelson's theatrical play (1996), and the film's dialogue suffers as a result; it is overwritten and does not trust the cinematic medium enough to tell the story (quite unlike *Diamonds of the Night*). Nevertheless, Nelson's film is among the most explicit in showing the mechanics of industrialized death. Nelson bases the details of the event on the account of Dr. Miklos Nyiszli, a Hungarian Jew, and Dr. Josef Mengele's assistant in the medical experiment section of the camp. Despite its shortcomings, it dramatizes one of the most significant uprisings within the concentration camp, only made possible through a well-coordinated co-operative effort and a tremendous amount of courage and self-sacrifice. Female internees in Birkenau working at the Union Munitions Factory in Brzezinka smuggled out small amounts of gunpowder day by day. These small amounts of gunpowder were then slipped into the clothing of corpses, which were carted off to the crematorium. It is through this network of conspirators — using corpses as a vehicle — that gunpowder was smuggled to the Sonderkommando, who then fashioned improvised explosive devices that destroyed Crematorium IV. Partisans as well left weapons at the perimeter of the camp for the Sonderkommando, allowing the men to mount a small yet valiant fight against overwhelming force.

What this film does well is its unrelenting insistence on depicting the actual mechanisms of mass murder at work, clearly and explicitly. Few films go so far to show the grim aftermath of mass execution — the vomit, feces and blood-smeared walls, the process of cleaning up human filth, the extraction of gold fillings from the dead, and the gruesome task of moving bodies from the gas chamber to the crematorium where they were summarily burned. Although the film is dialogue-heavy, it relents to the cinematic medium at the moments when it really matters — moments of genuine cinema that allow the image to speak for itself; for instance, Schlermer, one of the Sonderkommando, stands at the end of the hall pounding a bottle of some unknown alcohol as the camera slowly tracks in on him (fig. 4.1). It is not clear what he is doing, where he is, or what he's waiting for until finally we hear the exhaust fans trip on. And from here, Schlermer, and the others who then join him, put on gas masks and move into the gas chamber — this tracking shot, dramatically lit, conveys without a word of dialogue the enormous and complex emotional weight the Sonderkommando carry. As forcefully and convincingly as Claude Lanzmann argues for a prohibition of such images, here we have a representation of the acts many of his interviewees from his 1985 documentary *Shoah* participated in, and as much as we might be inclined to pay deference to Lanzmann, perhaps we can appreciate the testimonies of the Sonderkommando all that much more with this dramatization.

Figure 4.1

And for all of its verbose indulgences it does not over-sentimentalize, it is not overly melodramatic, and it refuses to paint characters with broad strokes — good versus bad — at least insofar as the Sonderkommando are concerned. "In other words," Janet Ward concurs, "despite the rebels' achievement — half the crematoria are destroyed and not rebuilt — this film resists the temptation of a more universally applicable conventional heroism into which resistance narratives of the Holocaust might fall."[20] Indeed this film marks a turn in the depiction of the Holocaust victims. Axel Bangert argues that *The Grey Zone* "appears to indicate a qualitative change in filmic Holocaust memory, as it challenges the widespread image of Jews being murdered as a homogeneous and largely passive victim group."[21] As futile as their fight might have been, *The Grey Zone* casts off the Jew-as-victim, while never resorting to jingoistic sentiments.

Edward Zwick's 2008 film *Defiance* is one of the few films with a "happy ending." A dramatization of a true story, *Defiance* features Tuvia and Zus Bielski, Jewish brothers who are forced to flee into the forest when their Belorussian shtetl is liquidated. The Bielski brothers establish a camp where they take in other Jews, and form a clandestine community complete with an armed militia. Zus Bielski decides to join forces with the Russian partisans, leaving Tuvia to command the encampment, which struggles to survive the harsh environment. When the German forces finally discover the encampment, the band of Jews is forced to flee, and like the story of *Exodus*, Tuvia leads the group through the swamps and eventually to safety. When the German forces, with far superior firepower, including tanks, beset the group they are saved (just in a nick of time) when Zus and other partisans arrive to counter the German assault. In classic Hollywood form good vanquishes evil, and the spectator is treated to a thrilling story of Jewish empowerment.[22]

The constellation of good versus bad characters — illustrating a Manichean worldview — necessitates a narrative strategy that dehumanizes the villains. Nazis (or their collaborators) are generally not characters as such but representatives of clear-cut evil. Zwick's *Defiance* effectively mobilizes this strategy. The undeniable adrenaline rush that the spectator experiences while watching the film — especially in the final Exodus sequence, when the Germans beset the band of Jews — is rooted in the fact that the representatives of evil are not represented as agents but as pawns sacrificed to the service of the uplifting and action-packed narrative. In the climatic battle sequence the Germans are depicted in medium long shots, or long shots, with very little or no recognizable facial features. They are largely disembodied, merely extensions of their weapons, instead of characters. Moreover, the Germans are not afforded subjective shots. The climatic sequence is little more than an American Western, where American frontiersmen (Jews) fend off the marauding Indians (Germans). The Jewish characters, on the other hand, are given close-ups; they're fully embodied, and are privileged with subjective shots. There is no question that the strategy is effective in creating an exhilarating film, but it comes at the expense of nuance.

POLITICAL COMMITMENT

Committed political resistance is effectively another kind of "spiritual" resistance; faith is place not in God but in the Socialist cause. Wanda Jakubowska's 1947 film *The Last Stage* is emblematic of politically motivated forms of resistance,[23] and is unmistakably and unapologetically colored by Socialist politics. As discussed in the second chapter, Jakubowska was a member of the Polish Communist Party and active in the resistance. She was arrested and was eventually sent to Auschwitz-Birkenau where she met Gerda Schneider. The pair collaborated together to develop the script for *The Last Stage* while interned.

Jakubowska's film features the solidarity of female internees in Auschwitz, and Jakubowska makes a moving and defiant account of the concentration camp experience. She situates the act of resistance itself as the focus of the film, rather than an individual character. As a result individual characters are less important than their commitment to the struggle against fascism, and the Nazi oppressor. In fact, despite national, religious, and cultural differences the characters unify against a common enemy. Among the principal characters — such as they are — Marta works as a translator and is a Polish Jew; Anna, the committed communist of the group, is a German nurse; and Eugenia is a Russian doctor. Almost all of the major characters die, but as Annette Insdorf observes, and to reiterate the point, "the central character, which is the Cause, remains — a whole greater than the sum of its parts."[24]

Jakubowska places a premium on ideological alignment, and thus she foregrounds political solidarity among the internees over ethnic or national identification. "Jewishness" effectively dissolves into the Babel of the concentration camp, but is nevertheless omnipresent in the *mise en scène*; Jewish characters are there, as Judith Doneson observes, but "in the background, marching silently into the gas chambers."[25] And so even despite its stanch depiction of defiance, even this wonder of a Holocaust film conforms to the conventions of rendering the Jew-as-victim. Read cynically, we might say that the faceless mass of Jews marching to their death are condemned to do so precisely because of their individuation as Jews, rather than joining the selfless Cause, which knows no ethnic, cultural, or national difference. The one Jewess character in fact, Martha, "is brought into the resistance — made a hero — by the gentile organizers."[26] Martha earns her "stripes" so to speak, not as a Jewess, but as an individual who has submitted to the political ideology of the Socialist resistance organizers.

Solidarity is exhibited early on in the film. In its opening moments a pregnant woman, Helena, nearly falls over during roll call. She picks herself back up with the help of the other women, who give her words of encouragement. The entire group is punished for the weak-kneed woman, and told that they're all to stand at attention for an extended period of time. The entire group performs as a kind of collective midwife, in locked arms the entire group, like a gentle rolling oceanic tide, sway side to side to comfort the woman in labor (fig. 4.2).

Figure 4.2

Inside the barracks where the child is born, the other internees huddle around the newly born child as the nurse cleans it. We see nothing of what is happening beyond the huddled women, but from this circle where the newborn is being bathed, a light emanates; as if the newly born baby boy signifies some "ray of hope" (see fig. 2.2). An SS officer, whistling as he walks, passes the barracks, though, and hears the sounds of a crying baby; he stops, and then goes about his business. Later the SS officer returns and asks where the mother and the child are. The barrack nurse says that the mother died during birth — swapping a recently deceased woman for the new mother; this is similar to the swap that happens in Gillo Pontecorvo's 1959 film *Kapò*, allowing the principal female character to hide her Jewish identity and adopt the persona of a recently deceased common criminal.

While the body swap in *The Last Stage* gives Helena a new lease on life, her little boy is condemned to death. The SS officer does not want to give the child the chance to grow up, to his mind only to become a criminal or a murderer, ironic considering who is sitting in judgment. (A similar scene is also found in *Escape from Sobibor*.[27]) One might imagine that Helena would succumb to the grief of having her newborn child torn from her, and murdered so coldly. But rather than sinking into the abyss of despair Helena instead becomes one of the leaders of the resistance movements in the camp.

When Martha first arrives in the camp, and after being "processed," she learns what really happens there by quizzing an experienced internee. Seeing the smokestacks belching smoke she naively asks, "What is that factory in the background?" The other internee scoffs a bit, "A factory? It's the crematorium where the prisoners are cremated. Now burns those who arrived with you. Did you have a family? Nonsense! Some day we all go through the chimney, and we'll meet together again." The film turns towards the melodramatic — in that emotionally charged moments are heightened with cinematic embellishments, the music swells, and the revelation about the truth of the camp is cut over a series of dissolves — Martha's confounded and grief-stricken expression, the smoke ascending towards heaven, finally cuts to a portrait of Hitler.

The choreography of the camera and lighting articulate the oppressive nature of the concentration camp. While the film trades heavily in the currency of verisimilitude, this in itself is not enough; it is lighting and the cinematography that lends power to the narrative. Liebman and Quart credit the cinematography team — Boris Monastrysky, Karol Chodura, and Andrzej Ancuta — that

> opted to shoot many of the exterior scenes in high-angle long shots that focus on the arranged, choreographed masses of prisoners — standing, even swaying, in rows on the Appellplatz, or being angrily threatened and beaten by Kapos and guards as they march off to work. These shots also pick up the light eerily reflecting off the water in the drainage ditches and puddles through which the often exhausted inmates had to trudge, highlighting one aspect of the oppressive quality of daily existence in the camp.[28]

Liebman and Quart identify the scene where Helena is in labor as exemplary, but in fact *The Last Stage* establishes a representational strategy; many of the compositional devices and choreographed cinematography serve as a model for future Holocaust films, from Alain Resnais's 1955 documentary *Night and Fog* to Steven Spielberg's 1993 film *Schindler's List*. These include tracking shots that exhibit the "remainders" of extermination — suitcases, clothes — or the tilt from Jews marching into the undressing barracks up to the crematorium chimney belching flames and putrid smoke. Even beyond using the film as a template a number of documentaries have made use of *The Last Stage*, including *Night and Fog*, which incorporates some of the footage as if it were archival material[29] (fig. 4.3; fig. 4.4).

Figure 4.3

Figure 4.4

While the Cause is the protagonist of the film, the antagonist of the film is the mélange of cookie-cutter Nazis, embodiments of sadistic evil. The Nazis for the most part are unfeeling robots that blurt out fascist diatribes. Aleksandra Slaska who plays the Superintendent of the Women's Block (and later finds a similar roll in Andrzej Munk's 1963 film, *The Passenger*, as Liza an SS guard) is an icy blonde whose stern expression cuts to the quick. In the constellation of female characters Slaska's character in *The Last Stage* embodies the antagonist's position; a fervent believer in the Nazi agenda, even dressing down colleagues who do not exhibit the steely resolve required to execute their assigned mission: "Gentlemen, I see that you don't realize the importance of the task the Fuehrer entrusted our camp with. That's the great task first of all to clear Europe from all racial and political inferior elements. The only way is extermination."

The ending of the film is characteristically Socialist Realist, with its caricature of the selfless sacrificing heroine, Martha, preaching the virtues of communist solidarity to the masses up to her very last breath. Mounting the gallows, with the camp assembled to watch the execution, Martha kicks the rotund commandant off the platform as Allied bombers soar overhead. Like cockroaches the Nazis scurry for cover, cowering at the sight of the Allied planes (in the context of the film and Martha's speech it is suggested that the planes are Soviet). Earlier when Martha was escorted to the gallows one of her fellow internees slipped her a knife, which she uses to slit her wrists, denying the Nazis the satisfaction of killing her. But before she dies she professes to her fellow internees that the Nazis are doomed. Martha in her final moments not only preaches the party line, but is also framed in the style of Stalinist era Soviet aesthetics — Martha is transformed into a statuesque figure, monumentalized in a low-camera angle, framed against a brilliant sky (fig. 4.5). This final sequence — though undoubtedly over the top in its Socialist Realist aesthetic — is premised on a real event, and modeled after the legendary internee Mala Zimetbaum. (Chapter 11 discusses the Zimetbaum case in more detail.[30])

Figure 4.5

LOVE, TRANSCENDENCE, AND SPIRITUAL RESISTANCE

Love, transcendence, and spiritual resistance were the few forms of resistance available to some of those caught up in the Nazis' systematic extermination of European Jewry. Sharing certain affinities with Wajda's *Kanal*, sexuality plays a key role in Jewish defiance in Brynych's 1962 film *Transport from Paradise*, set in Terezín.[31] The Judenrat (Jewish Council) was commissioned by the German authorities of Terezín to generate lists of internees to be transported, where they faced almost certain death in a Nazi extermination center. Lisa, a young attractive internee, is given the opportunity to escape the next transport when the newly appointed deputy chairman of the Judenrat propositions her; in return for sexual favors she could save her life, and get off the transport list. Lisa refuses, but she does accept an invitation to sleep with a handful of young men — all on the transport list and bound for death. Lisa meets the young men in their room, and has sex with each of them individually. "By means of understatement and graphic restraint, Brynych repudiates any potential pornographic charge," Ilan Avisar insists. "The adolescents' sexual act is an initiation to life, signifying both newly gained maturity and reproductivity; in this scene, however, it is motivated by the characters' knowledge of their imminent death."[32] While figures like Alvin Rosenfeld adamantly refuse to acknowledge that sexuality was a part of the Holocaust, and he very well might be correct, denying sexuality is to deny the humanity of the Holocaust victim, and here Brynych figures sexuality not as a means of titillation but as a defiant affirmation of life.[33]

Sean Mathias's 1997 film *Bent* is also another example where love prevails. Rather than identifying as queer, Max, when interned at Dachau, prefers to simply identify as Jewish. In the Sisyphean universe of the concentration camp, he is made to carry large rocks from one place and stack them in another. When he is finished stacking all the rocks, he is made to carry the rocks back, repeating the process in an endless loop. He falls in love with a queer-identifying internee, Horst, and while never touching one another develop an intimate relationship using only their imaginations. Imagination and fantasy are vehicles of escape, present in a number of other films including Radu Mihaileanu's 1998 film *Train of Life* (discussed in the succeeding chapter), and *The Pianist*, where for instance the central character Wladyslaw Szpilman, who is in hiding, is forced to only imagine playing the piano for fear of alerting other occupants in the building to his presence.

Building off an incredibly rich tradition of filmmaking about the Polish Resistance, Polanski's 2002 film *The Pianist* situates art as a form of resistance to Nazi brutality, and situates Chopin's music as a way to transcend the earth-bound suffering brought by the Nazis. Fryderyk Franciszek Chopin, born in Warsaw in 1810, holds a special place in the heart of the Polish national spirit. The film, set in Warsaw in 1939, begins with an act of artistic-fueled resistance. In a radio studio Wladyslaw Szpilman is playing Chopin's "Nocturne in C sharp minor" as artillery begins to rain down on the city. The producers in the radio station tell Szpilman to stop playing, but he refuses and continues as shards of plaster rain down. He finally is forced to stop when a blast blows out the windows of the studio.[34] Szpilman, our principal character, is not a hero as such, but rather a bit of a dandy and survives as a matter of chance, good luck, and the generosity of others. "If the pianist, Wladic Szpilman, is no hero," Lawrence Kramer observes, "his nation's iconic composer, Frédéric Chopin, may take over the role in the form, almost literally in the person, of his music."[35] Polanski himself says that the film is optimistic because, "The victim survives, thanks to his passion for the arts, and for music in particular; thanks to his willpower."

The film, however, relies on the Jew-as-victim motif precisely in the ways that Doneson outlines it. The reliance on this motif, though, is not entirely a product of narrative construction, as the film is premised on real events. Nevertheless time and again Szpilman relies on the charity of Gentiles to shelter him; even in the latter part of the narrative, a German officer shelters him. As an artist Szpilman is rendered as having a fragile disposition, rebuffed when he wants to join the resistance, too delicate to carry out hard labor, the consummate onlooker rather than taking action, and at one point succumbing to malnutrition — needing to be nursed back to health by Gentiles. Szpilman, however, is not the site of resistance; rather it is Chopin that materializes as the true site of resistance.[36]

Like all other Jewish families, the Szpilman family is impacted by the ever more degrading laws imposed by the occupational government: prohibitions about Jews entering parks, making it compulsory to display of the Star of David, and finally the relocation of Jews into the ghettos. Frustrated, Szpilman visits a member of the resistance but is rebuffed. Nevertheless, this is where Szpilman meets Majorek, an organizer in the resistance.

While the rest of his family is deported to the East — a euphemism for sending Jews to the death camps — Szpilman is pulled from a line of deportees to remain behind in the ghetto. Finding compatriots in the resistance, Szpilman helps to smuggle guns and munitions into the ghetto with shipments of food. With Majorek's help Szpilman makes contact with Janina, an old non-Jewish friend, who helps him slip out of the ghetto. He is then sent into hiding; the Polish resistance arranges a flat for Szpilman not far from the ghetto. From his window, he watches the Warsaw Ghetto Uprising (April 19 through May 16, 1943) unfold;

he sits alone in the dark as his comrades just a few yards away fight and die.[37]

Once again, in Szpilman's new hideout adjacent a German hospital and police headquarters, he has front row seats to the anti-German insurgency; on August 1, 1944, Polish resistance fighters launch the opening salvo of the Warsaw Uprising. This will result in a long campaign with heavy tolls on both sides, but the Polish resistance is not especially well organized, and Germans launch a counter insurgency and effectively level the city, systematically going from building to building, and blowing them up, or setting them ablaze. (The Russians essentially let the Germans quash the Polish resistance because it was not advantageous to them to have a strong Polish nationalist force when the German occupation finally collapsed.) Szpilman's flat is locked from the outside, and when word comes that the building is about to be blown up, he has no way of getting out. Szpilman watches as a German tank takes position and begins bombarding the building. Szpilman narrowly escapes and finds refuge in the bombed-out hospital across the street. But when the Germans come back through this section of the city, they systematically set each building on fire. Again making a narrow escape, Szpilman lurches out the back of the building, and hops over a wall to discover the ruined Warsaw before him in all its magnitude, a long crane shot moves upward to reveal an apocalyptic sight.[38]

Rummaging through the ruined city Szpilman comes across an opulent home, pock-marked with the scars of war. Finding a can of pickles he attempts to open it, but the racket calls the attention of the house's occupant, an SS officer. Calmly, the German officer, Captain Wilm Hosenfeld, asks what Szpilman is doing there, or if he works in the house. "No," Szpilman answers. Hosenfeld then inquires what Szpilman's occupation is. "I am . . . I was a pianist," Szpilman replies. "Come here," the German officer says, leading Szpilman to the next room where there is a piano. "Play something," Hosenfeld commands in a calm tone. With Chopin's "Ballade m 1 in G minor, Op. 23," Szpilman "disarms" the Nazi, so moved by his playing the Nazi retreats to a chair; he sits and listens in utter awe.[39] Although Szpilman throughout the film has been depicted as a delicate waif, at the piano the force and passion with which he hammers out the notes materialize as a transcendental form of resistance. The lighting of the scene also embellishes this transcendental character; a beam of light bathes the emaciated Szpilman with an almost sacred aura.[40] Indeed, music effectively saves Szpilman from a sworn enemy, as the dumbfounded Hosenfeld asks, "Are you hiding here?" Szpilman nods yes. "Jew?" Again Szpilman nods yes. "Where are you hiding?" the German inquires. "In the attic," Szpilman responds. Satisfied that the hiding place is sufficiently secret, Hosenfeld asks, "Got any food?" Szpilman gestures to a can of pickles, and the German leaves.

This scene, where Szpilman belts out Chopin's "Ballade," is effectively the climax of the film. Although the war (and the film) is not yet over, the enemy is vanquished here, crushed under the massive weight of transcendental beauty. "Music" in Szpilman's case Alexander Stein argues, "can serve compound defensive or coping functions in transforming our perceptual and sensory experience of time to evoke temporally distant events or reminiscences, provoke a heightened or accelerated anticipation of a future moment, induce or relax states of tension, or seeming to altogether suspend time's ineluctable forward movement." The climax slowly culminates into a thunderous crescendo; music engenders a "discursive narrativism" that carries with it "a sense of time's passage, of a beginning traveling towards an end."[41] The incredibly moving performance carries us from beginning (appropriately, recall that film begins with Szpilman playing Chopin) to the triumphant end (the film ends with Szpilman playing a concert). Polanski's choice of music, much more dramatic than what Szpilman played in real life, is "filled with fantastic, dramatic moods," Stein observes. Asserting that Chopin's "Ballade" is the climax of the film, corresponds with Stein's conclusion: "Two themes are developed which are transformed, made more complex and subjected to dramatic vicissitudes, leading to a turbulent coda, where, by its virtuosic climax, supreme tension yields ultimately to profound emotional relief."[42]

The following morning, after Szpilman's impromptu piano performance for Hosenfeld, we discover that the residence is a Nazi beehive, buzzing with countless Germans planning military operations, and the officer that Szpilman played for, the commanding officer. After finishing some business, Hosenfeld furtively slips away to the attic to bring food for "his Jew." When the Russians are poised to roll into the city the Germans pull out, but before doing so the commanding officer brings "his Jew" a final stock of provisions.

The film relies on the formulaic conventions of what we associate with Hollywood films, in the neat and tidy restoration of social order. Szpilman does indeed return to the radio, and we pick him up where he was abruptly interrupted at the beginning of the film during the German bombardment, playing Chopin live in a newly refurbished radio station. The closing shot of the film is set in an opulent theater; Szpilman plays the piano, this time accompanied by an entire orchestra. Lawrence Kramer finds the conclusion, and specifically the evocation of Chopin's "Nocturne in C sharp minor," "too pat: it simply observes the Hollywood rule of moralizing by making a big repetition, something as often done with music as with words." Kramer later goes on to say,

> Chopin's iconic standing formed a seductive veil over the proceedings, and so did the visual paraphernalia that it commanded: the rebuilt studio, the plush concert hall, the pianist's healthy appearance and new tuxedo, the gleaming piano. Even the music is refurbished, retrieved from the silent keys in the safe house that the fugitive dared not touch.[43]

While perhaps *The Pianist* panders to our desire for tidy dramatic narratives, as Michel Chion argues to the contrary, the film nevertheless

> suggests that after the horror of the Holocaust everything can go on as before, as if the music remained absolutely intact, untouched by events, and in this capacity were a symbol of the indifference of the universe. Unlike painting, for example, music is

something that carries no traces, that cannot be marked, and that has no scars. It remains untouched by history, by events, by horror.[44] *Is this true?*

Part of the miracle of the post-Holocaust world is that humanity, despite the horrors that were perpetrated, managed to survive.

NAZI HUNTERS

One theme that plays out in the image of the defiant Jew is the Jew as a stealthy and cunning covert agent. William A. Graham's 1996 *The Man Who Captured Eichmann* is an empowering and uplifting film, about the clandestine Mossad mission to abduct Adolf Eichmann, the architect of the Holocaust, who lived under an assumed name in Argentina. In the spring of 1960 Mossad agents successfully abducted Eichmann, smuggled him out of the country to Israel, where he was put on trial and subsequently found guilty and executed. Ole Christian Madsen's 2008 film *Flame and Citron* — Flame and Citron are the code names of the principal characters, Bent Faurschou-Hviid (Flame) and Jørgen Haagen Schmith (Citron) — depicts the Danish resistance (though not Jewish) and is set in the style of a neo-noir gangster film, in the tradition of *The Untouchables* (Brian De Palma, 1987). Nazi hunter films, such as *The Man Who Captured Eichmann*, or for that matter Franklin Schaffner's 1978 film *The Boys from Brazil*, typically entertain fantasies of revenge, where good vanquishes evil.

Quentin Tarantino's 2009 film *Inglourious Basterds* satisfies our fantasies for revenge against Nazi barbarity. The opening shots of the film could have been torn from the pages of a child's picture book, with rolling bucolic French hills, and it contextualizes the film as a fairytale, even beginning with, "Once upon a time." The film harbors no pretense of historical fidelity, or to verisimilitude. As a revenge fantasy, though, Tarantino plumbs the depth of our psyche, potentially revealing a discomforting truth about our morbid fascination with violence, even Holocaust violence.

This is not the first Holocaust revenge fantasy film; rather, it comes in the tradition of films like Brynych's 1967 film *I, Justice*, where a group of Czechs abduct Hitler, dishing out a brutal punishment which leads to a very slow painful death. Or even István Szabó's 1999 film *Sunshine*, which illustrates how the power shifts in Hungary fostered the brutal Communist-sponsored inquisition to purge the state of fascists in the second half of the twentieth century. Ronald Neame's 1974 cloak-and-dagger thriller *The Odessa File* justifies Peter Miller's assassination of a former Nazi, Eduard Roschmann, on the grounds that Roschmann killed Miller's father; a "good" German soldier, unlike the sadistic and heartless Roschmann. *Inglourious Basterds* in certain respects is similar to many of these, insofar as they satisfy our desires to exact revenge, but Tarantino's film in the end interrogates this strange pretension in cinema to locate pleasure in killing and the spectacle of violence.

Although the film pays no deference to history, like all of Tarantino's films it is characteristically meta-cinematic — a film about film — and is encyclopedic in its cinematic references. This film is different from Tarantino's other work, though, in that it goes beyond trivial encyclopedic references, and is rather heuristically inviting the viewer to contemplate the cinematic form and *how* it represents violence. Tarantino seems to have moved from trivial historian to film theorist. This is particularly true of the latter part of the film, where the scheduled French premier of *Nation's Pride* screens in Shosanna Dreyfus's movie theater, catering to the Nazi elite, including Hitler and Goebbels.[45] In the film we see a German sniper taking out Americans left and right, as they fall head over foot from windows high above the street, characteristic of any typical American Western. Hitler laughs with giddy exhilaration, Goebbels likewise giggles like a little girl, at the spectacle of wholesale slaughter, as the German marksman, Fredrick Zoller, picks off American soldiers. Hitler's euphoria at the spectacle of violence taints our own visual pleasure, if not frustrating it altogether.

Having intelligence that most of the Nazi elite will be attending the premier, The Basterds — a band of Jewish American soldiers — orchestrate a plan to blow up the theater and assassinate the German leadership. Dreyfus has plans of her own, in the opening of the film her family is executed by the "Jew Hunter," Hans Landa, and she too has similar plans to exact revenge. Although things do not go exactly as planned, Dreyfus does in fact set the theater ablaze while locking the leadership in the theater. Two of The Basterds, including the "Bear Jew," played by Eli Roth who directed the *Hostel* films, discussed at length in Chapter 9, manage to assassinate Goebbels and Hitler in their balcony seats; the Bear Jew riddles Hitler's body with automatic weapon fire at close range and in slow motion. Perched above the theater in Hitler's balcony seat the two Basterds then proceed to indiscriminately pick off Nazi officers and officials like shooting fish in a barrel, mowing down people with automatic weapons. Brian De Palma's films are clearly evident in this scene; the carnage in the burning theater is clearly taken from the bloody end of the prom sequence in *Carrie* (1976),[46] but also in the spectacle of slow-motion gunfire we might detect the traces of De Palma's 1983 film *Scarface*.[47] In the traditional narrative cinema (and particularly Hollywood) violent scenes are designed to exhilarate the audience, to deliver a thrill, and while Tarantino delivers on these expectations, it is nevertheless undercut by the enjoyment that Hitler derives from the wholesale murder witnessed in the film just moments before. That the spectacle of violence also takes place in a movie theater begins to point back at the spectator. We might feel a rush of adrenaline as the Bear Jew stands over Hitler's prone body, pumping it full of lead, but our own giddy euphoria is made uneasy in its relation to Hitler's own response to *Nation's Pride*.

In the closing scene of the film the audience is uncomfortably placed in the position of the conniving Landa, assuming his visual perspective. The Nazis for Tarantino, as David Denby has it in his *New Yorker* review, "are merely available movie tropes — articulate monsters with a talent for sadism. By making the Americans cruel, too, he escapes the customary division between good and evil along national lines, but he escapes any sense of moral accountability as well."[48] While Denby is quite correct on the former counts — indeed, as a fairytale the film relies on defined tropes of evil, but at the same time it does not go so far as create a clearly defined Manichean worldview either — where Denby gets things wrong, however, is on the latter point regarding accountability. More so than any other film he has done in the past, Tarantino seems to hold filmmaker and spectator alike quite accountable, complicit in the fantasies of revenge. This fact is emphasized in the closing moments of the film when Lieutenant Aldo Raine, the commanding officer of The Basterds, carves a swastika on the Landa's forehead with a buck-knife. English phrases like, "if the shoe fits," and "the shoe is on the other foot," is something of a running joke through the final chapter of the film, and this latter phrase is appropriate to the narrative, but it also functions with respect to the viewing experience. The spectator is uneasily positioned in the shoes of the Nazis; the pleasure we commonly derive from the sadistic voyeuristic gaze is compromised. Not only is this gaze subject to critique in the theater scene, but also in the closing moments of the film, because when Lieutenant Raine carves the swastika on Landa's forehead, this is done in a POV shot; the spectator is literally placed in the Nazis' shoes, branded with the swastika.

Although not as forceful or polemic, *Inglourious Basterds* meets up with Pier Paolo Pasolini's 1975 film *Salò, or the 120 Days of Sodom*, which likewise explicitly places the spectator in the position of fascist libertines. In both films the spectator's identification is aligned with the fascist characters. Pasolini leaves the spectator no other option in terms of identification, and he constantly, and very consciously, aligns the camera's gaze with the libertines. In Tarantino's film our gaze is aligned with Landa, who, despite his cruelty, is nevertheless a seductive character. While Pasolini forces our alignment with the libertines, in *Inglourious Basterds* we are relatively easily seduced by Landa's smarmy cunning, a character who, as Denby describes, "takes an intellectual pleasure in devilry."[49] Landa is the consummate example of the clinical sadist. Where these films part company, though, is that in *Salò* power and violence are inflicted upon others, and we are made to "enjoy" the spectacle, whereas in the final moments of Tarantino's film violence is visited upon fascist characters. And while the pleasure that we derive from the violence exhibited against the Nazis is then in some way given allowance — the bad guys get what they deserve — Tarantino complicates the pleasure in the revenge fantasy. Although Denby questions Tarantino's accountability, he might have got it right when he said, "In a Tarantino war, everyone commits atrocities."[50] Indeed, Tarantino might have turned a corner here, and is perhaps asking us to interrogate the pleasure that we derive from spectacles of violence.

Chapter Five

Holocaust Comedies?

INTRODUCTION

[handwritten: same criticisms made of film]

One of the "problems" with the genre of comedy is that it is generally considered less sophisticated (read: incapable) than the more so-called "noble genres" such as tragedy, or conventional (historical) drama. And as a consequence is not well suited to deal with a topic as grave as the Holocaust. As Hayden White is keen to point out, our cultural assumptions lead us to presume that a horrific historical event of the Holocaust's magnitude is only suitably represented in more "refined" genres that coincidentally trade in the currency of verisimilitude. Comedies, on the other hand, are prone to "clowning around," to exaggeration (read: distortion), and absurdity. Holocaust comedies generally do not support the underlying and often unspoken agenda of conventional narrative films — even when great artistic license is taken — to convey the idea that "this really happened."[1]

This is not to say, it must be stressed, that Holocaust comedies inherently malign truth. Like other genres that garner less cultural esteem — including horror, and exploitation — comedy, David Brenner agrees,

> can afford to show or say what "serious" modes of representation dare not. . . . If comedy is a mode of representation that resists the impulse to censor or to respect taboos, how might it be contrasted with tragedy, which also claims to speak the brutal truth? In what ways does comedy come closer to the reality of catastrophic events?[2]

Laughter and the feeling of dread (as evoked by the horror genre) are effectively two sides of the same coin. The genres of horror and comedy regularly utilize material that is characterized as taboo, or culturally sensitive. Both genres elicit from the spectator a physiological response; with horror films the spectator might jump, avert their eyes, furrow their brow at the sight of gore, while comedy compels us to smirk, laugh, and even in extreme cases, cry. There is then a potential purgative function that these genres can serve, though many critics point out the risks of trivialization and historical infidelity. These are genuine concerns; however, I am inclined to make allowances for representational strategies that exceed the narrow confines of the "noble genres."[3]

Some have argued that nothing is funny in the Holocaust and that laughter is unthinkable in the confines of the camp, but in fact there are examples of jokes being made in the context of the Holocaust. Many that cite the significance of humor argue that it functioned as a form of resistance, or a defense mechanism mobilized against the horrors of orchestrated violence. Steve Lipman's book *Laughter in Hell*, replete with period jokes, illustrates the ways in which laughter materialized even in the gravest moments. "Nothing about the Holocaust was funny," Lipman notes, but it is also important to acknowledge that by "appreciating the humor from the period we are not laughing at the victims or their suffering; we are simply recognizing that laughter was a part of their lives, a part nurtured by their suffering."[4] To deny humor is to deny yet another aspect of humanity. The almost instinctual reaction to Holocaust comedy is quite understandable, and certainly the product of well-founded concerns about how the Holocaust will be remembered, forgotten, or even denied.[5]

What makes the vehement criticism surrounding films like *Life Is Beautiful* so strange is that humor is entrenched in the Jewish tradition; why wouldn't the Holocaust be treated in the comedic genre? Some critics have seemingly forgotten, Omer Bartov reminds us,

> about the Jewish tradition of humor and its relationship to pain and persecution, about the specific role humor and fantasy played in attempts to survive or at least maintain a semblance of normality and humanity during the Holocaust, and about the tradition of "black," "gallows," or "concentration camp humor" in literary and cinematic representations of the Holocaust and other horrors of modern warfare, going back at least to the aftermath of World War I.[6]

Radu Mihaileanu, who made one of the most significant Holocaust comedies in the latter part of the twentieth century, *Train of Life* (1998), freely admits that he was profoundly moved by Steven Spielberg's 1993 film *Schindler's List*. However, the Romanian filmmaker was not entirely satisfied either. "We can no longer keep telling the same story of the Shoah in the same way, solely in the context of tears and horror," Mihaileanu says.

> My theory was to change the language but not the context. I wanted to tell the tragedy through the most Jewish language there is — the tradition of bittersweet comedy. It was a desire to go beyond the Shoah — not to deny or forget the dead, but to re-create their lives in a new and vivid way.[7]

The television program *Seinfeld* in 1994 aired an episode entitled "The Raincoats" that parodies *Schindler's List*, and illustrates the ways in which the comedic genre can function as a meta-narrative critique. In this two-part episode Newman discovers Jerry making out with his girlfriend, Rachel, in the movie theater during *Schindler's List*. Jerry's long-time nemesis, Newman, squeals, explaining to his parents, "He was moving on her like the stormtroopers into Poland."[8] The episode concludes with a parody of the melodramatic ending of *Schindler's List*. At the airport Jerry, Elaine, and Aaron (Elaine's boyfriend) bid farewell to the Seinfelds. At the entrance of the jetway Aaron laments, "I could've done more." Elaine scoffs, "You did enough." "No," Aaron retorts, "This watch, this watch could've paid for their whole trip. This ring is one more dinner I could've taken them out to." The episode functions as a meta-narrative critique, if only by virtue of parody. The mere re-casting of the *melodramatic form* utilized in *Schindler's List* in the comedic genre invites us to "look again" at the subject in a different light. The episode, whether it was intended to do so or not, interrogates *how* Spielberg tells the Schindler story.[9]

There is something of a difference between parodying Nazi buffoonery or rendering Hitler comedically and locating humor in the context of Nazi crimes.[10] There is a long list of films that feature Hitler gags. Jerry Zucker's 2001 comedic road movie *Rat Race* features one of the funniest. Randy Pear (played by Jon Lovitz) in a series of mishaps stumbles to a podium before a crowd of World War II veterans to explain the situation, but his impaired speech comes out as gibberish, and his expository gestures resemble the overwrought gesticulations of the German dictator (fig. 5.1). This is truly a hilarious sequence, but it is not necessarily a recasting of Hitler, though, but rather of Chaplin's parody Adenoid Hynkel.

Figure 5.1

In the late 90s a series of Holocaust comedies were released, including *Life Is Beautiful*, *Train of Life*, and *Jakob the Liar*. "Significantly," Slavoj Zizek observes, "all three films are centred on a lie that allows the threatened Jews to survive their ordeal."[11] Zizek views this convergence of Holocaust comedies as symptomatic of the shortcomings of the Holocaust tragedy, specifically citing *Schindler's List* as an impetus for the rise of Holocaust comedies. Where Zizek sees duplicity in Spielberg's representation of the Nazi executioners, specifically Amon Goeth, comedy on the other hand, "at least accepts in advance its failure to render the horror of the Holocaust."[12] *accepts that it cannot render the horror*

Whether it's laughter as "the best medicine," laughter as a mobilized defense, or laughter as an aggressive act of ridicule, comedy has been utilized to represent the Holocaust. Terrence Des Pres argues that, "laughter is hostile to the world it depicts and subverts the respect on which representation depends."[13] The carnal — be it sexuality, or laughter — is part of what makes us embodied beings, to be human, and trying to rob the victims of the Holocaust of this does them a great disservice; even in its most crass forms jokes, humor, and laughter offers an inkling of human dignity in an inhuman situation.[14]

COMEDY AS PROPAGANDA

During the war, and even leading up to it in certain cases, comedy was mobilized as a weapon against an incredibly formidable enemy. One of the earliest is Jules White's 1940 film *You Nazty Spy!* a Three Stooges short, and parodies the Nazi regime; Moe parodies Hitler in the character of Hailstone, Curly satirizes Goering as Gallstone, and Larry plays Goebbels as Pebble. The comedy team utilizes their characteristic physical humor, and eventually end up being eaten by lions.

The television series *Hogan's Heroes* (1965–71) serialized Nazi buffoonery; this weekly dose of bumbling Nazi antics owes a debt to earlier films such as *To Be or Not to Be* (Ernst Lubitsch, 1942), the short *The Lambeth Walk — Nazi Style* (Charles A. Ridley, 1942), and of course the single most important comedy, Charles Chaplin's 1940 film *The Great Dictator*.[15] These satirical films illustrate how treachery might be reconceived as a laughing matter. In the post-war era, though, attitudes shifted after the ghastly crimes of the Nazi regime saw the full light of day. "Had I known of the actual horrors of the German concentration camps," Chaplin recounts in his autobiography, "I could not have made *The Great Dictator*; I could not have made fun of the homicidal insanity of the Nazis." Chaplin adds that he "was determined to ridicule their mystic bilge about a pure-blooded race. As though such a thing ever existed outside of the Australian Aborigines!"[16] At the end of the day, *The Great Dictator* is less about the Holocaust than it is about intolerance and the tyranny of fascism.

Indeed, the war and realization of the Nazis' crimes against humanity made satirizing Hitler and the Nazis a perilous venture — for fear of offending Holocaust survivors, and the millions that died. With time, however, we have witnessed an increase of comedic routines that come at the expense of Hitler, or the Nazis. Roberto Benigni's Chaplinesque routine in *Life Is Beautiful* is an exceptionally funny dressing down of absurd racial theories. Appropriated many times over for comedic effect, Oliver Hirschbiegel's 2004 dramatic narrative *Downfall* is something of a YouTube phenomenon; reconfiguring the climatic moment when Hitler (played brilliantly by Bruno Ganz) learns that Berlin is on the brink of falling, sending the Fuehrer into a rage, YouTube posters have changed the subtitling, altering the meaning of the scene.[17] The appropriation of *Downfall* is more in the spirit of *The Lambeth Walk — Nazi Style* than *The Great Dictator*; nevertheless, it is illustrative of the changing attitudes about the appropriateness of making jokes about Hitler, the Nazi regime, and their policies.

Chaplin turned lampooning the German dictator into an art. Only a few days separate their birth — Chaplin was born on April 16, Hitler on April 20, 1889 — and the physical similarities between the two were recognized well before Chaplin's film. It is inconceivable to think it now, but at the time in 1939, because of the American isolationist policy, Chaplin's anti-Nazi film was set on a collision course with film censors and destined to be banned. Chaplin had to make the film independently (investing $2 million of his own money), as it clearly went against the official American position, and general public opinion. Michael Richardson in fact observes that Chaplin's portrayal of Hitler, at the time, was not provocative because it breached some ethical boundary with respect to representing the Holocaust, but rather that it was "too insulting of Germany and Hitler."[18] Although the reaction to Chaplin's film prior to the war was tepid to say the least, when the United States declared war on the Axis Powers Hollywood was quickly mobilized in the war effort.[19]

In *The Great Dictator* Chaplin plays both a Jewish barber and Adenoid Hynkel, the dictator of the fictional country Tomania. As in life, there is a striking resemblance between the barber and Herr Hynkel. Many of the key characters are given very thinly veiled names, bearing phonetic traces from which they derive: most obviously the Phooey, Adenoid Hynkel, is a parody of the Fuehrer, Adolf Hitler; the Nazi Minister of Propaganda Joseph Goebbels is dubbed Garbitsch; the German Luftwaffe chief, Hermann Göring, is given the name Herring. While the famously decadent Göring is transfigured as a diminutive fish, the infamous Goebbels — a chief architect of the Nazi platform — is cast as someone who spouts "garbage." The Italian dictator Mussolini does not escape Chaplin's ridicule; Napaloni is the dictator of Bacteria. Napaloni and Hynkel tangle in games of trying to one-up the other, constantly jockeying for the upper hand. Typical of Chaplin's physical comedy, on one occasion in a pair of barber chairs each dictator cranks their seat higher than the other, until they hit the ceiling and come crashing down (fig. 5.2).

Many of the gags in *The Great Dictator* are premised on near-homonyms or other forms of word play, such as we find with the thinly veiled character names. Chaplin replaces the potent symbol of the swastika, with two "x", the "Double Cross," as the emblem is called in the film. Obviously, this too is loaded with satirical meaning. To double-cross means to perpetrate an act of deceit on two parties. Certainly, this is an apt characterization of the Nazi regime that not only betrayed European Jewry — many of whom held German citizenship — which is an obvious understatement, but the regime also betrayed all of Germany, leading the nation headlong into a catastrophic war under false pretense and brazen scapegoating.

As with many comedic scenarios, the plot of *The Great Dictator* is premised on mistaken identity. The Jewish barber and Hynkel share an uncanny resemblance, while the source of jokes in the film is at the same time a serious lambasting of the Nazis' eugenic platform. That the upper echelon of the Double Cross cannot distinguish between the Phooey and a Jew is the comedic thrust behind the film. This also materializes in the stand-up routine of the title character in Elijah Moshinsky's 1993 *Genghis Cohn*, where Cohn compares the stereotype of a Jew as

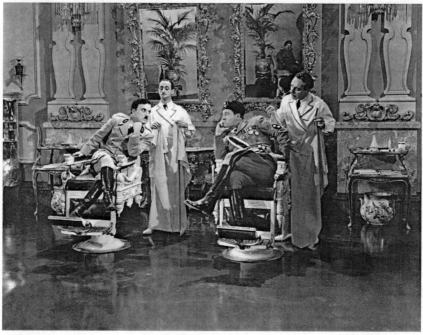

Figure 5.2

a loud talking and gesticulating figure to the haranguing and wild gesticulations of the Fuehrer. Although not a comedy, the irony of Agnieszka Holland's 1990 feature film *Europa Europa* is that the principal character, Salomon "Solly" Perel, a Jew, assumes the name Josef "Jupp" Peters, and joins the Hitler Youth, hiding in clear sight among the wolves. Whether it is Hynkel who is confused for the Jewish barber who escapes a concentration camp, or the Jewish barber who is confused for the Phooey, *The Great Dictator* continually points to the absurdity of intolerance.

In addition to the theme of intolerance, Chaplin pokes fun at the megalomania of dictators. Ilan Avisar argues that Hynkel is an embodiment of Satan, the anti-Christ, and that Chaplin aims to equate Hitler with evil. The argument Avisar posits is certainly interesting, although tortured, but nevertheless is probably not too far off the mark. If there is any devilish agent in *The Great Dictator* it is Garbitsch, who plays Mephistopheles, promising the world to Hynkel, feeding his ego. Garbitsch fuels Hynkel's imagination, claiming that if the world will be purged of Jews he will rule a pure Aryan world, "They will love you," Garbitsch says, "adore you, they'll worship you as a god." This startles the dictator; gasping Hynkel jumps out of his seat, and sends him climbing the curtains (literally) in fear (fig. 5.3). Left to ponder the future, Hynkel scurries down the curtains, and prances over to a large globe, imagining himself, "Emperor of the world!" Lofting the globe in the air, Hynkel dances with it in his characteristic way, until the globe (which is nothing more than a large balloon) explodes (fig. 5.4). The Faustian theme — where a character is promised the world, if they only give their soul to a fascist cause — is fairly common, but *The Great Dictator* certainly is among the first to do so.[20]

Figure 5.3

Figure 5.4

In order to proceed with world domination, the Tomainian government needs to secure a loan from Epstein (a Jew), to finance the invasion of Osterlich. When Epstein refuses to lend the Hynkel regime money because of the persecution of his people, the Phooey is enraged. Expecting to deliver a speech that evening, Garbitsch hands Hynkel his notes, but the dictator proclaims that he will not need them, "What I say will not be directed to the children of the Double Cross, but to the children of Israel!" Cutting to the Jewish ghetto, the barber prepares to go on a date with Hannah (played by Paulette Goddard, Chaplin's third wife). As the couple walks down the street, they stop at a street vendor, and the barber asks for two Hynkel buttons, but just then Hynkel's speech cracks the (unrealistic) peace of the idyllic ghetto. Hynkel's speech — which is utter gibberish — is inflected with the fiery vitriol that Hitler was known for, and it blares across the ghetto from loudspeakers. The inhabitants of the ghetto scatter, stricken with fear. The stormtroopers soon follow, breaking shop windows, overturning vendor carts, and attacking Jews. The assault permits Chaplin to include a number of physical gags, which are quite funny, but certainly in retrospect these lighthearted treatments of Nazi brutality are the most disturbing element of *The Great Dictator*. In one instance, for example, coming to the aid of the barber, Hannah hits a stormtrooper over the head with a pan (fig. 5.5), which prompted Theodor Adorno to conclude that "*The Great Dictator* loses all satirical force, and becomes obscene, when a Jewish girl can bash a line of storm troopers on the head with a pan without being torn to pieces."[21]

Figure 5.5

Ernst Lubitsch's 1942 comedy *To Be or Not to Be*, like *The Great Dictator*, also uses mistaken identity as a source of humor. Many critics dismissed as anemic a 1983 remake of the film, directed by Alan Johnson, but often attributed to producer Mel Brooks, because it lacked the punch of the original. On the eve of the Second World War, August 1939, a Polish theater group is preparing to perform a theatrical play featuring a cast of Nazi characters, including Hitler. To prove his acting prowess, Bronski, who plays the part of Hitler, walks the streets of Warsaw. A crowd gathers at the curious sight of Hitler wandering the streets of Warsaw, alone no less, but Bronski is disappointed when a girl breaks through the crowd of curious onlookers to ask, "May I have your autograph, Mr. Bronski?" Famously, during a rehearsal in the opening moments of the film when Hitler (i.e., Bronski) enters the scene, the entire casts salutes him, "Hiel Hitler," to which Bronski responds, "Heil myself." The theater director stops the rehearsal, "That's not in the script." Bronski protests, "But it'll get a laugh." The director pleads with his cast, "This is a serious play, a realistic drama."

The Polish government, however, given the political climate, feels that it would be inappropriate to stage something that might be considered inflammatory. While the theater group never gets to perform their Nazi play, they do get to play "real Nazis," using their acting skills and costumes to fool the Gestapo set on eliminating the Polish underground. *To Be or Not to Be* shares company with other more "serious" films that establish a link between the Nazis' love of pageantry and the spectacle of theater. "Instead of countering fiction with truth," Michael Richardson notes, Lubitsch "answers theater with more theater."[22]

Walt Disney also mobilized as part of the war effort. Disney produced a number of animated films, including technical training films and propaganda films as part of the campaign against the Axis powers (sadly, many of these films resorted to racist stereotyping to berate the enemy, e.g., buck-toothed depictions of Emperor Hirohito). Hitler's wild gesticulations and overwrought oration were ripe for animated lampooning. Many of these films took Chaplinesque gags far beyond what is possible in live-action film. Jack Kinney's 1942 eight-minute animated short *Der Fuehrer's Face* features Donald Duck, who dreams that he's living in Nazi Germany, or Nutzi Land as it is called in the short. Donald and apparently everyone else in Nutzi Land work like slaves and live off sparse rations. All aspects of life are strictly regimented, and Nutzi iconography permeates all matter of it — when the cock crows first thing in the morning it gives the Nazi salute and squawks, "Heil Hitler!" Numbers on a clock face are replaced with swastikas, the blades of a windmill are in the form of swastika, the wallpaper in Donald's dreary flat is emblazoned with swastikas, even in the natural landscape trees and shrubs are shaped as swastikas (fig. 5.6).

Figure 5.6

Donald's strictly regimented daily routine includes working in a factory, assembling artillery shells for the Nazi war effort. Many of the same gags found in *Der Fuehrer's Face* are taken directly out of Chaplin's 1936 film *Modern Times*. The greedy industrialist in Chaplin's classic, modeled after the historical figure of Henry Ford (known as an anti-Semite and German sympathizer), demands that his factory labor force work at breakneck speeds. Chaplin's unnamed character tries to keep up on the assembly line before he is sucked into the factory machinery, and going certifiably insane, is eventually driven off in an ambulance. There is no industrialist as such in director Kinney's short film, but rather Hitler, and the disembodied agents of Nazism, which materialize in menacing form, including: rifles with bayonets, jackbooted guards seen only from the waist down, rendering them more machine than human, and a loud speaker proclaiming, "Is this not wonderful? Is not our Fuehrer glorious?" and later, "Faster, faster, faster!" (fig. 5.7; fig. 5.8) In the clearest appropriation of the famous factory scene in *Modern Times*, Donald struggles to keep up with the ever-increasing speed of a conveyor belt, screwing on the tops of artillery shells (fig. 5.9; fig. 5.10). And just like Chaplin's character, Donald also goes "nuts," exclaiming, "I can't stand it!" (fig. 5.11)[23] While these animated shorts, and films like *The Great Dictator*, aimed to reveal the lies behind the Nazi agenda, other Holocaust comedies employ characters that lie, or create imaginative fantasies, in order to protect victims of Nazi persecution.

Figure 5.7

Figure 5.8

Figure 5.9

Figure 5.10

Figure 5.11

FANTASIES AND LIES

Comedies are partial to flights of fancy and the absurd, and in Holocaust films the comedic is typically called upon to mediate the horrors that the characters encounter. Whether it is intended to instill hope, to shield against the harsh realities, mobilized as a form of defiance or to ridicule the oppressing agent, or a device that alleviates tension, the comedic in Holocaust films typically manifests as a character's imaginative musings. "No matter what the difficulties, the hero finds a way out," Slavoj Zizek observes regarding Holocaust comedies. "However, if the comic dimension stands for the triumph of life at its most opportunistically resourceful, we should remember that the life which survives is not simple biological life but a fantasmatic ethereal life unencumbered by the constraints of biological reality."[24] Indeed, in the face of imminent destruction, the survival of a character (or characters) against the most improbable odds is the stuff of comedy. Whether it is the return from the dead of Genghis Cohn in the form of a dybbuk in Elijiah Moshinsky's 1993 adaptation *Genghis Cohn*, the game that is played in *Life Is Beautiful*, or even Kurt Gerron's 1944 cabaret "Karussell" performed at Theresienstadt, the most improbable and absurd situations are the wellspring of comedy and stave off horror, if only for a brief moment. Zizek encourages us to

> Recall a standard Tom and Jerry cartoon: Jerry is run over by a heavy truck, dynamite explodes in his mouth, he is cut to slices, yet in the next scene he's back again with no traces of the previous disasters. The stuff of comedy is precisely this repetitive, resourceful popping-up of life — no matter how dark the predicament, we can be sure the small fellow will find a way out.[25]

In the Holocaust comedy, in fact, the protagonist might not "find a way out" in the end — Jacob Heym in Frank Beyer's 1975 film *Jacob the Liar* in all likelihood went straight to a gas chamber, the same character in Peter Kassovitz's 1999 version is executed immediately prior to the liquidation of the ghetto, Guido sacrifices himself to save his son in *Life Is Beautiful*, the entire narrative of *Train of Life* is a whimsical fantasy of the village idiot, Shlomo, who is a concentration camp internee — nevertheless the fantasies, the sharp comedic barbs that laugh in the face of suffering and overwhelming oppression locates humanity in the abyss of catastrophic suffering.

Frank Beyer's 1975 film *Jacob the Liar* was adapted from Jurek Becker's novel, which was premised on the author's own personal experiences. In 1999 Peter Kassovitz remade the film. Set in a Polish ghetto in 1944, Jacob is caught out after curfew and ordered to report to the police headquarters to ask for his deserved punishment. Wandering through the halls of the German authorities, Jacob overhears a radio broadcast; the radio announcer reporting that, "During a ferocious battle our courageous troops stopped the Bolsheviks 20 kilometers before Bezanika." This is profound news, and ferreted away behind a door, Jacob whispers under his breath, "My god, he just said 'Bezanika,'" knowing that the Soviets are advancing through Poland, and indeed, not all that far away from the ghetto. As it turns out, the clock in the German officer's office indicates that curfew is still a few minutes away, and rather than trouble himself the officer tells Jacob to go home. The following day during work-detail, one of Jacob's fellow ghetto internees, Mischa, is at his breaking point, and believes that a carriage in the rail-yard contains potatoes, knowing full well that if he is caught he is a dead man. "I'll be shot before I starve," he says, resigned. Jacob stops Mischa, explaining that the Russians are near, and that he heard it while in the police headquarters. Not only is the news too good to be true, the very fact that Jacob was in the police headquarters and lived to tell about it makes such news quite improbable. Ironically, to convince Mischa that the news is *true* Jacob resorts to *lying*: "I'm in possession of a radio." And so starts the slippery slope of lies. Mischa in quick order tells others about the news and Jacob's radio; soon the entire ghetto knows and looks to Jacob for a sliver of hopeful news.

Jacob has no family, but cares for Lina, a ten-year-old orphan. She too gets wind of Jacob's supposed radio, and begs him to let her listen to it. He eventually relents and treats her to a special "radio performance." Insisting that Lina remain seated at one end of a room, Jacob hides away behind a partition where he pretends to turn on his radio. Even though Lina peeks around the corner to see that it is really Jacob merely pretending, the child suspends all disbelief — despite the truth, akin to fetishistic disavowal — and "believes" that she's been listening to Jacob's radio (fig. 5.12). During Jacob's radio performance he tells a story of a sick princess, who needs a cloud to recover. None of the king's men could figure out how to capture a cloud, until the gardener asked the sick child what clouds are made of. "Every child in the world knows that they're made of cotton balls." As Jacob recites the story, Beyer cuts away to Lina's fairytale imagination of the story of the sick princess, full of vivid color and fantastic *mise en scène* (fig. 5.13). At the conclusion of the film, the entire ghetto is liquidated. In the cattle-car Lina peers out the small window, and asks Jacob if the story of the sick princess is true. "Of course it is," he reassures her. In the final line of the film Lina asks, "Aren't clouds made of cotton balls?" before the film cuts to black.[26]

Figure 5.12

Figure 5.13

1999 remake (handwritten annotation)

Peter Kassovitz's 1999 version, *Jakob the Liar*, follows effectively the same narrative, and is also premised on Becker's novel. The muted earthen grey colors of the ghetto in the opening scene weigh heavily on the spectator, but Jakob's voiceover brings some levity to it, making the ominous tone a bit more bearable. "Hitler goes to a fortune-teller," Jakob begins, "and asks, 'When will I die?' And the fortune-teller replies, 'On a Jewish holiday.' Hitler then asks, 'How do you know that?' And she replies, 'Any day you die will be a Jewish holiday.'" The joke does not deny the morbid tone of the *mise en scène*, it simply makes it just a bit easier to tolerate. And this little preamble sums up the entirety of the plot, with which we are already aware. The voiceover continues as the camera pans down from the ghetto street to Jakob, seated on a tree stump near the ghetto wall. "So you ask me as a Jew, 'How could you tell a joke like that at a time like that?' That's how we survived, and those were some of the things that kept us going." Suddenly a single sheet of newspaper, set aloft on the wind like a kite, flies over the ghetto wall. Jakob tries to grab it, but the wind carries it away. Lawrence Baron argues that this opening scene, with the newspaper whimsically floating in the air, is a reference to the white feather in Robert Zemeckis's 1994 film *Forrest Gump*, conveying "the original sense of Jakob as a simple man in the right place at the right time."[27]

Although there is some ambiguity in the ending of Kassovitz's *Jakob the Liar*, as with the conclusion of *Life Is Beautiful* the lies that Jakob tells effectively come true. At the conclusion of Kassovitz's film, following Jakob's public execution, the character speaks from beyond the grave, saying in voiceover,

> So that's how it ended. I never got a chance to be the big hero and make my big speech. I swear, I had a speech all prepared about freedom and never giving in, but somehow, yes, that's how it ended. And they all went off to the camps, and were never seen again. But maybe it wasn't like that at all.

Turning from the most likely conclusion — death in a concentration camp — to the most improbable scenario, Jakob's voiceover continues to explain that, 50 kilometers outside of the ghetto the train was intercepted by Russian troops. While Giosuè gets his tank at the end of *Life Is Beautiful*, advancing Russian forces save the ghetto inhabitants.

An American band, mounted atop a Russian tank, performs an upbeat swing tune, "The Beer Barrel Polka," as prophesized in one of Jakob's most outlandish lies (fig. 5.14). There is significant melodrama in the closing moments of *Jakob the Liar* attributable to the form's trope of being "too late." As Jakob reported, the Russians were indeed closing in on their position, and while in fact Jakob fabricated stories of the Allied forces closing in on German positions, his lies were not too far from the truth. When the Russians intercept the train carrying Lina and the others, we see Lina — without audio — mouth "Jakob." This is immediately followed by a flashback of Jakob and Lina dancing in what used to be Jakob's café. That sensibility of being "too late" manifests in these closing moments: *if* Jakob had only held out just a bit longer, *if only* . . . the comedic absurdity of an American band mounted atop a Russian tank, and the melodrama elements are a potent mix that tug at the heartstrings. The "Hollywood ending" with the Russians saving the convoy, as the filmmaker explains in his commentary, "is really the last lie."

Figure 5.14

Based on the novel *The Dance of Genghis Cohn* by Romain Gary, Elijiah Moshinsky's 1993 adaptation, *Genghis Cohn*, takes a comedic approach to the dybbuk narrative. Originating in Jewish mysticism, the dybbuk is a wandering soul that inhabits a living body to complete unfinished business. (The dybbuk is discussed at some length in Chapter 9.) Although more akin to a possession than a haunting, in *Genghis Cohn* the dybbuk manifests in a ghostly form. Moshinsky's film opens in a Berlin cabaret in 1933, where the principal character, Genghis

Cohn, is doing a comedic ventriloquist act with a Hitler puppet. Following his performance outside the venue, Brown Shirts set upon the comedian.[28] Three years later in a Vienna cabaret, Cohn wears the clothes of an Orthodox Jew, and explains as part of his comedic stand-up routine, "You know why Hitler doesn't like the Jews? Because they are small, and they are dark, they talk too loud, and, and, and they gesticulate too much," as he tears away his jacket, false beard, side-locks, and hat, to reveal that underneath he's wearing a swastika armband, and a Hitler-mustache. In his new guise he repeats the same refrain, but in a different tone, "They are small, and they're dark, and they gesticulate too much." (fig. 5.15) Once again, Cohn is beset by Brown Shirts following his act.

Figure 5.15

Finally, in Warsaw, 1939, Cohn plays to a silent crowd and asks, "How do you kill a Jewish comedian? Uh, well, the same way that you kill any comedian, you don't laugh at his jokes," which elicits nothing but an eerie silence. In the previous two scenes, Cohn is shot in medium shot with warm lighting; in the Warsaw act, though, he is shot in close-up in a dark smoky venue, leaving the character in a cold and vulnerable environment. Persevering with his routine despite his reception, he says, "When a comedian's act doesn't work he says, 'I died.' I died in some of the classiest places in Europe, but in the end, I finally died in . . .", which is immediately followed by an abrupt cut to an exterior shot in full daylight. Cohn, now in concentration camp garb, along with a number of other Jews, exits the rear of a transport vehicle and marches to a ditch dug in the forest where they're to be lined up and shot. The shocking contrast between comedic routine and killing is quite jarring, and the simple matter-of-fact *mise en scène* of the execution is actually very close to the Wiener film, the only known existing film depicting the Einsatzgruppen in action. Rather than go quietly into the night, Cohn, in Yiddish, yells at his executioners, "Kiss my ass!"

The commanding officer of the garrison that executes Cohn, Otto Schatz, rises to the rank of Commissioner of Police in post-war Germany. He successfully hides his war crimes by convincing the Americans that he was merely a private in the Wehrmacht. Cohn returns as a dybbuk to possess/haunt his executioner. Just like Cohn's act in the opening scene, Schatz becomes a puppet manipulated by the unseen ventriloquist Cohn. The comedian lives on through the Commissioner, ordering a chopped liver sandwich, and taking out *Anne Frank's Diary* from the library. In the course of conversing with his unseen interlocutor, others in earshot of Schatz take his comments out of context, or find them inappropriate. While visiting the Baroness, a widow, who shares a mutual attraction for the Commissioner, he suddenly and quite angrily blurts out when encountering Cohn's spirit, "Jews, Jews, everything is Jews!" Handing the Commissioner a drink, the Baroness implores, "Calm down Otto, there aren't any Jews here. Not any more." Increasingly, the Commissioner integrates Yiddish into his everyday speech, "shtup," "I'chiam," and takes a liking to traditional Jewish food such as gefilte fish and latkes.

There is some satisfaction in Cohn's capacity to exact revenge on his executioner, but the final resolution might not be all that productive. In the sanitarium Schatz is dressed in striped pajamas, not unlike the uniforms for concentration camp internees, and eventually he comes to terms with the objective of Cohn-as-dybbuk — to turn Schatz into a Jew, or perhaps more accurately into Genghis Cohn, whose life, like all the other victims of the Holocaust, was cut short. The former police Commissioner and former Nazi relents and gives up everything to open a kosher deli, and picks up Cohn's comedic career where he left off. Just as with the opening of the film, Schatz is set upon by neo-Nazis after leaving a nightclub. Prone on the ground, Schatz faintly utters in Yiddish Cohn's dying words, "*Kish* mir en toches."

Radu Mihaileanu's 1998 film *Train of Life*, released a year after *Life Is Beautiful*, is frequently paired with it.[29] Set in Poland during the Nazi occupation, a small Jewish shtetl hatches a plan to buy a train, and "deport" themselves, with the ambition of escaping to Palestine via the Soviet Union. The film, like *Life is Beautiful*, is a fairytale, a fantasy, and makes no pretense to verisimilitude. Some have argued that the film rearticulates tired Jewish clichés — the exaggerated gesticulations of quarrelling Jews, the penny-pinching accountant — while others view the mobilization of these tropes as indicative of the fairytale mode. "It is important to understand the role of Jewish humour, the role of cliché, the way in which we speak about ourselves," Mihaileanu says.

Cultural difference

> We do not have a documentary-type, objective way of speaking about ourselves. We have a very subjective, funny and extravagant way. This is Jewish humour, we speak a lot about ourselves, we do not criticise others so much. The French criticise the Belgians, the Rumanians the Bulgarians. The Jewish tell a lot of jokes about themselves . . . about their mother, about their rabbi, about their accountant, about God. They are always discussing with God.[30]

Indeed, this inward sensibility materializes in the fabric of the film, when crises arise, characters undergo existential exercises examining their place in relation to God, to their fellow non-Jewish brethren, their own community, and finally as individuals in a world turned upside down.

Made in the spirit of Lubitsch's *To Be or Not to Be*, the ruse of deportation is complete with Mordechai, the village woodworker, playing the part of an

SS officer with a small garrison of "German soldiers" that "guard" the train. A small contingent of the community goes off the rails so to speak, lead by Yossi, a recent communist convert, preaching a secularist and egalitarian message to his fellow deportees. As tensions rise and the urgency of the voyage intensifies, the "Nazis" — and specifically Mordechai in his role as commanding officer of the train — and the "communists" become the parts that they respectively play. Mordechai becomes increasingly more severe and totalitarian in his disposition, while Yossi inspires an insurrection, leading a mutiny of his comrades aboard the train, and "escaping" into the forest while the train is stopped.

Where Benigni's film is not distinctly Jewish, a fatal flaw in some critics' estimation, Mihaileanu's film, on the other hand, as already noted, exhibits a distinctly Jewish sensibility, perhaps to the point of exaggeration. "Mihaileanu," Lawrence Baron cites, "once belonged to Bucharest's Yiddish theater ensemble. His movie is steeped in Eastern European Jewish folklore, literature, politics, and religiosity." And adding to his credentials, Mihaileanu's "parents survived the camps while other members of his family perished."[31] The film does indeed focus on specific Judaic themes, such as language. Mordechai, in a scene preparing for his role as SS officer, says during his German language lesson, "It's odd. It's like Yiddish, I understand every word." His language instructor interrupts him, "German is rigid, Mordechai. Precise and sad. Yiddish makes fun of German. It has a sense of humor. To speak perfect German, and to lose your accent, take the fun out of it." Mordechai leans in, "We make fun of their language? Maybe that's why we're at war."

As the train makes its way east partisans prepare to blow up the rails and the train, believing that it's a German train. But of course the train is not on any of the train schedules and gets dubbed the "ghost train." The partisans are thwarted (thankfully) each time an opportunity arises to attack it, and are confounded by the train's erratic route. When the train stops for Shabbat, the partisans finally have a clear shot at the "Nazi" garrison. On their wireless radio the commander of the small band of partisans seeks permission to initiate an attack: "The Germans are praying too! . . . They're bobbing up and down, holding books." The superior on the other end of the wireless commands, "Hold on . . ." The exasperated partisan commander in the field exclaims, "Fucking war!" As the partisan commander waits anxiously, his superior at the other end of the wireless informs him, "It's confirmed: they're doing Sabbath prayers. They're of the Hebrew persuasion." The demoralized band of partisans eventually walks away. The train narrowly escapes yet another disaster, without ever knowing it.

Multiple times Mordechai is called upon to negotiate passage of his "deportation" train, on one occasion marching straight into the lion's den to retrieve one of their men captured by real Nazis following Yossi's mutiny. In the latter part of the film, transport vehicles block the tracks, and a Nazi officer informs Mordechai, "I have orders to requisition the train. You'll continue in trucks . . ." Mordechai protests naturally, and the two "Germans" stand off. While the two bicker, Shlomo comes to Mordechai's side, "Heil shalom! Mordechai, can't you hear his accent?" As it turns out, a group of gypsies had hatched a similar harebrained scheme, deporting themselves with transport trucks, with a contingent of fake

Nazis. The other "German" officer explodes in frustration in not be able to fulfill his duty as the group's "Nazi commanding officer." Mordechai consoles his brethren, "You can't imagine how I sympathize." The two groups merge, and board the train eastward.

Although Mordechai and the shtetl Rabbi are effectively the heroes of the film, leading the exodus of the community out of Poland and to the promised land, Shlomo the village idiot is nevertheless the principal character that propels the narrative forward; he doesn't speak much within the diegesis, but it's his crazy ideas that allow the community to evade disaster. *Train of Life* is bookended with Shlomo's voiceovers. At the end of the film Shlomo in voiceover says, as the train recedes into the distance, "Once in the Soviet Union, mostly everyone espoused the communist cause. Some went to Palestine, mostly the gypsies. Others went to India, mostly the Jews." In a dissolve, transitioning from the train to a close-up of Shlomo, similar to the opening, he continues to explain (in voiceover) what happened to his compatriots as he tweaks his head to the side, and the camera quickly zooms out to reveal that Shlomo is speaking to us from behind a barbwire fence and wearing a concentration camp uniform (fig. 5.16). "Well . . . almost true," Shlomo concedes before breaking into song. The fairytale elements of *Life Is Beautiful* and *Train of Life*, which are associated with the bookended voiceovers in both films, are about survival. In *Train of Life* Shlomo apparently allows for flights of fancy to escape the hell of the concentration camp, and to imagine that he and his community managed to evade capture, while *Life Is Beautiful* utilizes the game to protect the young Giosuè. *Train of Life* Mihaileanu says is not intended "to banalize, not to rewrite, but to keep the discussion going. I wanted to depict the tragedy of the Holocaust using the language of comedy, to use comedy to strengthen the tragedy. Laughter after all is another form of crying."[32]

Figure 5.16

Written and directed by Roberto Benigni, his 1997 film *Life Is Beautiful* stirred up a hornet's nest of critical and academic debate. Not since the 1978 NBC miniseries *Holocaust*, or Spielberg's 1993 *Schindler's List*, had a film about the Holocaust roused the praise and the ire of so many. Many detractors of the film parroted the conservative mantra that the Holocaust should be represented "as it really was," and also questioned Benigni's credentials (as a non-Jew) to play the part of a Jewish victim. Among the chorus of naysayers David Denby called *Life Is Beautiful*, in his *New Yorker* review of the film, "a benign form of Holocaust denial."[33] Denby's review ranks among the most critical:

> The enormous worldwide success of *Life Is Beautiful* suggests that the audience is exhausted by the Holocaust, that it is sick to death of the subject's unending ability to disturb. The audience's mood is understandable, but artists are supposed to be made of sterner stuff, and surely an artist cannot transcend what he never encounters.

He finally lambasts the conclusion of the film: "The audience comes away feeling relieved and happy and rewards Benigni for allowing it, at last, to escape."[34]

Benigni's father, Luigi, was in fact interned in a German labor camp, in Erfurt, when the Italians turned against the Germans in 1943. Weighing only 80 pounds when he was released, Luigi Benigni was nearly worked to death.[35] He later shared many stories about the experience, but always managed to inflect the harrowing with humor. As Roberto Benigni recounts,

> Night and day fellow prisoners were dying all around him. He told us about it, as if to protect me and my sisters, he told it in an almost funny way — saying tragic, painful things, but finally his way of telling them was really very particular. Sometimes we laughed at the stories he told.[36]

The film's principal character, Guido Orefice, played by Benigni, arrives in Arezzo, a small city in Central Italy, having arranged to work at a restaurant his uncle, Eliseo Orefice, manages. Ferruccio Papini accompanies him, having also secured work in Arezzo at an upholsterer. We are introduced to the pair as they are driving to Arezzo, but they lose control of the car when the brakes fail. In a throwback to the slapstick comedy of Chaplin, Guido urges a crowd, who have gathered to welcome the king, to clear the way, but the crowd mistakes Guido's urgent gesticulations as the fascist salute, and excitedly return the salute (fig. 5.17). Benigni's debt to Chaplin is incalculable, and he knows it; Guido's concentration camp number — emblazoned across his striped uniform, 07397 — is the same as the Jewish barber's in Chaplin's *The Great Dictator*.

Figure 5.17

Finally stopping to repair the faulty brakes, Guido walks to a small farmhouse where a woman, Dora, falls out of a barn and literally into his arms. The two bump into one another on other occasions and after a whimsical courtship — despite Dora being engaged to Rodolfo, a city bureaucrat — marry and have a child, Giosuè. As a Jew, Guido is subject to increasingly more restrictive laws and growing social intolerance. On Giosuè's fifth birthday, Guido, Guido's uncle, and Giosuè are summarily rounded up and deported. Dora, although not a Jew and not subject to deportation, insists on boarding the train carrying her family off to a concentration camp. At the camp, Guido, in order to protect his son from the horrors of the camp, pretends that they're playing a game, and that the prize — after reaching 1,000 points — is a real tank. In the end Guido succeeds in protecting his son until the end of the war, and mother and child are reunited, but Guido pays the ultimate price to protect his child.[37]

The film is framed with voiceovers, and we don't learn until the end of the film that it is the adult voice of Giosuè. The opening is enigmatic, as a figure carrying a child (Guido and Giosuè — characters we are not acquainted with yet) walks into a thick fog, and as voiceover conveys, "This is a simple story, but not an easy one to tell. Like a fable, there is sorrow and, like a fable, it is full of wonder and happiness." Like Quentin Tarantino's 2009 film *Inglourious Basterds*, which begins in full disclosure, "Once upon a time . . .," here too Benigni prompts the spectator not to confuse this fanciful tale with reality. The film then cuts to an exterior shot of the countryside, and a title reads, "Arezzo, Italy, 1939." *Life Is Beautiful* is perhaps the single most moving Holocaust film, and its emotional intensity is attributable to the comedy in the film; the laughter in the film makes its heart-breaking ending ever more charged. Guido orders his son to hide, and after the Germans flee and the concentration camp empties, Giosuè finally emerges from his hiding place; suddenly from around the corner an American tank rolls right up to him. Giosuè is awestruck, and exclaims, "It's true!" Mounted atop the tank Giosuè sees his mother in the procession of newly freed internees, and exclaims, "Mommy!" The voiceover that began the film closes the film, "This is my story. This is the sacrifice my father made. This was his gift to me."

There is a string of Italian films that in one form or another deal with the Holocaust, most of which locate responsibility elsewhere. Liliana Cavani's 1974 film *The Night Porter*, Luchino Visconti's 1969 film *The Damned*, Lina Wertmüller's 1975 film *Seven Beauties*, and Bernardo Bertolucci's 1970 film *The Conformist* all locate the source of fascism in sexual perversion, as a mental ailment, and situate it as a distinctly German pretension. Pier Paolo Pasolini's 1975 film, *Salò, or the 120 Days of Sodom*, on the other hand, is an exception to this, and draws on clinical sadism, which at its core is the practice of reason, unguarded by ethics. This is the subject of the following chapter.

Unlike films such as *The Night Porter* or *The Damned*, *Life Is Beautiful* "is not limited to the failure of German civilization," Carlo Celli observes. "*Life Is Beautiful* does not gloss over the responsibility of the Italian fascist regime that permitted and aided the Nazi crimes."[38] In this respect Benigni's film might even go further than Pasolini's *Salò*, which locates responsibility in Enlightenment

[handwritten annotation: everyone is guilty]

rationality, and holds Western civilization as a whole (including contemporary viewers) accountable. At their core *Salò* and *Life Is Beautiful* are the most congruous, despite their glaringly obvious differences. While Pasolini exhibits the systemic operations of fascism allegorically in his adaptation of Sade's salacious and hyper-violent novel, *The 120 Days of Sodom*, Benigni turns fascism into farce, where Guido repeatedly demonstrates an "ability to appropriate and recast authoritative language for his own purposes [which] is also used to his amorous advantage."[39]

Systems — whether its race policies, or the deportation of Jews — are the butt of Guido's jokes. On a couple of occasions Guido makes a point of noting to Giosuè that, "You see? It's all organized!" to deflect anxiety about the deportation and concentration camp regime. Tired and scared, Giosuè asks, "What game is this?" This is a stroke of genius, and Guido excitedly confirms Giosuè's question, "We're all players. It's all organized. . . . If somebody makes a mistake, they get sent right home. That means you have to be very careful. But if you win, you get first prize!" Giosuè asks, "What's the prize?" Hesitating as he thinks, "First prize!" Uncle Eliseo stoops down and says excitedly, "It's a tank." Disappointed, Giosuè says, "I already have one." Guido assures his son, "This one's a real tank! Brand new!" Skeptically, Giosuè asks, "Real?" "Yes!" Guido answers, "I didn't want to tell you." When an SS officer taps Uncle Eliseo on the shoulder and orders other men to step aside as well, Giosuè asks, "Where's Uncle Eliseo going?" Perhaps knowing what this means, but nevertheless hiding it from Giosuè, he says, "He's on another team. It's all organized. Bye, Uncle." The game — and its rules — functions as an inversion to the Nazis' organization, an inversion of systematized regimentation of Nazi execution of the Final Solution.

The game is the critical trope of *Life Is Beautiful.* Just as *Salò* utilizes clinical sadism and the libertine's strict adherence to their code to demonstrate the evacuation of ethics from reason under the Nazi regime, the rules of the game in *Life Is Beautiful* work against dehumanization. When a camp guard barges into the barracks, he asks if any of the deportees speaks German. Guido, despite being ignorant of the German language, raises his hand. The stern-faced German guard proceeds to explain the camp rules in German, but Guido's "translation" is for the benefit of his son, instead explaining the rules of the game. "The game starts now," Guido commands sharply, approximating the German's inflection, but coming nowhere close to the content of his speech. "Whoever's here is here, whoever's not is not. The first one to get a thousand points wins. The prize is a tank! Lucky him!" Guido continues to "translate" the rules of the game.[40] The objective of the game — with its strict rules and regiment — is to preserve humanity, to "protect" Giosuè from the inhumanity of the concentration camp. Ironic and antithetical to the application of Nazi systematic implementation of the Holocaust, Guido's system — the rules of the game — was designed to save life, whereas the Nazis' systemized brutality was designed to humiliate and kill.[41]

Earlier in the film, while working as a waiter in Arezzo, Guido makes the acquaintance of a German doctor, Lessing, who, like Guido, has a passion for riddles. By happenstance Dr. Lessing is the camp physician where Guido is interned, and he believes that the doctor will help him and his family get out of the camp. The doctor arranges for Guido to work as a server in the officer's quarters. During service, Lessing feigns clumsiness — dropping his utensils, and a bottle of brandy on another occasion — to get Guido's attention, without calling attention to the fact that the German officer desperately wants to converse with the Jewish internee. Urgently, the doctor leans in to speak to Guido, as if to convey important information, "Pay attention," as Lessing begins to recite a riddle. Frantically, Lessing implores with Guido to help. Dumbfounded by Lessing's blindness to the suffering all around, Guido leaves the German officer to wallow in his mental anguish.

Dr. Lessing is set in contrast to Guido. Lessing enjoys games as well, is obsessive about riddles, but he cannot see beyond them. The system, the logic of riddles, swallows Lessing up, without any regard to humanity. Critics and scholars frequently compare Lessing to Mengele, a physician who conducts his medical duties with the utmost professional care, but without an ounce of humanity, and acting according to his duty selects those not fit enough to work to die. While Lessing cannot sleep, plagued by a riddle he cannot solve, he is not in the least bit disturbed by his role in conducting mass murder. Millicent Marcus argues that Guido's encounter with Dr. Lessing in the concentration camp is a "red herring, intended to disabuse us of any conventional expectations for a comprehensive happy ending. In the case of the riddle, Guido's game work is insufficient, and Nazi behavior remains an insoluble enigma."[42] Marcus is correct in observing that Guido's encounter with Lessing in the camp disabuses us of any expectations — our initial thought that he is a "good" Nazi — but there is no enigma here. Benigni follows Pasolini's lead on this count (and a handful of scholars on the subject): Lessing is a clinical sadist who is not a cold-blooded beast but rather a character enamored with the instrument of reason, divorced of ethics or any sense of human sentimentality — a true sadist.[43]

Chapter Six

Sadism and Sexual Deviance

INTRODUCTION: WHAT IS SADISM?

The colloquial concept of sadism — pleasure derived from the pain of others — obfuscates its profound philosophical origins. Indeed, in some cases the victim–perpetrator relationship set within the Holocaust — be it in film or in life — merits this rather colloquial designation. But in other cases to simply characterize a perpetrator as "sadistic" lacks a degree of nuance, and is perhaps too easy. Hastily yielding to the term "sadism" provides us with a name for what we imagine to be "unthinkable" or utterly "inhumane."

In Holocaust films sadistic characters all too often materialize as tawdry. In exploitation films, for example, Nazis are typically depicted as sick and twisted, deriving giddy pleasure from the administration of pain. In more "serious" films colloquial sadism materializes to draw distinct lines between good and evil. In Roberto Rossellini's 1945 film *Rome, Open City*, for instance, a Catholic priest is set in contrast to a German officer, who employs torture to extract information. Pitting the priest against the Nazi establishes a clear divide between the virtuous victim and the sadistic perpetrator. This is the most common manifestation of Nazi sadism in film, but it does not conform to what will be dubbed here as "clinical sadism."

Made just three years after the war Alfred Hitchcock's 1948 film *Rope* might figure as an example of clinical sadism. At the beginning of the film Phillip and Brandon strangle one of their associates, David Kentley, in their New York apartment and hide his body in a chest in the middle of a their living-room. The pair of killers hosts a dinner party that evening, leaving the chest in clear sight. During the dinner party Rupert, a former instructor of the young assassins, speaks rhetorically on the merits of murder, arguing that it would "solve" innumerable problems, including overpopulation and troubles getting theater tickets. He explains that murder should be an art, and, "As such, the privilege of committing it should be reserved for those few who are really superior individuals." Brandon adds, "And the victims, inferior beings whose lives are unimportant anyway." One of the dinner guests, and David's father, Henry Kentley, is agitated by the capricious discussion of murder, and interrupts, "Probably a symptom of approaching senility, but I must confess I really don't appreciate this morbid humor." Henry is puzzled and troubled that Brandon truly appears to believe in the idea of superiority, and suggests that his position is no different from that of Hitler. "Hitler was a paranoid savage," Brandon implores. "All fascist supermen were brainless murderers. I'd hang any who were left. But then, you see, I'd hang them first for being stupid. I'd hang all incompetents and fools. There are far too many in the world." Henry has enough of Brandon's diatribe, "Then you should hang me. I'm so stupid, I don't know whether you're serious or not." Throughout the film Brandon drops hints regarding the act of murder committed just hours earlier and revels not only in the erotics of killing but also in intellectually outstripping his guests. And it is this latter trait that is associated with the clinical form of sadism.

The term "sadism" derives from the infamous French author, Donatien Alphonse François Sade, the Marquis de Sade, who wrote some of his most notorious works during the Reign of Terror. Sade cloaked his critique of the Republican movement behind an allegorical veil. On the surface Sade's stories are encyclopedic catalogues of perversion, but beneath the surface his discourse on libertinage (sadism) illustrates how strict systematized reasoning fosters a dehumanization of victims, and evacuates all human sentimentality from acts of cruelty. The basic principle of clinical sadism — of libertinage — is this: *the practice of reason unchecked by ethics*. In the wake of two world wars scholars began to query: What happened to the Enlightenment project? What happened to the Kantian principles of logic and reason that were intended to elevate humanity? What went wrong? And, finally, some began to wonder: Was Sade prophetic? Is the libertine, in fact, the enlightened subject *par excellence*?[1]

The parity drawn between Kant and Sade is one of deep profundity and significance. "A lot — everything, perhaps — is at stake here," Slavoj Zizek writes, and subsequently asks, "is there a line from Kantian formalist ethics to the cold-blooded Auschwitz killing machine? Are concentration camps and killing as a neutral business the inherent outcome of the enlightenment insistence on the autonomy of Reason?"[2] Even matters regarding sex for the libertine is not premised on passion but on duty. Indeed, and despite our preconceived notions otherwise, any inspection of the Sadean volume will reveal that the sexual acts, no matter how benign, or vicious they may be, are all executed under strict guidelines, and within highly controlled environments. (These tropes — strict guidelines, and a controlled environment — are important features in the *torture porn* genre, which is addressed in the succeeding chapter.) There is nothing capricious or spontaneous about the libertines; that is to say, no action is perpetrated through love, or genuinely erotic feelings. The sadist when it comes right down to it is enslaved to reason, and what gives the sadist pleasure is intellectual superiority. While Nazi sadism in film most commonly materializes in the colloquial sense, there are, however, cinematic representations of clinical sadism. This chapter surveys variations on the sadist motif.

THE MENGELE MODEL

Ilse Koch and Dr. Joseph Mengele are two of the primary historical archetypes on which sadistic characters are frequently premised. (Koch is subject to discussion in Chapter 8.) Mengele was a clinical sadist. He veiled his barbarity behind the veneer of science. As some witnesses have reported, for example, during childbirth, "Dr. Mengele took all correct medical precautions . . . rigorously observing all aseptic principles, cutting the umbilical cord with greatest care, etc. But only half an hour later he sent mother and infant to be burned in the crematorium."[3] Mengele's naked cruelty emerged from the neutralization of reason, where the pursuit of scientific knowledge was stripped of any human compassion.

The Mengele motif is evident in Ingmar Bergman's *The Serpent's Egg* (1977). Annette Insdorf says of the film that it "presents three ominous aspects of 1923 Berlin: anti-Semitism; a ravaged economy; and scientific curiosity gone wild, severed from moral considerations."[4] This last aspect — scientific reason unchecked by any moral compass — exemplifies clinical sadism. Set between the two great wars, where the seeds of Nazism were sowed, Bergman's film features a Mengelesque sadist. Abel Rosenberg and his bother are Jewish circus performers, and find themselves out of work and down on their luck. In the early moments of the film Abel, stumbling drunk, discovers that his brother has committed suicide. Abel's sister-in-law (and now widow), Manuela Rosenberg, tries to support them emotionally and financially. An old family friend, and Manuela's occasional lover, Dr. Hans Vergerus, furnishes her with a flat. Abel very reluctantly agrees to share the flat with Manuela, as he finds Vergerus quite disagreeable. Abel recalls that as a child he and Vergerus used to play together and in one instance found a cat and tied it up; Vergerus vivisected it — to watch its heart beating.

Recollections and suggestions like this paint quite a disturbing portrait of the clinician. Vergerus, effectively a prototype of what is to come in the Nazi era, is the harbinger of Dr. Josef Mengele. He is yet another character in a line of pasty icy cold blond-hair blue-eyed devils, similar to Wolfe Aschenbach or Martin von Essenbeck in Luchino Visconti's *The Damned* (1969), or Helmut Wallenberg in Tinto Brass's 1976 exploitation picture *Salon Kitty* (the latter two both played by Helmut Berger). We do not learn much about Vergerus — aside from short anecdotes and brief allusions — the truth of his character and his activities is made known only at the climax of the film. When Abel returns to the flat he discovers that Manuela is dead. As Abel shakes Manuela's lifeless body, the flash of a photographic bulb goes off, leading to the discovery that all the mirrors in the flat are two-way mirrors, surveying the flat with motion and photographic cameras (fig. 6.1).

Figure 6.1

Voyeurism and sadism in film tend to go hand in hand, and the conclusion of *The Serpent's Egg* makes this connection fairly explicit. A network of passages leads from the two-way mirrors in the flat to Vergerus's lab. Unbeknown to them, Manuela and Abel are guinea pigs in one of Vergerus's medical experiments. When Vergerus enters the room, the unfazed clinician invites Abel to "Look at the screen and you'll see some interesting pictures. They were taken during our experiments here at the St. Anna Clinic." In the films that Vergerus shows Abel the human subjects either resort to killing themselves, killing someone else, or go certifiably insane. Vergerus reveals that his brother killed himself as a result of the experimental drug Thanatoxin.

Continuing with the survey of experiments, Vergerus discusses one of their most recent studies of Kapta Blue, a nearly odorless gas that alters behavior and produces radical shifts in emotion. Placing his hand to his head, Abel realizes that this is precisely what has been done to him and Manuela; both of whom who have been argumentative and emotionally strained of late. We infer that ultimately this is what leads to Manuela's death. The use of gas — although not necessarily intended to be lethal in this case — is an uncanny specter of what is to come with the Nazis some 20 years later. With a devilish chuckle Vergerus claims, "I'm not a monster, Abel. What you have seen are the first faltering steps of a necessary and logical development." In his deference to reason and the pursuit of scientific knowledge, Vergerus reveals himself to be a sadist.

Vergerus's project of clinical observations, captured on film, establishes clear power relations between clinician and subject. The mastery of the field of vision corresponds to the sadist's imperative to operate within a hermetic universe, controlling the parameters of what is seen. Numerous other films that have sadistic elements evoke voyeurism in some fashion, including Liliana Cavani's 1974 film *The Night Porter* where the principal male character, Max, films new inductees into the concentration camp with his penetrating camera, and the libertines at the conclusion of Pier Paolo Pasolini's 1975 film *Salò, or the 120 Days of Sodom* who in the film's finale watch a spectacle of torture as if at the opera.

FASCISM AS ILLNESS

Pre-war German industry is central to the plot of Luchino Visconti's film *The Damned*, featuring the Essenbeck family, wealthy industrialists. Geoffrey Nowell-Smith observes, regarding the family, that "their private destinies cannot be separated from those of the State, and the rise of Nazism involves them both in political accommodations and in personal disintegration."[5] Although Visconti lays blame for the rise of Nazism at the feet of the industrialists,[6] perhaps contrary to his own intentions what materializes in the film instead is the idea that Nazism is the product of a disturbed mind.

Joachim Von Essenbeck, the patriarch of the family, in the opening moments of the film announces a successor to the Essenbeck Steelworks. Moments before his announcement it is learnt that the Reichstag — the seat of the German government — is on fire; this historical event, which took place on February 27, 1933, is a critical turning point in the Nazis' rise to power. Von Essenbeck, prone to making purely pragmatic decisions, and in light of the political climate, feels compelled to name a vice-president that it is on good terms with the fascists.

Herbert Thallman, who was originally in line to be the successor, is deposed in favor of Konstantin Von Essenbeck, a member of the SA. Thallman protests, quite prepared to submit his resignation, but lashes out against the patriarch's quick acquiescence to the blowing of political winds, "Right or wrong," the Steelworks always comes first, he blasts. "That has always been your creed. You sent your son to the slaughter, so you could say: 'See the Essenbecks put children and cannons into the world with the same sentiment.' And with the same sentiment they'll be buried." Later Thallman admits to his progressive leaning nephew, Gunther Von Essenbeck, that "Nazism, Gunther, is our creation; it was born in our factories, nourished with our money."[7]

The patriarch of the family, Joachim, is no sadist, but the logic that he employs establishes fertile ground for it to grow and flourish. His practical decision making, *despite* his own ethical reservations and disgust with the Nazi regime, establishes a precedent for the succeeding generations: reason, logic, needn't be hampered by ethical reservations. The narrative, though, rather than pursuing the clinical form of sadism, turns towards the more colloquial form, simply conflating sadism with sexual deviance.

The blond blue-eyed devil Wolfe Aschenbach is an SS officer who plays the role of Mephistopheles, seducing successive generations with the promise of power, and in turn ensures that Essenbeck Steelworks continues to supply the regime with munitions. In different ways, Aschenbach, the consummate puppet-master, manipulates Frederick Bruckmann, his lover Sophie Von Essenbeck, and finally Martin Von Essenbeck and even the progressive-thinking Gunther Von Essenbeck. Bruckmann and Aschenbach are cousins. The seduction of power manifests as a contagious disease, polluting the minds of the Essenbeck family. (This idea — fascism as a contagion — manifests in films like *Apt Pupil*, discussed in Chapter 3.)[8]

The Faustian plot is woven into the *mise en scène* of the opening and the closing of the film, which features shots from the Essenbeck Steelworks. Huge cauldrons of molten steel bubble and belch forth sparks of red-hot steel, trading in the popular vision of Hell. The closing shot of the film features Martin Von Essenbeck, the newly anointed proprietor of Essenbeck Steelworks, standing at attention in his SS uniform, giving the Nazi salute. The camera slowly zooms in, bringing his face into tight close-up, and a cross-dissolve is used to transition between this close-up and the succeeding shots of Essenbeck Steelworks, effectively illustrating Martin's pact with the devil, or in other words, *The Damned* (fig. 6.2).[9] The Faustian plot device is a common motif in Holocaust films, where Nazis (and their collaborators) are seen "making deals with the devil" in exchange for power (e.g., Nicole's accession in rank in Gillo Pontecorvo's 1959 film *Kapò*), or alternatively the Nazi is depicted as an agent of evil (this is subject to discussion in Chapter 9).

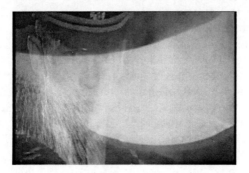

Figure 6.2

A close relative of the Faustian plot device — or Nazi as agent of evil — is Nazism as a form of sickness. And this latter character-type is usually dressed in some way in the discourse of colloquial sadism — various forms of sexual depravity. Sophie Von Essenbeck's son, Martin, is a dandy and effeminate. Coded as homosexual, we eventually learn that he's been seen going to "one of those clubs." We are introduced to his character during the stage performances of the Essenbeck grandchildren to celebrate their grandfather's birthday. While Gunter treats the patriarch to a little Bach, Martin "Einen Mann, einen richtigen Mann," appears in cabaret drag.[10] Figured as utterly decadent, and antithetical to high culture, Martin is figured as morally suspicious.

Visconti conflates homosexuality with pedophilia, and ensures that Martin is coded as an unredeemable deviant. Early in the film he seduces his young cousin as they play hide-and-seek. Later he seduces a young Jewess, Lisa, probably 9 years old, bringing her a gift of a wooden horse, "a veritable horse of Troy," Claretta Micheletti Tonetti calls it, "hiding danger and death inside its peaceful appearance."[11] The young girl after the apparent sexual encounter becomes ill, making Martin desperately anxious, fearing that he might be found out. Silently slipping into the sick girl's room, Martin checks up on her. Without a word Lisa, pasty and feverish, gets up from her bed, mounts the stairs to the attic and hangs herself.

Martin goes into hiding following this incident, and Konstantin Von

Essenbeck, the crass SA member, takes advantage of the situation to momentarily grab control of the Essenbeck Steelworks. Aschenbach, an SS officer, won't stand for it, though, and in a purge modeled after the Night of Long Knives, crushes his SA rival (fig. 6.3). Visconti "makes a sharp distinction between the mob fascism of the SA squads and the efficient militarism of the SS, identified with the New Order and with the Nazi state itself."[12] During the purge, it is Friedrich who "personally dispatches the coarse and cretinous Konstantin . . ."[13] Visconti aestheticizes the massacre of the SA. "The naked bodies of the SA are carefully grouped in entanglements that could have been conceived by a Renaissance painter, and they are systematically slaughtered in what is a disquieting combination of horror and artistic expression."[14] Aschenbach once again goes to work manipulating characters; eventually, he makes Martin's "indiscretion" go away, in exchange for his allegiance to the SS.

Figure 6.3

At the end of the film, Martin, assuming the familial throne, hosts the wedding for Frederick and his mother. During the wedding the couple is asked if there are any hereditary diseases in the family — both answer in the negative, but Martin is figured as clearly sick, and his presence in the frame seems to contradict Sophie's response. Martin, to ensure that the wedding party is lively, brings along some of his friends, and in effect turns the family estate into "one of those clubs" (fig. 6.4). Couples engage in explicit displays of affection, and the rooms are adorned with a multitude of Nazi flags and banners. Immediately following the simple ceremony Martin escorts the newlyweds to another room to present them with his gift: a matching pair of cyanide capsules. Inspired by Hitler and Eva Braun's suicide in their Berlin bunker, Frederick and Sophie dutifully take their own lives. Some critics are incensed by the conflation of sexual depravity and Nazism. Richard Schickel for instance writes: "To imply a cause-effect relationship between sexual perversion and political perversion is historically inaccurate and socially irresponsible."[15] Perhaps "socially irresponsible" is too strong, but the conflation of sexual perversity — tinged with sadism — is tawdry to be sure; it is just too easy. Nevertheless this vision of the sadistic Nazi — a sexual deviant — is a common motif repeated *ad nauseam*.[16] Indeed the Naziploitation genre (discussed in Chapter 8) rests on this basic motif.

Figure 6.4

MASTER AND SLAVE

Liliana Cavani's 1974 film *The Night Porter* is set in post-war 1957 Vienna. The principal male character, Max, is a simple night porter at Hotel zur Oper, but with a sordid past; he is a former SS officer and a member of a clandestine group of former Nazis. The group holds regular meetings, where they conduct "mock trials" of the members. These are intended to serve three purposes: first, to root out any incriminating information that might be harmful to the "accused" and at the same time jeopardize the group as a whole — witnesses that might testify against them are executed, and any pilfered archival documents discovered during the investigation are summarily burned at the conclusion of the mock trial; second, the trials serve as a dress-rehearsal should in fact a member be sent to a tribunal; and, third, the trials are intended to be therapeutic, absolving the members of guilt, or more accurately assuaging their anxiety, assured that any damning evidence has been destroyed. Max is "on trial," but the clandestine circle of former Nazis become alarmed by a mysterious female witness that might still be alive, Lucia, the central female character in the film.[17] She is indeed alive, and by coincidence staying in Max's hotel with her husband, who is conducting a performance of "The Magic Flute."

As in Sidney Lumet's 1964 film, *The Pawnbroker*, Max, once confronted with Lucia, is inundated by a surge of wartime flashbacks. During the war the teenaged Lucia was interned in a concentration camp — it is never clear what her offense was, or what her heritage is exactly, though one thing is certain, she is not Jewish — and from first sight she captures Max's imagination. Max films the new inductees, who are stripped bare, and seizes on Lucia, examining her nude waif body. These flashbacks come abruptly, short at first, but as the film progresses they increase in duration, again similar to *The Pawnbroker*. Lucia too experiences the same thing; once she sees her former master, she desperately wants to leave Vienna, haunted by the memory of her past, which she thought she had escaped. But she is conflicted, at once yearning to return to her domineering partner, and her role as submissive, but at the same time filled with dread because of what might come of it. Again, echoing the use of flashbacks in *The*

Pawnbroker, as Lucia wanders through a curio shop, she finds a dress, which leads into a flashback where Max gives his internee-mistress a dress. These associative flashbacks are a common motif in *The Night Porter*, allowing the present and the past to bleed into one another.

During a performance of "The Magic Flute" — conducted by Lucia's husband — Max and Lucia, separated by a couple of rows of seats, exchange a series of knowing glances. Cut into this sequence is the "seduction" of Lucia while interned in the concentration camp. In a series of flashbacks we see Max, the camp "doctor," taking Lucia from her bed; in a later flashback we see her hands chained to a bedpost, as the camera pans down to her ashen face, Max looms large over her, as he begins to caress her bound body. He mimes fellatio, slowly moving his index and middle finger in and out of Lucia's gaping mouth. Tied to the bed, it is unclear where pleasure is located, with Max and his assertion of physical prowess, with Lucia who seems to revel in her submissive role (which she seems to confirm in the latter part of the film), or is it perhaps even mutual?

In the practice of bondage, domination and sadomasochism (BDSM) — which is yet again different from Sade's theory of libertinage — the submissive wields most of the power, dictating how far an encounter can go. The power relations in these practices are a little murky, because while the domineering partner executes "punishments," the submissive controls the situation: "yes," "no," "go," "stop," or some predetermined safeword.[18] This instability — the murkiness of power structures, and the *reliance* of the master on the slave — is what materializes in the opera sequence, where Lucia is placed in a love triangle, caught between her husband the conductor, and Max, between her past and her present. In "Signifying the Holocaust: Liliana Cavani's *Portiere di Notte*," Marguerite Waller offers an insightful analysis of this scene: "Mozart's problematic opera, about a woman, Pamina, who first seems to be imprisoned and later 'saved' within a rigidly hierarchical masculinist regime, becomes associated through the complex intercutting of sound and image, with *both* Lucia's relationships." The three-tiered sequence — "The Magic Flute," Lucia and her husband, Lucia and Max — resists bifurcating the narrative or the characters into neatly consigned camps: "Surely a clean-cut American conductor is good, an uptight ex-Nazi sadist, torturer night porter is bad."[19] Cavani makes no allowances for such an easy distinction.

Although Max and Lucia are aware of one another, it takes nearly an hour into the narrative before the primary characters directly interact with one another. Their first encounter spreads the gamut of emotions and physical expression — anger coupled with love, and violence paired with gentle affection. Max, going to Lucia's room, angrily asks why she has come: "Have you come to give me away? Have you?" as he begins to beat her. Throwing her to the floor, he insists on an answer, "Why, why, why?" Once on the floor, though, for a brief moment, violence turns to tenderness. As they both rise Lucia runs for the door, but Max stops her. Once again a violent struggle gives way to tenderness as the two embrace; Lucia pulls Max to floor as they chuckle, a giddy laughter that is charged with nervous sexual excitement. Max urges Lucia, "Ah, no, no . . . too fast, too fast," and that it has been, "Too long! Too long!" Confounded and soaked in sexual excitation as they roll on the floor, "Tell me. Tell me!" Max exclaims. In response Lucia screams, "I want you!" Again Max looks to her, "Tell me what to do. Tell me what to do. Tell me what to do!" Lucia screams, "No!" (Again, this invites comparisons between the on-screen relationship and the practice of BDSM, where the submissive controls the situation.) Collecting themselves, Max confides in her, "I love you so."

Lucia's husband moves on to the next performance in Germany, leaving Lucia behind in Vienna. Still conflicted, she considers whether she should return to her home in the United States, or should she stay with her domineering lover. Eventually, Lucia takes up residence in Max's apartment and they start where they left off in the concentration camp, reacquainting themselves with the master–slave relationship. As she unpacks her luggage, hanging her clothes in the wardrobe she finds Max's SS uniform, which she strokes nostalgically. Making coffee, Max spoon-feeds Lucia. While a romantic gesture, it also demonstrates how he, as master, assumes complete control over his submissive partner. Lucia returns the favor with fellatio, which cuts to a flashback of a similar sexual encounter between the pair in the concentration camp.

In one of the most memorable scenes of the film, Lucia, now Max's well-established submissive mistress in the camp, performs — effectively as Salome[20] — in a makeshift concentration camp cabaret. Topless, and in highly fetishistic gear, Lucia dons black oversized-trousers held up by suspenders, an SS officer's cap, and most striking long leather gloves. The fetishistic application of Nazi regalia in visual culture — be it film, Stalag book covers, or some other art form — typically feature jackboots, but in this case Lucia's long black gloves take the place of this common fetishistic trope to great effect (fig. 6.5). As a "gift" for her performance Max has a box sent over to his table where he and Lucia are seated. She peels away a piece of linen concealing its contents; inside is the head of Johann, a fellow internee that used to, according to Max's account, torment her. She had simply asked that he be transferred. As Max recounts later to the Countess, chuckling as he does, "I don't know why, but suddenly the story of Salome came into my head. I couldn't resist it." The Countess flatly comments,

Figure 6.5

"You were always insane, and you still are." "Sane, insane, then. Hmm, who's to judge," Max retorts. As if to admonish the Countess, he says with a slightly dubious tone, "And just you remember, we're both in the same boat," as he wags his finger. The reference to "being in the same boat" cuts two ways, because while on the one hand it functions as a stock phrase suggesting their shared Nazi past, at the same time it also recalls an earlier incident where Max murders a fellow member of the clandestine circle — Mario, an Italian — by drowning him as they fished from a boat.

The Night Porter trades heavily in the colloquial vision of sadism. Sickness pervades the narrative in multiple ways, and is offered as the motivating factor for Max's sadistic disposition (and perhaps Lucia's masochistic sensibility as well). Klaus, the key investigator of the clandestine group, says, "Max had imagination. He had fun passing himself off as a doctor, to have a chance at making sensational photographic studies." Here Max is implicitly compared to one of the archetypes of Nazi sadism, Dr. Josef Mengele, by "passing himself off a doctor." The pretense, however, of being a concentration camp "doctor" is fairly transparent in Klaus's view of it, quite unlike the figure of Mengele who cloaked his acts of treachery behind the veil of scientific research. Under the ruse of "making sensational photographic studies" the rationale falls flat, and rather than conforming to the strict rules of clinical sadism reveals Max to be anything but a sadist. Rather, he's nothing more than a simple pervert, a "peeping tom" making sensational photographs[21] (fig. 6.6).

Figure 6.6

As found in *The Serpent's Egg*, voyeurism goes hand in hand with the sadist motif. There is a difference, though, in Holocaust films where the power of the gaze goes unquestioned, such as found in Steven Spielberg's 1993 film *Schindler's List*, discussed in Chapter 3, where there is the repeated eroticization of female victims. "The handling of the outside audience's look through the look of the inner audience builds up a clear process of identification between the external spectators (us) and the internal (the Nazis)," Marga Cottino-Jones says of *The Night Porter*, "thus completely eliminating any distinction between 'us' and 'them.'"[22] Films that have a degree of self-reflection regarding the discourse of looking — such as we find in *The Night Porter* — are often more successful in inviting the spectator to question the very nature of representing the Holocaust. Films that utilize cinema's voyeuristic strategies without appealing to the spectator's heuristic devices (e.g., *Schindler's List*), on the other hand, operate in a closed circuit. They tell rather than engage with the spectator, demanding very little viewer engagement and rarely if ever asking the spectator to question their own viewing position. This is not to suggest that didactic films are inherently more successful, and indeed finding subtle nuanced ways to elicit the spectator's critical faculties is generally more preferable. The breaking down of barriers between the seen and the seer, and interrogating the spectator's viewing positions, are all significant features of *Salò*, which is discussed in the following section.

In the end, *The Night Porter* only addresses power relations in the abstract, with little bearing on the historical world wherein the Holocaust unfolded, and the power structure of the concentration camp. Teresa de Lauretis agrees:

> In *The Night Porter* it is not Lucia's experience (her victimization, initiation, and subsequent unbreakable bondage to her oppressor-Father-lover) that serves as a metaphor for the infamy perpetrated by the Nazis on humankind, but Nazism and the atrocities committed in the camps that are the allegorical framework chosen by Cavani to investigate the dialectics of the male-female relationship in our contemporary, post-Nazi, society.[23]

Figuring the film in these terms actually places it much closer to Don Edmonds's 1975 film *Ilsa: She-Wolf of the SS* (discussed in Chapter 8) than Lina Wertmüller's 1975 film *Seven Beauties*, to which *The Night Porter* is frequently compared, because *The Night Porter* registers contemporary sentiments regarding gender power dynamics. By placing it in the same camp as *Ilsa* the intention is not to disparage Cavani's film; there is no question that the quality of her film far surpasses Edmonds's exploitation classic. Rather, what both films do is to employ the Holocaust as a narrative device to explore power dynamics, be they gender roles, male anxieties regarding the liberated woman, or female sexual agency.

While *The Night Porter* and *Seven Beauties*, both films made by women, "have been vehemently criticized by eminent male Holocaust survivors for muddying our understanding of the 'truth' with their sexual allegories of concentration-camp power relations,"[24] Marguerite Waller observes, they nevertheless shed light on the ways in which the Holocaust has (and can be) used to elaborate on social-cultural mores. "These comparisons," Marguerite Waller astutely concludes, "do *not* serve to minimize the horrors of the Holocaust; on the contrary, they keep them relevant. They signify the Holocaust, not as the unthinkable Other, but as one distinctly possible effect of the misogynistic signifying situation through which we, who share this history and culture, are ourselves articulated."[25] Indeed, one of the greatest dangers is to relegate the Holocaust to a fixed point in history, as an event that is *over*, or *finished*. While the camps have been liberated and a reunited Germany has entered the world of nations again, the discourses (i.e., clinical sadism) that made the Holocaust possible are still very much with us today.[26]

Although our immediate response is to treat Nazism or fascism as abject — dismiss it as monstrous, as an anomaly in the history of the West — nothing could be more dangerous. Fascism, Nazism, totalitarian nationalism, is every bit a product of Western culture as the Model-T Ford, as capitalism, Impressionist painting, polio vaccines, and so forth. And it is precisely in these terms that we can think of Sade as prophetic. As with the humanist tradition in general, Susan Buck-Morss reminds us that the Nazis too envisioned "a society beyond material scarcity, and the collective, social goal, through massive industrial construction, of *transforming the natural world*." And while fascism maintained an "open hostility to many aspects of modernity," she continues, it also "shared in this mass utopian dream"; a dream it must be added that — in the context of Nazi Germany — called for the eradication of Jews and other non-Aryan elements.[27]

SALÒ, OR THE 120 DAYS OF SODOM

Anyone interested in civics must see *Night and Fog* and *Salò*.

— Jean-Claude Biette

Salò, or the 120 Days of Sodom, Pier Paolo Pasolini's 1975 adaptation of the Marquis de Sade's infamous novel, *The 120 Days of Sodom*, is an allegorical approach to fascist violence. The film is set in fascist Italy, 1944–45, in the Republic of Salò, the last holdout of Italian fascism in Northern Italy propped up by the Nazis. Although the narrative is peppered with real historical references, it is ostensibly an allegorical representation of the Holocaust. Pasolini's adaptation of Sade's novel is well aware of the French scholarship regarding sadism.[28] Although Pasolini has been accused of making simple analogies[29] — Nazism is like sadism — the spectator profits most when viewing *Salò* through the Sadean lens, where beneath the spectacle of violence lurks a profound cultural critique. Indeed, out of all the films discussed in this chapter, *Salò* is by far the most judicious representation of clinical sadism and its relationship to Nazism.

Remaining faithful to Sade's novel, Pasolini begins *Salò* with the four libertines finalizing their villainous scheme. According to the libertines' design, they begin by enrolling guards or escorts; as for them Sade writes, "the young men whom we propose henceforth to designate as fuckers, the size of the member was the sole criterion: nothing under ten or eleven inches long by seven or eight around was acceptable."[30] Pasolini does his very best to follow these strict guidelines.

Following the conscription of the fuckers, the libertines begin the abduction and selection of their young subjects. Special attention is given to the buttocks of the young prospects. Sade writes of the girls' inspection, "The slightest defect in this part was grounds for immediate rejection."[31] If the young prospect passed this initial inspection, she was ordered to strip, or was stripped, and naked, she passed and passed again, five or six times over, from one of libertines to the other, she was turned about, she was turned the other way, she was fingered, she was handled, they sniffed, they spread, they peeped, they examined the state of the goods, was it new, was it used, but did all this coolly and without permitting the senses' illusion to upset any aspect of the examination.[32]

In *Salò*, Albertina, for example, is an attractive young woman, yet when she cracks a smile one of the libertines notices that she has a gap in her teeth (fig. 6.7), and she is summarily rejected.

Figure 6.7

Just as in Sade's narrative, in *Salò* the libertines methodically approach the inspection of each subject, examining their teeth, buttocks, penis, breasts, social status. "This done," Sade writes,

the child was led away, and beside her name inscribed upon a ballot, the examiners wrote *passed* or *failed* and signed their names; these ballots were then dropped into a box, the voters refraining from communicating their opinions to one another; all the girls examined, the box was opened: in order to be accepted, a girl had to have our four friends' names in her favor.[33]

The selection of the boys unfolds in the same manner. These inspections that take place in Sade's novel and unfold on-screen in *Salò* are analogous to the selections in Nazi concentration camps, where Nazi doctors segregated the fit, which were sent to work in the camp, from the sick, the weak, and the frail who were sent to the gas chambers.[34]

Despite the fact that these young subjects are integral to the narrative, we hardly learn a thing about them. They are largely speechless and generally nameless. They are nothing but objects for the libertines' amusement. Here the abducted subjects find some likeness to the *Muselmänner*, a word used in the concentration camps identifying the hopelessly "weak, the inept, those doomed to selection."[35] Primo Levi's firsthand narrative, *Survival in Auschwitz*, suggests that it is the *Muselmänner* that are "the drowned," and "form[ed] the backbone of the camp, an anonymous mass."[36] As in Levi's personal accounts, the characters in

Salò remain anonymous and are doomed from the very start. It is through them, however, that the narrative works, the libertines' subjects are the backbone of the film's plot. And even more horrific in *Salò*, some of the young subjects who survive are interpolated into the libertine's universe and, as a consequence, are given names, identities; they are no longer objects, or props, they, in fact, accede to the position of active agent. (These assimilated characters might have some affinities with the kapo in the camps.)

After these preliminary procedures — collecting the adolescent subjects — the libertines, along with their freshly procured subjects, head to their rendezvous at Château de Silling. In Sade's novel the trip to the château is perilous. But to ensure that no one escapes, or likewise, so that no one discovers them, the novelist writes, "a fine wooden bridge" was especially constructed to traverse a deep chasm. However, upon the final convoy's arrival it "was destroyed immediately . . . and from this moment on, all possibility of communicating with the Château de Silling ceased."[37] No bridges are destroyed in *Salò*, but a convoy of military and civilian vehicles meanders through the picturesque mountains of Northern Italy much as Sade depicts his crew. Like Sade's novel, the convoy in *Salò* traverses a bridge, which appears to span a deep chasm. The camera, only for an instant, catches at the edge of the frame a road sign that reads "Marzabotto." An incidental or insignificant detail we would imagine, unless we recognize the historical gravity of this site.

This Northern Italian village bears the scars of Nazi atrocities. Marzabotto maintained a long Socialist and Communist tradition; during the war the community explicitly opposed itself to the fascist regime. Additionally, Stella Rossa, the partisan group associated with this particular district, routinely launched acts of sabotage against fascist infrastructure. Retaliating for their sustained resistance against the fascist regime, and for their acts of sabotage, the Germans annihilated the village of Marzabotto in May 1944.[38] The Nazis executed its entire population, as well as those in its immediate vicinity; at least 1,830 people died at the hands of the Nazi troops.[39]

This historical reference and others like it in the film demonstrate one of the clear problems with the allegorical device, and its guarded approach among Holocaust scholars who routinely demand that representations of the Holocaust be realistic.[40] Allegory, as a parallel narrative, necessitates the spectator to traverse between these diegetic paradigms — the historical world and the fictional narrative. But ultimately the allegorical narrative explicitly invites its spectator to *interpret* the narrative before them, and the act of interpretation is precisely what makes some Holocaust scholars uneasy; in general they prefer expository narratives (e.g., documentaries, or clearly defined coherent narrative films) leaving little room for interpretation. From this perspective spectators cannot be trusted to formulate their own understanding of historical events; coddled like children, spectators must be dictated to.

The Marzabotto sequence in *Salò* is a pivotal scene and is of monumental importance to the narrative. Like the bridge in Sade's novel, the bridge leading to Marzabotto marks the point of no return. The château as an impregnable "candyland" of depravity begins to resemble something like a concentration camp. The convoy hauling the libertines' captives is analogous to the cattle carriages transporting Jews into the Nazis' factories of death.

When the convoy arrives at the château the abducted subjects — guarded by the SS and the fuckers — disembark from the vehicles and assemble before the four libertines who set down the laws under which they'll live. The Duke begins,

> Weak, chained creatures, destined for our pleasure. I hope you don't expect to find here the ridiculous freedom granted by the outside world. You are beyond the reach of any legality. No one on earth knows you are here. As far as the world is concerned, you are already dead.

Pulling a book from his coat pocket, "Here are the laws that will govern your lives." He hands the book to his fellow libertine, the Magistrate, who opens the book and proceeds to read,

> Punctually at 6:00 the whole group must assemble in the so-called Orgy Room where storytellers, in turn, will sit and tell a series of stories on a given subject. Our friends can interrupt any time and as often as they like. The aim of the stories is to stir the imagination. Any lewdness will be allowed.

After the rules have been read, the Magistrate with a scowl closes the book of laws and the Duke orders the fuckers, "Now, all inside. Make them go in!" And the subjects, like new inductees into a concentration camp, file into the libertines' complex. In complete accordance to clinical sadism, the subjects are at once under the jurisdiction of libertinage, and sealed within the hermetic space of the château. There is a hint at the possibility for a rupture in the hermetic universe with the rustling about of the servants, but the libertines effectively seal off any fissures that might spoil the site where the sadistic rituals are to unfold.

Everything is meticulously planned in keeping with the sadistic disposition. One of the most disturbing episodes in the film at first glance seems like an act of capricious cruelty, but instead it is a carefully crafted act of humiliation and degradation. During the selection of the female subjects we learn that Sophie's mother died trying to save her. Each of the storytellers take turns showcasing each of the female candidates for the four libertines; when Sophie is introduced the storyteller explains, "She cries for her fool mother, who jumped into the river to defend her and drowned right before this angel's eyes." Standing naked before the libertines, Sophie weeps, eventually falling to her knees with grief. In response the libertines rise to their feet, pleased to no end, smirk and revel in the abducted adolescent's misery; they will capitalize on this later.

One of the storytellers recounts an incident where she in her youth in pursuit of sexual pleasure recalls that her mother "that evening, was more intolerant than usual. She begged me not to go, to change my life and . . ." "And then?" the

Magistrate interrupts. "I couldn't resist temptation. I killed her." The Duke then interjects, "It was the only thing to do." He continues and reveals that he too dispatched his own mother. Eventually, outside the frame Sophie's weeping catches the Duke's attention. Feigning ignorance, the Duke asks, "Why is that child crying?" Signora Vaccari reminds the group, "Your talk has reminded her of her mother. Recall, she died trying to protect the girl." "Splendid!" the Duke replies, and continues, "Come, I'll console you!" The girl again falls to her knees, begging, "Pity. Respect my grief," and continues to plead for mercy. Angrily, the Duke orders the fuckers to undress her immediately. Intoxicated by this sight, the Duke says, "This whining is the most exciting thing I've ever heard." She implores that the libertines free her from this misery and show compassion by killing her now so that she might join her mother. But the Duke retorts, "You'll be punished and deflowered at the right moment." The Duke purposefully steps into the middle of the Orgy Room, unbuckles his belt, drops his pants, squats down and defecates. "Come, little one. It's ready," the Duke reports. "On your knees!" Sophie on all fours crawls over to the fresh turd. Grabbing a spoon, the Duke demands, "Come on. Go on. Eat." Handing the distraught girl the spoon, he says, "Take this spoon." Tentatively, she reaches for the spoon and scoops up a spoonful of faeces. "Eat!" the Duke commands. Gagging, she chokes down a spoonful of faeces, as the grinning Duke looks on excitedly (fig. 6.8). Although the scene is played off as a capricious act of cruelty, the subject of the storyteller's story, the Duke's matricidal account, and the faeces eating were calculated to torture Sophie, whose fragile disposition and trauma were already known.

Figure 6.8

In the Orgy Room the storytellers convey titillating episodes designed to incite the lubricious desires of the libertines. Their position on a stage solicits the voyeuristic gaze. The stories are accompanied by a piano, gesturing towards the history of the cinema where silent films would be accompanied by a live musical performance. *Salò* is an incredibly self-conscious film, and clearly invites the spectator's heuristic faculties by including these allusions to the cinema and the spectator's gaze. The libertine's hermetic universe is permeated only by the spectator's voyeuristic gaze, puncturing an otherwise sealed-off world.

The camera and the cinematic image facilitate the spectator's gaze to pierce the libertine's hermetic world. The meeting of two different worlds — the libertine's and the spectator's — forms a division, a boundary; the spectator creates excess by looking in on the hermetic château and Pasolini fuses our identification to the libertines.

Just as the storytellers are commanded to provide salacious tales to fuel the four libertines' imagination, they also aim to captivate the film's spectators. Sade explains in *The 120 Days of Sodom* that the libertines assembled in a circular room every day to hear one of the four storyteller's episodes; they each sat in recesses that faced the center of the room. The storyteller, as if on a stage, sat in the center. Sade tells his readers,

> in this position she was not only well before the four niches intended for her auditors, but, the circle being small, was close enough to them to insure their hearing every word she said, for she was placed like an actor in a theater, and the audience in their niches found themselves situated as if observing a spectacle in an amphitheater.[41]

Pasolini adopts this theatrical staging, and this is where the spectator's implication begins.

The libertines take turns to watch their villainous scheme play out in the grand finale; they watch the events unfold in a beautiful high-modern Mackintosh chair, perched above the château's courtyard. Here the sadistic rites unfold: rape, beatings, murder, buggery, and necrophilia. As if at an opera, the libertines witness the spectacle through binoculars while seated in their high-modernist chair, in a room decorated with numerous modern paintings. The *mise en scène* suggests human progress, in the form of modernist décor, but is juxtaposed with barbarity.[42] The coupling of modernity, or human progress, and barbarity is the dialectic of enlightenment, such as Adorno and Horkheimer posit it.

During this climatic scene the Duke turns the binoculars around, looking through them wrong-way round. Here Pasolini uses the common cinematic practice of the shot/reverse-shot to confirm our identification with the libertine. The spectator sees, at first, a close-up of the libertine as he turns the binoculars wrong-way round; the camera then cuts to the libertine's assumed perspective. Not only is the scene suddenly distant, providing a "new perspective" on the affair, but our identification with the libertines is substantiated. The camera assumes the perspective of the libertine — the camera, and the libertine's perspective is at this point indistinguishable.[43] (See fig. 3.36, and 3.37.) Pasolini brings us to the sight/site of horror, and yet we discover that the horror we sense — with fascination and revulsion — is not one that comes from without, but within. We are sick with our own fascination with the spectacle of horror, and by distancing our perspective through the inverted binoculars Pasolini insists that we meditate on the nature of cinema and our fascination with violence.

The final sequence is comparable to a scene in Alfred Hitchcock's *The Birds* (1963). The lead male character, Mitch Brenner, notices that the seductive playgirl, Melanie Daniels, is crossing Bodega Bay in a hired boat. She does not know it, or at least she feigns not knowing, as Mitch watches her through a pair of binoculars. Hitchcock uses the same shot/reverse-shot that Pasolini does. Both objects of either sequence — that is the median shot in both films — aim to satiate our voyeuristic expectations. While Hitchcock offers the fetishistic vision of Melanie, Pasolini delivers sadistic violence; both fascinate us. This self-reflective practice is similar to some of the other films considered in this chapter — *The Night Porter* and *The Serpent's Egg* — as well as Quentin Tarantino's 2009 film *Inglourious Basterds,* and Michael Haneke's work, discussed in the chapter on horror. The spectator is not necessarily repulsed by the exhibition of torture, although the final scenes of the film are undeniably horrific, but more poignantly, by our own abject fascination. Very few Holocaust films ask us to contemplate our fascination with the horrific spectacle of the concentration camp and Nazi brutality; *Salò* does.

Holocaust films typically draw clear boundaries between the interior space of the narrative and the space that the spectator inhabits. *Salò*, however, refuses to draw clear lines, allowing those clear inside/outside boundaries to break down, placing the spectator within the libertine's rank. In addition, Holocaust narratives routinely cast the Nazi as the epitome of evil, a monster and completely unsympathetic, and subsequently impossible to identify with. Such an arrangement bolsters the ego of the spectator by creating a them/us distinction; it allows us to situate the monstrous characters on the side of utter evil, and places us on the side of righteousness. *Salò* does not allow for such a Manichaean worldview, by placing our identification with the libertines, who are at once every bit as monstrous as one would expect, but also figures of the Enlightenment *par excellence.*[44]

In the final sequence of *Salò*, two boys listen to the radio. Carl Orff's "Carmina Burana: Veris leta facies" is playing, but one of the young men changes the channel. Instead of the solemn Orff the selected radio channel plays a more popular dance tune, the same that is heard during the opening credits. One of the boys asks, "Can you dance?" The other responds, "No." The boy encouragingly says, "Let's try." They set their rifles aside and begin to dance. One asks, "What is your girlfriend's name?" The other simply replies, "Margarrette." With this incredibly banal set of shots the film concludes. The promised heterosexual coupling ("What's your girlfriend's name?"), the casual tone, all suggest normalcy. Although the film ends with murder, buggery, blood, and horror, the heterosexual coupling conveys a sense of "normalcy." The music, the popular jig, which is heard at the very beginning of the film, also closes it, and brings us full circle; absolutely nothing has changed, and the spectator's presence has not altered the libertine's hermetic universe in the slightest.

Chapter Seven

Body Genres I: Melodramatic Holocaust Films

↓ tears in viewer

INTRODUCTION

This chapter and the two following it are informed by Linda Williams's concept of the "body genres," films that provoke a visceral response in the spectator. Williams identifies melodrama, horror, and pornography as the constituents of the body genres. Each of these genres elicits a physiological response; with melodrama — especially the weepie — spectators are brought to tears; the horror genre startles us, making us jump from our seats, gasp, or cringe or avert our eyes at the sight of gore; and the objective of pornography is the sexual arousal of the viewer.

Williams observes that these genres — melodrama, horror, and pornography — share one common feature: exhibition of bodily excess. In fact the display of the body in these films tends to interrupt or impede narrative progression. "It would not be unreasonable," Williams argues, "to consider all three of these genres under the extended rubric of melodrama, considered as a filmic mode of stylistic and/or emotional excess that stands in contrast to more 'dominant' modes of realistic, goal-oriented narrative."[1] What is important here is that all these genres permit the display of bodily excess, and this materializes in a number of different ways: first, "there is the spectacle of a body caught in the grip of intense sensation or emotion"; second, forms of ecstasy that manifest in the field of vision as an "uncontrollable convulsion or spasm — of the body 'beside itself' with sexual pleasure, fear and terror, or overpowering sadness"; and, third, "it is the female body in the grips of an out-of-control ecstasy that has offered the most sensational sight."[2] There is a reciprocal relation of sensations, and "the success of these genres is often measured by the degree to which the audience sensation mimics what is seen on the screen."[3]

In the physicality of the body genres Williams suggests that there is a degree of violence inflicted upon the viewer. The viewer is manipulated in one way or another, and because there is "a sense of over-involvement in sensation and emotion." In response to the manipulation associated with body genre films we have developed colloquialisms that express the implicit violence inflicted upon us, the viewing body: we refer to the weepie as a "tear jerker," and a horror film as a "fear jerker," or we resort to even cruder terms, "it scared the shit out of me." Further, Williams writes that we can add pornography to this list of corporeal colloquialisms because "some people might be inclined to 'jerk off.'"[4] Like the manipulation of a marionette, the viewing body is "jerked around" when watching body genre films. Following James Twitchell's research, Williams calls our attention to the Latin root of "horror," which comes from *horrere*, meaning "to bristle, shudder" and specifically references the physiological response of making one's hair stand on end, which once again points to a certain manipulation and/or physical violence exerted onto the viewing body.[5] Geoffrey Nowell-Smith also reminds us of the origins of the term "melodrama," which "originally meant, literally, drama + melos (music) and this eighteenth-century sense survives in the Italian *melodrama* — grand opera. In its early form melodrama was akin to pastoral, and differentiated from tragedy in that the story usually had a happy end."[6]

Alan J. Pakula's 1982 film *Sophie's Choice* is exemplary of a Holocaust melodrama (this film is addressed in more detail in the subsequent section of this chapter). As much as the narrative focuses on Sophie and her traumatic experience, though, the principal character is in fact Stingo, Sophie's neighbor, who is infatuated with her. In this film the burden of the (mentally) tortured woman, Sophie Zawistowski — the woman who sacrifices more than anyone could bear — elicits from the viewing body an empathic response; we are expected to share in the tortured woman's crushing sadness. But what do we gain by this experience? Is there pleasure derived from the sadness that we might experience? Does this position the viewer in a sadistic relationship to Sophie's hyper-masochism? At least in Moretti's view of it, which again Williams draws on, the melodrama is in effect cathartic, it releases tension in the form of tears, "which become a kind of homage to a happiness that is kissed goodbye. Pathos is thus a surrender to reality but it is a surrender that pays homage to the ideal that tried to wage war on it."[7] Williams reads this optimistic perspective as subversive, as it transforms the "woman's genre" and the subsequent viewing position from a passive/masochistic one, to an active one that *despite everything* strives towards happiness. Such a formulation is hard to situate in relation to the narrative of *Sophie's Choice*, until one realizes that the desire that is never fulfilled is not Sophie's but rather Stingo's. Again we are returned to an ethical question: Does our catharsis (and presumably Stingo's) come at the expense of Sophie's grim fate? Does this narrative have more to do with our desire to "save" or "rehabilitate" Sophie, who is utterly and hopelessly consumed by the guilt of having to choose one child over another, than it does with dealing with the weight of survivor-guilt? And by finding catharsis through an identification with Stingo, does this leave the

Holocaust survivor in the gaping void of melancholia and utter hopelessness? These questions go beyond the intended scope of this chapter, but they point to some troubling concerns about mobilizing the melodramatic genre to represent the Holocaust.

Finally, then, the "negative" feelings associated with the body genres (e.g., sadness, masochism), might not exactly correspond to the viewer's experience. Leaving aside the ethical problems that the example of *Sophie's Choice* raises, it is possible to see how "tear-jerkers," or the horror film for that matter, might be read against the grain, where "negative" feelings might have "positive" effects. Such a conclusion of course is in perfect keeping with the Aristotelian discourse on narrative — where pity and fear give way to catharsis. Williams concludes that it

> may be wrong in our assumption that the bodies of spectators simply reproduce the sensations exhibited by bodies on the screen. Even those masochistic pleasures associated with the powerlessness . . . are not absolutely abject. Even tear-jerkers do not operate to force a simple mimicry of the sensation exhibited on the screen.[8]

In other words, we need to continue to explore the "function" of the body genres, and ask who is served by such narratives, and although I do not expect to arrive at *the* answer, I hope instead to offer some observations regarding the treatment of the Holocaust in the body genres and their effects upon the viewing body.

When representing the Holocaust, American films tend to lean towards the melodramatic genre, while historically European films relied less on this form. Ilan Avisar observes that in Czech cinema it is not until Zbynek Brynych's 1962 film *Transport from Paradise* that "most of the eastern European films on World War II were what Antonín Liehm called a kind of western, showing clear-cut moral conflict with both good guys and bad guys bigger than life, in accordance with conventional cinematic, melodramatic connotations that one finds in classic Hollywood westerns."[9] Rather, many European films — and especially Eastern European films — were didactic, drawing from the varying traditions of realism, and frequently focusing on resistance narratives (see, for example, the chapter on defiance). But this is not to say that these films were completely devoid of the melodramatic, and in fact André Bazin notes that when an Italian Neo-Realist film is reduced to its plot, the films are "moralizing melodramas." Despite this, though, "on the screen everybody in the film is overwhelmingly real."[10] And indeed, from the 1947 film *The Last Stage* by Auschwitz survivor Wanda Jakubowska, to Andrzej Wajda's 1957 film of resistance *Kanal*, and Gillo Pontecorvo's 1959 film *Kapò*, all these films — which trade heavily in the realist aesthetic — the shocking verisimilitude sometimes collapses under the excruciating weight of melodramatic pandering.

Pontecorvo, for instance, laments his own detour into the melodramatic genre. In his film the primary female character is a young 14-year-old French Jewess, Edith, cultured and mild mannered. We are first introduced to her during a musical lesson — harpsichord — in a handsome apartment. But this tranquil opening takes a sudden and dramatic turn from the cultured world of classical music lessons to the brutal realities of a Nazi concentration camp. With a bit of luck and some assistance, she is able to escape her ultimate fate by assuming the identity of a recently deceased French woman — Nicole Niepas — a common criminal, trading in her yellow star for a black triangle.[11] She quickly learns the ropes — stealing, using her body and consorting with German guards for food and better conditions, standing up for herself, beating fellow internees, and so forth (fig. 7.1). Nearly forgetting who she is, Edith not only acts like Nicole, she in effect becomes her, and as a result she eventually becomes a kapo.[12]

Figure 7.1

She eventually falls for a male internee, a Red Army soldier, Sascha, and begins to drop her defenses a bit. She maintains the façade of a kapo, and thus does not arouse sympathy. She is selfish, flogs people, and even at one point betrays Sascha by ratting him out to a German guard; Sascha is severely punished — forced to stand in place in front of the electrified fence, shirtless, all night long — but despite this continues to have amorous feelings for the young woman. Superhuman in stamina, and in undying love, Sascha is the stock romantic lead that we might associate with melodramatic narratives. Eventually, he — along with a host of other male internees — plans an escape, which involves setting Nicole up to sacrifice herself for the sake of others. She is sent to shut down the power to the high-tension wire; however, this will automatically trigger an alarm and she will not be able to escape alive. Nicole only later learns that her mission means certain death, but despite this she carries through with it and after being shot, her dying wish is to have the last vestiges of the Nazi regime removed from her clothes — and dies, not as Nicole, an agent of the regime, but as Edith (fig. 7.2).

The bond that develops between Sascha and Nicole/Edith is "the greatest error movie people can commit," Pontecorvo laments, "we underestimated the possibilities of the public." He continues,

Figure 7.2

> We forgot the fact that when you speak through any situation to eternal themes in the
> human condition, you always have the hope of reaching an audience. So we censored
> ourselves and inserted this horrible episode of a love story between the soldier and
> the girl. Its style was completely different from the rest of the film, and it made the
> section melodramatic.[13]

There is no need to close the door on the truly cathartic potentiality in the
melodramatic genre, but there is certainly a risk that the genre might be judged
as trivializing the very subject it seeks to represent. As Ilan Avisar observes,
while Pontecorvo never sought to "exploit the extraordinary background of the
Holocaust to enhance melodramatic action," what he has done, though, for all
practical purposes is "to exploit melodramatic action to upstage the historical
events."[14]

It's not just the love story, however, that situates *Kapò* in the melodramatic
camp but the treatment of the female character, who undergoes an incredibly
brutal transformation. By becoming Nicole, Edith must in effect kill herself —
denying her own Jewish identity to survive. A similar transformation occurs in
Agnieszka Holland's 1990 film *Europa Europa*, where the young male protagonist,
Salomon Perel, assumes the identity of Josef Peters, and not only denies his
Jewish identity but is compelled to join the Hitler Youth and eventually *fights*
as a German soldier no less; an utterly absurd plot were it not based on a true
story. Unlike in *Kapò*, though, the protagonist in *Europa Europa* does not face
nearly the same degree of mental or physical torment, and subsequently the film
reads more as a "straight" dramatic narrative, with little or no melodramatic
inclinations. Conversely, Nicole's brutality, which inhabits her flesh, as if pos-
sessed, manifests in the explicit sadistic swings and blows she delivers, but at
the same time materializes as a radical masochism directed inward. (These
features — possession and sadomasochism — eerily follow the disposition of
female characters in both the exploitation and horror genre, as discussed in
the succeeding two chapters.) And, finally, in keeping with the conventions of
the melodramatic narrative, she is made to pay the ultimate sacrifice, giving up
her own life so that others might live. But more than this, though, she does this
willingly, as if to absolve herself.

If we judge *Kapò* to be less than a success, it is probably because it falls in between genres — not quite a realist film (such as we might associate with Pontecorvo, who made *The Battle of Algiers* in 1966), and not a straight dramatic film either given its detours into the melodramatic. And as for the latter, as Williams informs us, success is "often measured by the degree to which the audience sensation mimics what is seen on the screen."[15] Irrespective of the degree of success, what is made abundantly clear here is that if we reduce it to one of its most significant trademarks the melodramatic genre profits from the suffering of women.

TORTURED MOTHERS

Since the 1960s there has been an increasing trend of sexually terrorized female characters in the genre of horror films, Alfred Hitchcock's 1960 film *Psycho* is perhaps the most obvious example. But Linda Williams also observes that the melodramatic body genre also trades heavily in the torture of women. Alan J. Pakula's 1982 film *Sophie's Choice* is exemplary of the melodramatic variety of the body genres, and its title character suffers tremendously from self-loathing and guilt. Williams succinctly summarizes the genre: melodramatic weepies address "women in their traditional status under patriarchy — as wives, mothers, abandoned lovers, or in their traditional status as bodily hysteria or excess, as in the frequent case of the woman 'afflicted' with a deadly or debilitating disease."[16] Isn't the title character, Sophie Zawistowski, all of these things?

What perhaps sets Sophie apart from the treatment of other women in the melodramatic genre is that her affliction stems from her traumatic experience in a concentration camp; her ailment, though not physical as such (although her mental trauma manifests in physical symptoms), is nevertheless deadly because it propels her towards the seemingly inescapable conclusion: suicide. To arrive at this dire conclusion Sophie's affliction leads her headlong into an abusive relationship, where her partner Nathan Landau habitually abandons her, only to "get back together," and once again begin the cycle of mental and physical abuse. In addition she is predisposed to bodily hysteria and excess — she drinks to get drunk, she is anemic and is subject to fainting spells, she bears the scars of at least one earlier suicide attempt, has a veracious sexual appetite, and is prone to melancholia and tears. Sophie is the archetypical female character in melodrama that exhibits "bodily hysteria or excess."

The tear-jerker — and *Sophie's Choice* is certainly that for some viewers — calculates its effects according to a temporal code. Citing Franco Moretti's work, Williams argues that "what triggers our crying is not just the sadness or suffering of the character in the story but a very precise moment when characters in the story catch up with and realize what the audience already knows." Stingo, in *Sophie's Choice*, is too slow to realize that Sophie's course leads towards one inevitable conclusion. When "desire is finally recognized as futile," this is the temporal moment that is likely to elicit tears from the audience, and this happens in *Sophie's Choice*, because it is not until Stingo finally realizes that his desire to be with Sophie (and ultimately to "save her") is useless; it's already too late.[17]

The film, and the novel that it's based on, hinges on the physical and emotional torment that Sophie endures, as she effectively atones for her sins. Whether it succeeds in capturing this torment is debatable. William Styron, the author of the novel, felt that Pakula held back, claiming, "that he felt the movie slighted the sadomasochistic eroticism of the book."[18]

The conflation of sex and violence comes just within the first several minutes of the film. Recently having let a room in a Brooklyn home, Stingo is made aware of the boarder directly above him, through her boisterous daytime love-making sessions, as evidenced in the unmistakable sounds that echo through his room and the chandelier that rattles overhead. We soon learn that the boarder is Sophie. Day gives way to evening, and passionate love-making yields to inflamed quarreling; outside Stingo's door we hear Sophie plead with Nathan not to leave. Stingo steps out of his room and sees, halfway up the stairs Nathan, violently holding Sophie by the arms, pinning her against the banister. She insists that they "need each other," but he responds, "I need you like some goddamn insufferable disease. I need you like a case of anthrax, hear me?" He continues to let into her, listing off a litany of other diseases, "I need you . . . like death! Hear me? Like death!" Despite all this, Sophie pleads with Nathan not to leave. "Go back to Krakow, baby. Back to Krakow!" Nathan implores, as he makes his way down the stairway (fig. 7.3). At the base of the stairs he turns to see Stingo, and letting out a small chuckle he says, "Well, good evening. Did you have a good time? Did you enjoy our little show? Do you get off on a little bit of eavesdropping?" After Nathan leaves — not before ridiculing Stingo's American Southern accent, and his literary aspirations first — Stingo asks, "Are you okay?" to Sophie, who is left sitting on the stairs sobbing; she is quick to apologize for Nathan's behavior, insisting that he's not really like that.

Figure 7.3

Nathan's dialogue points to a fixture of the melodramatic genre: the spectacle of violence visited upon women. This is only the beginning of the torment that

Sophie endures, and shortly after this violent scene, Stingo notices Sophie's tat-too — a metonym of Holocaust violence, and a sign of things to come.

We eventually learn that Nathan is mentally ill, explaining his mood swings that vacillates radically, between nearly uncontainable jubilance, to violent fits of rage. Although he puts up the front of working in the medical profession, he is in fact consumed with hunting down Nazis, and the history of the Holocaust. During one of his many passionate fits of anger — fueled by a jealous rage, thinking that Sophie is sleeping with another man — he queries just why Sophie managed to survive, while millions of Jews died. Stingo sits idly by as Nathan begins to interrogate Sophie. "Tell me why you inhabit the land of the living. What splendid little tricks and stratagems sprang from that lovely head of yours? To allow you to breath the clear Polish air, while the multitudes of Auschwitz choked slowly on the gas." Once again pinned into a chair, the tearful Sophie thrusts her hands forward, covering Nathan's mouth in an effort to silence him, but he screams, "Explain! Explain!" Phyllis Deutsch observes that, "This scene is shot from overhead, so it looks like the 'lovers' are fucking. As Nathan shouts at her, Sophie whimpers, cries, and, in her halting little-girl English, begs him to stop. The scene ends with a convulsive orgasmic shudder on the part of both parties."[19] The bodily excesses that we associate with melodrama abound here — from Nathan's excited and lurid probing of Sophie's body as he lambasts her, to Stingo's childish but well-intended attempts to reason with Nathan, physically placing himself between the pair, and Sophie's cowered whimpering and spas-modic masochism shouting at Stingo not to get involved, finally pushing him out of the room so that she might take her punishment.

Just as Nathan demanded an "explanation!" Stingo too will want an explana-tion, and while he does not exorcise the same sort of violence, his desire to "know," his insistence, brings Sophie back to the source of the trauma governing her melancholic character. While she is drunk, alone, and sitting in her room with the lights off, Stingo approaches Sophie and says, "Sophie, I want to understand, I'd like to know the truth." She hesitates a bit, "The truth doesn't make it easier to understand." Finally, Sophie relents, and mutters, "Oh, the truth, the truth . . ." and turns to stare directly into the camera and begins narrating her life in Poland during the war era. The scene is inter-cut with a series of flashbacks. She explains that when she was arrested, she was transported to Auschwitz along with her two young children. When the train arrived at Auschwitz, the Germans made their "selections." "Jan, my little boy," she explains, "Jan, my little boy, was sent to the *kinderlager*, which was the children's camp." She pauses a bit, "And my little girl, Eva, was sent to Crematorium II. She was exterminated." Melodramatic films tend to heighten cinematic signification during particularly poignant moments, so as Sophie begins to tell her story the camera moves in for a tight close-up, and when we learn of her daughter's death, the film cuts from a freeze frame of her daughter's profile in the train, to a slow cross-dissolve of the smokestacks of Crematorium II belching out black smoke and ash. Sophie nevertheless holds back and does not reveal the whole story; the choice that she was compelled to make happens later.

Running away with Stingo, alone in a hotel room, Sophie finally reveals her darkest secret. Throughout the film Stingo has fantasized about Sophie, and in his childish romantic vision of life he believes that they can "settle down" and have children. "You should have another mother for your children," Sophie scoffs. Stingo insists, "Only you." But Sophie will not have it, "It would not be fair to your children to have me as their mother." Confiding in Stingo, Sophie begins, "I'm going to tell you something. I'm going to tell you something I never told anybody." Insisting upon a drink first to muster the courage, she returns to the site of trauma, her arrival at Auschwitz. "It was spring, you know, and we arrived there at night. It was a beautiful night." As she narrates the film slips into another flashback. During the selection an SS officer, seeing Sophie, comments on how beautiful she is, and that he'd like to sleep with her. She is struck with fear, and can hardly speak, or respond to his questions. As he walks away she speaks up, "I am a Pole," she exclaims in German, "I was born in Krakow! I am not a Jew! Neither are my children! They are *not* Jews. They're racially pure. I'm a Christian. I'm a devout Catholic." He turns to her, as she cowers, holding her young daughter whose face registers nothing but fear. "You're not a communist?" he asks. She shakes her head, "No." "You're a believer." "Yes, sir. I believe in Christ." With a slight smirk, he queries, "You believe in Christ . . . the Redeemer." He continues, "Did He not say, 'Suffer the little children to come unto Me?'" Gesturing for a response, Sophie vaguely nods her head, "Yes." "You may keep one of your children." Confounded by what he has just said, Sophie asks, "I beg your pardon?" "You may keep *one* of your children. The other one must go," he responds. "You mean, I have to choose?" With a sadistic grin, thinking he has given her some sort of gift, "You're a Polack not a Yid. That gives you a privilege, a choice." Shuddering, shaking her head, "I cannot choose. I cannot choose," she says under her breath. The SS officer begins to lose his patience, "Choose! Or I will send them *both* over there! Make a choice!" Protesting, Sophie says, "Don't make me choose! I can't!" He repeats his threat, "I'll send them both over there." This continues as Sophie begins to crumble under the emotional weight of having to choose between her two children, and the officer becomes increasingly belligerent. He orders a nearby guard, "Take *both* children away!" Sophie finally relents, "Take my little girl! Take my baby!" As the screaming infant is torn from her arms by a German guard she incants, "Take my little girl!" hysterically (fig. 7.4). Sophie is reduced to a voiceless scream, very much like the conclusion of Sidney Lumet's 1964 film *The Pawnbroker*. The scene is utterly heart-wrenching, and is tremendously emotive.

This powerfully affecting scene works on us at many levels, drawing on many of the signature tropes of the melodramatic form: first, the tortured body, second, the "unfit" mother, third, disillusion of the familial unit, and, fourth, disruption of generational succession. Although Alvin Rosenfeld responds to William Styron's novel here, his sentiments could just as easily apply to Pakula's film:

> Here it needs to be noted that Sophie represents a new and singularly perverse type
> of sex object that is beginning to emerge in the writings of certain authors drawn to

Figure 7.4

the most unseemly side of the Holocaust — namely, she represents in her abused and broken body, the desirability of the Mutilated Woman.[20]

While melodramatic form trades heavily in the spectacle of tormented women, the Holocaust film revels not just in torment but the tortured body. Sophie's body withers before us: anemic, ashen, gaunt, self-hating, masochistic, and suicidal.

Sophie, like many female characters in the melodramatic genre, is an "unfit" mother. Despite the fact that she had effectively no choice to make, she nevertheless blames herself; when Stingo insists that Sophie would be a great mother to their children, she has no illusions about this, and shoots him down quickly with, "It would not be fair to your children to have me as their mother." And from the perspective of the spectator, Sophie is held at least partly accountable here, as a Catholic Pole perhaps she could have easily avoided her fate. The choices that she makes in effect placed her children in jeopardy.

And among these "poor" choices was Sophie's decision to leave her husband for another man. At the heart of the matter is Sophie's sexual agency; her desire for a man other than her husband — the father of her two children — breaks the family unit. Viewed from this perspective, the Holocaust has very little to do with the film; rather, it functions as mere hyperbole: there is hell to pay if a woman expresses sexual desire, becomes a sexual agent.[21] On the surface of things the film portrays Sophie as innocent and enduring grave injustices, but on closer inspection the subtext of the film suggests otherwise: it is all Sophie's fault. And, finally, it is precisely because of her "poor" judgment that her children are swallowed up in the Nazis' machinery of death.

The strong emotional charge in the melodramatic genre frequently corresponds to a female character's transgression, in some fashion stepping outside socially prescribed roles. Like Sophie, Elsa, in Mark Herman's 2008 film *The Boy in the Striped Pyjamas*, is ultimately figured as a bad mother. This is despite the fact that she embodies the portrait of the "good wife" to her husband, an SS officer recently appointed the commandant of a concentration camp. Elsa even demonstrates relative kindness to the internees that work as servants, and strives to foster serenity within the household by willfully ignoring the truth of what is unfolding just beyond the garden wall. But according to Katharina Von Kellenbach it is the "good wife" that ultimately made genocide possible: "Women's love nourished and condoned the violence, rewarded and soothed the perpetrators, and normalized and sanitized a world that was profoundly disordered and depraved."[22] Here perhaps is another manifestation of the Nazi taint, poisoning the well of motherhood.

And this thesis certainly works in the context of *The Boy in the Striped Pyjamas*. The family's youngest child, Bruno, a six-year-old boy, and central character of the story, pays the ultimate price for the self-delusion fostered by the "good wife." Tapped to be the commandant of a concentration camp, Bruno's father moves the family to a rural villa immediately adjacent to the camp. Eventually, Bruno befriends a Jewish internee, Shmuel, the boy in striped pyjamas, without understanding the circumstances. In fact, Bruno is gassed to death along with his young friend, Shmuel, and the audience is inclined to sympathize with Bruno's mother (although she is on the "wrong side"), who in the closing moments of the film delivers a dramatically choreographed scream of anguish over the loss of her son (fig. 7.5).

Figure 7.5

The editing, *mise en scène*, and cinematography amplify the emotional weight of the scene: Bruno sneaks into the camp after putting on "striped pyjamas," and his fate is sealed when he is swept up in the liquidation of a barrack. As Bruno marches into the gas chamber, his parents discover that their child is missing. In the pouring rain they begin their panicked search for their child, which is dramatically cross-cut with the doomed internees (and Bruno) undressing for a "shower." The pile of Bruno's discarded clothing, and shovel used to dig under the fence, is discovered first by Bruno's father and shortly thereafter his mother at the perimeter of the camp. In the rain Bruno's father — realizing that he is too late, and that his son has just been gassed to death — lets out a scream, "Bruno!" which echoes through the camp, and with that Bruno's mother knows what has become of her son. The profound grief is emphasized in the clichéd use of rain. Soaking wet and sobbing, Bruno's mother kneels down, clenching her son's clothing at the perimeter of the camp and screams to the heavens, the camera, in an all too elegant crane shot, replicates her gesture, and rises in a heavenly ascent. This shot at the same time is a ghostly figure of Bruno's disembodied self — as smoke and ash, spewed forth from the crematorium — leaving this world. Bruno's mother, on the outside of the camp, is left to negotiate her role in the Nazis' program. Likewise Bruno's father, who is inside the camp, is left dumbfounded, as the camera tracks around his speechless character. The various cinematic techniques that are called upon to make this closing scene more dramatic also are intended to elicit emotion in the viewer. One hardly feels anything for the anonymous mass that is executed in the closing moments of the film (however, the gassing scene is among the most explicit), but we do "feel" for Bruno's parents. In this case, we identify with Bruno's parents, not as Nazis as such as, but as parents.

Setting Bruno's mother, Elsa, outside the camp establishes a thin partition between a safe feminine domestic space and a masculine space which is inscribed with barbarity and violence, and this is in marked contrast to the sadistic Ilsa in Don Edmonds's 1975 film *Ilsa: She-Wolf of the SS*, the subject of the following chapter. Elsa remains outside the barbwire perimeter, in effect still "distancing" herself from the "masculine world of brutality" despite what she can no longer disavow. Ilsa, on the other hand, is inside that world, and engages with the workings of the concentration camp, what Katharina Von Kellenbach identifies as "men's work."[23] The constellation of gendered roles in the Nazi genocidal program though is firmly re-inscribed in *The Boy in the Striped Pyjamas*, and it is mobilized for melodramatic purposes.

While Elsa garners spectator sympathy, she ultimately bears the responsibility for her son's tragic death. Sophie too raises conflicting emotions; while there is no question that the spectator grieves for her; the narrative nevertheless foists responsibility for her tragic circumstances on her "wayward" sexuality. Elsa, on the other hand, is subject to the Nazi taint; she is a "bad mother" because she's a "good Nazi wife," and she is tortured for it.

SUFFER THE LITTLE CHILDREN . . .

As with the figure of women, the suffering of innocent children is also a common motif in melodrama, which was evident in *Sophie's Choice* and *The Boy in the Striped Pyjamas*. Using the innocent child motif is a salient rhetorical strategy that wields enormous emotive potential. Holocaust films certainly are not the only ones to rely on the innocent child motif; this of course is also a common trope of Italian Neo-Realist films. In the wake of the atomic bombings of Japan the innocent child motif was employed to great effect in Japanese cinema. The motif manifests in various forms, from Keiji Nakazawa's comic book series *Barefoot Gen*, which was subsequently made into an animated feature film in 1983 directed by Mori Masaki, to the absolutely heartbreaking animated film *Grave of the Fireflies* directed by Isao Takahata in 1988, and perhaps even Katsuhiro Otomo's 1988 animated cult classic *Akira*.

Grave of the Fireflies and *Barefoot Gen* are quite similar in their focus on adolescent and pre-adolescent characters. As with both of these narratives, the primary characters, although only children, are left to fend for themselves during the war and its aftermath. These two narratives, Susan Napier observes,

> share in the collectivity of the Japanese memory as well as individual autobiographical accounts of personal suffering. In this regard, they attempt to 'speak for history' in a personal voice that, through the power of vivid images of suffering, destruction, and renewal, becomes a collective voice of the Japanese people.[24]

As Napier indicates, both of these narratives are essentially family melodramas, and it is precisely for this reason that both *Barefoot Gen* and *Grave of the Fireflies* are such highly emotive narratives. Moreover, because the narratives are seen through the eyes of children, the narratives themselves embody a sense of innocence and senselessness. Employing the innocent child motif in Holocaust films is used for much the same purposes, to highlight the utter senselessness of the scapegoating of Jews and other so-called "undesirables."

More than simply using the child within a narrative, but positioning the narrative from their perspective, seeing through a child's eyes so to speak, can be an incredibly potent rhetorical device serving at least two purposes. First, as already suggested, it serves an emotional function. The destruction of the familial unit creates a narrative that is inherently designed to "pull on the heartstrings," and at the same time give the narrative a "universal" appeal, that is to say everyone has a mother, father, etc., and thus can identify with a character or cast of characters, at least in these most fundamental terms. In *Barefoot Gen*, for example, Gen watches his father, sister, and brother burn to death, helpless to do anything to save them. In *Grave of the Fireflies* the mother of the two child-protagonists dies, leaving them orphans. While many might not be able to comprehend the catastrophic destruction wrought by the atomic bombs, or the struggle to survive in a wartime environment compounded by food scarcity, we can nevertheless appreciate and identify with the pain and trauma of familial loss. Likewise Holocaust films frequently utilize the innocent child motif; relying on an empathetic identification based less on historical reality and more on recognizing that the characters occupy a place in a familial constellation.

Familial structure is precisely what is at stake in the 1978 NBC miniseries *Holocaust*, directed by Marvin Chomsky, which by no small coincidence bears the subtitle *The Story of the Family Weiss*. We do not necessarily identify with this fictionalized family in the specifics of who they are, but in the generalities of their positions in the familial structure. For example, the youngest daughter of the Weiss family, Anna Weiss, is raped by a small group of Germans on New Year's Eve; the trauma is such that she no longer speaks, and languishes in a near vegetative state. As a Jew trapped in Berlin, Anna's mother is unable to seek medical attention for her daughter. Inga Helms Weiss, Anna's sister-in-law and a Christian, takes the youngster to a clinic. She is subsequently sent to a sanitarium for the mentally challenged and disturbed. She, along with the rest of the group, is gassed. The experimental gas chamber, using engine exhaust to asphyxiate the "undesirables," invites an emotive response from the spectator. Whatever feelings the spectator might experience over Anna's fate — a traumatized rape victim, murdered in an early experimental gas chamber — these feelings have less to do with the violence visited upon the character and more to do with an empathetic response to the suffering endured by the family. The loss of a child, a daughter, or a sister is what spawns a spectator's emotional response. Ultimately, it is tampering with the familial structure that is the operative component to the melodramatic genre and its strong emotive charge.

The second purpose for situating the narrative from the perspective of children is to play on that sense of innocence for ideological purposes. Napier discusses the reconfiguration of Japanese history as a "'victim's history,' in which the Japanese people were seen as helpless victims of a corrupt and evil conspiracy between their government and military."[25] Situating the narrative from the perspective of children, then, allegorically represents this particular vision of "victim's history," where the child, the sign of innocence *par excellence*, is representative of a helpless people oppressed by a radical nationalistic regime. Further, it relieves the people of Japan from any sense of responsibility for its brutal colonial advances into Asia.

Akinori Nagaoka's 1995 animated feature *Anne no nikki* is a recasting of the Anne Frank narrative in the Japanese anime form, and utilizes the melodramatic tropes of the innocent child. And while the Holocaust is relatively alien to Japanese culture, Nagaoka's animated film is every bit as emotive precisely for the same reasons *Barefoot Gen* or *Grave of the Fireflies* elicits an emotional response in Western audiences. The Anne Frank narrative is "ready-made" for the melodramatic form, and every film version plays it this way.

Nagaoka's animated version is quite similar to George Stevens's 1959 film *The Diary of Anne Frank*, which is probably the most well-known film adaptation. *The Diary of Anne Frank* was first published in 1947, translated into English in 1952, adapted for the stage in 1955 — having a stint on Broadway — before it was finally adapted into Stevens's movie.[26] Well over a dozen films (including documentaries and television miniseries) have been made from the book since 1959.[27] The popularity of the Anne Frank narrative is based in the melodramatic sensibility — the innocent child motif, the torment directed at the female character. The source material is in effect "prepackaged" melodrama, and the subsequent cinematic representations — while rearranging certain plot elements — work with content that is ripe for the genre.

Stevens's film opens with the return of Otto Frank, Anne's father, to their former attic hideout. Slowly mounting the stairs and wandering through the small attic, he finds traces of his family's former life; memories and the physical toll of Auschwitz weigh heavily upon him. Finding Anne's glove, Otto bows his head and sobs. The shopkeepers who hid the Frank and Van Daan family, Kraler and Miep, find Otto rummaging through the ruins of his former attic-home, and welcome him back to Amsterdam. No one is left and Otto is overwhelmed by grief, fueled by the memories of his home, his friends, and the city. "I — I — told Anne if I got back here, I'd find her book," he says. "Anne's diary?" Miep asks, "It's where she left it." She reaches down and pulls it off a shelf, handing it to the grief-stricken Otto.

As mentioned earlier, melodrama relies heavily on temporal discontinuity, and it looms larger here. The diary — a metonym of Anne, and her life — signifies that sense of "too lateness." It is as if Otto, as he clutches Anne's diary, is clinging to her very frame, but it is only an uncanny specter of her, a bitter-sweet return that slips through his fingers — an apparition. It is in fact too late; she is dead. Signaling the melodramatic moment, violin strings swell during this spectral encounter. From this melodramatic moment, we enter Anne Frank's world, through the very flesh of her words; slowly dissolving from the open pages that Otto reads aloud to when the family first goes into hiding (fig. 7.6).

Figure 7.6

As in fairytales, children's literature, and melodrama the separation of family members is a common emotive trope — separation between children and their parents, usually children who get lost, run away, or are abducted — tug at the heartstrings. When a new member is welcomed into the attic-hideaway, Albert Dussell, he updates his fellow stowaways about the fate of the Jews of Amsterdam. Dussell tells them of the death camps, and that many people have been dragged from their homes. Desperate of word about her best friend Sanne de Vries, Anne's classmate, she asks, "Do you know the de Vries?" "They're gone," Dussell responds. Offering more details, Dussell adds, "She returned home from school to find her parents gone. She was alone for two days, and then they came and took her away." "Gone?" teary-eyed Anne wonders. Later Anne questions Dussell about his family and we learn that he is alone, never married, no family whatsoever. This baffles Anne, frightened of the prospects of being alone. Being torn from one's family, of being separated from one's parents, literally gives Anne a nightmare. Anne sees her friend, Sanne, and hordes of other forlorn women lined up, in striped pajamas, in a concentration camp. Tearing apart the familial unit, which preoccupies Anne, is the very fabric of melodrama.

Innocence materializes not only by virtue of the characters themselves but also in the very discourse of the narrative. In the Stevens's film, when Anne is chided by her mother for being ungrateful for their relative safety the youngster lets into her, "We're young, Margot, Peter and I. You grown-ups have had your chance. Look at us. If we begin thinking of all the horror in the world, we're lost. We're trying to hold on to some kind of ideals, when everything — ideals, hope — everything is being destroyed," finally shooting a glance towards Peter. "It isn't our fault the world is in such a mess. We weren't around when all this started." Anne's mother angrily interrupts, "Now you listen to me," but Anne won't have it. "So don't try to take it out on us," as Anne leaves the room. Hans Van Daan retorts in disbelief, "She talks as if we started the war. Did we start the war?"

The love story that develops — the amorous relationship that grows between Anne and Peter — is also figured within the melodramatic pretense of being "too late." In the closing moments of the film Peter and Anne, alone, stare outside through the broken skylight, shattered earlier during a bombing raid. They try to cheer each other up, imagining what they'll do when they get out of their secret hideaway. Sirens close in on them, they've heard them before, but this time the Germans are coming for them. As the sirens continue the young couple embrace and kiss, as the music swells right on cue, embellishing the melodrama (fig. 7.7). But the consummation is interrupted; it is too late as the Germans arrive, shouting, whistling, and banging on the door.

Figure 7.7

The *coitus interruptus*, the disruption of the formation of a familial unit — as embodied in the budding relationship between Peter and Anne — is indicative of the formulaic "unhappy ending." The melodramatic genre compels action towards the restoration of social order and the imperative that things are set "right," but at the same time the genre, at its most emotive (and sometimes most successful) wallows in the exact opposite, the disruption of social structures. In melodramatic Holocaust films filial order is turned on its head, where parents survive their children. This is evident in *Sophie's Choice*, the NBC miniseries *Holocaust*, and in *The Diary of Anne Frank*. Geoffrey Nowell-Smith observes that melodramatic narratives enact conflicts in sexual maturity and proper accession within the familial system. "In addition to the problem of adults, particularly women, in relation to their sexuality, the Hollywood melodrama is also fundamentally concerned with the child's problems of growing into a sexual identity within the family, under the aegis of a symbolic law which the Father incarnates."[28] The "problem" then within the melodramatic narrative is finding a suitor (outside the incestuous matrix), to perpetuate proper family order. Anne is "too close" to her father, and channels this libidinal energy towards Peter. One of the most striking features of the Anne Frank narrative is that we witness the transition of her character — she enters the attic a girl and becomes a young woman. Her sexuality, and her desire for Peter, are key features of the melodramatic form.

The poignancy of the narrative is that Anne is left somewhere in between the possible legitimate positions in the familial constellation — wife, daughter, sister. She vacillates between daughter and (presumed soon-to-be) wife, and this also calls attention to the vacillation of patriarchal agents between the old and young generation. Anne's shift between daughter to (presumed soon-to-be) wife signifies the change of orbital patterns, where once Anne's world revolved around her father, Peter's gravitational pull signifies a shift in patriarchal order. Peter, however, like Anne is also in between, not quite old enough to "rightfully" occupy the position of patriarchal agent. The profound grief that we feel for Anne is that she is blocked from occupying her "proper" place, and is left instead in an abject state, somewhere in between daughter and wife. Nevertheless, once again, as indicative of the body genres, it is the female character Anne's suffering that carries the burden of the narrative's emotional charge.

Chapter Eight

Body Genres II: Pornography and Exploitation

INTRODUCTION: SEXUAL THEATER

Susan Sontag describes a strange underworld fascinated with Nazi iconography in her essay, "Fascinating Fascism." She attributes the fetishistic eroticization to power relations, where the SS exercises "total power over others and . . . treat[s] them as absolutely inferior."[1] The SS uniform further contributes to the erotic sign system of power, by at once physically containing the subject, and at the same time fostering an erect stature.[2] The fascination with Nazi paraphernalia has less to with the historical realities and what it signifies, and more to do with sadomasochistic role-play. "Between sadomasochism and fascism there is a natural link," Sontag posits. "'Fascism is theater,' as Genet said. As is sadomasochistic sexuality: to be involved in sadomasochism is to take part in a sexual theater."[3] This same fascination with Nazi paraphernalia and the Holocaust setting materializes as sexual theater in both the pornographic and exploitation genres.

This sexual theater is yet again different from the more nuanced presentation of sadism found, for example, in Pier Paolo Pasolini's 1975 film *Salò, or the 120 Days of Sodom*. The pornographic and exploitation genres, however, are not known for nuance. Victims are typically mere foils for the violent and/or eroticized plot, and little regard is given to the character (or characters), be they victim or perpetrator. Instead, in the case of the sadistic character they tend to be one-dimensional images of pure evil, or easily dismissed as deranged. Victims, likewise, are little more than props on which the sadistic operation of power is exercised.

In the exploitation and pornographic genres there tends to be little regard for the industrialized nature of the Holocaust, and these films foist responsibility for abject crimes onto a "sick" character, or a band of characters, as opposed to the very mundane realities of a bureaucratic system that assimilated ordinary men and women into the machinery of mass murder.[4] To be sure, though, some of the sensational acts of atrocity that materialize in these films are grounded in factual events. Human medical experimentation is a common trope of the Naziploitation genre, but here the intent is not to represent the historical record but to titillate the viewer with sadistic spectacles, or "gross-out" gore. The title character of Don Edmonds's 1975 film *Ilsa: She-Wolf of the SS* — premised on the historical figures Dr. Joseph Mengele, and Ilse Koch, the "the Bitch of Buchenwald" as she was commonly known in the press — conducts medical experiments to prove that women have a high pain threshold and are fit for military service.

Sexual exploitation is another common theme in pornographic and Naziploitation films, and the "Joy Division" — concentration camp brothels, which used female internees as sex slaves — often serves as a setting. Lee Frost's 1969 film *Love Camp 7* is an exemplary case of this plot device. Yehiel Dinur's 1955 novella *The House of Dolls* (which he published under the pseudonym Ka-Tzetnik 135633, deriving from the German acronym KZ — *Konzentrationslager* — and the numerals referring to the former internee's concentration camp number) rendered in explicit, if not pornographic, detail sex slavery in the concentration camp and popularized it among exploitation filmmakers.[5] Although this novella is set apart as a legitimate reflection of the Holocaust, it is nevertheless frequently positioned not that far removed from the "illicit" Stalag literary genre, which Omer Bartov describes as "a type of pornographic literature that circulated in Israel of the time [i.e., post-war], written by anonymous (but most probably Israeli) writers, replete with perverse sex and sadistic violence."[6] More often than not these pulp fiction novels were set in a concentration camp, or POW camp. In some cases Stalag novels feature SS women torturing American airmen who, for one reason or another, are interned in a German camp. Similar to the iconography that we see in Edmonds's *Ilsa*, the covers for these lurid tales are highly fetishistic — buxom SS women whipping bound shirtless men; Ari Libsker's 2008 documentary *Stalags* explores this salacious literary genre.

Although an altogether different scenario, the Lebensborn program is also a common plot device for Naziploitation films. In effect an Aryan breeding program, its architect Heinrich Himmler first introduced Lebensborn facilities to offset a declining birth rate with children of "good stock," but the program eventually evolved and expanded its scope and agenda as Germany became increasingly desperate to replenish its ranks. Milan Cieslar's 2000 film *Spring of Life* is set in a Lebensborn home. Films that employ the Lebensborn program as a plot element tend to be less explicit in their sadism, but nevertheless salacious owing to their subject. It should be added though that these films are perhaps a departure from the Holocaust film, since the stories revolve around manufacturing the "master race," rather than the destruction of European Jewry. Naziploitation films, however, are not known for their commitment to historical fidelity, so these plot elements — the Joy Division and Lebensborn program — sometimes intermingle in the most unusual ways. Tinto Brass's 1976 film *Salon*

Kitty, in effect, does this: using Aryan sex servants, not for reproductive purposes, but rather to "service" Nazi officers on leave.[7]

In the context of these films, though, these specific and ghastly historical events are taken in isolation, and not situated in the larger systematic processes enacted to exterminate European Jewry, and other "undesirables," in the middle of the twentieth century. The Holocaust in these cases is used as a mere plot device, and robbed of its profound historical significance. Nevertheless, these films, despite their crass character and general disregard for historical fidelity, are social artifacts that register certain attitudes about the process of representation: revealing a certain morbid fascination in the voyeuristic spectacle of the Holocaust eliciting a sensual response in the spectator — sexual arousal, titillation, revulsion — characteristic of the body genres.

THE GENRE OF NAZIPLOITATION

Art historian and critic Clement Greenberg describes kitsch as parasitic; like a vampire, kitsch feeds off "genuine culture," as he describes it, drawing "its life blood, so to speak, from this reservoir of accumulated experience."[8] Exploitation by this definition is exactly that: kitsch. The origins of the Naziploitation genre are traceable to many of the films that are discussed in the previous chapter on sadism, namely Liliana Cavani's 1974 film *The Night Porter*, Pier Paolo Pasolini's 1975 film *Salò, or the 120 Days of Sodom*, Luchino Visconti's 1969 film *The Damned*, and perhaps to a lesser extent Bernardo Bertolucci's 1970 film *The Conformist*. It is no accident, then, that the vast majority of the Naziploitation films were released between 1975 and 1977, quick on the heels of *The Night Porter* and *Salò*.[9] Mikel J. Koven situates Naziploitation films in almost the same terms: "What emerges from a study of these films' influences and precursors is a genetic/generic code that moves downward from 'art' films like Visconti's through Brass's glossy but salacious re-working, into the Nazi sexploitation period proper."[10] Koven explores how Naziploitation films brazenly replicate "serious" films about sadism, and the Holocaust. In one case he notes how closely the plot of Cesare Canevari's 1977 film *Gestapo's Last Orgy* follows that of Cavani's *The Night Porter*. But true to the conception of kitsch, Koven concludes that the comparison between these "cultured" films and their less esteemed counterparts "end at . . . [the] surface level," because while a film like Cavani's is "*about* sexual exploitation," Canevari's film *is* "sexual exploitation."[11]

As stated earlier, while the events depicted in Naziploitation might have some bearing, in fact the tendency within these films is to showcase isolated depictions of grotesque suffering — torture, rape, gruesome medical experiments — as sheer spectacle, they are generally viewed outside the larger historical context of the Holocaust. The exploitation film is especially complex, because it is frequently designed to elicit sensations from the viewing body by combining elements of horror and pornography — two of the body genres — and thus mixing sexual stimuli (pleasurable feelings, sexual arousal) with violence and gore (feelings of displeasure, repulsion, or disgust). In the Naziploitation genre women are most often the targets of abuse. More often than not female victims are in the state of undress; they are paraded about and made a spectacle of. If men are subjected to any sort of violence it is commonly handled in one of two ways: either they are dealt with quickly, with little or no suffering as such, or they are foils for the monstrous Nazi female, who effectively turns their male victims into women, either by castrating them, penetrating them in some form, or making them plead "like a little girl."[12]

The torture of women, which Linda Williams identifies as endemic to the melodramatic genre, manifests literally in the exploitation genre. Gillo Pontecorvo's 1959 film *Kapò* exemplifies the tortured treatment of the female character. As discussed in the previous chapter, the primary female character, Edith, assumes the identity of a deceased French woman, Nicole, a common criminal, and becomes a kapo. Transitioning from Edith to Nicole, the female character steps outside "proper" gender role, in effect acting as an agent of phallic power. Edith's transgression cannot go unpunished; she accepts her violation and sacrifices herself to atone for her offense. In her melodramatic death Edith casts off the accoutrement of the Nazi regime (read: phallic power), and returns to her "rightful" place: a self-sacrificing, compliant (Jewish) woman without agency.

Whereas the tradition of melodrama is to render phallic power in authority figures, or other symbolic ways, representations of phallic punishment are made more explicit in Naziploitation. For instance, in *Ilsa: She-Wolf of the SS*, Ilsa administers electrical shocks to female victims with an electrified dildo (fig. 8.1). They are also whipped, strapped and bound, and literally beaten into submission. When the tide turns at the end of the film and Ilsa is made to pay for her crimes — namely exercising phallic power — the American detainee, who is endowed with an unyielding member, ties her up and leaves her for dead. A German compatriot, finding Ilsa bound to her bed, instead of saving her shoots her in the head, which explodes in a gruesome spectacle. Where melodrama tends to be subtler in the casting of phallic punishment, in exploitation it materializes in more explicit ways, as in *Ilsa* — an electrified dildo, whips, the American's erect penis, the German's gun.

Figure 8.1

Viewing positions tend to be very different in exploitation films, compared to their more culturally esteemed counterparts. In *The Night Porter* and most especially *Salò*, the viewing body is consciously aligned with subjective perspectives, and in the latter film the audience is made painfully aware of their complicity in the spectacle of suffering. No such critical perspective is fostered in exploitation cinema. Rather, exploitation *promises* to deliver guilt-free spectacles of violence that treat the female form both as fetish object and a prop on which sadistic punishments are exercised. Comparing *The Night Porter* and *Gestapo's Last Orgy* Koven observes that in the latter film, "The spectator is positioned more or less objectively to the horrendous events on screen. The horrors are presented as if on some kind of Grand Guignol stage."[13] What Koven calls an "objective" viewing position does not invite the spectator to question their own visual pleasure, a film like *The Night Porter* or *Salò*, on the other hand, does precisely that. And it is in this respect, in its gross exaggeration, that the Naziploitation film shows the truth of films such as Steven Spielberg's 1993 film *Schindler's List* that use an "objective" viewing position.

ILSA: SHE-WOLF OF THE SS

Don Edmonds's 1975 film *Ilsa: She-Wolf of the SS* is exemplary of the Naziploitation genre. Made on a shoestring budget, and shot in only nine days, the film was put into development following the box-office success of Lee Frost's *Love Camp 7* in 1969. The so-called "Sultan of Sleaze," David F. Friedman, produced both films and secured the use of the former set of *Hogan's Heroes*, the popular comedy television series about Allied soldiers in a German POW camp, in a feat of low-budget ingenuity.[14] The set in fact was scheduled to be razed to make way for a condominium development, allowing the film crew free rein over its use and destruction, which would later figure into the film's production and appeal.

The success of *Ilsa: She-Wolf of the SS*, and its subsequent cult status, led to a number of other films that used the Nazi concentration camp as a plot device for salacious and sadistic spectacles. Despite the fact that the title character is killed in the first film — such a trivial detail hardly matters in the exploitation genre — in quick succession three sequels to the first *Ilsa* film were released: Don Edmonds's 1976 film *Ilsa: Harem Keeper of the Oil Sheiks*, and one year later *Ilsa: the Tigress of Siberia* directed by Jean LaFleur, and finally the 1977 unauthorized film *Ilsa: the Wicked Warden* directed by Spanish director Jesus Franco.

The influence of this series of films has continued on in the work of subsequent filmmakers. As a fan and aficionado of the exploitation genre, Quentin Tarantino also draws from the *Ilsa* films. In the faux 2007 double-feature *Grindhouse* (Quentin Tarantino and Robert Rodriguez), between the two feature films *Death Proof* (Quentin Tarantino) and *Planet Terror* (Robert Rodriguez), a series of fabricated trailers are screened, including *Werewolf Women of the S.S.*, directed by Rob Zombie, which in many respects is a composite of the most popular Naziploitation films.

In an interesting turn of events, which illustrates the earlier discussed debates over authenticity in Holocaust films, Friedman removed his name from the film after a falling out with the Canadian financer of *Ilsa: She-Wolf of the SS*. According to Friedman, the latter party added the title card at the beginning of the film, in effect apologizing for the film:

> The film you are about to see is based upon documented fact. The atrocities shown were conducted as "medical experiments" in special concentration camps throughout Hitler's Third Reich. Although these crimes against humanity are historically accurate, the characters depicted are composites of notorious Nazi personalities; and the events portrayed, have been condensed into one locality for dramatic purposes. Because of its shocking subject matter, this film is restricted to adult audiences only. We dedicate this film with the hope that these heinous crimes will never occur again.

The statement is signed, "Herman Traeger, Producer," curiously, one of Friedman's many pseudonyms. In opposition to the "Herman Traeger" statement, Friedman and Edmonds fully acknowledge that the concentration camp setting was a mere narrative device to exhibit shocking and sensational material. Although Friedman and Edmonds have resisted the idea that *Ilsa* has any bearing on the "real" world, it is abundantly clear that the filmmakers drew on popular conceptions of the sadistic Nazi.

The primary character, Ilsa, is a composite drawing on historical figures such as the notorious doctor Mengele, the Angel of Death, and others who conducted medical experiments on concentration camp internees. (This much the film-makers openly admit to.) Her namesake, though, is assuredly premised on Ilse Koch, popularly known by various titles including "the Bitch of Buchenwald," "the Witch of Buchenwald," or "the Beast of Buchenwald."[15] As the wife of SS *Standartenführer* (Colonel) Karl Otto Koch, the commandant of Buchenwald, she exercised her privileged position with the utmost brutality. With all the privileges of an SS officer, but with no official office, she, the so-called "red-headed widow," was situated in an unusual position. Koch did not officially fall under the author-ity of the Nazi regime, and she had no official responsibilities; effectively she wielded power and authority, and yet answered to no one. Although operating under no official capacity she was prosecuted not once but three times: first, by the Nazi regime (for corruption, for which Karl Koch was convicted and executed, while Ilse Koch was acquitted); second, by the war crimes tribunal; and, finally, by the post-war German government.[16] Among her acts of naked cruelty, for which she was tried as a war criminal, "she allegedly had more than forty inmates killed for their tattooed skins. The report commissioned by the US Army immediately after the liberation of Buchenwald also documented the reign of terror of the 'homosexual' commandant Karl Koch and his 'nymphomaniac' wife Ilse."[17] With the case of Ilse and Karl Koch — proving that life can be stranger than fiction — one might see how historical events and figures can be used as narrative fodder.

The iconography of Ilsa's character in Edmonds's cult film points back to the historical record. In her regalia Ilsa is typically seen wearing a white shirt — unbuttoned to emphasize her buxom cleavage, of course, black riding boots, riding pants, and riding crop in hand. Such attire is not entirely usual to Nazi films, nor is it completely alien to the world of sadistic fetishism (closely associated with the exploitation genre), but what is particularly intriguing here is that most of Koch's abuses take place in an indoor riding ring, which was built on the grounds of Buchenwald by concentration camp inmates apparently at Ilse Koch's behest. In her "Transfixed by an Image: Ilse Koch, the 'Kommandeuse of Buchenwald,'" Alexandra Przyrembel's careful study of Ilse Koch recounts the infamous woman's war crimes trial, where Koch denied ever beating any of the internees with a riding crop, but admitted that the timber and the camp labor were cheap, and that the riding ring was not intended for her sole use.[18] In addition to the fetishistic accoutrement of horse riding (i.e., riding boots, pants and crop), it was popularly reported that Koch was inclined to wear revealing clothing, further evidence of her sexual deviance. The salacious court proceedings, along with testimonial accounts of Ilse Koch's sadistic character, prone to exact punishment with her riding crop, and her predilection for provocative clothing, were the catalyst for the fictional character of Ilsa. These details about Koch and her sadistic sensibility were widely reported in the press (which is discussed in more detail shortly).

In addition to the iconographic tropes that we can associate with Ilsa's historical precursor, the *mise en scène* of the film also owes a debt to the historical accounts of Koch.

Apart from the sexualized images of Ilse Koch, in which the scantily clad SS wife (occasionally on horseback) intervened in camp life, in the 1960s the organization of former Buchenwald inmates still referred to the "unusual perversity" of Ilse Koch, whose household allegedly contained a ghoulish collection of "shrunken heads, skulls and table lamps with shades made of human skin and other parts of human bones".[19]

Throughout Edmonds's film Ilsa is shown in a white blouse with cleavage exposed, and has an insatiable sexual appetite. She also conducts gruesome medical experiments, and collects body parts (e.g., penises) for her colleague in Berlin, characteristics clearly derived from the historical figure. *Ilsa: She-Wolf of the SS*, however, is more accurately a picture of male anxiety in the 1970s in the wake of the Women's Liberation movement, than it is a depiction of the historical horrors of the concentration camp. *Ilsa* is what (Western) patriarchal culture fears the most: a woman "on top," authoritative, and an independent woman with sexual agency. It is fitting that the film opens with Ilsa having sex with one of the male internees, on top, astride him. Gendered tropes, such as pink ballet slippers and beauty products lining an ornate vanity, quickly give way to a decidedly masculine and merciless individual. As the commandant of Medical Camp 9, Ilsa is the lord of her domain and exercises her privilege over it by conducting sadistic medical experiments, and using internees to satisfy her sexual desires.

In the first scene there is nothing that contextualizes the sex act with conventional representations of feminine sexuality. Rather, we find the couple in the midst of the coital act with the woman on top — in control and enthralled with pleasure. Immediately, it is clear that the "order of things" is not in line with the traditional patriarchal paradigm. Pleasure, though, in this opening scene quickly gives way to disappointment when Ilsa's male partner climaxes, despite her pleas to hold on, leaving the insatiable Ilsa unfulfilled. Sullenly, she slumps down and rests upon her spent sexual partner, saying under her breath, "You should have waited." Unsatisfied by her male partner, Ilsa retreats to the shower where she pleasures *herself*. Returning to the bedside, she orders two female associates to take the hapless man away; soon we find him in Ilsa's lab, nude and strapped to an examination table. Like the female praying mantis — which devours its mate — Ilsa and her two female accomplices castrate the internee and presumably allow him to bleed to death. The scene ends with blood pouring down a trough designed to capture and dispense with bodily fluids coming from the examination table.

Exploitation films tend to conflate the genres of horror and pornography, combining two of the body genres. Just within the opening moments of *Ilsa: She-Wolf of the SS*, the audience is "treated to" doses of embellished eroticism and violence. And even within the first few minutes of the film, it exemplifies the three general traits that Linda Williams associates with the body genres. Indeed bodies are "caught in the grip of intense sensation or emotion" — Ilsa's pursuit of erotic pleasures (and her sexual frustration charged with intense emotions), and the subsequent castration of her male partner. As for the latter experience, the male internee is lost in uncontrollable convulsions, a "body 'beside itself' with sexual pleasure, fear and terror," as he pleads with Ilsa not to "dis-member" him, giving way to screams of pain and agony. And, finally, "it is the female body in the grips of an out-of-control ecstasy that has offered the most sensational sight."[20] The female body here is "out of control" not only in Ilsa's penchant for violence (and the apparent perverse pleasure she derives from administering pain) but also in her insatiable sex drive. In addition, by castrating the male character, effectively making him a woman, the body strapped to the examination table writhes out of control. The spectacle of violence and eroticism gives rise in the viewing body, then, to a conflicting array of sensations oscillating between pleasure and repulsion.

The misogyny of patriarchal culture is projected in reverse, with highly embellished scenes of women perpetrating violence against and sexually exploiting men (and other women), rendering them as objects of satisfaction and when through casting them away like rubbish. Ilsa is not so much a vision of a real Nazi (or the real Ilse Koch), but rather she signifies the monstrous and what in the 1970s was perceived by patriarchal culture as the quintessence of evil: a woman with agency. Rendering the woman with sexual agency as a Nazi — the embodiment of absolute evil — is then nothing more than hyperbole. The Holocaust, in this case, is merely a narrative device — or an excuse — on which contemporary social anxieties are projected; the grotesque horror of the spectacle that we see on-screen amounts to an articulation of male hysteria.[21]

There are intersections, nevertheless, between the historical Ilse Koch and Ilsa, the harbinger of the Women's Liberation movement in the eyes of patriarchal culture. Ilse Koch was popularly believed among the Buchenwald inmates "to have penetrated a domain of power reserved for the male members of the SS or at most certain *Kapos* (inmates who supervised inmate labor). This interaction between the (apparent) confirmation and transgression of gender stereotypes is," as Przyrembel believes, "the root of the 'Ilse Koch phenomenon' after 1945."[22] The infamy of Ilse Koch, then, serves as a model for the negative stereotype of the "liberated woman," a woman in a position of authority and in control of her own sexuality. Ilsa is not castrated as such, but a castrator. One inmate, Mario, explains to Wolfe, that "Perhaps it is her way of punishing a man, who makes her feel like a woman, yet fails to satisfy her cravings for more, who knows. But only one thing is certain, once he has served her, it is the end of him as a man." Wolfe asks his fellow inmate, "And you?" To which Mario responds, "Yes I had her for one night. Better to live as half a man for the present . . . for revenge, I live only for revenge."[23]

Indeed, the objective of Ilsa's medical experiments in the 1975 film is to prove that women have a higher pain threshold than men, and thus should be permitted to serve in combat missions along with their male counterparts. To prove this point, Ilsa conducts excruciatingly painful experiments on female inmates (fig. 8.2). In one such case, we see a woman harnessed to an examiner's chair, her right foot is in a vice bloody and mangled, as one of Ilsa's female accomplices rips out the inmate's toenails, indicative of the body genres, the sound-design amplifies the scene with the sound of torn blood-soaked flesh and cracking toenails eliciting disgust from the spectator. The camera tilts upwards to reveal that the inmate's eyes have also been gouged out. As Ilsa's obedient guards continue with the gruesome experiment, Ilsa bitterly declares, "Berlin laughed at my theory. Soon I will give them documented proof, and they will laugh no more." One of her associates retorts, "They do not wish to believe it." To which Ilsa responds, "No, they are men; it is unthinkable to them that a carefully trained woman can withstand pain better than any man." These arguments about a woman's equal capacity to serve in the military resonate with the struggle for women's rights in the 1970s. A rather primitive and naïve psychiatric assessment of Ilse Koch in 1951 determined that "the multiplicity of her loves is explained by a thirst for vengeance because of her resentment at not having been born a man."[24] This diagnosis seems more symptomatic of a misogynistic culture than of Koch's actual ailment (criminal inhumanity), but what this illustrates is how the figure of Ilse Koch — a perversion of a "proper" woman in the popular imagination — might easily serve as a model for Ilsa the she-wolf.

In keeping with this misogynistic theme, it is fitting that the American character, Wolfe, defeats Ilsa in the end. He counters Ilsa's monstrous femininity with both an animalistic and machine-like prowess; Wolfe is capable of controlling

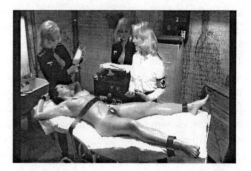

Figure 8.2

when he ejaculates, and thus can maintain an erection for an inordinate amount of time, controlling when he reaches climax. Wolfe, the character's name, also connotes animalism, and more than that, it is closely aligned with the monster traditions of Dracula (vis-à-vis enlarged incisors) and the werewolf, both of which are loaded with the implication of a boundless fecundity. In the film Wolfe's sexual prowess is also characterized as machine-like. Explaining his superhuman abilities to a fellow internee, Wolfe says, "I discovered that I can hold back for as long as I want. I still can. All night if necessary. I guess you can call me a freak of nature. Sort of a human machine. A machine that can set its control to fast, slow or never." In the lead-up to their first sexual encounter Wolfe says, "I will satisfy you." Ilsa responds, "Those are words." Wolfe returns, "I will satisfy you until you beg me to stop." "Do it then," Ilsa retorts. Once again, like the opening scene, the film cuts from the flirtatious dialogue to coital act and Ilsa is on top, "Please not now, no," and finally in the pitch of passion, "Now! . . . Harder, hurt me." She finally slumps down, collapsing on Wolfe's chest exhausted, while the camera zooms in towards his face, revealing a small knowing grin that she is no match for his sexual prowess. In the following cut, the tide has turned, now Wolfe is on top in the standard missionary position (suggesting that the order of things is changing "for the better"), and Ilsa says, "You're made of iron." Finally, Wolfe returns to the male barracks to everyone's amazement, strutting his stuff, set to an odd variation of "Yankee Doodle Dandy." Ilsa regards Wolfe as a prime specimen because of his prowess, and this boundless male fecundity cancels out Ilsa's insatiable sexual appetite; Wolfe's capacity to hold back, as he says, "just about drove her up the wall."

Ilsa calls upon Wolfe again to prove himself, because as she says, "No man can perform as you did, no man. . . . You must prove it." Ilsa enlists the help of her two faithful female guards as she watches Wolfe satisfy both women. Having proven himself, he says from bed, "Now you my beautiful commandant. But this time it will be different," Ilsa returns, "Tell me." "Take off your clothes," Wolfe commands, "I want you to undress, while I sit and watch you." As she begins to strip, Wolfe admonishes her, "No! Slowly. Show me yourself slowly." Here it becomes evident that the tables are turning, power is slipping from Ilsa, over to the representative of "proper" patriarchal power, Wolfe.

In the closing moments of the film, Ilsa exclaims to one of her faithful accomplices, "Fetch him I tell you, I need a real man." When Wolfe arrives in Ilsa's room he brandishes her riding crop, and as she stands before Wolfe half naked he runs the phallic instrument across her breasts, explaining how this sexual encounter will top all others. Wolfe orders Ilsa to get her silk stockings and then lie on the bed. When she begins to undo her bra, Wolfe stops her, saying, "No Ilsa, no. I didn't ask you to think, I ordered you to lie on the bed. Now do what I told you." She submits to his commands and Wolfe then begins to tie her arms and legs to the bedposts.

"Each of the three body genres" that Williams isolates "hinges on the spectacle of a 'sexually saturated' female body, and each offers what many feminist critics would agree to be spectacles of feminine victimization."[25] And this certainly holds true in *Ilsa: She-Wolf of the SS*; women are subject to sexually charged sadistic punishments — exhibited for the pleasure of the viewer. What perhaps sets *Ilsa: She-Wolf of the SS* apart from the conventions of the body genres that Williams establishes is that men are also subject to sadistic abuse and are likewise on display for the viewer's erotic consideration. The men that are subject to abuse, though, are routinely feminized — some are literally castrated. Horror stems not only from the brutally on-screen but also the horror of contemplating the male subject as an erotic "sexually saturated" body, eliciting the homophobia endemic to patriarchal culture.

It is important to note, however, that Williams does not partition the body genres into clearly gendered camps — it would be incorrect to say that melodramas appeal to an "innate" masochism found in the female disposition or, likewise, to ascribe the sadistic elements of pornography as "inherently" masculine — rather there is a certain "bisexual" vacillation that happens. "In slasher horror films," for example, Williams notes that, "we have seen how identification seems to oscillate between powerlessness and power."[26] This "oscillation between powerlessness and power" describes the visual pleasure one potentially derives from *Ilsa: She-Wolf of the SS*. Arriving at a similar conclusion, Rikke Schubart argues that the "function of the *Ilsa* series is the display of a perversion — male masochism — that is taboo and therefore fascinating."[27] Indeed, there is a conflicting set of feelings/sensations that occurs when watching *Ilsa* (or other Naziploitation films), a mix of fascination, revulsion and perhaps even erotic arousal. However, all of this is set against a narrative contextualized in the Holocaust, leaving the viewing body to wrangle with a range of conflicting sensations, and the ethics of deriving (visual) pleasure from the representation of suffering.

Where this reading of *Ilsa: She-Wolf of the SS* as a projection of male anxiety in the wake of the Women's Liberation movement might meet up with the historical realities of the concentration camp (and specifically with Ilse Koch) is in the field of vision. Looking is an active position; it is a position of agency and power. Thus in the discourse of the concentration camp and of films that are set in concentration camps, the act of looking is most frequently attributed to characters in positions of power and authority. In contrast, characters without agency — typically the anonymous mass of concentration camp internees — are subject to surveillance, to be seen, on display, and denied the power to look. Defiant characters — inmates who resist — are frequently given the power to "see." They survey the camp, measure up their guards, seek avenues of escape or survival, and find ways to evade *being seen*. Kitty Hart, for instance, speaks of becoming "invisible" in Auschwitz in the personal documentary *Kitty: Return to Auschwitz* (Peter Morley, 1979). Furthermore, it is in the realm of sight where character identification is affirmed; the spectator becomes intimate with the characters on-screen when we see through their eyes, perhaps even share in their agency and prowess. The power and pleasure associated with looking, the control and subjugation of those being looked at, however, is the very principle on which pornography operates.

PORNOGRAPHY

Typically, the concentration camp, the sadistic SS guard, bondage and other fetishistic accoutrements that we might associate with Nazi regalia (e.g., a riding crop, which is so closely associated with the infamous Ilse Koch) are employed flippantly in pornographic films. This, however, is not to say that the signifiers of Nazism are completely divorced from their "original" signifieds, that is to say, irrespective of how it is employed — be it in pornography, or some other genre — the loaded imagery that we associate with Nazism, and the meanings that we associate with it, still bear a relationship to its original source. For the most part, these appropriated motifs "work" precisely because of their origins, no matter how far removed from reality they might be. In their most abstract form, the iconography of Nazism is rooted in power relations.

And indeed, even more so than the exploitation genre, pornography —which by its very nature is rooted in fantasy — has absolutely no allegiance to historical fidelity. Concurring with these sentiments, Rikke Schubart advises, "to read Ilsa as a historical figure would be to read against the grain. She is a figure from S-M role-play, a dominatrix out of the erotic imagination and she masquerades in the literal sense of the term."[28] Nevertheless, while the exploitation genre at least pays lip service to narrative, disguising its sexual power play fantasies behind the concentration camp plot device, pornography on the other hand is less concerned with narrative, dropping the thinly veiled narrative pretense for a more explicit encounter with sexual role-play that trades heavily in the currency of domination and submission. Although he generally takes a conservative position on the representations of the Holocaust, Alvin Rosenfeld seemingly agrees here, because "one side of the Nazi appeal, for there is no denying that the promise of absolute lordship and absolute submission projected by the political program of the Third Reich speaks to sexual yearnings of a powerful and, it would seem, pervasive kind."[29] This is not to say that the historical realities of the Holocaust operated in these sexual terms, quite the opposite is true, but rather that the fantasy narratives of domination and submission adapt the Holocaust as a plot device as if it were "tailor-made" for S-M role-play.

There are in effect two variants of pornographic films that employ Holocaust-related imagery, both governed by a particular type of male character. In the pornographic films the male Nazi is figured as either all powerful and rules over the camp with impunity, and is governed by an insatiable sexual appetite and fecundity; or he is impotent, and while ruling over the camp exorcises his authority by *orchestrating* sex acts. In this latter case, the ruling male figure very well might employ, as his agent, a character or characters that resemble Ilsa: buxom women frequently outfitted in fetishistic gear. Regardless of the variant, almost without fail these films are either set in a concentration camp, perhaps without calling it as such, or some other outpost — a military encampment, or a military-operated/sanctioned brothel. At the conclusion of these films, because narrative is not necessarily the issue, the order of things might remain unchanged. In some films, however, there is a narrative resolution, and "proper" order is re-established.

Joe D'Amato's 1996 film *The Joy Club* plays on the motif of the prison brothel, taking its name from the so-called Joy Division. Just as the opening of *Ilsa: She-Wolf of the SS* is closely modeled after John Sturges's 1963 film *The Great Escape*, D'Amato models the opening of his film after Lina Wertmüller's 1975 film *Seven Beauties*. *The Joy Club* opens with archival images, searchlights scanning the night sky as aircraft are shot down. The American version of *The Joy Club* film includes a stilted expository voiceover explaining,

> War is hell. That's the old cliché. It's also true. And you need men to fight these wars. And these men need something to take their minds off the frontlines when they get a few days leave. And so the military brothel was born. They call it, "The Joy Club."

This is effectively where the narrative ends, and the film quickly launches into explicit sex. Nazi officers scrutinize female internees to determine their sexual aptitude for serving the Joy Club; this is the general narrative motivation for most of the film.[30] This same basic plot is evident in *Salon Kitty*. Pornographic films that use Nazi or Holocaust imagery are typically recasting the prison film genre.

In the case of *The Joy Club* the figure of the Nazi is all powerful and boundlessly fecund. While some pornographic films depict the SS officer as effectively impotent, here the SS officer is, as Susan Sontag says with respect to Nazi role-play, "the ideal incarnation of fascism's overt assertion of the righteousness of violence," and he exercises his "right to have total power over others and to treat them as absolutely inferior."[31] The female figures in these films, prisoner or not, Jewess or not, are typically rendered as inferior and subjugated, to be fucked (fig. 8.3). Interestingly, the SS officer conducts sexual acts (at least to begin with) with his clothes *on*, only allowing his erect member to protrude from his uniform to penetrate his female subject. The uniform contains the figure of the SS man, as if to shield himself from the taint of the outside world, and at the same time, to restrain his own virility.

Figure 8.3

Gail Palmer and Bob Chinn's 1980 film *Prisoner of Paradise* (aka *Nazi Love Island*), features porn star legend John Holmes, who plays Joe Murrey, an American sailor. After his ship is sunk by an enemy submarine, Joe washes up on a deserted tropical island in the South Pacific. With further exploration, though, Joe finds that the island is in fact inhabited; it is a small Nazi outpost monitoring American radio communications, and a single Japanese female soldier, Suke, guards the encampment. Held in the camp are two American female prisoners (Army nurses), who are used to sexually gratify the gluttonous and sadistic camp commandant, Hans. Under the commandant's authority are two female Nazi guards, Greta and Ilsa (of course). Hans is effectively impotent, but revels in choreographing sexual encounters; for instance, ordering Greta and Ilsa to have sex with their new detainee, Joe (fig. 8.4).

Figure 8.4

While trying to orchestrate an escape for his two American compatriots, Joe and the two American women are captured. At the behest of the commandant, Joe is made to satisfy Greta and Ilsa — at gunpoint — as well as forced to copulate with one of his fellow inmates. The Japanese female guard becomes enamored with Joe, and they too have sex, but under more amorous conditions, and uncoerced (i.e., not at Hans's order). During a scuffle between Greta and Ilsa — the latter is being too sympathetic towards their captives — Suke is accidentally shot, Joe is able to grab a gun during the confusion, kills his captors, and destroys the

Nazi compound. Text appears on screen to inform us that that on March 2, 1946, the American sailor and the two nurses — along with their five children — were rescued.

Employing Holocaust imagery for sexual excitation potentially reveals in explicit form the possibilities of a bodily enunciation; which is indicative of the body genres, although certainly ethically problematic. But nevertheless it points to the underlying problem in more "serious" genres; when conversing with his composer, Marvin Hamlisch, for *Sophie's Choice*, Alan Pakula told him, "The film is so emotional, the film is about such horror, that it runs the great danger of becoming emotional pornography. I would like something that gives a kind of dignity."[32] Though the pornographic film has little to teach us historically, it perhaps can tell us something about the problems of representing the Holocaust.

The appropriation of Nazi signifiers says something about the connotative values that we ascribe to these images; the power relations associated with Nazi iconography, and how evacuating historical meaning allows for the mobilization of signifiers in fantasies of power play. Taken more generally, though, it is possible to see how these power-play fantasies might correspond to the sadism associated with voyeuristic visual pleasure, where, for example, the victim might be subjugated to our epistemological gaze. *Nazi Love Island* says nothing of the Holocaust, but it potentially reveals the naked power relations that are invested in the iconography of the Holocaust: the visual pleasure (even despite our moral indignation) in the spectacle of violence, and the pleasure of knowing. "Out of Darkness," David Denby's review of Claude Lanzmann's 1985 documentary *Shoah*, observes that Lanzmann refuses to show us any archival imagery in his film, which Denby describes as having "an almost pornographic appeal."[33] Films such as *The Joy Club* and *Nazi Love Island* simply literalize this strange pornographic appeal of the concentration camp imaginary.

There is no intention to "save" or "rehabilitate" pornographic or exploitation films that appropriate Holocaust imagery, but as cultural artifacts they are worthy of our attention, and harbor the capacity to reveal the naked truth of representing the Holocaust. There is a twisted pleasure that one potentially derives from the representation of suffering. A film like *Sophie's Choice*, for instance, profits enormously from the Holocaust as a dramatic back-story. The pathos in *Sophie's Choice* is greatly amplified, and the subsequent cathartic experience that we derive from such dramatic stories comes at an incredibly high cost: the Holocaust as dramatic fodder. Theodor Adorno warned against such abuses of memory. The audience very well might be brought to tears with the melodramatic Holocaust narrative; the pornographic, on the other hand, titillates and invites sexual excitation. The visual pleasure that the exploitation and pornographic genres expect to elicit from its viewers hides nothing. As depraved as it might be, these films are honest in their intent.

Discussing novelist Ka-Tzetnik (Dinur) and the Stalag genre, Omer Bartov notes that the Holocaust continues "to serve as a site for sexual titillation and pornographic representation, often clad in the respectable garment of historical novels or films and asserting special importance (while arousing greater interest) by dint of dealing with a 'serious' topic."[34] But this brings us to an uncomfortable conclusion; perhaps the Naziploitation genre or other pornographic representations of the Holocaust illustrate a certain truism — if amplified, or exaggerated to be sure, though — that the graphic and horrific nature of Holocaust imagery elicits from us a degree of (negative) pleasure. These films are calculated to disgust and to titillate, and we might not care to admit it, but do they in the end merely point to the continued morbid fascination that we have with representing the Holocaust even in more "serious" genres?

emphasize our fascination w/ the Holocaust?

Chapter Nine

Body Genres III: The Horror Genre and the Holocaust

INTRODUCTION: THE BLOOD AND GUTS OF IT

Given the heinous nature of the Nazi genocide one would imagine that it was ripe for the horror genre. But very few films in the horror genre proper (as separate and distinct from the exploitation genre, as discussed in the previous chapter) actually deal with the Holocaust. Undoubtedly, the ethics of such an enterprise throws up a degree of resistance in this regard. But of those horror films that do in some respect represent the Holocaust, most deal with the subject by rendering the Nazi-as-monster, where the Nazi is figured as an embodiment of absolute evil with almost superhuman strength, the virtual spawn of Satan. As the agent of evil, the figure of the Nazi is typically responsible for opening the door to hell, or opening a Pandora's box, unleashing (supernatural) forces that "mortal men" should not be toying with. In Steven Spielberg's 1981 film *Raiders of the Lost Ark*, for instance, it is a band of Nazis that are responsible for unleashing God's wrath by opening the Ark of the Covenant. Michael Mann's horror-fantasy *The Keep* (1983) is also an example of this, where greedy Nazi soldiers open a portal to hell.

Although there are very few horror films that explore the Holocaust, Caroline Joan Picart and David Frank in their book *Frames of Evil: the Holocaust as Horror in American Film* argue that many American Holocaust films from the late twentieth century are structurally very similar to the conventions of American horror, and specifically the tropes associated with the American Gothic. Both Holocaust and horror films, drawing from Robin Wood's thesis, "identify evil as a breach with the ordinary, evil as intentional, the space of the monstrous other as dark and the site of the other, the victim in passive relief, and an unproblematic division

155

between ordinary time and the nightmare suffering and death." And whether this conflation is done "consciously or unconsciously framing the genocide as the ultimate horror film"[1] is indicative of the American approach to representing the Holocaust. Picart and Frank are quite correct in citing the need to examine Holocaust films through the lens of the horror genre, because as we have seen through Linda Williams's concept of the body genres, in representations of the Holocaust there is a complex meeting of fascination and revulsion that elicits a physiological response in the viewer. The Holocaust — whether represented in literature, survivor testimony, documentaries, history, or narrative fiction — has an undeniable hold on Western culture. While the weight of the Holocaust bears down on us with a crushing moral responsibility, echoed in slogans like "never forget," a morbid curiosity exists at the same time, one rooted in an oscillation between disgust and fascination with the (tortured) body. This incarnation of the Holocaust in the body itself is a dynamic that is historically rooted and mythologized by popular culture and, in particular, the horror genre.

The medicalization of the Holocaust is a socio-historical dynamic that extends far beyond the actual bodily atrocities which took place. Medical experiments and the figure of Doctor Josef Mengele are common tropes in the Naziploitation genre, as illustrated in the previous chapter, but this certainly holds true for the horror genre as well. The horrific medical experiments conducted on internees are a potent feature of the concentration camp imaginary. A cinematic incarnation of this is the torture porn genre that emerged in the early 2000s, integrating Holocaust imagery with post-9/11 images of tortured and abused detainees. Following the contours of the concentration camp and the human medical experiments conducted by the likes of Mengele, torture porn films find innocent victims imprisoned in grim environments, subject to vivisection, dismemberment and mutilation with grotesque instruments, testing the limits of the human body's capacity to endure suffering.

Filmmaker David Cronenberg's insistent investigation into the body can be seen as a predecessor to the torture porn genre, through his fascination with attempts to master, manipulate and perfect the human body. Indeed these tropes are hard to read outside the history of the Holocaust and Mengele's medical experiments.[2] Franklin Schaffner's 1978 film *The Boys from Brazil* similarly deals with monstrous reproduction, where in an effort to resurrect the Nazi regime, Mengele in his South American hideout deploys multiple clones of Hitler, with the ambition that a clone might eventually assume the place of his progenitor.[3] Residing throughout Cronenberg's work too is the fear of the monster coming not from without, but from within; where monsters lurk within regimes of authority (e.g., the medical profession, family, government), or within our very bodies. It is no surprise that, as Joan Hawkins observes regarding European cinema, "the Nazi doctor — a figure of some anxiety in postwar Europe (just where exactly had all those sadistic physicians gone?) — appears with increasing frequency in medico-horror tales."[4]

Whether explicitly representing the Holocaust, or simply following the contours of it — offering more of an impressionistic view — the horror genre evokes the sensation of fascination and revulsion. Traditional representations of the Holocaust invite our morbid gaze, but at the same time, owing to their "serious" form, permit for the disavowal of our own curiosity in the abject. This is done either by cloaking the Holocaust behind the veil of objectivity, as seen in historical narratives and documentaries, or dressing it up in the garb of "noble genres," such as dramatic narratives or tragedy. The horror genre, in this respect, is potentially more productive, because within this genre there is license, if not an expectation, to explore "the blood and guts" of it.[5] But more than this, the horror genre also deals with the existence of evil in the world, and the darker side of humanity.

NAZI: CONDUIT OF EVIL

David S. Goyer's 2009 film *The Unborn* is one of the rare exceptions of a Holocaust film that neatly fits into the horror genre proper. Certainly more characteristic of the horror genre than *Apt Pupil* or *The Keep* — the former being more of a thriller, and the latter having fantasy elements — Goyer's film is geared towards making adolescent audiences jump in their seats, loaded to the hilt with the conventions of the horror genre that (young) audiences come to expect: terrorized young nubile bodies in their underwear, ghostly figures that pop out of dark shadows, jump cuts emphasizing creepiness, a steel-blue/gray color palette to demarcate dreams and haunting sequences from the "real world," and an enhanced audio track that guides the viewer's reception of the film. Critics roundly panned the film for its generic thrills and its dubious venture into the Holocaust.

Similar to the discussion presented in the previous chapter on the genres of exploitation and pornography, Goyer's film further illustrates the ways in which the Holocaust has been appropriated by popular visual culture to negotiate contemporary social anxieties. *The Unborn* is analogous to *Ilsa: She-Wolf of the SS* insofar as the film is more about the anxieties of female sexuality — and more specifically pregnancy — than it is about the Holocaust. The Nazi, in this case, functions as a conduit through which the "aberrance" of female sexuality is unlocked.

The film's plot is built around Sofi Kozma, and her twin brother Barto, who were interned at Auschwitz. The twins catch the attention of the infamous "Angel of Death," Doctor Josef Mengele. Because of their unique scientific potential, twins offered Mengele the opportunity to conduct experiments on one, while using the other as a "control" subject. In addition to being interested in twins, Mengele was also interested in heterochromia, a condition that causes one iris to be a different color than the other.

In a parallel, contemporary time period, the film's primary character, Casey, who we eventually learn is Sofi Kozma's granddaughter, begins to have strange hallucinations, and is disturbed by a shift in her eye color from brown to blue. Although it is not apparent to begin with, this alteration in eye color refers to Mengele's experiments to artificially change eye color. Barto, as it turns out, was subjected to this very experiment, where the Nazi doctor injects a substance into the youngster's retina, only to have him die as a result. Two days later Barto awakes from the dead in the form of a dybbuk — a wandering soul, an entity rooted in Jewish mysticism — that inhabits his body. When Sofi realizes that Barto is no longer her bother, but rather some nefarious entity possessing his body, she kills him. The dybbuk then returns to haunt the successive maternal generations of the family, Sofi's daughter, Janet Beldon, and then finally her daughter, Casey. That the dybbuk haunts the maternal line, in the Judaic context, is certainly significant (Jewish heritage passes through the mother).[6]

The Unborn owes a great debt to Michal Waszynski's 1937 film *The Dybbuk*, which was based on Shloyme-Zanvl ben Aaron Hacohen Rappaport's play *The Dybbuk: Between Two Worlds*. *The Unborn* is by no means a "re-make" of this amazing film from the Yiddish theater, but many of the ideas derive from the dybbuk myth. The term "dybbuk" comes from the Hebrew, referring to glue, or attachment, and in the context of the kabbalistic text refers to a soul that is wandering, and finally *attaches* itself to a living entity and inhabits it.[7] Should a dybbuk inhabit a body, only a Judaic ritual exorcism can dislodge the possession.

Different from the figure of Pazuzu in William Friedkin's 1973 horror film classic *The Exorcist*, which is inherently malevolent, rather a dybbuk is a "soul which has not been able to fulfill its function in its lifetime, according to the doctrine, [and] is given another opportunity to do so by being sent down to earth again in the form of a dybbuk."[8] While quite distinct, dybbuk stories almost certainly influenced William Peter Blatty, the author of the novel *The Exorcist*, published in 1971. In his novel Blatty references, on more than one occasion, Traugott Oesterreich's 1921 book *Possessions: Demoniacal and Other: Among Primitive Races, in Antiquity, the Middle Ages, and Modern Times*, which cites a Russo-Polish Jew, Jacob Frommer, and his autobiographical account, witnessing with his own eyes "an exorcism that took place in the Polish Ghetto." Ira Konigsberg observes, however, "The victim was a Jewish girl, the possessor not a demon but the soul of a Talmudic student who had drowned himself after a short life of dissipation, and the exorcist a rabbi."[9]

A dybbuk is therefore not inherently evil, and to a limited degree this is acknowledged in *The Unborn*. While a dybbuk might well be the product of evil or malevolence brought about by some form of injustice, in the case of Goyer's film Nazis (and specifically Mengele) create a situation where a dybbuk might enter the body of a concentration camp victim. Like *The Keep* the Nazi functions as the conduit or agent of evil that opens up a portal to the netherworld, and while the dybbuk is not innately evil, and this sets it apart of the demonic figure in the Christian pantheon, it nevertheless comes from the world of the undead.[10]

However, like representations of Christian possessions, the body that is inhabited is frequently a young woman, and the possession manifests as a form of hysteria and/or depraved sexual behavior. The Christian vision of possession — which is so clearly presented in *The Exorcist* — is indicative of a Manichean perspective, where the world is neatly divided "between good and evil, between the power of God and the power of Satan." But as Konigsberg astutely observes, the Judaic worldview is distinctly different from this Christian perspective, where *nothing* is apart from God. Nevertheless, there is a division between worlds:

> The dybbuk is also the product of a vision that sees a binary opposition (in this case an opposition between this world and the next, between the living and the dead), but the impulse is towards unity and fusion. The dybbuk is the soul of someone lost between two worlds, a soul unable to inhabit its dead body and unable to inhabit heaven or hell because of its conduct while alive, but the drive of this soul is to be one with God and the universe.[11]

The dybbuk in *The Unborn* straddles the world of the living and the not yet existing (in other words *the unborn*), and in the opening scene Casey, during a morning run, discovers a jar with a human fetus. As she examines it closer, its eyes suddenly open with the predictable horror genre crescendo of sound and lightning-quick editing to match. This sequence turns out to be a dream, but nevertheless foretells of the nefarious intention of the dybbuk.

In Waszynski's *The Dybbuk* two rabbinical students, Sender and Nisan, pledge that their children shall wed — assuming one is a girl and the other a boy — but then a mysterious messenger admonishes that "Lives of the unborn should not be pledged." Eventually, the two friends part company, moving to different towns, and forget their vow. Following the birth of Sender's daughter, his wife dies. At the same time, while at sea Nisan's wife gives birth to a son, and the stormy waters claim Nisan. Before he is cast overboard he exclaims, "Sender, remember our sacred vow." The two children, Lea and Chanan, grow up without knowing each other, but fate brings them together. Not of means, Chanan eventually digs into the Kabala to unlock the powers of "black magic" in order to ascertain wealth, and finally win Lea's hand in marriage. Chanan willfully channels Satan's power to ascertain wealth, proclaiming, "Everything Jehovah created contains holiness. . . . there is holiness even in Satan!"[12] But when Chanan dies, Lea kneels beside his grave, and begs of her beloved, "Come, my bridegroom, I shall bear both our souls, like unborn children." (fig. 9.1) Here we see how this story serves as a template for *The Unborn.*

Figure 9.1

It is hard — if not utterly impossible — to read films such as Waszynski's *The Dybbuk* outside the history of the Holocaust. It is perhaps too much, though, to say that it is prophetic, but nevertheless contemporary specta- tors cannot help but to view the film through the lens of twentieth-century history.[13] Appreciating the context in which *The Dybbuk* is made is important; the film nevertheless locates its characters in a history of pogroms and of lives cut short. The dybbuk story is about lost souls, lives unjustly and prematurely interrupted. The profound resonance of this, in the wake of the Holocaust, is indicative of the poignancy of *The Dybbuk*. Superficially, these ideas can be found in Goyer's version of the dybbuk, taking up the burden of the *unborn* for instance; however, under his stewardship the narrative is reconfigured so that the maternal figure — and the maternal lineage, through which the Judaic heritage passes — is demonized.

The Dybbuk, while seeming "to be about generations, about parents and children, is strangely void of mothers and women figures in general."[14] With *The Unborn*, generations are precisely the issue, and specifically how one generation might haunt the proceeding generations. Goyer's film then might function as a literalized manifestation of second or third generation survivors riddled with "survivor guilt." The weight of the Holocaust, even when survivors elect not to speak about it (perhaps because they don't want to burden anybody with their traumatic memories), can be enormous and return to the succeeding generations as an uncanny specter, manifesting in forms of (survivor) guilt or melancholia. Although Mengele is the conduit for evil, Goyer does not necessarily locate responsibility there; rather, he places responsibility on Sofi, the matriarch of the family. And by doing so, perhaps there is less an expression of anger at Germans for the evils they visited upon the Jewish people than a violent resentment directed towards generations of Jews that have allowed the Holocaust to languish in the sinews of familial history. Mengele very well might be the plot device, but ultimately it is the maternal body that is the site of evil in *The Unborn*.

During an evening out at a nightclub Casey retreats to the restroom — feeling nauseous. After vomiting and resting up against the door in the bathroom stall she discovers a hole, a glory-hole. Around the hole in pen, a single eye is drawn (the hole figures as the pupil), and around it an inscription reads, "IN the

Figure 9.2

KINGDOM of the BLIND the ONE EYED MAN IS KING." (fig. 9.2) Hearing something from the adjoining stall, Casey looks through the hole, and what emerges is not a "one-eyed bandit" but a claw-like appendage and a deluge of bugs, Jerusalem crickets, followed by a torrent of reddish brown liquid, perhaps blood or fecal material (or both).

The hole is interesting in that it resembles the peephole in the gas chamber door (the peephole motif is discussed at length in Chapter 3). Furthermore, the cinematography — a slow tracking in towards the hole — is highly reminiscent of shots found in films such as Errol Morris's documentary *Mr. Death: The Rise and Fall of Fred A. Leuchter, Jr.* (1999) where the camera assumes a subjective point of view, embodying a character's look through the gas chamber peephole at Auschwitz (fig. 9.3). As mentioned before, the peephole is also featured in Todd Bowden's nightmare — oscillating between victim and perpetrator — in *Apt Pupil*. And Steven Spielberg's 1993 film *Schindler's List* utilizes the peephole motif to render Jewish women in a gas chamber/shower as part of the sadistically charged erotic spectacle. But here in *The Unborn* there is a refusal of the look. It is as if the peephole vomits, urinates, defecates, or ejaculates. The hole — and Casey's body — is in revolt.

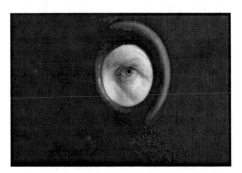

Figure 9.3

Casey, full of dread, says to her boyfriend, "It's getting stronger Mark, and I can feel it everywhere. And I think that it's strong enough to enter anyone now, even the dead." To which Mark responds, "So no place is safe?" "No, no, you see I don't think the world was ever safe, I think that we were all just trying to pretend like it was, but it's not." Typical of the Holocaust horror film, it is the Nazi that unleashes evil in the world. But this is a ruse, much in the same way that *Ilsa: She-Wolf of the SS* is also a cover for a deep-seated cultural misogyny, because what is at stake in *The Unborn* is fear of the female body — and especially pregnancy. The young nubile body — the ever fertile body, "it's getting stronger Mark," Casey says, "and I can feel it everywhere" — now conflates another type of "sexual perversity" with that of Nazi evil: female sexuality and the generative powers that she personifies.[15]

I would like to take Picart and Frank's thesis further, when considering *The Unborn*. Indeed, as with other Holocaust films, *The Unborn* superimposes the conventions of the horror genre over the Holocaust film. And while many horror films use the monster as an embodiment of abnormality, in this case there is a correlation made between the evil of Nazism and female sexuality and the generative powers of women. At first glance it might seem that *The Unborn* bucks certain conventions of the horror genre. Namely, the film does not conform to the "final girl" plot associated with the slasher films that emerged in the mid-1970s.[16] In these films, young adolescent women, and sometimes their young male counterparts, are systematically punished — i.e., hunted down and killed, usually with some sort of slashing instrument from which the sub-genre derives its name — for engaging in illicit sexual activity. If the young men in these films are dispatched, they tend to be done away with quickly (and almost always with their clothes on). The young women, on the other hand, tend to meet protracted and torturous ends, pleading and screaming for their lives, usually in some form of undress, in revealing pajamas, or underwear. In contrast to their counterparts, the "final girl," however, survives and frequently dispatches the killer/monster that stalks the group of wayward teens. She is typically cunning, boyish, and most importantly she is most often a virgin and rebuffs any sexual advances made towards her.[17]

This sets *The Unborn* apart from these earlier films, and the conventions of the slasher sub-genre. Casey has sexual intercourse but does not die, and nor does her male partner. In fact, we might say that Goyer offers us a conventional Hollywood happy ending. The prospects for a normative heterosexual coupling — one of the key ingredients to a happy ending — is all but assured, and more than that, the union between these two has borne fruit; we learn at the end of the film that Casey is pregnant with twins (of course).

The fact that Casey survives, despite the fact that she engages in sexual intercourse, and that she becomes pregnant out of wedlock, is somewhat unusual. However, on closer inspection we realize that the womb — and female generative powers — is the site of evil, or the gate through which evil is allowed to materialize. *The Unborn* in certain respects then merges Nazi medical experimentation and the figure of Mengele with the Frankenstein story. In both cases, the lab operates as an artificial womb. Victor Frankenstein and Mengele's ambitions are to create life — a power that only God and women are allowed to possess. While Frankenstein hopes to create life, Mengele aims to unlock the secrets of race, to facilitate the regime's ambition to breed — if artificially — a "superior" race.[18] Taboos around menstrual blood, in one way or another, center around the prohibition of tampering with generative powers — the ability to create life — and horror films frequently tap into this deep-seated anxiety about the female body. "From classical to Renaissance times the uterus," as Barbara Creed observes, "was frequently drawn with horns to demonstrate its supposed association with the devil."[19] Over and over again, pregnancy, the womb, female generative powers have been associated with evil. Drawing from Margaret Miles, Creed notes that the womb has been rendered as "'quintessentially grotesque'" and "that in Christian art, hell was often represented as a womb, 'a lurid and rotting uterus,'" and the horror film invokes these earlier traditions.[20] In Goyer's film then, hell on earth, the concentration camp, (re)materializes in Casey's pregnant body.

The pregnant body is abject because it is unclear where the division between one entity begins and the other ends; the line between mother and fetus, between life and not-yet-existing, is blurred. Cinematic depictions of possessions are frequently a thinly veiled exploration of the anxiety about pregnancy: one entity inhabiting another. The dybbuk as an inhabitant of another body parallels the abject state of the pregnant body.

The experience of being somewhere between the living and the dead — between existence and nothingness — is a relatively common motif found in representations of the Holocaust. Harry, the protagonist in the novel *The House of Dolls* written by Yehiel Dinur says, for instance, says, "These days a man has no way of knowing if he's already in the hereafter, or if he still has to wait for death. Everything is mixed up. Life and death in one brew. A hereafter that's not here, not after."[21] Goyer's film is more about the anxiety of pregnancy than it is about the Holocaust. In this case, the horror of the Holocaust — where "life and death [are] in one brew" — is projected onto the female body. Goyer conflates many of these ideas and associates them with dybbuk possessions. In one of Casey's dreams she has an out-of-body experience, where, floating above her bed, she witnesses the dybbuk (in the form of the young Barto), tearing opening her abdomen to inhabit her body, effectively, "the child's return to the mother's body"[22] (fig. 9.4).

Figure 9.4

In the end, Goyer's film is highly conventional in its gender politics, assigning the female character as morally suspect — she has sex outside of marriage — and is subsequently making her susceptible to evil. Here Casey is both victim and instigator. And when placing Casey in the lineage of a Holocaust survivor there are some unseemly conclusions to be drawn: that victims of the Holocaust somehow brought the catastrophe on themselves by something that they did. Indeed, a very problematic conclusion.

TORTURE PORN

In recent years a new type of horror film has emerged: the sub-genre of "torture porn." The term was coined by film critic David Edelstein in "Now Playing at

Your Local Multiplex: Torture Porn," in the January 28, 2006 issue of *New York Magazine*. The genre exhibits several consistent features. Unlike the slasher tradition where victims are stalked and preyed upon, in torture porn, victims are typically confined or imprisoned in some fashion and in most cases have it much worse. Where slasher victims are dispatched with a lethal blow from sharp, penetrating instruments, in torture porn, on the other hand, victims are not just impaled or cut, they are frequently dismembered, or in some fashion mutilated. Victims are indeed tortured, and not merely subjected to savage physical brutality, but also tormented emotionally and psychologically. Often forced to perpetrate acts of violence against others (in a bid to save their own lives), torture porn victims are faced with some sort of grievous choice usually involving bodily mutilation, or are simply allowed to languish in their own suffering knowing that they have little or no hope of surviving.

Victims suffer at the hands of sadistic characters that, despite having malice as a motivating factor, are nevertheless intelligent, cool, calm, and collected. Meticulous and premeditated, their actions, just as with Sade's libertines, establish and are governed by a set of rules, frequently manifesting as some sort of game (with rules that might be amended to suit the perpetrator).

And, finally, there are no satisfactory resolutions. Unlike the slasher genre, the last person standing, commonly known as the "final girl," is a resourceful and morally upstanding female character who vanquishes the villain, and subsequently brings about the restoration of proper order. In torture porn, on the other hand, the order of things does not change, and the villain might even walk away unscathed and unpunished. Where victims in slasher films pay for some sort of moral transgression, in torture porn characters perceive themselves to be innocent, are made to suffer needlessly, and are ill-equipped and/or confounded by what they did to deserve such a fate. Blissful ignorance might be transgression enough for a perpetrator to select a victim and to exact a punishment, and in one form or another victims frequently ask, "Why are you doing this?" Efforts to save victims are either thwarted or useless. This is due in part to the representatives of authority — doctors, police, agents of the state apparatus — who are either ineffectual or completely inept, or even at times complicit in the deadly game being played, creating an environment permeated by fear and hopelessness. At the conclusion of a torture porn film evil still exists in the world, and there is no overarching authority poised to set things right. Indeed, it is actually quite the opposite, where spectators leave a torture porn film knowing that evil lurks "out there," and could pounce at any moment.

It should be made very clear that the genre of torture porn is not directly related to the Holocaust or the tradition of Holocaust films. This recent development in the horror genre does, nevertheless, share certain *affinities* with the tropes of the Holocaust, and there are certain repercussions for the cinematic strategies of representing it.[23] Routinely, film critics characterize torture porn films as sadistic; Brian Price, for instance, observes, "Above all else, [Michael] Haneke's work is violent. It would be quite simple to describe Haneke as an immoral sadist who relishes in the desecration of the body as a form of entertainment."[24] Sadism, as discussed earlier, is a central trope of the torture porn genre; likewise, is also a central trope in the Holocaust film. This shared theme of sadism suggests the need to contemplate the strategies of representation and an examination of the relationship between Holocaust and torture porn films.

To further detail the characteristics of this sub-genre let us first consider one of the progenitors of torture porn, James Wan's 2004 film *Saw* (which at present has spawned six sequels). Torture porn films, and especially the *Saw* franchise, are typically framed within the critical discourse of the post-9/11 era,[25] or video games; briefly, let's review the latter, and I'll return to the former at the conclusion of this chapter. Adopting the parlance of video games, often characters are required to solve riddles, to navigate through spaces, to follow a set of prescribed rules, and characters plot against one another in a bid to survive (i.e., win); failure to do these things usually has lethal consequences. Jigsaw, the antagonist of the *Saw* series, for instance, ends the first film by saying, "Game over," before the screen fades to black.

There is much to gain by discussing the torture porn genre in relation to the discourse of video games; however, my subject here is not video games but rather how this genre might inform the practice of making and viewing Holocaust films. Representing the Holocaust as a game is not altogether out of the question, though. As Hayden White observes, the allegorization of the Holocaust as a cat and mouse game is precisely the strategy that Art Spiegelman adopts in his two-volume comic book, *Maus*.[26] The allegorization of the Holocaust — and Spiegelman's form, the comic book — at first glance compromises the factual content; however, Spiegelman's *Maus* is perhaps one of the most significant renditions of the Holocaust in the written form. Indeed, there is no question that *Maus* challenges our common assumptions regarding the "right" way to represent the Holocaust, and we might read the gamesmanship in torture porn — especially insofar as it relates to sadism — as similar to Spiegelman's abstraction; that is, the comic book form, and the allegorization of the narrative. While we can never directly superimpose the gaming elements of torture porn onto the Holocaust, we can nevertheless read this trope next to it, as the discourse of video games follows the contours of the sadist motif in Holocaust films.

In addition to the prism of video games, in critical literature torture porn is also contextualized in a post-9/11 political framework. Where *Saw* most explicitly employs the discourse of video games, Eli Roth's 2005 film *Hostel*, and his 2007 film *Hostel: Part II*, evoke the specter of 9/11.[27] Torture porn continually invites comparisons to the brutalities perpetrated by Americans through the so-called "war on terror," whether represented by the infamous photographs that came out of Abu Ghraib prison, or by the hooded detainees at Guantánamo Bay prison. As Kim Newman observes, "In a world where foreigners worry about winding up at the mercy of Americans, *Hostel* is about Americans being terrified of the rest of the planet."[28] And this fear that Americans sense is largely a product of their doing, because of a general disregard for world affairs, made bitterly palpable in that question that was never fully addressed in the wake of the 9/11 attacks: "Why do they hate us so much?" Clearly, the question has not been given much contemplation precisely because of what the answers might reveal about America's place in world affairs.

The two American male characters in *Hostel* — Josh and Paxton — are indicative of contemporary American attitudes. They're both "book-smart," both are presumably off to graduate school in the near future; Paxton eggs his more reserved friend on, encouraging him to be more adventurous because soon Josh will be writing his thesis, and he will be studying for the Bar Exam. On their European trip, sowing their wild oats before they embark on their imminent success, Josh and Paxton are the epitome of the American sense of entitlement; they are clearly privileged, arrogant, and believe the world is theirs to plunder (in this case specifically, European women are theirs to plunder). And yet despite their privilege, sense of self-assuredness, and their "book-smarts" they are also incredibly ignorant of the world that they inhabit.

In the film, Elite Hunting is a syndicate that caters to the sadistic tastes of rich patrons that pay thousands of dollars to do *anything* to another person — $5,000 for a Russian, $10,000 for a European, and $25, 000 for an American.[29] Young men in particular are lured to Slovakia with the prospect of finding young attractive women who will do *anything*. An abandoned Slovakian factory is re-purposed as a complete in-house torture facility, where the rich come to maim, dismember, and kill those unlucky souls ensnared by the syndicate.

"Why are you doing this?" is a question that is frequently asked during the course of a torture porn film. After being drugged, Josh, for example, finds himself hooded and strapped to a chair in a dark and dingy room equipped with a vast array of tools and surgical equipment. Once his torturer enters the room and unhoods him, he pleads for answers, "Who are you?" and "Where the fuck am I?" and then also, "I didn't fucking do shit to you, what the fuck!" and "Please, I didn't fucking do anything."[30] Josh, the smart and "responsible one" as Paxton refers to him, is utterly bewildered by his situation. All this pleading, though, distinctly resonates with that question: "Why do they hate us so much?"

In the slasher film the final girl brings about the conditions that allow for the restoration of order. In torture porn, however, the "final boy" might somehow manage to escape his torturer — perhaps even inflicting some "righteous" vengeance along the way — but they never bring about the same conditions that suggest that the world has been "set right." For instance, Paxton escapes the torture facility, even saving a Japanese woman along the way, and taking out a number of the syndicate as he makes his escape. After making his get-away on a train out of Slovakia, by chance Paxton hears the Dutch torturer on the train (the same man who killed his friend, Josh). Stalking him like prey, he kills him in a train-station bathroom, in a capricious act of passion (i.e., revenge). This sets Paxton apart from the torturers, who are sadistic in the clinical sense, and who are governed by reason and a set of rules (i.e., the syndicate's code); Paxton, on the other hand, is driven by emotions not reason.

Perhaps owing to Roth's own biography — descended from a European Jewish family — the *Hostel* films have the most distinct traces of the Holocaust. In *Hostel* the emblem of the torture syndicate is a bloodhound. All the torturers — and presumably all members of the syndicate — have the syndicate's emblem tattooed on their left arm (in *Hostel II* the tattoo is placed on the right arm, or the lower back). At first glance the moniker in itself is nothing special; however, this implicitly relates the members of the syndicate to the SS, many of which also had tattoos on their left underarm, indicating their affiliation with the Waffen-SS and the individual's blood type. Adopting the *blood*hound as the tattooed emblem might in some fashion meet up with the tattooed *blood* type of the SS.

The torture chambers in the *Hostel* series are located in an abandoned Slovakian factory. The factory is topped with a large smokestack, which echoes the profile of the concentration camp, where the crematoria smokestack — belching smoke and human ash — loomed large over the Nazi death camp. In addition, when the rich client is finished a large hunched-backed employee of Elite Hunting hauls bodies (or more frequently just body parts) into a room where they are then butchered into smaller pieces, and then tossed into the crematorium.

The *mise en scène* of *Hostel* is remarkably similar to Tim Blake Nelson's 2001 film *The Grey Zone*, which dramatizes the Sonderkommando uprising in Auschwitz-Birkenau. The aprons worn by Sonderkommando in *The Grey Zone* resemble the butcher smocks worn by the torturers in the *Hostel* series (fig. 9.5; fig. 9.6). The cart of dismembered bodies pushed by the undertaker in *Hostel* evokes the industrialized killing and disposal of bodies in *The Grey Zone* (fig. 9.7; fig. 9.8).

Figure 9.5

Figure 9.6

Figure 9.7

Figure 9.8

The oven, the smokestack, and the piles of mutilated corpses are hard, if not impossible, to separate from the images that we associate with the Holocaust. The furnace is precisely where Roth's 2007 film *Hostel: Part II* begins; an unseen undertaker rummages through a victim's belongings, setting aside valuables, and casting other personal possessions — clothing, a diary, photographs and postcards — into the flames, which resonates with the Nazis' plundering of loot collected from deportees.

Roth's films are an interesting confluence of cinematic history. The Japanese filmmaker Takashi Miike, an extreme filmmaker in his own right, makes a cameo appearance in *Hostel*; he plays an unnamed syndicate member, and when Paxton meets him as he is leaving the abandoned factory Paxton asks, "How is it in there?" Miike's character admonishes, "Be careful." Paxton then queries, "Why is that?" He responds with a slightly devilish grin, "You could spend all your money in there."[31] Quentin Tarantino produced both *Hostel* films, and then also cast Roth as Sergeant Donny Donowitz, the Bear Jew, in *Inglourious Basterds* (fig. 9.9). Donowitz's weapon of choice is a baseball bat that he takes to the head of captured Nazis, bludgeoning them to death; the bat is "signed by fellow members of his Boston Jewish community with names of their loved ones in Europe. He is so feared amongst the German military that some believe he is a golem."[32]

Roth's films specifically, and the genre of torture porn in general, also evoke an earlier film, John Schlesinger's 1976 film *Marathon Man*. In many ways, the content and the *mise en scène* of Schlesinger's thriller set the stage for the torture porn genre some 30 years later by pitting an innocent character against a sadist.

Figure 9.9

The primary male character, Babe, is a young graduate student in the History Department at Columbia University, writing a dissertation on tyranny. Babe's brother, Doc, however, is enmeshed in a world of international intrigue and inadvertently gets his young brother involved. The antagonist of the film Christian Szell has amassed a huge collection of diamonds, confiscated from Jews during the Second World War, and Szell believes that Doc, before dying, has divulged information about the diamonds to his younger brother. Babe is genuinely innocent, and knows nothing of the diamonds, but Szell has to be certain of this. Babe, then, functions much in the same way that the victims in torture porn do, and figuratively speaking, Babe could have fathered either Josh or Paxton; they are cut from the same cloth. Like Josh and Paxton in *Hostel*, Babe is also book-smart — attending graduate school — however, he is not especially worldly.

Set against Babe, a figure of innocence, is the sadistic antagonist: Christian Szell, a Nazi war criminal. We learn that in Auschwitz he was known as Der Weisser Engel (the White Angel), on account of his stark white hair. Obviously trading in the currency of the historical figure of Doctor Josef Mengele, the Angel of Death, Szell ran an experimental medical camp at Auschwitz.[33] Arranging safe passage for Jews for substantial payments in diamonds, Szell also extracted gold fillings from Auschwitz internees before sending them off to their death. This plunder would eventually end up in a safety deposit box in New York City, managed by Szell's brother, while Szell himself was in hiding in Uruguay. When Szell's brother suddenly dies in a fiery car wreck, Szell, at great risk of capture, arrives in New York to recover his plundered treasure. When his character is first introduced, the soft-focus camera tilts up to reveal a glass cabinet that includes human and animal skulls. In themselves the bones are not especially evocative; however, coupled with German newspapers, and other signifiers of "German-ness" adorning his secret hideaway, the cumulative connotative value meets up with the image of Ilse Koch.

Szell's character is an exemplary Nazi sadist, in effect a composite of both Mengele and Koch. A dentist by trade, he approaches his work clinically, and with the utmost professionalism. In terms of narrative content and form, a critical scene where Szell employs his dental trade to torture Babe establishes clear lineage between *Marathon Man* and the genre of torture porn. When Szell, with his two accomplices, enters the room where Babe is confined, he moves with purpose, opening his briefcase, and placing his toolkit matter of factly on a worktable. Szell is clinical in manner and speech, never once losing his temper, or letting his emotions get the better of him. Dressed in a three-piece suit, he retreats to the back corner of the room where there is a sink, removes his coat, and washes his hands as any doctor would.

Szell then asks, "Is it safe?" Of course, Babe is completely ignorant of the saga unfolding all around him, and is confused by the question. As Szell repeatedly asks, "Is it safe?" Babe searches for the answer that he wants to hear. Walking back over to the worktable, all the while calmly asking, "Is it safe?" Szell unfurls his tool kit, revealing an assortment of dental tools. Taking a pick and a dental mirror Szell proceeds to examine Babe's teeth, but not before some resistance and fidgeting from the reluctant patient. Poking about, Szell finally asks, "That hurt?" Babe manages, "Uh-huh." "I should think it would," Szell admonishes. "You should take better care of your teeth. You have quite a cavity here." And then abruptly Szell asks again, "Is it safe?" Babe begins to answer before Szell firmly launches into the cavity with his pick, causing Babe to lurch and scream in pain. Convinced that Babe knows something, he calmly applies some clove oil to Babe's tooth, "Isn't that remarkable?" he says with a gentle smile. Babe feels instant relief. Szell steps back, holding the bottle of clove oil and the pick, and begins, "Life can be that simple. Relief . . . discomfort. Now which of these I next apply, that decision is in your hands, so . . . take your time, and tell me . . . Is it safe?"

True to the sadist disposition, everything is meticulously planned. After this first round of dental procedures is over, Babe is dragged off to another room where he is allowed to rest. One of Szell's accomplices nurses Babe, administering more clove oil to relieve the pain. A government agent, Janeway, surreptitiously enters the room, dispatching Szell's accomplice with a knife, gunning down the other, and springing Babe from the clutches of the former Nazi. In the get-away car in an overwrought tone Janeway reveals the plot — telling him about Szell's treasure, and that Doc worked as a courier — he asks if Doc said anything before he died. Still, of course, Babe is clueless; he knows nothing of this international intrigue. The whole escape, however, turns out to be a ruse. When the car comes to a stop, Babe finds himself exactly where he started, and back in the hands of Szell's accomplices, who are very much still alive. In the true meaning of sadism, which is more about power and intellectual mastery, even the escape was intended to pump Babe for information. Babe once again finds himself in Szell's makeshift dentist's chair. This time, though, Szell brings out the electric drill and purposefully drills into a healthy tooth to inflict intense pain. He is finally assured that Babe knows nothing, and instructs his accomplices to "get rid of him." (It's little wonder that Josh's torturer uses a household drill.)

The *mise en scène* of this scene is very significant, and illustrates the intimate link between the genre of torture porn and the representations of the Holocaust. Although it goes relatively unnoticed during the torture scene itself, in its after-math it is clear that Babe is wearing a robe and white and grey striped pajama bottoms, evoking the attire associated with concentration camp internees. At the beginning of the torture scene, Babe finds himself in a dark room, immobilized, confused and struggling to get his bearings; it is a situation remarkably similar in many respects to Josh's predicament in the first *Hostel* film (fig. 9.10; fig. 9.11).

Suddenly, a single industrial light is turned on, and we discover that Babe is alone in a dingy room; his arms are strapped to the arms of a chair, and likewise his feet are strapped to the base of the chair. The room is relatively small and sparse, an office in a larger warehouse. Though modest by torture porn standards, Szell's collection of dental tools is laid across the makeshift worktable, and their display is intended to provoke anxiety not only in Babe but the spectator as well. Shots panning across the instruments of pain in torture porn films are used too, much to the same effect, arousing an anxious anticipation in the viewer and the hapless victim usually strapped to a table or chair. An earlier film which resonates with this trope, but predates these films, is Roberto Rossellini's 1945 film *Rome, Open City*, which exhibits many of the same characteristics: sparse room, a tortured subject strapped to a chair, ordinary household tools transfigured into instruments of torture (figs. 9.12–9.15).

Figure 9.10

Figure 9.11

Figure 9.12

Figure 9.13

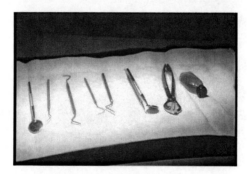

Figure 9.14

Figure 9.15

The banality of the space, the decor, and the instruments displayed before the victim are charged with a wholly different, more nefarious character. The everydayness of the objects, a drill, a dentist's pick, a chair are recontextualized here as weapons, and they are designed to evoke dread in the victim and the spectator, where the stability of the order of things is undone.[34] "The appearance of these common domestic objects in torture reports of the 1970s is no more gratuitous and accidental," as Elaine Scarry observes, "than the fact that so much of our awareness of Germany in the 1940s is attached to the words 'ovens,' 'showers,' 'lampshades,' and 'soap.'"[35] The figure of Mengele (and the characters that are derivatives of him, including Szell) then also fit in this, as the acts of a man of science, of medicine, whose pledge to "do no harm" are radically turned on their head.[36]

Whether in life or in art, the environment that an individual who is subjected to torture inhabits "is limited to the room and its contents; no other concrete embodiments of civilization pass through the doors."[37] The signature enclosed space in torture porn films corresponds to the sadist's reliance on a hermitic universe, where within a strictly defined space nothing is abject. And from this perspective it is possible to see how the torture chamber in torture porn films is an overdetermined site, alluding to the concentration camp, the libertine's universe in Sade's novels, and to earlier cinematic renditions of torture. While the space where pain is administered in *Marathon Man* is relatively sterile albeit a bit dingy, what distinguishes it from its torture porn progeny is that in the latter genre the torture chamber typically exhibits abject symptoms that the former illustrates in more clinical ways. The torture chamber in the torture porn genre is frequently dank, dark, damp space colored in the various shades of fecal matter. And in the fecal palette the torture chamber in torture porn buts up against the conceptualization of the concentration camp, which has been referred to as *anus mundi* — the asshole of the world. (Most of *Saw* interestingly takes place in a bathroom.)

Torture porn films do not paint a neat Manichean worldview, victims are not always likable characters, and when given the chance the victims prove to be just as brutal as the perpetrators. The perpetrators of torture — especially in the *Hostel* films — are not homogeneous, or depicted as nefarious to the core; and this is probably torture porn's most distinct characteristic relative to the tradition of Holocaust films, which is apt to construct narratives of good versus evil.

In Michael Haneke's films the clear division between good and evil is dissolved completely; violence seems to well up from nowhere. Retrospectively grouped into the torture porn genre, which properly speaking only emerged after 9/11, Haneke's work deals with the existence of violence (or perhaps evil) in the world, but a violence whose exact source is somewhat ethereal. Disorientation, riddles or games are plot devices that are associated with the German/Austrian filmmaker's work. *Benny's Video* (1992), *Funny Games* (1997; 2007), and *Caché* (or *Hidden*, 2005) constitute Haneke's "glaciation trilogy." The first film of the trilogy highlights the proximity of the Bosnian conflict, relative to the seemingly indifferent Austria. In *Hidden* mysterious videotapes with ghastly child-like illustrations appear on the doorstep of a French family; who and exactly why the videotapes are made is never explicitly revealed — they appear like uncanny specters. The videotapes and the violence associated with them materialize like the return of the colonial repressed, an impressionistic manifestation of the lingering guilt over the crimes perpetrated against Algeria and Algerian immigrants. As with all the films in the "glaciation trilogy," malevolence appears like a ghostly apparition in *Funny Games*. Haneke made essentially two identical versions of this film: first, a German film in 1997, and then again ten years later in 2007 an American version. In the films, two young men arrive at an exclusive summer vacation spot, a lake dotted with holiday homes, and they skip from one house to another taking families hostage and then savagely and coldly killing each one.[38] The antagonists of *Funny Games* pepper their victims with riddles and little games, and are the consummate clinical sadists. Haneke toys with the spectator's pretension for violent retribution too, but never satisfies our desire for revenge.

Of course one of the things that shocked us so profoundly in the mid-1990s is that the imagery that came out of Serbian concentration camps resonated so closely with that of the Holocaust; emaciated figures languishing behind barbwire fences were nothing short of uncanny. All of our pleading of "never again" seems to have fallen on deaf ears, and now followed by successive genocides — Rwanda, and Darfur. Haneke's film *Benny's Video* is to one degree or another responding to European apathy to events happening (again) in its midst.

In an interview speaking about *Hidden* Haneke says that the film is about guilt, "how one lives with guilt." Although the film deals with the post-colonial experience in France, he insists that this theme could be situated in any country or time, because as he says, "In any country, one can find a secret hidden by the 'common sense' of that country." Casting off the yoke of memory (or history) is how we generally negotiate guilt, or actually more precisely responsibility for the past. The primary male character, Georges, for instance, abdicates his responsibility: "I was only six, how am I supposed to remember?" Max Silverman argues that this denial of guilt, as expressed by Georges, consciously or not allows Haneke to incorporate the

> iconography of the Holocaust to invade a narrative ostensibly about colonial and postcolonial relations between France and Algeria. The abduction of children, disappearance, and denials of guilt have become central elements in our cultural vocabulary of racialized violence and trauma and oblige us, even unconsciously, to view one event (colonialism) in the light of another (the Holocaust).[39]

Haneke moves the torture porn genre closer to Pasolini's *Salò* and Tarantino's *Inglourious Basterds* in their admonishing gestures that point to our complicity in the voyeuristic thrill associated with violent spectacles.[40] Haneke in this sense is the antidote to torture porn. Haneke probably never will represent an historical event "as it really was," for the medium of film inherently abstracts events — it is always already pure artifice. "The danger with the catastrophe genre in Hollywood," Haneke observes, "is that it's one of exaggeration, so it makes catastrophe seem attractive — something we can enjoy because it's so unrealistic. My work consists of trying to reach people on an emotional level, raising the level of audience identification as high as possible by avoiding overt stylization or exaggeration."[41] Haneke does not speak about the Holocaust, he speaks next to it; in the contours of his work are the key elements that concern representations of the Holocaust (e.g., the nature of sadism, viewing positions, the responsibility to memory/history, our proximity to violence and our willful overlooking of it).

In his discussion with Anthony Lane, Haneke does not want to specifically locate his 2009 film *The White Ribbon* as a Nazi film, "It's a film about the roots of evil. It's about a group of kids who are preached certain ideals and become the judges of others — of those who have pushed this ideology onto them."[42] He goes on to explain that stringent ideological positions spread across the political, social and religious spectrum, and are not the sole property of twentieth-century fascism. Haneke embraces, rather than runs from the darker side of the human psyche, saying that "There is no crime I couldn't have committed. . . . It is so easy to say, 'Oh no, I would never do that,' but that's dishonest. We are capable of everything."[43] It is next to impossible to read Haneke's films outside the context of Nazism, their institutionalized violence, and the Western world's disavowal of the Holocaust by locating it in particular culture and historical moment; Haneke's work is about forgetting, about denial, and the inability to take responsibility.

Strategies for representing the Holocaust have much to learn here. For there is a delicate balance to reach: it is arguable that explicit and unadulterated representations of horror are imperative — after all, shouldn't representations of the Holocaust strike us to the very core? But how does one do that without (re)violating the victims? Contemplating the genre of torture porn, Edelstein queries, "Fear supplants empathy and makes us all potential torturers, doesn't it?" The genre of torture porn upsets the conventional narrative constellation, and places us uncomfortably close to the agents of evil. Be they horror films or not, in Holocaust films Nazis, of course, are typically cast as the epitome of evil, and in the standard clear division of cosmic order, the victims of Nazi persecution are subsequently positioned on the side of utter goodness, and through an identification with these characters, we, the spectators, are comfortably placed on the side of the righteous. Especially now, in the wake of 9/11, and Abu Ghraib, water-boarding, bound and hooded prisoners, Guantánamo Bay Prison, the detention facility at Bagram Air Base, aligning spectator identification with righteousness seems laughably naïve at best, and downright duplicitous at worst. Our faith in the Manichean worldview has collapsed, and the consequences of this perhaps necessitate a new critical viewing position of existing Holocaust films, and might require future films to reconsider the nuances of Holocaust narratives and characters, especially when rendering perpetrators.

Chapter Ten

Holocaust Documentaries I: Telling It Like It Really Was

INTRODUCTION: DOCUMENTARY MODES

One of the problems with the documentary form is that it is burdened with a supposed allegiance to objectivity, an expectation that it will provide a transparent window onto the past. This erroneous colloquial understanding of the documentary form places an undue burden on the genre to convey *the* unadulterated account of what has happened. Building from this, when presented with a testimonial account — where a witness speaks — there is an expectation on the part of the spectator that the documentary offers us unfettered access to the historical referent: to the event itself embodied in the witness, who, after all, was there and saw history unfold before their very eyes. The objective of this chapter, and the following three chapters on the subject of Holocaust documentaries, is to offer a survey of some of the different rhetorical strategies used to represent the Holocaust in non-narrative forms, and at the same time challenge some of our commonly held assumptions about what a Holocaust documentary is, or even should be.

The esteemed documentary film scholar Bill Nichols outlines a series of documentary modes — expository, observational, interactive, and poetic — that will be productive in our discussion of the documentary form. The vast majority of Holocaust documentaries fall within the expository mode, or have certain expository elements, which "address the viewer directly, with titles or voices that advance an argument about the historical world."[1] There are countless Holocaust films (especially if we include in this the glut of World War II documentaries), and the vast majority of these rely on the "voice-of-God" convention, a voiceover narration that guides the spectator's reception of the visual material, following the tradition of journalistic reportage, which has been "the primary means of relaying information and persuasively making a case at least since the 1920s."[2] Persuasive commentary addressing the spectator is the governing rhetorical principle of the expository mode. The visual material, which serves as illustration or counterpoint, and the use of nonsynchronous sound, typically in the form of voiceover, substantiates the appeal made to the spectator. The editing strategy in expository documentary works in the service of the commentary, establishing and maintaining "rhetorical continuity more than spatial or temporal continuity."[3]

The majority of documentaries, which air on television, conform to the conventions of the expository mode. Michael King's 2009 documentary *The Rescuers: Heroes of the Holocaust*, for instance, details the lengths to which some individuals went to save Jews from fascist authorities via a deliberately articulated argument and framing. The film chronicles, just to cite one example, the Japanese consular agent in Lithuania, Chiune Sugihara, who arranged for Jews to obtain visas to leave Nazi occupied territory, and find safe passage to Japan, eventually settling in Shanghai, which at that time was under Japanese rule.[4] Constructed from survivor interviews, voiceover narration set to archival footage, and illustrative cutaways the film's commentary stresses the heroism of its subjects, and compels us to think likewise. The expository mode utilized in *The Rescuers* accommodates the inclusion of interviews, but generally in this mode, "these tend to be subordinated to an argument offered by the film itself, often via an unseen 'voice-of-God' or an on-camera voice of authority who speaks on behalf of the text,"[5] which is precisely what historian Sir Martin Gilbert's role is in the film.

The observational mode largely conforms to the conventions associated with direct cinema, or cinéma vérité, where events are allowed to unfold before the camera, with limited or no use of voiceover narrative or other practices that might frame the recorded event. Furthermore, where the expository mode might introduce archival information — or some other form of extra-diegetic material — the observational mode is prone to take a "fly-on-the-wall" approach and assemble footage from an unfolding event. And while in the interactive mode the filmmaker is prone to intervene with the events taking place before the camera, the "observational mode stresses the nonintervention of the filmmaker."[6] Many Holocaust documentaries, discussed further in Chapter 11, where individuals go on voyages of "personal discovery," utilize the observational mode. And because the observational mode is largely beholden to the present tense — what is happening at the instant the camera is rolling — "the observational film most readily addresses contemporary experience," whereas the expository and interactive modes are more amenable to historical investigations.[7] And perhaps more than any of the other modes, the observational mode invites our voyeuristic gaze because we are invited to look in on an event, which in some cases might be profoundly personal and private.[8]

James Moll's 2006 documentary *Inheritance* relies primarily on the observational mode. The film tracks the journey of Monika Hertwig, the daughter of Amon Goeth, the commandant of the Plaszow concentration camp (featured as the primary antagonist in Steven Spielberg's 1993 film *Schindler's List*), to come to terms with who she is, and who her father was. Only one year old when her father was hanged, and told that he died during the war, Hertwig eventually learns of her father's past, and after seeing Spielberg's film became "sick with the truth." In an effort to try to understand, and to in some sense assuage her own guilt, Hertwig writes to survivor Helen Jonas, a Jewish internee in the camp who lived in the commandant's home as Goeth's servant. Just 15 years old at the time, Jonas has vivid memories of Goeth's cruelty, and as she puts it, "his need to kill." The camera follows their meeting, at the Plaszow memorial site, which is contemptuous, filled with false starts, and tenuous gestures from Hertwig; the filmmaker does not intervene (aside from simply being present), but rather observes Hertwig's perhaps misdirected search for forgiveness echoed in her refrain, "I'm not my father." As Nichols argues regarding the observational mode, Moll's application of it draws on the traditions of "classical narrative fiction, [where] our tendency to establish a repertoire of imaginary relationships with characters and situations prospers on condition of the filmmaker's presence as absence."[9]

Where Moll keeps his distance in *Inheritance*, indicative of the observational mode, the interactive mode on the other hand presents the filmmaker as a social-actor within the film itself, not only conversing with or interviewing subjects, but shaping and interacting with the events that unfold. The interactive mode "stresses images of testimony or verbal exchange and images of demonstration (images that demonstrate the validity, or possibility, the doubtfulness, of what witnesses state)."[10] Many of the most significant Holocaust documentaries, which feature testimonial accounts, utilize the interactive mode; *Shoah* (Claude Lanzmann, 1985), and *Hotel Terminus* (Marcel Ophüls, 1988) are two clear examples of this. The interview is a common rhetorical device in the interactive mode, and as Nichols notes, this "raises ethical questions of its own: interviews are a form of hierarchical discourse derived from the unequal distribution of power, as in the confessional and the interrogation."[11] And this hierarchal relationship is frequently, and quite painfully, on display in *Shoah* as Lanzmann sadistically prods victims to recount traumatic memories, sarcastically cajoles bystanders, or simply lies to perpetrators in order to "get the story."

Where Lanzmann forcibly places himself into *Shoah*, an interactive documentary need not have an embodied filmmaker. James Moll's 1998 film *The Last Days*, for instance, is assembled from a series of interviews, including ones with five Holocaust survivors; his intervention "arises out of the selection and arrangement of the evidence provided by witnesses rather from a voice-over commentary."[12] The film showcases the experience of American citizens, all Hungarian immigrants, who survived the Holocaust; among them is the late congressman Tom Lantos (Democratic representative from the state of California). Not only are each of the stories compelling but the case that Moll makes — spoken through the survivors — is that killing Jews was more important to the regime than even winning the war. It's not until the eve of the war in mid-1944 that the Nazis began to mobilize against Hungarian Jews, and begin deporting them to death camps; hence the title *The Last Days*. Applying the interactive mode, while not being embodied in the film, such as Lanzmann is, situates the interviewees as a conduit through which Moll makes his argument.

While the three modes previously discussed keep the tacit contract between objectivity and the documentary genre intact, the poetic mode stresses form and thus the "constructedness" of documentary, and consequently holds no pretense of objectivity. The poetic mode is concerned not just with rhetorical *content* but also with the *form* and emphasizes stylistic and aesthetic embellishments. The poetic mode, insofar as it emphasizes form, shares affinities with what Nichols calls the reflexive mode, which tends to highlight rather than conceal the ways in which a film is constructed. In this self-awareness the concern of documentaries that employ the reflexive or poetic mode is not simply *what* the content of the film is, but *how* the subject is addressed.[13] And because the reflexive and poetic modes are largely shorn from the moorings of documentary conventions (e.g., linear narrative, discourse of sobriety), there is a tendency for these films to be highly stylized.

The Holocaust films of the Hungarian filmmaker Péter Forgács — *The Maelstrom: A Family Chronicle* (1997), and *Free Fall* (1997) — are exemplary of the poetic mode. Forgács's films exhibit certain reflexive traits too, though, insofar as his authorial hand is present in the compiling, manipulation, and editing of the footage. All of these films, discussed in Chapter 13, are assembled from home/ amateur movies, and the recontextualization from the domain of private home movies to public documentary is implicitly marked with Forgács's signature. The filmmaker lovingly reconstructs the lives of families otherwise lost to oblivion. Since the source of the footage is home movies, Forgács is able to interrogate the origins of the footage, who is shooting it, and for what purpose, certainly not for a documentary about the Holocaust. Since Forgács's films are constructed from small snippets of a family's life, or a private individual — usually record- ing momentous occasions like birthdays, weddings, the birth of a child — the filmmaker showcases what most documentaries try to conceal: the fragmentary nature of historical knowledge, the fissures in what we know, and what is pos- sible to know. If conventional documentaries rely on narrative fetishism — the presumption that an event can be (completely) knowable, and can be contained in a tidy narrative package — then the reflexive and poetic modes are the antithesis of this; it is not an acquiescence of the limits of historical knowledge, rather it is an acceptance that knowledge is inherently fragmentary, and efforts to represent it in the reflexive and poetic modes are part of an *ongoing* effort to work through history, rather than presuming that a subject — especially something as traumatic as the Holocaust — can be definitively explained.

This chapter surveys what we might consider the most conventional documen- tary form, the expository mode. It takes issue with commonly held assumptions about the documentary genre, that it is a transparent window onto the past, and illustrates the ways in which the expository mode constructs rhetorical arguments using interviews, archival material, and other framing devices (e.g., voiceover).

THE EXPOSITORY HOLOCAUST DOCUMENTARY

Laurence Jarvik claims that his 1982 film *Who Shall Live and Who Shall Die?* "invites the viewer to form his own judgments, and therefore has no narration. It was produced privately, with no partisan, organizational, or governmental support."[14] Such a statement is naïve at best and dubious at worst. All documentary films have a perspective, and the veil of supposed objectivity in *Who Shall Live and Who Shall Die?* is in fact very thin indeed. The film addresses the delayed Allied, and specifically the American, response to save the Jews from the atrocities being committed by the Nazi regime. From the outset of the film, through the use of title cards and archival newsreels, a clear premise is established: the United States knew about the systematic destruction of European Jewry but stood idly by and allowed the genocide to continue. Through a series of interviews with numerous survivors, Jarvik demonstrates that even early in the Nazis' rise to power Jews looking for an escape out of Germany found no place to turn to. "America didn't open the doors for us," one survivor laments. The film is constructed in three chronological parts: pre-war efforts to relocate German Jews, the Allied response to the treatment of Jews in Nazi-occupied territories, and finally post-war reflection on the magnitude of the Holocaust. Although *Who Shall Live and Who Shall Die?* never employs the voice-of-God narrator — there never is any need for it — Jarvik's use of interviews and the newsreel footage speaks on his behalf, and this strategy of presenting a particular point of view is exemplary of the expository mode.

Through a series of interviews and archival newsreel footage *Who Shall Live and Who Shall Die?* illustrates numerous frustrated efforts to find German Jews a safe haven prior to the outbreak of the war on September 1, 1939. These included the establishment of the Jewish colony of Sosua in the Dominican Republic.[15] There was also the sorrowful voyage of the steam-liner *St Louis*, carrying over 900 Jewish refugees that sailed from Hamburg, but was denied entry to Cuba and the US and forced to return to Germany where a number of the refugees eventually ended up in concentration camps.[16] And finally there was an organized but limited effort to "repatriate" Jews (against British law) to Palestine. Time and time again Jewish refugees found doors closing. Jarvik also interviews US government officials and employs newsreel footage to illustrate that the American isolationist policy prior to 1941 exacerbated this problem. Not only did American foreign policy dramatically clamp down on Jewish refugees finding safe haven in the US, but it also set a precedent for other countries to limit or deny altogether an exit for Jews trying to escape the ever increasing oppression of the Nazi regime.

Finally, as the United States entered the war, Jarvik's film ponders why all efforts to either destroy or damage the infrastructure of mass murder (e.g., bombing railway lines leading to Auschwitz), threats of retaliation for use of chemical weapons by Germany to dispatch Jews, or efforts to negotiate with German officials (e.g., buying Jewish lives) never materialized. When the true magnitude of the Holocaust was revealed with the liberation of the concentration camps, Jarvik asks John Pehle, Executive Director of the War Refugee Board, what he felt about the documentary footage from the liberations, "The feeling of any civilized human being: it's hard to believe that such things could have happened." Jarvik returns, "And the work you did?" "Late and little, I would say." Immediately from this acknowledgement that too little was done, the film cuts to a group of children freed from Auschwitz, rolling up their sleeves to reveal their tattooed serial numbers. The juxtaposition of an authorial agent, an official in the American government, next to the signifier of innocent victimization — without being blatantly didactic — makes a dramatic closing argument. The careful crafting of the film, as Annette Insdorf observes, "results in a profoundly disturbing document that is certain to offend many viewers,"[17] and although she does not say as much, the film points if not to American complicity in the genocide especially late into the war, then to a failure in American moral leadership.

Unlike *Who Shall Live and Who Shall Die?* Lydia Chagoll's 1979 short documentary *They Came From Far Away* relies extensively on the voice-of-God narrator indicative of the expository mode. Written, edited, and directed by Chagoll, the film offers several fascinating diversions from the expected conventions of the expository mode. To begin with, a woman, Cicely Sandford, narrates the film — an unusual choice, because the voice-of-God, as a commanding figure of authoritative knowledge, is frequently associated with a deep male voice, and reflects the ingrained patriarchal values of the form.[18] Sandford's narration is clinical in its delivery and commanding, and the female narration seems befitting to the principal subject of the film: the treatment of women and children in the concentration camp. Sandford details the brutal practices of the Nazis and the grave toll the conditions of the camp took on the internees.

They Came From Far Away offers two key types of visual imagery to provide support for Chagoll's scripted narrative. The film begins with photographic archival images, and at its midpoint integrates drawings created by concentration camp internees, primarily children. This powerful imagery, which, because of its simplicity in some circumstances might jeopardize the supposed "authenticity" of a documentary, here is nearly as incontrovertible as a photograph, lending "authoritative weight" from its authorship. There is a certain metonymic quality to the illustrations, forming a nexus between the traumatic experience of children in the Holocaust and the present tense of the film. Guiding the spectator's framing of this imagery is the voiceover commentary, which elicits the spectator's sympathy.

Mike Rossiter's 1995 film *Nazi Designers of Death* uses expert testimony and a rhetorical editing strategy to look at the intricacies of engineering mass murder at Auschwitz. The position of the film — in this case, that tremendous engineering efforts were mobilized to solve the problems of killing and disposing of thousands of human bodies — is given voice primarily through the historian and architect Robert Jan Van Pelt (who is also featured in Errol Morris's 1999 documentary *Mr. Death: The Rise and Fall of Fred A. Leuchter, Jr.*, which is discussed in Chapter 13). Indicative of the expository mode, Rossiter utilizes the documentary device of expert testimony (e.g., historian, professional in subject at hand) to make a persuasive case. While it seems as though it is Van Pelt who is speaking on his own accord, as if he would be making the case whether the camera was present or not, it is rather quite the opposite, it is the *film* that speaks through him. The film effectively stages a ventriloquist act, where expert testimony is given on behalf of the film.

The editing strategy employed in *Nazi Designers of Death* functions in a similar way. Unlike in narrative cinema where editing is used to establish temporal and spatial continuity, in expository documentaries the mechanics of editing instead support "rhetorical continuity."[19] Russian footage of the liberation of Auschwitz is used as a backdrop for the voiceover narrator, who explains that in 1945 when the Soviet Army liberated Auschwitz "members of the KGB took all the documents that they could find, and transported them to a secret library in Moscow." Rossiter then uses a cutaway to a contemporary shot of Moscow, a cold snowy industrialized landscape, and then before the voiceover continues cuts to an interior of a clinical hallway, bathed in the colors that we associate with drab Soviet bureaucracy, "There since 1945, access to these documents has been denied to anyone." The interior hallway shot — presumably in the secret library — is framed through a peephole in the door, and as the narrator mentions a denial of access, the peephole is slammed shut with a loud thud, and the screen cuts to black. The imagery corresponds to the audio track — however, not in the form of archival footage, but as an abstracted visual tapestry, something akin to mood music in narrative cinema, that supports the scripted voice-of-God narration. The imagery in this case is there to establish a *mood*, to give the *feeling* of an *exoticized* Russia closed for nearly half a century behind the Iron Curtain, where significant archival documents were secreted away, unseen until now by Western historians. The use of cutaways — to essentially fill the image track, analogous to use of non-diegetic mood music in narrative features — is a common feature of the expository documentary.

The six-episode 2005 series *Auschwitz: Inside the Nazi State* co-produced by KCET/BBC is an exceptional expository documentary on the historical development of Auschwitz from its earliest days as a POW camp to its eventual transformation into a factory of death. This documentary utilizes many different cutaway devices in the service of its rhetorical objectives. As an expository documentary it is largely instructive in nature, making extensive use of Linda Hunt's distinctive voiceover narration. The series utilizes highly produced re-enactments, dramatizing historical events. The re-enacted cutaways are generally desaturated, but in certain cases colors, for instance red Nazi festoons, might be highlighted for dramatic effect. The drained color scheme establishes a stylistic code that sets the re-enacted scenes apart from the documentary diegesis. The documentary also makes use of computer-generated imagery (CGI) to reconstruct facilities that no longer exist, including the gas chambers at Auschwitz. These animated cutaways follow the color scheme established with re-enactments. In addition to re-enactments and animated sequences, the series also includes exceptionally rare archival footage, including early tests of a gas chamber. The array of cutaway devices greatly enhances the instructive rhetoric of the series.

There are effectively two films in one in Kurt Gerron's 1944 documentary *The Fuhrer Gives a City to the Jews* (or *Theresienstadt*; *Der Fuhrer Schenkt den*

Juden Eine Stadt), one film effectively comments on the other. On the one hand, there is an interesting example of Nazi-produced propaganda directed by a camp internee, and on the other hand there is a meta-cinematic study of the first.[20] Originally shot in the summer of 1944 and finished in March of 1945, all known prints of the completed film were lost after the war; it exists today in a fragmentary state. And as an example of Nazi propaganda one might assume that Joseph Goebbels had a hand in its creation, but conflicts in the regime kept the film outside the jurisdiction of the Ministry of Propaganda. Its introductory title cards leave no doubt about its intentions — not as a piece of propaganda as such but as a historical record, or a study of the Nazi propaganda machine. Imprinted at the top right corner of the film, just so there is no confusion while the film is running, "staged Nazi film" anchors the film as a heuristic exercise. When we are tempted to buy the lies presented on film, thinking to ourselves, "It doesn't seem so bad," the labeling intends to disabuse the spectator of any such idea.

Reading the film as an example of Nazi propaganda, it easily fits within the paradigm of expository documentary, bearing many of the conventional trademarks associated with it — for instance, voiceover narration and dressing the rhetoric of persuasion in the guise of "neutral information." As for the meta-cinematic film, though, this could be read one of two ways, first as having the qualities of a reflexive documentary precisely because it directs our attention to the production of the original 1944 film. On the other hand, though, it does not necessarily call attention to the production of the meta-film, the 1991 reconstructed film, and in this respect it might share more affinities with the expository mode because the titles at the beginning of the film, and the omnipresent "staged Nazi film" emblazoned across the top right corner of the screen functions in exactly the same way that the voice-of-God narrator does, dictating precisely how the images on-screen are to be read. While there are indeed some fascinating reflexive elements of *The Fuhrer Gives a City to the Jews*, the film is read through the lens of the expository mode here (a film such as this illustrates how Nichols's documentary modes need to be mobilized in a nuanced way, rather than treating them as rigidly fixed paradigms).

The film features the Theresienstadt concentration camp, or Terezín as the locals called it, which was situated in Nazi-occupied Czechoslovakia, about 40 miles north of Prague. Theresienstadt was quite different from the other camps; it was specifically established as a showcase camp, opening in the fall of 1941 where many of the "cultured Jews" of the Nazi-occupied territories were sent. Officially, Theresienstadt was decreed an "autonomous ghetto" by the Nazis, but in reality it was a transit camp where internees would eventually be transported to the East, a euphemism for a transport destined for a death camp. Many transported from Theresienstadt ended up in Auschwitz.[21] The director of *The Fuhrer Gives a City to the Jews*, Gerron, was one of Theresienstadt's "cultured" internees; he famously starred along with Marlene Dietrich in Josef von Sternberg's 1930 film *The Blue Angel*, playing Kiepert, the magician. Among the high-profile examples of the Nazis' charade at Theresienstadt was an opera, "Brundibar," performed by internee children, and staged for the Danish Red Cross (June 23,

1944), designed to silence any rumors that the Germans were systematically killing European Jewry. Prior to the visit by the Red Cross conditions were quite bleak, but after continued pressure from the Danish government — following the detention of 450 Danish Jews — Nazi officials embarked on a beautification campaign to spruce up the camp before the Red Cross arrived, and in order to mitigate the overcrowding 7,500 internees were transported to Auschwitz.[22] The shooting of Gerron's film took place several weeks following the Danish Red Cross's visit.

Gerron was interned on February 26, 1944, and during his internment organized a cabaret in the camp. Obviously, the documentary film *The Fuhrer Gives a City to the Jews* was not his idea, but rather created at the behest of the SS, which supervised the film every step of the way. The shoot took 11 days and Gerron, as Karel Margry contends, was effectively demoted to assistant director midway through the shooting. The Prague-based production company Aktualita had been brought in for the shoot, and its managing director Karel Pecency stepped into the role of director. Gerron nevertheless remained on set and organized the production. Regardless of his role, Gerron would never see the finished film; he was transported to Auschwitz on October 28, 1944, where he was immediately sent to the gas chamber (the following day Himmler ordered the gas chambers shut down). Aktualita handled the post-production of the film, and cut it to the liking of German officials. Donning the guise of neutral reportage, the film supposedly demonstrated just how good life was in Nazi concentration camps. However, by the time the film was completed the world was well aware of the truth.[23]

It is interesting to compare Malcolm Clarke and Stuart Sender's 2002 documentary feature *Prisoner of Paradise* to *The Fuhrer Gives a City to the Jews*. The former film is a biographical documentary of Gerron, examining his status as one of Germany's most famous actors and filmmakers, his flight from the Nazis, internment and eventual execution at Auschwitz. A good deal of Gerron's Theresienstadt footage is used in the Clarke/Sender documentary to construct their film, which allows them also to seamlessly slip from the present into the past.

The film opens with two contemporary aerial shots of Theresienstadt; the second shifts from color to black and white and utilizes visual effects to age the contemporary material — adding scratches, a degree of graininess, and fluctuating tonal values — before the film cuts to era footage. By "aging" the contemporary shot the filmmakers create a smooth transition into the subsequent shots from the war era. The opening of *Prisoner of Paradise* effectively enacts the "transparent window" motif in this series of shots, suggesting that the spectator is about to get a rare look into the unmediated past. In addition to the opening shots a number of other contemporary shots (e.g., shots taken from a train) are highly desaturated, almost entirely drained of all color, similar to the reenactments in *Auschwitz: Inside the Nazi State*, and are used as cutaways to maintain the illusion that the spectator is seeing things how "they really were."

These editing and compositional "conceits" are indicative of the expository mode. *Prisoner of Paradise* applies other expository conventions as well, including voiceover narration, and an editing strategy that privileges rhetorical cohesion. For instance, when Gerron moves to Paris as the environment becomes increasingly hostile towards Jews in Germany, the voiceover narrates over stock aerial footage of the city of Paris "renowned for its tolerance and culture," cutting to a Parisian gate with the Eiffel Tower in the background, "there was perhaps no other city in Europe more welcoming to creative artists." In the proclamation that the city is "welcoming," the gate flings open, offering a visual analogue to the voice-of-God narration. This is set to non-diegetic music, which is marked with an accordion further signifying "Frenchness." The aerial footage, the gate flinging open, and the non-diegetic score have nothing to do with Gerron, but form an audio/visual tapestry that embellishes the rhetorical cohesion of the documentary narrative.

As a Holocaust victim Gerron's case is somewhat unusual insofar as he left behind a vast body of *very public* visual evidence, appearing or starring in many films, as well as working as a director and having a successful stage career. On certain occasions *Prisoner of Paradise* utilizes this material detached from its original narrative source, and deployed as "stock footage." For instance, the voiceover narrator informs the spectator that living in Paris wasn't easy for Gerron, and he had to forfeit many of the luxuries he enjoyed in Germany, as the camera zooms into a contemporary shot of Gerron's Parisian apartment. The voiceover continues by noting that this is "certainly a step down from the grand style of his Berlin apartment, but far from uncomfortable." The film then cuts to a narrative-fiction film, where a character (played by Gerron), obviously intoxicated and surrounded by others, reaches into his pockets and pulls out some cash, "The only worry was how to pay for it. The high-life Gerron loved so much was now beyond his means, yet despite being almost penniless he could still be enormously generous." The sentiments of generosity are cut with images from a narrative film of Gerron pouring champagne for his fellow revelers (fig. 10.1). Shorn from the original context of a narrative film, it is Gerron himself that serves as the visual analogue working in the service of the documentary's rhetorical assertions.

Figure 10.1

This is all the stranger, as it is precisely this narrative strategy that Fritz Hippler utilizes in his 1940 Nazi propaganda film *The Eternal Jew* (sometimes given as *The Wandering Jew*), which in fact *Prisoner of Paradise* references.[24] Hippler's film, although filled with lies and designed with nefarious intentions, adopts the very documentary form that *Prisoner of Paradise* uses, and like the latter film recontextualizes the image of Gerron, torn from a narrative feature film, but in this case frames the images in such a way to render Gerron as the anti-Semite's archetype of the gluttonous Jew who enjoys grotesque humor. The narrator recites in *Prisoner of Paradise*, over a freeze frame of *The Eternal Jew*, which itself is extracted from a comedy featuring Gerron (fig. 10.2): "Taking clips from some of his best known roles the Nazis chose Gerron to symbolize everything they despised about the Jews. He was unwittingly used in a sophisticated propaganda campaign designed by Goebbels to set the stage for an unthinkable future." The irony of such a double reappropriation goes unaddressed, seemingly without any sort of self-reflection about its own use of clips from Gerron films. This is not to suggest that *Prisoner of Paradise* is in some fashion morally suspect; there is no intention to equate the two films either. Rather, the intention here is to indicate *how* the documentary genre recontextualizes original source material for its own rhetorical purposes.[25]

Figure 10.2

THE POWER OF THE ARCHIVE

There is little doubt about the power and potency that archival materials offer us, particularly given the Nazis' history in veiling their genocidal program behind secrecy and euphemisms. There is nevertheless a risk in relying heavily on archival visual material to generate meaning. Such images are prone to be treated as fetish objects, and by acquiescing in the available visual archival material — figured as representative of *the* Holocaust — we might heedlessly accept these "substitute" images for those things that have no visual representation. There is in fact no visual record of the gas chambers *in operation*; this does not mean, however, that they did not exist. In addition, fixating on the existing body of the visual archive potentially prompts a foreclosure in critical engagement. What frequently warrants the spectator's most considered reflection is not what *is* represented, that which *manifests* in visual form, but what *is not* represented (or cannot be represented). Claude Lanzmann refused to incorporate archival material into his documentaries for similar reasons (discussed in the following chapter).

Insofar as our understanding of the Holocaust is premised on archival material, Elizabeth Cowie contends that the visual record of it presents us with something of a paradox because, "seeing does not translate into a simple and proper knowing."[26] Despite the adage, "seeing is believing," the rhetoric of the image is always contingent on innumerable considerations, for instance, framing and composition of the image, the interplay of audio design (e.g., music, voiceover narrative) with the image, the ways in which that visual material might be contextualized in a documentary narrative diegesis (e.g., labeled, set in a particular editing strategy), and so forth. Holocaust deniers are just as apt to use some of the *same* visual material to "prove" their point. They might, for instance, point to the vivid carnage at Bergen-Belsen (fig. 10.3) where hundreds, if not thousands, of bodies lay strewn across the open areas of the camp as evidence of the fact that people died of disease (e.g., typhus), and not an orchestrated plan to commit genocide. And in a sense such a reading of the material is not altogether "wrong," although it has to be pointed out that one also has to *willfully* ignore a preponderance of other evidence to arrive at such a preposterous conclusion. Bergen-Belsen was not an extermination camp, and in fact many of those that died in Belsen died as a result of disease and malnutrition.

Figure 10.3

The archival visual material recording the liberation of the concentration camps is some of the most potent — epistemologically and emotively — film ever recorded.[27] *Memory of the Camps*, created under the supervision of British media magnate Sidney Bernstein, is a documentary made from footage shot by Allied forces immediately following the liberation of Auschwitz, Bergen-Belsen, Buchenwald, Dachau, Ebensee, Ludwigslust, Mauthausen, Ohrdruf, and other camps. The film is commonly but mistakenly attributed to Alfred Hitchcock.[28] While he functioned as an advisor to the film (he was friends with Bernstein), he is not the film's director. The intention of the film was to illustrate to the German people the magnitude of the Nazi regime's crimes against humanity; however, it was ultimately not finished until 1984, when it was exhibited at the Berlin Film Festival. The film that exists today is incomplete and only hints at its original intended scope and purpose. The graphic nature of the imagery used is nevertheless nothing short of horrific.

The film opens with clips from Leni Riefenstahl's famous 1935 film *Triumph of the Will*, setting the stage to indict the regime as the architects of genocide. Immediately following is some of the most horrific but iconographic imagery from the Holocaust. Harry Oakes and Mike Lewis of the British Army's Film and Photographic Unit (AFPU) shot this documentation of the liberation of the Bergen-Belsen camp on April 15, 1945.

The Bergen-Belsen footage depicts massive pits filled with emaciated corpses, and former guards and administrators of the camp carrying thousands of bodies to the hastily dug mass graves. Many, if not familiar with *Memory of the Camps*, have seen bits and pieces of these shocking images in other films, which have utilized this archival material. While the power of these images has been drawn on repeatedly and has effectively come to signify the horrors of the Holocaust, Toby Haggith astutely observes that, "the scenes at Belsen, however appalling, do not represent the Holocaust."[29] Haggith reminds us that "Belsen was not an extermination camp; Auschwitz-Birkenau, Chelmno, Sobibor and Treblinka were, and people died there because they were murdered within hours of arriving, not through disease or starvation."[30] The iconography of human suffering and abjection embodied in the Belsen footage, has — right or wrong — effectively become *the* representation of the Holocaust, though, and documentaries that examine the Holocaust in general, or a camp like Auschwitz, might utilize the Belsen imagery as a "substitute," because of the scarcity of archival visual material documenting other camps, or because of the sheer potency of the imagery itself.

It appears that the original concept of the film was to utilize Bergen-Belsen and Auschwitz as bookends, detailing some of the most vivid displays of the Nazis' contempt for humanity. The body of the film was then filled out with other illustrations of the horrors perpetrated on behalf of the German regime. Jovial German women, for instance, are seen coming to the Buchenwald camp to discover the truth of the genocidal program. On exhibit besides countless corpses are the artifacts associated with the infamous Ilse Koch (although the film never names her), tattooed human skin, a lampshade fashioned from human skin, and two shrunken heads of Polish escapees who were recaptured.[31] (Koch and her crimes are discussed at some length in Chapter 8.)

In the latter part of the film there is an abrupt break. The Russians liberated Auschwitz on January 27, 1945 and *Memory of the Camps* indicates that a Russian cameraman shot the final segment of the film. This footage however, was never delivered. Instead title cards inform us that, "The reel is missing, but the script is intact. This is how the narration concludes." As the film continues, it returns to the footage shot at Bergen-Belsen. The Auschwitz reel was intended to be the most damning, because Auschwitz-Birkenau was specifically designed as a death camp, and it was the Nazis' largest industrialized center of mass murder. The narration is didactic in its conclusion, proclaiming that: "Thousands of German people were made to see for themselves, to bury the dead, to file past the victims. This was the end of the journey they had so confidently begun in 1933. Twelve years? No, in terms of barbarity and brutality they had traveled backwards for

12,000 years. Unless the world learns the lesson these pictures teach, night will fall. But, by God's grace, we who live will learn."

A similar film attributed to Billy Wilder, *Death Mills* (1945), was also made the same year and was intended to be shown to the German people.[32] As the opening title card indicates, the film was not intended for the American public, and is not to be screened "without permission of the War Department."[33] *Memory of the Camps* and *Death Mills* in fact share some footage in common, and this film too exhibits some of the most iconographic images that we associate with the concentration camps. The similarities are no accident, because of their shared footage and original intent. *Memory of the Camps* was something of an amorphous production, relying on American and Russian collaboration in addition to the AFPU.

Adopting the rhetoric of reportage, *Death Mills* is situated comfortably in the expository mode, and employs the voice-of-God convention throughout. In some of the imagery Allied forces commanded the nearby townspeople, municipal officials, and Nazi authorities to take a tour of a camp that sat on the outskirts of their town. In one shot we see cheerful citizenry marching off to Buchenwald. "They started their trip as if they were going on a picnic. After all, it was only a short walk from any German city to the nearest concentration camp." Faces turn glum, though, when they encounter what lies beyond the barbwire fences, "But there was no picnic behind the barbwire, death was the only one that visited here." Much of the same footage is used in *Memory of the Camps*, and narrated in a similar way. In the parade of Germans filing past evidence of crimes committed supposedly on their behalf, the sight visibly horrifies some. The narrator in *Death Mills* does not offer reprieve for these ordinary Germans, illustrating how German industry and farming was complicit in the Nazis' factories of death.

In the latter part of the film Wilder makes effective use of montage, coupled with a brooding voiceover narration. Juxtaposed with the image of Germans filing past row upon row of corpses from the concentration camps, Wilder cuts in the throng of crowds at the Nuremberg Rally (documented in *Triumph of the Will*). Wilder uses cross-dissolves (fig. 10.4) to emphasize this by superimposing imagery from the past and the present tense of the film: these people cheering for the Nazi Party are the same people that now hang their heads in shame and sickened by the abject horror. The film begins with a parade of ordinary Germans marching with shovels and 1,100 crosses intended for the graves of the victims that suffocated when the Nazis locked them in a barn and set it ablaze, and this is where the film ends as well. In the closing shot, the narrator offers a final admonishment: "Remember, if they bear heavy crosses now, they are the crosses of the millions crucified in Nazi death mills."

While *Death Mills* clearly "manipulates" the material, through voiceover commentary and image juxtaposition, Hitchcock advised Bernstein to use a different approach in the making of *Memory of the Camps*. Concerned that many would think that the liberation footage was fabricated, he suggested a particular editing strategy to foreclose any such notion. The editors of the film were counseled to "avoid all tricky editing and to use as far as possible long shots and panning shots

Figure 10.4

with no cuts, which panned for example from the guards onto the corpses."[34] Also, in order to connect the concentration camp to the outside world Hitchcock advised that the film should include "German villagers being forced to visit one of the liberated camps."[35] The editing and compositional strategy that Hitchcock suggested is characteristic of the ethnographic genre, which is also concerned with capturing "objective truth." The conventional shooting code of an ethnographic film frequently utilizes medium long shots, or long shots. The camera is situated as *outside* the space of examination, positioned as an "objective" observer of an event. There is an inclination to shoot from a distance because the connotation of close-ups is that a filmmaker is being "partial" (in all senses — i.e., revealing a certain preference, and not showing the whole picture, or on the other hand hiding something), thus the wide-angle shot is perceived as capturing events in context. Close-ups, when they are used, are employed to provide specific "forensic" detail as Toby Haggith calls it — a tattooed serial number, the facial expression of a corpse, etc.[36] And in keeping with this "objective" perspective the camera is typically fixed; camera movement, if there is any, is usually limited to smooth pans, tilts, or tracking shots (e.g., from a vehicle) with the intention of keeping the figures on screen within the center of the frame and fully embodied.

These compositional strategies are intended to preserve the integrity of the spatial field, but the privileging of the long take is the editing device that safeguards the veracity of the temporal dimension. The long take embodies "real time," which is imagined as more truthful. Editing always suggests choice, and threatens to undermine the integrity of temporal continuity. If, however, a long take is not practical, say for example when footage is simply not available, or unusable for one reason or another, in the place of "real time" as embodied in the long take, the use of rhetorical narrative helps to bridge the discrepancies between "film time," and "real time." An inspection of *Memory of the Camps* reveals that these are precisely the strategies deployed, and what are often associated with the ethnographic genre. This is perhaps what sets *Death Mills* apart: its employment of more visible and faster-paced editing.[37]

The unflinching rawness of the imagery presented in *Memory of the Camps*, perhaps even in its admission that its last reel is missing, leads one to imagine that the documentary offers unmediated access to the horrors of Nazi brutalities. These images, though, are every bit as constructed as any other documentary, so when this Allied footage was being considered for the film, and how to construct the narrative:

> There was much discussion as to what could be released to the newsreels . . . although the only sequences which [Peter] Tanner [brought on to edit the film] recalled actually being ordered deleted by the censor were of a British sergeant kicking a German guard, and American film of a [camp] guard being stabbed by an inmate with a concealed knife just after the leading vehicle had smashed open the gates of the camp.[38]

While the objective of *Memory of the Camp* was to condemn the regime, and in no uncertain terms foist responsibility upon the German people, the filmmakers (and British and American authorities) also had no intention of conveying the message that Germans should expect to face vigilante justice (as sweet as it might have been for viewers sympathetic to the Allied forces); this was not the narrative that they wanted to convey.

And the cameramen who shot these images were not unreflective conduits of unmediated reality. Quite to the contrary, the cinematographers were well aware of their responsibilities, both in terms of military operations (e.g., propaganda), and to humanity writ-large. Harry Oakes and Mike Lewis of the AFPU had specific ideas in mind while shooting. While Oakes tried to locate specific angles that evoked the horror of the scene, "Lewis recalled incorporating a spade that looked like a cross near a grave to give the image extra symbolic power."[39] Haggith also calls attention to some of the more obvious "allegorical references in the framing, notably naked male bodies splayed, martyr-like"[40] (fig. 10.5). Subsequently, even when conforming to the conventions that we associate with ethnographic film, the image is never neutral. Haggith agrees, he concludes, that "we can appreciate this archival footage [i.e., Oakes and Lewis's] as a highly mediated visual record of the camps, which has in turn constrained and influenced the work of those directors who have chosen to incorporate it in their films about the Holocaust."[41]

Figure 10.5

Death Mills was the product of a decision to make a shorter film, and to get it out to the German public as quickly as possible. American authorities felt that they could not afford to wait for several more months, which was the timeframe that the Bernstein film was working with. (*Memory of the Camps* runs approximately an hour, whereas *Death Mills* is only 20 minutes.) Owing in part to the American production and release of *Death Mills*, Bernstein's film eventually was shelved. Internal politics and the fact that the film was dependent on the Russians delivering a copy of their footage for the last reel (which never arrived), the project simply fell by the wayside. The power of the images of sheer horror transcend everything, however; the raw index of human suffering and brutality seem to cut through the politics of representation, through the crafting of narrative, and pack an emotional punch like nothing else.

Chapter Eleven

Holocaust Documentaries II: Testimonials

INTRODUCTION: THE ART OF TESTIMONY

The previous chapter discussed some of the general cultural assumptions about the documentary genre, and specifically that the documentary form is burdened with a presumptive fidelity to objectivity, that the genre is perceived to be a conduit through which an unmediated accounting of the Holocaust is transmitted. Documentaries perpetuate these problematic assumptions by adopting modes that veil their construction — as outlined in Bill Nichols's expository, interactive, and observational modes discussed in the previous chapter — operating under the illusion that narratives "tell themselves;" as if unprompted they emerge organically on-screen. And when documentaries incorporate witnesses into their narrative — manifesting in the form of testimony — the presumption is that the documentary provides the spectator with unassailable admittance to what "really happened." No matter how you cut it, though, or from which angle you approach it, testimony is, and always will be, an art form. Documentaries that rely heavily on testimonial accounts frequently adopt the interactive mode, where the filmmaker/interviewer is a social actor in the diegetic space, exchanging with the filmed subject. However, other testimonial forms attempt to mediate the participatory exchange in an effort to preserve the illusion of organic conveyance — from historical event to narration.

Institutions like the Fortunoff Video Archive for Holocaust Testimonies[1] and the Shoah Foundation Institute for Visual History and Education, and academic disciplines (e.g., history, oral historians) have tried to mitigate the problematic venture of collecting testimonies by applying some standard guidelines on how testimonial accounts are to be recorded and conducted. The Shoah Foundation, which is housed at the University of Southern California, has amassed "nearly 52,000 videotaped testimonies from Holocaust survivors and other witnesses, [and] is the largest visual history archive in the world."[2] They have established protocols for the ways in which interviewers should interact with the subject providing testimony, as well as a formalized procedure for shooting them.

Founded in 1994 by Steven Spielberg in the wake of the success of *Schindler's List* (1993), the Shoah Foundation has trained over 2,000 interviewers in 24 countries.[3] Testimonies have been recorded in 32 different languages and from 56 different countries. The scrupulous effort to maintain consistency and quality is maintained by professionals in the field, including Holocaust historians and oral historians. The objective of these codified structures is to garner from each testimonial account "a life history and describes events before, during, and after the war."[4]

A life history is expected, according to the Shoah Foundation guidelines, to average anywhere from a two to two-and-a-half-hour recorded testimony. Interviewees are encouraged to structure the testimony chronologically, and the interviewer should only interject when the subject finds it difficult to express themselves, or is jumping from one chronological moment to another. Consistent with strategies in historical discourse, chronological narrative coherence is at once a logistical organizing principle, but it also bridges fissures in a "life history" compressed into a finite space. As the mission of the Shoah Foundation is to collect testimonies, not interviews as such, the guidelines suggest that, "The ideal interview consists of open-ended questions that allow the interviewee's testimony to flow."[5] Although prompting and steering the testimony is generally avoided, the guidelines for the interviewer do suggest that when videotapes in the videocamera are changed, they "should use the tape breaks to give the interviewee encouragement, and to point out topics that may have been omitted and topics that will be covered in the next tape."[6] Claude Lanzmann, the director of the 1985 film *Shoah*, addressed at length later, reveals that getting witnesses to speak can be challenging, "Some [witnesses] were crazy and incapable of conveying anything. They had lived through experiences so extreme that they could not communicate anything."[7] The task then for documentary filmmakers (or historians for that matter) is to *assemble* narratives from which the spectator might derive some meaning.

The Shoah Foundation testimonies are an incredibly rich site for research and learning, and the database that the foundation maintains makes the task of conducting searches exceptionally easy. Researchers can search names, or keywords, and by adding search criteria can increasingly refine these searches, by, for instance, providing additional keywords, or searching for testimonies in a specific language, etc. Once a search has been sufficiently narrowed, the database will not only direct the user to a specific testimony, but to the precise moment in the testimonial account that addresses the researcher's selected subject. It is accessible at 24 institutions in five different countries.[8]

To ensure relative consistency between the tens of thousands of testimonial accounts each interviewer is provided with training, and videographers are provided with a set of guidelines, with the general expectation that interviewees will be set at three-quarter profile in soft high-key lighting. For the most part witnesses deliver testimony in their homes.[9] As outlined in the protocols for videographers, the composition of the Shoah Foundation testimonies is in keeping with the conventions of ethnographic film (discussed in the previous chapter), trading in the currency of "objectivity" by maintaining a critical distance from the subject, and remaining "outside" the field of examination; aside from the initial introduction interviewers are instructed to remain off-screen and limit their inter-actions. The subject delivering testimony is not fully embodied as they typically are in ethnographic film, though, which is heavily reliant on long and medium long shots; rather, the testimonies are presented either in medium or medium close-up. The Shoah Foundation guide for videographers directs camera operators:

> Once the interview has begun you should very slowly zoom in to a comfortable close shot. Be sure to avoid extreme close-ups. Once the close shot has been established, do not zoom in or out. Such camera moves would add editorial comment to the testimony, thereby compromising its historical validity.[10]

Elsewhere the guidelines indicate the importance of *not* cutting during pauses or emotional breakdowns because, "These are historical testimonies, raw archi-val footage, the content of which is considered valuable material to scholars, researchers, academicians, etc."[11] It is clear that the testimonial accounts are couched in the discourse of "objectivity," attempting to mitigate — wherever possible — influencing the delivery and reception of the testimonial account.

Housed at Yale University, the Fortunoff Video Archive for Holocaust Testimonies takes a different approach. Where the Shoah Foundation goes at great length to mitigate the impression of an editorial hand, specifically in the videography, the Fortunoff Video Archive utilizes compositional strategies that we associate with narrative film. A select group of testimonies are readily available online, and a quick survey of these reveals some striking differences, compared to the Shoah Foundation testimonies. To begin with, the video material accessible online has been edited into 30-minute excerpts, but perhaps more significant than the fact that the online material has been edited is that the aesthetic strategies differ quite widely. While the Shoah Foundation encourages videographers to frame the witnesses in three-quarter profile, with the Fortunoff testimonies tend to be framed more or less straight on. In addition, while the Shoah Foundation requires videographers to frame the subjects in "a comfortable close shot," which typically materializes as a medium close-up, the Fortunoff tes-timonies are shot in a variety of different ways — anywhere from a medium long shot to a very tight close-up. The Shoah Foundation all but forbids videographers from zooming in or out on a subject, fearing that such techniques compromise the historical validity of the testimony; Fortunoff videographers (apparently) are under no such obligation, and are free to make creative decisions during the shoot. What results is a very different treatment of Holocaust testimony.

Just to take one example, the testimony that Auschwitz survivor Helen K. (HVT-8035) provides concludes on a fairly dramatic note. She recounts how, after being separated from her family and her husband, she was reunited with her husband. The interviewer, sitting off-screen, asks, "What did you say when you first saw your husband again? What did you say to each other?" Giving a sigh, framed in close-up (shoulders up) Helen K. says, "Oh, I don't know." Shaking her head, and stumbling on her words slightly, struggling to keep her emotions in check, "This, you know, the man I married and the man he was after the war, wasn't the same person. And I'm sure I was not the same person either when I was at sixteen." With this emotive testimony the videographer slowly zooms in to get an even tighter close-up, as she continues to convey her increasingly emotive story. The videographer's pretension to zoom in corresponds proportionally to the emotional charge of the testimony that continues to ratchet up, until finally the shot lingers in a very tight close-up.

Although the tone and genre of testimony remains intact, the framing of the Fortunoff testimonies changes the meaning. The *form* changes the *content*, and if not changing it, then, *adding* something to it. The zooming into a close-up effectively says, "this is important," "this is dramatic," compelling the audience to feel likewise, but also — if only unconsciously — directing the spectator to what elements of the testimony are deemed most significant. The videographer is editorializing here, embellishing a testimony with the aesthetics of dramatic narrative, as Jean Epstein notes, "The close-up is an intensifying agent because of its size alone." But in the shift of proportions, Epstein adds later, "Pain is within reach. If I stretch out my arm I touch you, and that is intimacy. I can count the eyelashes of this suffering. I would be able to taste the tears."[12] This is precisely why the Shoah Foundation outlines such rigorous protocols for the videographer. This is not to say, however, that the static camera is neutral; the static camera utilized in Shoah Foundation testimonies is effectively contextualizing the testimonies in the discourse of science by adopting the techniques that we might associate with ethnographic films — the outside "objective" observer. The truth is, no matter which way you cut it, the art of testimony is always already subjective.[13]

Focusing on a single subject very quickly reveals other problematic issues with testimonial accounts, and the artistry required in utilizing them in documentary films (or narrating history). Let's take, for example, a search that I conducted at the Shoah Foundation, typing the keyword "Mala Zimetbaum" into the keyword database. Zimetbaum was a Polish-born Belgian Jew interned at Auschwitz; Wanda Jakubowska's 1947 film *The Last Stage* is a fictionalized account of her story (discussed in Chapters 2 and 4). A well-trusted internee, Zimetbaum worked as a translator and "runner" couriering information from one end of the camp to another. Taking advantage of her privileges, Zimetbaum, along with a male internee, Edek Galinski, escaped, only to be recaptured sometime later. To make an example of her, Zimetbaum was to be hung in front of the female internees in Birkenau; however, before the Nazis could execute her she slashed her wrists with a razorblade and slapped a German officer. There are 49 testimonial accounts catalogued in the Shoah Foundation video database that reference

Zimetbaum, 11 of which are in English. Owing to the fact that this event took place in the women's camp, most of the testimonial accounts are from women. Every single one of these testimonial accounts is different, and some of them are utterly irreconcilable.

A number of the accounts describe Zimetbaum slashing her own wrists with a razorblade. Eva Baumohl says that the razorblade was hidden in her hair, while Sylvia Fishman says that it was hidden in her shoe, and Malvina Mira Gold-Kornhauser recalls Zimetbaum hiding the instrument in her shirt pocket; others are not sure how she got the razorblade, but report that she slit her wrists. While some vividly describe this detail, many of the accounts make no reference to a razorblade whatsoever, or to Zimetbaum's bleeding wrists.

In Fishman and Gold-Kornhauser's account Zimetbaum strikes a German officer, while Pearl Pufeles simply says that some blood dripped on an officer, and others make no mention of this. In some accounts Zimetbaum is taken away, and in others (Dora Freilich, Lea Ganik, Magda Moldovan, Pearl Pufeles) she is hung; Sari Roer reports that she was hung days later. One of the things that sets Pufeles's account apart from so many of the others is that she recalls both co-conspirators being executed at the same time, saying that Galinski was hung first.

There are certain elements of these testimonial accounts that simply cannot be rectified; the discrepancies are simply too vast to bridge. There is no intention to discredit any of the testimonies. We must accept the testimonies in the spirit that they are given: the utmost sincerity. The point here is to illustrate that testimonial accounts are inherently imperfect — memories fade, recollections can get confused, context might radically change one's perspective, inaccuracies might mingle with "faithful" accounts of an event. What we must come to terms with is acknowledging the artistry in delivering and utilizing testimonial accounts, and perhaps most of all, realizing that there *is no* transparent window onto the past. We might never be able to assemble *the* truth, or *the* history of the Holocaust, but it is possible to construct *a* truth, and *a* history of the Holocaust.

This is precisely why Claude Lanzmann, director of the 1985 documentary *Shoah* (unrelated to the Shoah Foundation), says that, "Memory horrifies me: recollections are weak. The film [*Shoah*] is the abolition of all distance between past and present; I relive this history in the present."[14] To one degree or another, the Shoah Foundation also recognizes the fragility of memory, and urges its interviewers *not* to intervene if an

> interviewee cannot recall a particular fact about his/her experience, or says something historically inaccurate (e.g., an incorrect date or fact), the interviewer should refrain from directly correcting or confronting the interviewee. Instead, interviewers are encouraged to try to verify the correct information gently, by asking a clarifying question, or to probe deeper in order to trigger the memory.[15]

But "probing deeper" into a memory is no guarantor of accuracy; this misses the point altogether.

MARCEL OPHÜLS'S TRILOGY OF INDIFFERENCE

Marcel Ophüls's *Trilogy of Indifference* consists of three long documentaries — *The Sorrow and the Pity* (1969; US 1972), *The Memory of Justice* (1976), and *Hotel Terminus: The Life and Times of Klaus Barbie* (1988) — that in one respect or another take the Nazi era, the atrocities that the regime perpetrated, and what has happened in the wake of the war as its subject. Ophüls insists, though, that "None of the films I've done — and especially not *Hotel Terminus* — is about the Holocaust. The link between cynicism, callousness, indifference, complicity, and crimes against humanity is what the film is about."[16] Nevertheless, the subject of *Hotel Terminus* is Klaus Barbie, who was stationed in Lyon (France) as head of the Gestapo, responsible for the torture and killing of members of the French Resistance (including its leader Jean Moulin), and the deportation of Jews. His reputation earned him the moniker "The Butcher of Lyon." The Hotel Terminus is where the Gestapo Headquarters were located in Lyon. In all probability Barbie was allowed to escape after the war, and worked for American intelligence. He is also alleged to have helped train paramilitary groups in Bolivia where he found refuge. Although he previously enjoyed the protection of the right-wing Bolivian government, in 1983 with a change in the government, Barbie (who was living under the alias of Klaus Altmann) was extradited to France where he stood trial for crimes against humanity. He was convicted a few years later, given a life sentence, and died in prison at the age of 77.

One of the strategies that Ophüls employs in *Hotel Terminus* is to juxtapose interviewees — one might say that Barbie reveled in beating people, and another saying that he would never sully himself in such a way. One might say that Barbie was a raging anti-Semite, while another suggests that he was nothing of the sort. Whatever the truth might be, we frequently find that there is a stark contrast between various accounts that are irreconcilable, and it is left to the spectator to determine where the truth might lie. Repeatedly in *Hotel Terminus* Christmas trees and Christmas decorations materialize in the domestic *mise en scène*, inviting an unsettling and stark contrast between Christian values of fellowship, charity, and brotherly love in relationship to the hatred, barbarity, and inhumanity embodied in the figure of Barbie. Like *Shoah*, Ophüls predominately utilizes the interactive mode, exchanging with his interlocutors, and functioning as a social actor within the frame. And while some of the tactics that Ophüls and Lanzmann use share certain traits — snide condescension directed towards ignorant or anti-Semitic interviewees — what sets Ophüls apart from Lanzmann is his penchant for humor. For instance, when Ophüls interviews Álvaro De Castro, a Bolivian associate of Barbie, he leaves the interviewee in a hotel room for an untold amount of time. De Castro fidgets, chats with the crew, checks his watch periodically. "Well, the time here," De Castro jokes, "in Bolivia, there's no 'official' time. Nothing's official." Ophüls notes that, "De Castro must be getting impatient in there," which is then cut to a shot of De Castro checking his watch. Ophüls finally enters from an adjoining room wearing a bathrobe. De Castro asks, "You were asleep?" Ophüls apologizes for being late and his appearance, feigning altitude sickness.

In a series of attempted interviews with former Gestapo, Ophüls arrives at people's doorsteps. Mounting the stairs of an apartment building, Ophüls is greeted at the door of Karl Heinz Muller, former Gestapo chief stationed in Toulouse, and asks, "Tell me: what crimes against the Reich could a 2-year-old girl commit?" The elderly Muller waves his hand in disgust and reaches to close the door, without saying a word. Muller hesitates for a moment, though, and then begins, "That little girl . . . I didn't even look . . . Whoever was there, signed. If I'd separated the little girl . . ." Offering this garbled feeble response, he gives up saying, "Oh, what's the use?" and then abruptly closes the door, loudly latching the deadbolt. Ophüls, somewhat bemused, smiles, "Wie bitte?" throws up his hands, and says, "Merry Christmas," as a Christmas carol is edited into the non-diegetic aural space; shots of storefronts decorated with Christmas decorations adds to the bitter irony of the interaction.

Ophüls searches for Bartelmus, one of Barbie's Gestapo deputies, and who dealt with Jewish affairs in Lyon. For his crimes Bartelmus was only given 10 years in prison. When he arrives in Trippstadt we are only offered shots of the town, and what is presumably the Bartelmus home. Ophüls politely asks off-screen, "Mrs. Bartelmus, is your husband here? I wanted to speak with Mr. Bartelmus." The (off-screen) voice of Mrs. Bartelmus diminutively responds, "I know, but my husband has no comment." A shot of a second storey house window closing from the inside corresponds to Mrs. Bartelmus's refusal on behalf of her husband. What follows is indicative of Ophüls's more comical approach to the subject. He strolls through some backyard gardens and calls, "Herr Bartelmus? Herr Bartelmus?" kneeling down to take a look under a garden tarp, "Herr Bartelmus?" as he looks inside a composting bin. In his absence, Bartelmus's mugshot is cut into the scene. Finally, a voice off-screen calls, "Excuse me, what are you looking for?" Suddenly encouraged, Ophüls answers, "Herr Bartlemus." "You won't find him there!" a neighbor calls from her second storey balcony. Ophüls is eventually asked to leave, so he takes his hide and seek game elsewhere. At a gas station a woman filling up her Mercedes laments that, "Old people should be left in peace, not hounded from place to place." Ophüls returns, "And the children who never grew old?"

Interactions such as these make for a pleasurable viewing experience (such as it can be given the subject matter), but it also serves a function: to extract information from the interviewee, and not just in what they say but also in their physical reaction to Ophüls. "To the extent that the film may be *about* the interactions itself," indeed the doors that literally slammed in Ophüls's face, non-cooperative interlocutors, these "failed" interviews say a great deal. A film like *Hotel Terminus*, as Bill Nichols argues, "leads less to an argument about the world than to a statement about the interactions themselves and what they disclose about filmmaker and social actor alike."[17] The revelations that material-ize come not simply from what is said but in the interactions. Moreover, editing contrary positions, or when accounts are juxtaposed one against another, these collisions of ideas generate meaning. "History and our historical imagination," Nichols observes, "is what is at stake." As with numerous other documentaries, in *Hotel Terminus* there is a strident contrast between the public history of the war era, and personal negotiations with it. "History and what we make of it is the excess that we engage through the representation of bodies. The documentary film is an active reassemblage of the body as the repository of personal meaning and of a utopian unconscious of collective values."[18] What *Hotel Terminus* illustrates is that there are sometimes discrepancies in the individual repositories of memory and official discourse that manifests in those collective values. And what Ophüls figures into his films "as subtextual acknowledgement, is that history hurts."[19]

Lanzmann and Ophüls share certain elements in common, but one of the things that distinguish the two is that the latter utilizes archival material, whereas Lanzmann famously has argued against its use. In Ophüls's case there is a tendency to use archival material for rhetorical purposes, rather than establishing any sort of spatial or temporal continuity, which is more indicative of the expository mode. For instance, when Ophüls interviews Wolfgang Gustmann, a former SS officer, at one point Gustmann recounts his meeting of Barbie, and vouches for his moral character, "I thought he was a fantastic guy," he says. In a shocking exchange Gustmann boasts of his service in the SS and is distinctly and unapologetically proud of it. After his diatribe, he notes, "I met Klaus Barbie in 1945, through a buddy. I was soon deeply impressed, and thought he was a great guy. It may sound far-fetched, but my dogs were just crazy about him. And I thought an animal could clearly tell the difference between good and evil." Perhaps somewhat taken aback, Ophüls asks, "Dogs?" As Gustmann confirms this there is a cut to archival material of a deportation (a common piece of footage found in numerous other documentaries including *Night and Fog*), where at the feet of some SS men is a dog. "What kind?" Ophüls asks. "Dachshunds," Gustmann replies. The archival image has nothing to do with the specifics of what Gustmann is addressing — i.e., the footage does not depict Gustmann's dog, nor does it have anything to do with Gustmann's relationship with Barbie — but it adds something to the rhetoric of the documentary, namely undercutting what Gustmann says by contradicting the suggestion that an animal can sense the difference between good and evil, as evident in the happy-go-lucky dog following on the heels of SS men who are in the process of deporting Jews.[20]

While Ophüls's films exhibit many of the characteristics of an interactive documentary, there are also expository elements as well. Ophüls does not shy away from promoting a specific point of view, and proclaims, "there is no such thing as objectivity! *The Sorrow and the Pity* is a biased film — in the right direction, I'd like to think — as biased as a Western with good guys and bad guys. But I try to show that choosing the good guy is not quite as simple as [the movies make it seem]."[21] Objectivity is not the issue here, though, as Ophüls's film are consistent with the characteristics of the expository and interactive modes, where a rhetorical argument is generated through the integration of archival material and the collection of exchanges between Ophüls and his interlocutors.

CLAUDE LANZMANN'S SHOAH

Shoah is a fiction rooted in reality . . . [22]

Claude Lanzmann's 1985 documentary *Shoah*, which runs over nine and one-half hours, is the quintessential Holocaust film. The filmmaker shot 350 hours worth of footage over the course of 11 years in 14 different countries.[23] He traveled between Europe, Israel, and the United States to assemble this vast body of eyewitness testimony. Lanzmann's film has received a lot of critical attention, almost all resoundingly positive, and rightfully so because not only does it convey invaluable "first-hand" accounts of the machinery of death, but it also subtly critiques the discourse of testimony and the documentary form by staging interviews in highly charged environments, using cutaways to various sites associated with the history of the Holocaust, and refusing to use archival footage.[24] In fact, in a very public dispute with Jean-Luc Godard, Lanzmann recently stated that were he to find actual footage of the gas chambers *in use* (no such footage has ever been found) he'd destroy it.[25] His reasoning being: that such a film would become a "fetish" object, fossilizing the Holocaust in the past, and would quash the important ongoing critical debates about how to represent the Holocaust.[26] This refusal to use archival material, and instead relying on testimony, was a guiding principle from the very beginning of his 11-year journey. Lanzmann is a very self-aware filmmaker, acknowledging the limits and the power of the documentary form to represent the Holocaust.

Shoah exhibits many of the traits of the interactive mode, which incorporates the filmmaker as a social actor within the film itself. Lanzmann not only converses with his subjects on-screen, but in one way or another he shapes or interacts with the events in the scene. The interactive mode, as Nichols uses it, tends to emphasize testimonial accounts or interlocution set to illustrative imagery that either support or contradict what a witness states.[27] What sets Lanzmann's work apart from so many other documentaries that utilize similar rhetorical strategies is that he makes no pretense to document *the* Holocaust, as if it were something that could be encapsulated into a single narrative. Lanzmann accepts that our knowledge of the Holocaust is inherently fragmentary and that there are parts that "cannot be conveyed."[28] This is why Lanzmann finds representations of the Holocaust — like the NBC 1978 television miniseries *Holocaust*, or Spielberg's 1993 film *Schindler's List* — so reprehensible, because the presumption is that the Holocaust is *knowable*, contained within the tidy sanitized narrative package, "that permit all kinds of reassuring identification. *Shoah*, however, is anything but reassuring."[29] The dramatic imperative — in the conventional three-act structure that most narrative films conform to, for instance — relies on a satisfying resolution, and for Lanzmann the Holocaust is not something that can be, or even should be, *resolved*.[30] Rather, it needs to be placed into a continuum of human experiences that requires continued re-evaluation.

Lanzmann avowedly refuses to characterize *Shoah* as a historical film (no doubt, though, he is keenly aware of the significance of the historical content in it); instead he approaches the Holocaust as a filmmaker, and is thus concerned with the dramatic impact within a scene, and constructing a compelling narrative. And although there is an inclination to organize a film such as this in chronological order, the architecture of the film is based on the principle of thematic coherence. Lanzmann rules out of hand linear narrative, or a narrative structure organized according to historical chronology, precisely because it harbors the potential to evoke a sense of closure, which is the last thing that Lanzmann wants. Insisting that *Shoah* is a work of art, not a documentary as such, the film works against the notion that it is merely a record of static memories. Lanzmann adamantly asserts that

> a film on the Holocaust has to be set out from the principle of the rejection of memory, the refusal to commemorate. The worst moral and artistic crime that can be committed in producing a work dedicated to the Holocaust is to consider the Holocaust as past. Either the Holocaust is a legend or it is present; in no case is it a memory.[31]

The magnitude, the scale, the horrific nature of the Holocaust lays before us a nearly insurmountable problem in representation. How then does one set about giving the Holocaust representational form, in the overwhelming sense of absence, sites that no longer exist, a lack of visible evidence, memories that have faded or lapsed into senility, the millions of corpses that have no voice, a tangled web of Nazi secrecy, lies, and euphemism? "I started precisely with the impossibility of recounting this history," Lanzmann says. He continues,

> I placed this impossibility at the very beginning of my work. When I started the film, I had to deal with, on the one hand, the disappearance of the traces: there was nothing at all, sheer nothingness, and I had to make a film on the basis of this nothingness. And, on the other hand, with the impossibility of telling this story even by the survivors themselves; the impossibility of speaking, the difficulty — which can be seen throughout the film — of giving birth to and the impossibility of naming it: its unnamable character.[32]

This is not to mean that Lanzmann acquiesces in an inability to represent the Holocaust. Quite to the contrary, it compels him forward in a Sisyphus-like fashion to probe further and further, acknowledging all the while that he will never fully *know* the Holocaust.[33]

The interactive mode allows Lanzmann to side-step some of the pitfalls of the more conventional expository documentaries. Where the expository mode tends to rely on archival material, which effectively necessitates speaking in the past tense, Lanzmann prefers "to make a film from life, exclusively in the present tense."[34] Lanzmann is present in the film with his interlocutors, circumventing the need for a voiceover narrative that dictates how the images on-screen are to be read. There are voiceover narratives in *Shoah*, though, spoken through the body of the witness. Filip Müller, a member of the Sonderkommando at Auschwitz, describes his harrowing duties, which he finds incredibly difficult to do, and he didn't want to speak about it. Lanzmann shot his testimony over the course of three days. The nature of the shoot made it impossible to use it as it was and necessitated the use of contemporary cutaways to the site Müller narrates: "The landscape lends the words an entirely different dimension, and the words reanimate the landscape."[35] Where other testimonial accounts are staged — e.g., the Bomba barbershop sequence, discussed shortly — in Müller's case "the staging is created by the editing."[36]

While *Shoah* is most comfortably situated in the paradigm of the interactive mode, there are elements of the expository mode evident in the film as well. Specifically Lanzmann incorporates historian Raul Hilberg, who functions as an "expert witness," testifying to certain aspects of the history of the Holocaust. Although Lanzmann adopts many of the same interview strategies, Hilberg's function is to contextualize the individual testimonies in a larger historical framework, which is more indicative of the expository mode.

Lanzmann is particularly interested in the machinery of death, and subsequently he focuses on subjects that are intimately familiar with the business of killing. *Shoah* is preoccupied with the "special squads," or Sonderkommando — Jews enlisted to do the dirtiest of work, guiding victims into the gas chambers, removing bodies from and cleaning the gas chambers after an execution, and cremating or otherwise disposing of the corpses. Likewise Lanzmann is preoccupied with agents of mass killing, the perpetrators. By focusing on the Sonderkommando and perpetrators he generates the clearest possible picture of the actual practice of genocide.

> I did not just want just any witnesses. There are many deportees. There are swarms of them, as an anti-Semite would say. But I wanted very special types — those who had been in the very charnel houses of extermination, direct witnesses of the death of their people: the people of the "special squads."[37]

Although bystanders are also featured in the film, because of their unique ability to testify to the specific mechanics of death, the Sonderkommando, and the perpetrators, are figured as privileged witnesses.

Many of the most memorable and poignant scenes in *Shoah* — and not to mention filled with some of the most impressive details about the actual workings of the machinery of death — are self-consciously staged. And despite the fact that Lanzmann stages scenes, this in no way impugns the testimonial account, rather his staging embellishes the scenes with heightened dramatic tension. Lanzmann's aggressive interviewing strategy is perhaps a product of his own background. A French Jew, Lanzmann fought in the resistance. Fearlessly confrontational, and willing to go to almost any means to recovery testimony, Lanzmann's film privileges the "need-to-know" over everything else, even his own personal safety.

Eliciting testimony from perpetrators necessitated adopting a pseudonym and clandestine recording tactics. On one occasion, though, family members of a German war criminal, a member of the *Einsatzgruppen*, discovered his concealed microphone and camera, leading to a physical confrontation where Lanzmann was severely beaten. As a result Lanzmann had to be hospitalized. The material from this incident disappeared.[38]

In his interview with former SS Unterscharfüher, Franz Suchomel, stationed at Treblinka, Lanzmann lies to his interviewee, saying that his identity will not be revealed; "Mr. Suchomel," Lanzmann says, "we're not discussing you, only Treblinka. You are a very important eyewitness, and you can explain what Treblinka was." Suchomel then responds, "But don't use my name." He reassures one of his key witnesses, "No, I promised."[39] Suchomel is also unaware that his interlocutor is Jewish. Shot with a hidden video camera, Lanzmann extracts from the former SS guard precise details about the machinery of death in Treblinka. Disregarding even a modicum of social etiquette, Lanzmann showed Suchomel, and others, false papers to disguise his identity and his real intentions. "I showed with arrogance that I lied to these men. And why not? Didn't they lie to Jews when they massacred entire families? They didn't respect the fundamental priority — life — so why should I observe moral rules with them?"[40] Ophüls admires Lanzmann's tactics. "I can hardly find the words to express how much I approve of this procedure, how much I sympathize with it," he says. "This is not a matter of means and ends, this is a matter of moral priorities."[41]

Annette Insdorf marvels at what *Shoah* achieves: "it contains no music, no voice-over narration, no self-conscious camerawork, no stock images — just precise questions and answers, evocative places and faces, and horror recollected in tranquility."[42] Insdorf is correct on all counts, save for one: "no self-conscious camerawork." *Shoah* is layered with incredibly evocative and resonant camerawork, which by its very nature is self-conscious. "I have a strong sense of urgency to relive all of it," Lanzmann insists,

> to retrace the steps. In Sobibor, when I ask where the boundary of the camp was, I go across the imaginary line; it becomes real. The zoom in to the sign "Treblinka" is a violent act. And for the tracking shot into Auschwitz, I push the dolly myself. If the film is a resurrection, it's because of how I was compelled to do it.[43]

Whether we are speaking of a dolly shot simulating the experience of a train pulling into Auschwitz, the strategic staging of a scene (e.g., the Bomba sequence), the penetrating zooms during dramatic moments, the hand-held camera walking through the ruins of a concentration camp as an interviewee details their experience, all of these shots are highly composed, self-consciously constructed scenes accompanying invaluable testimonies for effective purposes.

For the most part the film frames the testimonies as talking-heads, or so it seems at first glance. Stuart Liebman asserts that *Shoah* explodes the conventions of the talking-heads genre, making it radically different from a host of other films.[44] On occasion, as an individual details their memories of certain events, say for example a specific concentration camp, the camera will traverse the same narrated space, but obviously in its post-war state. The temporal and spatial disconnect between what is being described and the shots of a desolate and lonely landscape acknowledge the deficit in the documentary's ability to faithfully reconstruct a witness's account. And this is especially true of the Holocaust, because while these testimonial accounts are moving, and without doubt faithful to the individual's memory (with the possible exception of some of the Polish bystanders who seem to have rather selective memories, if not quite fantastic recollections, of Jewish deportations), we nevertheless run up against the frustrating fact that there is a *lack* of visual or tangible evidence.[45] Although the testimonial accounts are highly charged — historically and emotionally — the cutaways in *Shoah* are shockingly absent of corroborating content; we are dumbfounded not by what is presented but rather by the barrenness of the landscape, the melancholic void. These Holocaust sites are very different, and the horror that these places witnessed have long since been covered in grass or pristine snow. The spectator's desire for (visual) evidence for what happened there, to verify what is being said, is always frustrated.[46] But these melancholic voids "mean" something, and *mise en scène* plays a major part in the communicative power of the film.

The Treblinka site, like many of the others, is vexing, because there is "nothing" there, a monument stands where the death camp once stood. The Germans razed the camp, all traces of it have vanished, just as Lanzmann asserts: "The sites I saw were disfigured, effaced. They were 'non-sites' of memory [*non-lieux de mémoire*]. The places no longer resemble what they had been."[47] How then to represent something that is no longer there? What strategies are utilized to reincarnate what has been subject to erasure? In the combination of audio design, editing, and cinematography how does one set about making something from nothing?

Lanzmann's interview with Suchomel is exemplary of the techniques found in the film that negotiate this tremendous absence which fills the film; discussing the "funnel" — a 13 foot wide pathway that Jews, stark naked, were corralled through leading directly to the gas chamber — Lanzmann asks what the "funnel" was made of, if it was made of solid walls? Without recourse to what Suchomel actually describes, the film uses a cutaway of the site, now marked with thousands of broken erect stones; the camera uses long meditative takes of the landscape with long silent pauses, allowing the spectator to reflect on the void presented on-screen.

In Simone De Beauvoir's review of *Shoah*, which she showers with praise, she says that Lanzmann's film "succeeds in recreating the past with an amazing economy of means — places, voices, faces. The greatness of Claude Lanzmann's art is making places speak, in reviving them through voices and, over and above words, conveying the unspeakable through people's expressions."[48] Indeed, form is given to nothingness through the combination of editing, strategically cutting in cutaways to the sites that witnesses address; the cinematography, with the ghostly zooms, pans, tracking shots, which evoke the haunting presence of the dead; and the voices of the witnesses, which are then layered over and integrated into the sequences. For instance, as Suchomel describes the victims of Treblinka marching up the funnel to the gas chambers, the slow zoom is an ethereal gesture, a disembodied trace of the countless souls that marched off to their death. And this is all done without music, archival footage, or other motifs filmmakers adopt to negotiate what *is not there*. Lanzmann is unyielding in this respect, and has steadfastly adhered to an anti-mimetic principle: "the pictorial reproduction of the awful circumstances in which the Jews met death is not essential for — indeed, is a hindrance to — anamnesis, the calling to mind of the process of their death."[49]

The ability to make "places speak," and evoke the specter of the victims, is an artifact of carefully crafted scenes. "There are a lot of staged scenes in the film. It is not a documentary," Lanzmann insists. "The locomotive at Treblinka is *my* locomotive. I rented it at Polish Railways, which was not so easy to do, just as it was not a simple matter to insert it into the traffic schedule."[50] Just as in narrative film, Lanzmann *directs*, as he recalls while shooting the locomotive arriving at Treblinka, he told the conductor, "'You are to get up into the locomotive and we are going to film the arrival at Treblinka.' I said nothing else." Lanzmann then continues to explain, "We arrived at the station; he was there, leaning out, and on his own, he made this unbelievable gesture at his throat while looking at the imaginary boxcars (behind the locomotive, of course, there were no boxcars). Compared to this image, archival photographs become unbearable."[51] While there is artifice in the film, and Lanzmann is the first to say so, there are also details that invite the uncanny ghosts of history to materialize on-screen.

Despite the fact that the scene is completely "artificial," the Abraham Bomba sequence is one of the most compelling and emotive moments in *Shoah*, if not the history of cinema.[52] Lanzmann is the first person to admit that *Shoah* is contrived; nothing but a pure construction, and the Bomba sequence is exemplary of this. His encounter with Bomba is macabrely staged in a Tel Aviv barbershop, which Lanzmann rented to shoot this scene. The testimony told in the context of a barbershop at once produces something of "poetic beauty," and at the same time elicits the uncanny (that which is ghostly and disturbing). Bomba, who had worked as a barber all his life, was a member of the Sonderkommando while he was interned in the Treblinka concentration camp. It was his responsibility to cut women's hair immediately before they were gassed to death. Having previous knowledge of Bomba's experience — in fact, Lanzmann had already interviewed him privately — Lanzmann decided to shoot the scene in a barbershop and filmed Bomba's testimony as he cut someone's hair. In a 1990 Yale University seminar Lanzmann said that he "tried to create a setting where something could happen."[53] He continues,

> I knew what I wanted from him, what he had to say. There was a fantastic tension for him and for me. The tension was physical in this barber shop where nobody understood what was going on because all the other barbers were Hebrew-speaking

of Moroccan or Iraqi origin. . . . [Bomba and I] were a kind of island in the middle of the barber shop, a kind of ghetto, with an extreme tension.[54]

Indeed Lanzmann got what he wanted. Bomba set in this uncanny situation, provoked by Lanzmann's questions and almost sadistic insistence, broke down, momentarily seized with the weight of his own account, incapable of speaking.

Had the Bomba sequence been arranged as a conventional talking-head format, say, just for example, in Bomba's home, it is unlikely that the scene would have been as emotive for Bomba, or the spectator. Such self-conscious arrangements are in stark contrast with Ophüls, who routinely interviews his subjects in their domestic space. As Bomba maneuvers around a man seated in a barber's chair, he recounts his experience as he trims the man's hair. He explains that the Germans wanted to use the women's hair for their own purposes (i.e., to make fabric), and then gestures how he, in a team of 16 barbers, cut women's hair quickly. The women were lead to believe that they were just getting their hair cut immediately before taking a shower, but within minutes after having their hair cut the women would be gassed to death. Lanzmann, speaking about this scene, notes that Bomba's body speaks, so when he asks, "What was your first impression when you saw all these naked women and children coming for the first time?" Bomba "turned away and did not respond."[55] The gesturing of turning away is an embodied denial, a literal turning away from a question that Bomba doesn't want to address. "Every expression of feeling demonstrates something," Lanzmann says, "and conversely, every proof of this sort is itself a form of emotion."[56]

On one occasion a transport of women came in from Bomba's hometown, and some of these women were his friends, people he knew. The terrified women asked, "Abe, this and that, what are you doing here? What's going to happen with us?" Bomba then rhetorically asks, "What could you tell them?" Immediately, he begins to recall the experience of a fellow barber, recounting, "What could you tell, a friend of mine, he worked as a barber, he was also a good barber, in my hometown," and then, with the slight hint of a cracking voice, "when his wife and his sister . . . came into the gas chamber . . ." Bomba's voice clearly cracks on the last phrase before his testimonial narrative abruptly stops, unable to get the words out. At the same time, at the beginning of this highly charged moment of silence the camera zooms in for a close-up of Bomba's face, as we see his facial muscles wince with emotion. As Bomba continues to cut the man's hair he tries to collect himself. Analogous to the conventions of a typical narrative film, this highly emotionally charged moment is emphasized by the cinematic composition by zooming in on the character — in this case Bomba — during a moment of heightened emotion. In cinematic terms there is little or no difference between melodramatic fiction and documentary, a zoom in signifies an intensified emotional state and directs the audience in how they should respond.

But aside from the content and the compositional cues, the scene is swallowed up in a painful silence. This excruciating silence is finally broken by Lanzmann's off-screen voice, "Go on Abe, you must go on." To which, while still trimming the man's hair and still tightly framed, Bomba faintly shakes his head indicating that he cannot, or will not go on. Again, Lanzmann insists, "You have to." Bomba responds, shaking his head, "I can't do it, it's too hard." Lanzmann implores, "Please, we have to do it, you know it." Bomba says, "I won't be able to do it," shaking his head, and pacing around the man seated in the barber's chair. "You have to do it," Lanzmann continues to insist, "I know it's very hard. I know and I apologize." Presumably looking directly at Lanzmann, who is somewhere off-screen, Bomba says sternly with a resentful stare, "Don't keep me long with that, please." Persistent, Lanzmann says, "Please you must go on." Bomba sharply adds, "I told you today's going to be very hard." Under his breath Bomba goes on and utters a few more words. Having apparently collected himself, he suddenly says, in a normal tone, "Okay, go ahead." Lanzmann too proceeds without missing a beat, asking, "So what did he answer when his wife or sister came?" Bomba then goes on to explain that the barber did the best he could for them, "to stay with them a second longer, a minute longer, just to hug them, and just to kiss them, because they knew that they would never see them again." And with that heart-wrenching conclusion the sequence ends. Through Lanzmann's imaginative arrangement the emotional charge of Bomba's testimony is significantly heightened. While a historian is supposedly charged with offering an "unadulterated" narrative, the (documentary) filmmaker on the other hand makes "additions" to the narrative through any number of possible cinematic devices (e.g., framing, editing, music, visual composition, setting), and Lanzmann takes full advantage of the cinematic arts to convey a powerfully charged testimony.[57] And while Lanzmann is a skilled cinematic craftsman, he does not overdo it; there is no music, there is nothing sentimental in *Shoah*. The Bomba sequence not only provides a revealing glimpse of a real historical event, but it is also an excellent example of how cinematic choreography — the zoom of the camera as the emotional tension reaches a peak, the long pregnant pause, the uncanny *mise en scène* — can create tremendous dramatic effect. As Lanzmann himself says, "I knew it would be hard to go back . . . and that's why I shot it in the barbershop: I wanted to reactivate the scene — and for Bomba to have scissors in hand."[58]

As testimony is the most common narrative form to convey an eyewitness account, there is always an *addition* to the *content* of the narrative even if that *addition* is only the imposition of *form*, the genre of testimony itself. To Lanzmann's credit, he is acutely aware of this. Unlike historians who generally attempt to "conceal" the constructed nature of their narrative, as a filmmaker Lanzmann self-consciously constructs *Shoah*.[59] Despite the "little lies"[60] that Lanzmann allows himself he is never malicious with the "truth" of the historical event. Transmitting factual events necessitates a degree of deformation in order to make them intelligible — structuring information into a narrative. But it is this very necessity that leaves historians, and specifically Holocaust scholars, especially anxious.

Chapter Twelve

Holocaust Documentaries III: Personal Documentaries

INTRODUCTION TO PERSONAL DOCUMENTARIES

The observational mode of documentary filmmaking is closely related to the personal documentary and many times the two approaches are discussed in similar contexts. Personal Holocaust documentaries are frequently about discovery of one kind or another. Adopting the strategies that we might associate with direct cinema, or cinéma vérité, an observational documentary unobtrusively records an individual or a group as they embark on a voyage of discovery. A survivor might return to the concentration camp where they were incarcerated, or the child of a survivor might retrace their parents' experiences. Whereas an expository documentary typically addresses its subject in the past tense, the observational mode is always in the present tense, recording events as they happen. The "fly-on-the-wall" strategy that characterizes the observational mode has the potential to invite a voyeuristic gaze, as we are allowed to peer surreptitiously into a private world. The unacknowledged and non-responsive filmmaker in the observational mode, as Bill Nichols posits, "clears the way for the dynamics of empathetic identification, poetic immersion, or voyeuristic pleasure."[1]

One element that distinguishes the observational mode from interactive documentaries is that the former frequently documents social actors in transit, as opposed to the subject's familiar domestic space. Airplanes, taxis, buses, and trains figure prominently in observational documentaries, effectively adopting the characteristics of the road movie genre and integrating them into a non-narrative practice. As with the road movie, in observational documentaries the destination in itself is not necessarily the objective; rather, it is what is discovered along the way.

Personal documentaries do not always adhere strictly to the observational mode, however, and might take advantage of a number of different rhetorical

211

strategies. Devices that we associate with the expository mode might in some way be utilized to contextualize a personal documentary. The use of voiceover narration, for instance, could come from the disembodied filmmaker, or the subject of the film, and even in some cases the subject and filmmaker might very well be one and the same, such as with Manfred Kirchheimer's 1986 film, *We Were So Beloved*, and Irene Lilienheim Angelico and Abby Jack Neidik's 1985 film *Dark Lullabies*. In some cases filmmakers even employ re-enactments for illustrative purposes; Steve Brand's 1984 film *Kaddish* uses re-enactment to visualize past events, and even dreams that haunt one of his interviewees. Also more indicative of the expository documentary is the use of archival material that might have nothing to do necessarily with the specifics of the personal narrative, but is illustrative and serves the rhetorical purposes of the personal account.

For example, Nina Koocher's 2007 film *How Much to Remember: One Family's Conversation with History*, which aired on many PBS stations, bears many of the characteristics indicative of the observational mode but also avails itself of other strategies. Holocaust survivors Morris Elbaum and Celia Rothstein Elbaum take their adult children and grandchildren on a trip to Poland to visit sites charged with personal memories: the gravesite of Morris's father and elder brother, Auschwitz, where Celia was interned, and Chelmno, where most of Celia's family perished. When Jews were corralled together for deportation Celia explains, she and her family were forced to leave all their possessions behind. "That's why I have not a single picture of my father or mother," she says. On the journey, Ann (Elbaum) Rosen, Celia's daughter, says, "I had never heard that story. . . . I heard many sporadic stories about the war, but that was not one that she spoke about." In personal documentaries such as these, it is not uncommon for the children of survivors to make new revelations about their parents during the shoot. But of course survivors too might make revelations of their own; Celia, for instance, discovers the cruel efficiency and efficacy of the Chelmno death camp, which obliterated all traces of those that died there, including her father and extended family. Upset and frustrated, she protests that there should be a marker indicating where the victims were from. Her son tries to explain to her that this may be impossible to determine, but she cannot understand, or in all probability *refuses* to understand this. In this case, "understanding" amounts to acquiescence in the utter and complete obliteration of her family.

Departing from the observational mode, interviews with family members allow for reflection on their journey. These interviews, bearing the marks of the expository mode, help to contextualize footage shot in Poland. Like voiceover narration, which directs the viewer in how to read certain imagery, the interviews function as commentary, and indicative of the personal documentary, meanings differ from one person to the other.

In the final interview with Celia Rothstein Elbaum, she reflects on the visit to Chelmno: "I felt sorry I went, it was a mistake." Before she went she could disavow the fact that everyone was gone, "but when I went there the reality hit very hard," she says. The subsequent cut to the empty space of the Chelmno site functions much in the same way that a flashback does; it is as if the cutaway to the Chelmno site is a subjective shot from Celia's perspective and reconfigured as a personal reflection.[2] Lamenting that her family disappeared without so much as a trace, she says, "My whole life was there, and I didn't see nothing. Do you understand that? You can't. You can't understand that feeling, no." In Celia's view the journey was a "mistake," and she regrets having gone, because for her there was only a melancholic void. For her it's not what she finds on her journey, but rather what she does not find; for her the discovery is a vast nothingness that swallowed up her father, her relatives, aunts, uncles, cousins, and girlfriends. Morris's granddaughter, Sally Rosen, reflects as she stands before the grave of Morris's father (and elder brother), "It was his moment, it was his father, and after 50 years of not being in Poland he was able to be there and say, 'good-bye,' one more time." Through the interview, meaning is attributed to the family's journey: while Celia views the journey as a *mistake*, Sally instead interprets it as *closure*, two divergent but highly personal views.

In many personal documentaries the narrative is cast as a journey, voyage, discovery, recovery, return, or reflection on unfinished business. This is frequently manifested in the titles of these films: *Kitty: Return to Auschwitz, Return to Poland, Now . . . After All These Years, Hiding and Seeking: Faith and Tolerance After the Holocaust, Reminiscences of a Journey to Lithuania.*[3] While those framed as road movies have more in common with an individual's need to discover something about themselves, the detective/mystery genre, on the other hand, shares the traits of historical quests as personal missions.[4] The sections below, *Who Was I?* and *Who Am I?* discuss journeys of individual discovery, and share affinities with the road movie, while the final section *The Personal Is Political* illustrates where personal convictions or personal memories are mobilized for political ends and bear traces of the mystery genre.

WHO WAS I?

This question "Who was I?" is often (if implicitly) asked in personal documentaries that examine the life of a survivor. Typically many years removed from the horror of the Holocaust, a survivor featured in a personal documentary reflects on what they did to survive. The person that they are in the contemporary moment of the observational film is very different from the person that they were during the Holocaust.

In *Kitty: Return to Auschwitz* (1979) Peter Morley follows Kitty Felix Hart back to Auschwitz where she was interned for two years as she explains "who she was" during those formative years in her life. In contrast to who she was in Auschwitz, Hart is now a radiologist in Birmingham, and living a relatively normal life. A Polish national, Hart was only 12 years old when the Germans marched into her town of Bielsko. She and her mother evaded detection for another four years, disguised as "Aryans," and working in a German labor camp. When Hart was 16 they were discovered and deported to Auschwitz-Birkenau.

Characteristic of the personal documentary employing the observational mode, Hart and her son arrive at the front gate of Birkenau in a taxi. Prior to their arrival the pair was wired with radio-microphones so that Morley could capture Hart's initial candid reaction to the camp, and follow them unobtrusively from a distance. Hart gets out of the taxi and marches under the gate with some trepidation, at times covering her eyes, saying she feels a bit sick. In an interview with the filmmaker, Morley, assuaging the viewer's anxiety about the fidelity of what unfolds, asserts, "Nothing was staged. I just followed her, and didn't even know — when the taxi arrived at Auschwitz — whether she'd turn right back and leave."[5] This film, more than any of the other personal documentaries discussed here, conforms most closely to the observational mode, as evident in Morley's assertion, "I just followed her."

Thirty-three years had lapsed since Hart was last in Auschwitz, but it all comes back, slowly at first, then, clear as day. "Pretty vast, isn't it," her son David comments. "Just wait and see," Hart returns quickly. Just beyond the main gate of Birkenau, she says, "Now wait a minute, wait a minute, I got to find my bearings here." The pair proceeds into the camp, walking parallel to the ramp where arriving deportees disembarked from their cattle-cars. Hart breaks down only about 20 yards into the camp. She queries her son, "Do you know why you're here?" She goes on to lament the fact that Holocaust deniers are out spreading lies, and wants her son to know what happened, so that he too can pass this on to his children. Morley's camera crew followed the pair two consecutive days, as Hart guided them all (her son, filmmaker, and crew) through the camp, revealing its darkest secrets.

Hart adopted a number of different strategies to stay alive, and as the pair traverses the grounds of the camp she explains just how she managed. "See I had realized one very important thing, the best thing to do in this camp was to do nothing. Be invisible, I mean, hide, hide," Hart explains, with such a vast population it was possible to go unnoticed, to be discreet. By becoming "invisible" one could avoid the brutalities meted out by the kapos or SS, and the untold hardships endured in labor detail. Another tactic was "to carry bodies," Hart explains. "I mean it was very hard work, but, (a) you didn't do external work, and (b) the dead body had a ration bread, piece of bread, the dead body had one change of clothes, and it wasn't any good to this dead body." She explains that the goods that she acquired weren't necessarily for her as such, but rather used to buy access to washing facilities, or to share with her mother who was in the hospital block.

When the pair arrives at the toilet barracks Hart explains in some graphic detail the procedures and protocol of using the "toilet" — a long concrete slab with a series of holes. The internees working on the *scheissekommando* (the shit squad) scooped feces out from the latrines and carried it to the cesspool. Although Hart does not go on to mention this, the work detail for the scheissekommando, despite the obvious grim nature of it, had its advantages: work was by and large indoors, the stench was such that the Germans and the kapos didn't bother going into such places. As vile as the work was, the scheissekommando had its advantages.

At this point in the film, it breaks from the established hand-held observational style. A long tracking shot follows the long line of open holes used as toilets, referencing an almost identical sequence in Alain Resnais's 1955 film *Night and Fog*. Clearly meant to be illustrative of the ghastly nature of the camp, the stylized shot — with its smooth mechanical movement — is something of a notable departure from the established style of the film.

Hart had the "fortune" of her mother's company, who worked in a hospital block. When Hart contracted typhus, her mother was able to nurse her back to health, and when necessary hide her during selections. After recovering, Hart stayed on in the hospital ward as staff, and when people died she had to load their bodies on to trucks. Some of Hart's friends were convalescing in the ward when Mengele determined that the entire block needed to be liquidated. Hart explains this to David, as they stand on the empty site where the hospital block once stood. "Everyone had to be loaded on [to the trucks], and I had to load my friends on . . ." Hart lets her head fall, hands covering her face as she is overcome by emotions. "That finished me, that finished me," Hart says; and it was only her mother who stopped her from throwing herself on the electrified fence.

In voiceover narration we are told that Hart eventually was transferred to "Canada," a facility in Birkenau where the clothes and personal possessions of those sent to the gas chambers were sorted out, and then sent to Germany.[6] Because of the bounty that was amassed in this section of the camp it was dubbed "Canada," a nation perceived to be a land of plentitude. Hart was 17 years old when she arrived in "Canada." From her barracks in the "Canada" section, Hart had a full view of the killing operation. Next to her barracks was a patch of grass, and during the hot summer days, she and her fellow internees would sunbathe, as people disappeared into the undressing barracks only to emerge as smoke and ash.

While the film begins and ends with interviews with Hart, before and after her trip, the body of the film is observational. One of Morley's colleagues suggested that a reporter go along with Hart and interview her as she walked the grounds of Birkenau. "I felt that it would be an intrusion," Morley says, "and might stifle Kitty's natural style of delivery." Having faith in Hart's knack for conveying events and personal experiences, Morley concluded that he was "pretty certain that once she entered Auschwitz-Birkenau, she would take control of the situation and pour out her recollections to David, peppered with anecdotes. This was going to be a very raw film, and its style, if one can call it that, was one of restraint — purely observational."[7] Like Claude Lanzmann's 1985 film *Shoah*, Morley insisted that no archival footage be used, because the "word-pictures Kitty painted in people's minds were far more graphic than old newsreel film."[8] When people refuse to listen, however, no "word-picture" is vivid enough, and this is precisely what is documented in Mark Cousins and Mark Forrest's 1993 film, *The Psychology of Neo-Nazism: Another Journey by Train to Auschwitz*, which also features Hart as one of its subjects.

Cousins and Forrest's film illustrates one of the pitfalls of the observational mode, in precisely the way that Morley feared would happen in *Kitty: Return to Auschwitz* — the unpredictability of human subjects. The film's opening title card reads:

In this film four "neo-Nazis" will travel by train from different parts of Europe, to meet in Berlin. They think this is where the film will end. It will not. In Berlin we will ask them to go onwards to Auschwitz, the Nazi death camp, to meet Kitty Hart.

Neo-Nazis say there were no homicidal gas-chambers in Auschwitz. Kitty Hart saw these gas-chambers with her own eyes.

Steven Cartwright from Glasgow, a member of the British Nation Party a far-right-wing group, Gerhard Endres from Vienna, Erik Sausset from Paris, and Ewald Althans from Munich participated in the film. The problem, however, inherent to the observational film, is that a subject is relatively free to do as they please. Cartwright, for example, while in Germany refuses to speak to a German Jew, saying that he has no need to explain his political beliefs to him. Despite the pleas from one of the filmmakers, Cartwright refuses to co-operate.

Hart meets the four neo-Nazis at the far end of the Birkenau camp, towards the ruins of the crematoria. When Hart is introduced to the gang of four, she begins with an off-handed compliment: "Well, hello, how are you?" Shaking Althans's hand, she continues, "Well, it's very nice to meet some phony Nazis, because I have met so many real Nazis, so it's very nice to meet some new-Nazis." "Neo-Nazis, not phony Nazis," Althans corrects her, "if you call me a phony Nazi I'm not interested in a conversation any more." Hart stands corrected, "Okay that's fine, the new-Nazi, that's good for me, great . . ." clapping her hands in exasperation. As Hart in vein tries to convey her story, Althans and some of the others begin to protest bitterly; Endres finally says, "Learn your history," as the gang of four walk away. The observational documentary is effectively over at this point; the social actors that are supposed to discover the truth and have some sort of revelation instead simply walk away. Hart nevertheless goes on to testify to what she witnessed in Birkenau for the rest of the film.

One of the dangers of an observational documentary is that the filmmaker relies on a certain amount of serendipity, and his or her social actors' continued indulgence in the filmmaking itself. There is an expectation, or at least a hope, that the chance encounters between social actors will result in dramatic moments captured on film. Placing Holocaust deniers with survivors — in a death camp no less — is a sure way to generate dramatic conflict *up to a point*, because without the antagonism between the social actors there is *no* film. *The Psychology of Neo-Nazism* could be characterized as a failure so to speak, not only because the four Holocaust deniers fail to be persuaded to see the idiocy of their position, but because the social actors — the protagonists of the film, who are expected to undergo some sort of change or transformation — walk away and are never heard from again. They enter the film as neo-Nazis and leave the film neo-Nazis (perhaps even emboldened).

Pierre Sauvage's 1988 film *Weapons of the Spirit* begins with the filmmaker's blunt voiceover statement: "I'm a Jew born in Nazi-occupied France." This is recounted over a still photograph of Sauvage's father holding the filmmaker in his arms, then only a baby. Sauvage continues to outline some of the details of the Holocaust that ripped his family apart, and as he says, "burned my roots." Despite the horrors that rocked Europe, the Sauvage family found refuge, along with many others, "sheltered in a village in the mountains of France." To make the film, he states, "I returned there to find out why." The people of Le Chambon doubled their population by sheltering 5,000 Jews and Sauvage documents his own quest to discover what motivated their efforts to protect the refugees.

Also working with an expository strategy, Sauvage incorporates archival footage to help contextualize his journey. For example, he makes use of fascist propaganda incorporating a period French newsreel documenting "The Jew in France," an exhibition in Paris, which aimed to "prove how France was the victim of her sense of hospitality, and was infested with Jewishness" and that Jews instigated the war and brought about France's ultimate defeat.

Sauvage reveals that many in the Le Chambon region were Protestants and persecuted in the predominantly Catholic France; the film implicitly argues that this history made the people Le Chambon sympathetic to the Jews' plight. For the people of Le Chambon, it was simply the right thing to do. The widow of the Pastor of Le Chambon during the war professes, "Each person, each day, did what seemed necessary. People ask about our organization. If we'd had one, we would have failed! You can't just plan something like this. As challenges arose, each person acted on their own." The widow does admit that "My husband had influence, but he didn't know everything! It was a general consensus."

At least one famous personality settled in the region at the time of the war. During his journey Sauvage learns of "a young Frenchman who had come to the area of Le Chambon for his health and . . . began to write a new novel." This Frenchman was none other than Albert Camus, and the novel that he wrote during the war in Le Chambon was *The Plague*, which Sauvage describes as "an allegorical novel inspired by those times." Ilan Avisar observes that Camus's novel "can be considered the literary model for *Transport from Paradise* [Zbynek Brynych, 1962] and also is a clue to the understanding of Brynych's spiritual background. The philosophy espoused and expressed in Brynych's art is modernist existentialism."[9]

By the end of the film, Sauvage never discovers what the exact motivation was for this community to go to extraordinary lengths to protect Jews. But as is revealed, there was no orchestrated plan to save people, or to harbor enemies of the Nazi regime (and by extension the Vichy regime), nor was it about being good Christians. Rather, the choice amounted to what was humane and what simply was natural to their disposition. In an interview regarding *Weapons of the Spirit* with Bill Moyers, Sauvage reveals that his parents did not speak that much about Le Chambon, and in fact, Sauvage's parents did not reveal their Jewish identity to him until he was 18 years old. The making of the film gave Sauvage an opportunity to find out more, not only about the people of Le Chambon, and how his parents managed to survive, but more importantly to discover who he was.

WHO AM I?

The conclusion of Manfred Kirchheimer's 1986 film *We Were So Beloved* asks a series of meditative questions about his relationship to the Holocaust and is characteristic of the personal documentary that explores the question: Who am I? As the children of survivors began to come of age, important questions emerged about their responsibility of carrying the weight of surviving the Holocaust on their shoulders; this is the wellspring of a number of personal Holocaust documentaries.[10]

Over a long shot of elderly Washington Heights residents congregating on park benches, he ruminates, "In this journey, through the complexities and contradictions of survival, I have returned to my former home in search of answers. I wanted to resolve questions that have been with me for most of my life, questions that would not let me rest." Kirchheimer's parents were able to immigrate from Germany in 1936 to the United States, when the filmmaker was just 5 years old. The family settled in Washington Heights neighborhood, which would become a thriving European Jewish community, sometimes referred to as the Fourth Reich, or Frankfurt-on-the-Hudson.

In his fifties, Kirchheimer began to interview family members, prominent figures in the community, and some of his contemporaries. Kirchheimer is dogged by questions about the victims and perpetrators alike. What would he have done to survive? Or would he have stuck his neck out to save others, as some German gentiles did? Although many of the questions that Kirchheimer directs towards his interviewees are about the past, they effectively function as foils on which to measure his own character.

Kirchheimer juxtaposes an interview with his father — a German Jew — with Louis Kampf, a contemporary of the filmmaker. His father describes the deportation of Polish Jews from Germany into concentration camps. And acknowledges that they looked down upon the Polish Jews: "I was told don't . . . the Polish Jews aren't as good as the German Jews, that's a kind of arrogance, of course, right?" The filmmaker asks his father, "So you were ashamed of those Jews?"

> Sometimes, yes, to see them on the street, and begging, and trading goods door-to-door; on the other side, we felt sorry for them, because they had no money. They came from poor Russia you know, they had pogroms, and they didn't make much money there, they lived in ghettos, they were suppressed there . . . we German Jews were patriots, patriots, and educated a different way.

This is a striking admission, which also led to a false sense of security among the German Jews, who never imagined that they were next.

Louis Kampf witnessed the tension between these Jewish factions aboard ship crossing the Atlantic:

> There was practically a war going on between the Eastern European Jews and the German Jews, and the German Jews looked at the Eastern Europeans as Ausjuden who got them into trouble with the Nazis, that was one of the particular myths, that came out of the thirties. That if it only had been for the Ausjuden, the German Jews would have been okay inside Nazi Germany.

While the two deliberate on the past, Kirchheimer is silently meditating on his own character, wondering if — despite his vigilance — he harbors similar prejudices within his soul.

"If the situation had been reversed, would you have hidden Jews, the way that many Gentiles did?" he asks his father. "I told you before I couldn't do it, because I'm a coward, I would have never done such a thing. Because the danger of it." The elder Kirchheimer's honesty cuts to the bone.[11] "How do you feel about the Gentiles that did it?" Kirchheimer asks. "Terrific. It's wonderful. They are real heroes." Kirchheimer pushes his father on this point. "Because from nature I am a coward, I'm afraid of everything. That's the reason, oh boy, I would've never done it . . ." Shaking his head, he says, "I thought of my family first, and my relatives to save them. And that was the idea, but I wouldn't have taken in any other Jews." Cutting to a photograph of a German street, presumably in the 1930s, the filmmaker includes the non-diegetic sound of wind howling through an open space, suggesting not only the barren nature of the image but of the moral weakness expressed by his father. This leads to one of the underlying questions of all personal Holocaust documentaries: "Is my honest father speaking for me as well? Would I hide a fellow human being in a Nazi world? What kind of person am I? What kind of a mensch? Will I ever know? Do I want to know?" Again, the interviewee here functions as a foil for Kirchheimer to address questions about his own disposition.

With most of these personal films there is also an existential angst. Kirchheimer says, "For every boy and girl that made it, there are as many that didn't. When I played ball with Louis Kampf, Max Frankel, and Walter Hess in those days I never detected an awareness that we almost didn't make it. That we are almost not here." There is the looming cloud of mortality over these documentaries, not so much about those that were killed during the Holocaust, but more so regarding a realization that one easily could not have been born. Growing up in the United States, while German and European Jews suffered terribly, weighs heavily on Kirchheimer. "I was so lucky, I felt it then, and I can still feel it today."

Irene Lilienheim Angelico and Abby Jack Neidik's 1985 film *Dark Lullabies* is another example of a personal documentary, at its core sharing similar concerns found in Kirchheimer's film. The film begins with the story of Lilienheim's parents, who soon after they were married were sent to separate concentration camps. Not until adulthood did Lilienheim fully understand her parents' struggle, when her father shared with her a manuscript that he had written detailing his experience. He ruminates in a voiceover on the experience of being in Dachau in April of 1945, a meditation that is almost singularly focused on hunger, "I'm tried of thinking; I would only like not to be hungry." A shot of contemporary Dachau is followed by a shot of Lilienheim peering out a train window, who in voiceover explains that after her parents were reunited, they emigrated to the United States and began a new life, and as with many Holocaust survivors tried to protect their children from the horrors they had seen. As she says, "They would try to spare me, their child, the horror that they left behind. Thirty-five years later I'm on a train in Germany trying to understand the experience that separates me from my parents." The train, the journey, and the quest to understand are indicative of the personal film.

Despite that Lilienheim's parents rarely spoke about their Holocaust experience, she nevertheless felt it, as she says, "in images and impressions." Lilienheim locates similar experiences in a group of other children of survivors, and laments in voiceover, "Most children of survivors have no grandparents, no uncles or aunts, there are no family photo-albums, no trinkets to pass on. Not even a photograph around which to imagine a whole life that was wiped out in the war." A visual memory is then reconstructed in the following shot through archival images of Jewish children playing, and non-diegetic Jewish folk music.

When Lilienhiem arrives in Germany she discovers that Germans — of her generation — had similar experiences. With both shame and guilt, many had little idea of their parents' experiences, and how their family or their neighbors were complicit in the Holocaust. In one account, a German woman shares that a site that had been simply described as a cemetery turned out upon further inspection to be a former concentration camp. She recalls having gone to the site and, digging with her bare hands, discovering shards of broken plates, revealing that it was at one time inhabited. "This was very hard for me to accept, because I felt as I had been cheated out of my history." The woman explains, "I lived here for 20 years, but I was missing a part of the history that belonged to the place. I was never told about it, and that's why I never learned to ask questions about it. This was a very important discovery for me."

Lilienheim also interviews children of perpetrators in order to understand how it is possible to reconcile individuals who might be loving parents on the one hand, and, at the same time, agents of death in the Nazi regime. She reads a passage from Elie Wiesel to the granddaughter of Robert Mulka, who was the adjutant to Commandant Rudolf Hoess at Auschwitz:

> Yes, it is possible to defile life and creation and feel no remorse. To tend one's garden and water one's flowers but two steps away from barbwire. To be enthralled by the beauty of a landscape, make children laugh, and still fulfill regularly, day in and day out, the duties of a killer. Have the killers been brutal savages, or demented sadists, the shock would have been less, and also the disappointment.

The facial muscles of Lilienheim's interlocutor tense up and fidget as she stares downward, and Lilienheim finally asks, "I'm trying to understand, a man like your grandfather, who can seem gentle to his granddaughter, even kind, and can do these things, I'm trying to understand and I don't understand, and I'm wondering if you understand yourself?" Clearing her throat, she shoots a gaze upward towards the ceiling, "No, I cannot understand this." Struggling to find a way to express it, she says, "It seems as if there are two souls, in the mind of those people, and also in the mind of my grandfather." Lilienheim asks how she has come to terms with these "two souls," and Mulka explains that being your own distinct person is among the most important things, to know oneself. This of course is the driving force of Lilienheim's whole quest.

Lilienheim's German associate, Harald Lüders, asks, "Did you come to find out something about Germany, or did you come to find out something about yourself?"[12] Similar to *We Were So Beloved*, while Lilienheim directs her questions outwards to survivors, children of survivors, children of perpetrators, and neo-Nazis, they ultimately serve a personal function, and are turned inward. What lurks beneath the surface is a questioning of what Lilienheim herself would have done, had she been placed in the same situation.

Steve Brand's 1984 film *Kaddish* features the Klein family; the patriarch, Zoltan Klein, a Holocaust survivor, and his son Yossi Klein (Halevi), who is profoundly affected by his father's story and tries to negotiate his place in the world. While many personal films involve a physical journey, North America to Europe for instance, *Kaddish* documents more of an inner personal journey, where Klein Halevi discovers more about himself than he does about his father and his experience. Unlike many Holocaust survivors who hid their past from their children, Klein Halevi's father did no such thing. While his mother would read him Dr. Seuss for bedtime stories, his father, on the other hand, would tell him stories about wartime, Europe, and how he managed to survive the Holocaust. *Kaddish* is situated somewhere between the expository and observational modes and is largely structured around interviews with the Klein family, shot over the course of five years.

Some interviews function as exposition to situate events, while others, and this is particularly true of interviews with Klein Halevi, reflect on events as they are in the process of unfolding. Also on a few occasions Brand uses re-enactments to visually represent the interviews. In one instance, when Zoltan describes his forest hideout, a hand-held camera offers a point of view perspective walking through a wooded area. As Zoltan continues to describe the bunker, saying it was "about 4 feet high, and 5 or 6 feet long, and 10 or 8 feet wide," two men are shown digging out a space roughly matching these dimensions. He continues, "and we buried ourselves there May the 2nd, 1944, and we didn't see the sun till October 27th, 1944. I never would have believed that we would survive that."

Breindy Klein, Zoltan's wife, notes that her husband was haunted by terrible dreams of being back in the bunker, and being discovered by Nazis. Once again Brand cuts to hand-held footage in the wooded area, but this time the camera movement is decidedly more frantic, as if taken from Zoltan's perspective during one of his nightmares. This shot in particular has strong affinities with the POV shots that are the trademark of slasher films, specifically Sean S. Cunningham's 1980 hit *Friday the 13th*. Although these POV shots in the slasher genre are typically associated with the monster, in *Kaddish* the shot resonates with profound fear and anxiety of the subject being hunted. This is somewhat unusual for a documentary — although not unheard of — because not only are we given a subjective shot, but also it's a subjective shot from the dream-life of a social actor.

This fear and anxiety no doubt permeated Klein Halevi's adolescence — and he says as much — but perhaps most shocking are the words that he uses to describe the suppression of these feelings. "I grew up so controlled, everything was so in, that it was almost as if my real life was just underground, subterranean. And all my emotions were underground." The specific words here, "underground" and "subterranean," evoke the specter of his father and the experience of hiding in the bunker, where of course, for the sake of survival, one needed to maintain "control" of one's emotions. In Klein Halevi's case these anxieties are eventually channeled into Zionist politics, leading to his immigration to Israel. The transgenerational trauma that is evident here, where children of survivors experience some degree of angst relevant to the Holocaust, is also explored in other films such as Orna Ben-Dor-Niv's 1988 documentary *Because of That War*, Jack and Danny Fisher's 1983 film *A Generation Apart*, Kartherine Smalley and Vic Sarin's 1987 film *So Many Miracles*, and the German film by Harald Lüders and Pavel Schnabel *Now . . . After All These Years* (1981).

THE PERSONAL IS POLITICAL

Many personal documentaries have political elements — whether it is the film's point of view or the subject documented — where the personal is politicized. This is certainly evident in *Kaddish* in Yossi Klein Halevi's Zionist persuasion, a political position that is perhaps not shared by the filmmaker. The work of Marian Marzynski — specifically his 1981 film *Return to Poland* and his 1996 film *Shtetl* — is of a different order, however, but by no means less political. *Shtetl*, a Frontline production that originally aired on PBS, exhibits many of the tropes of the observational mode, following the filmmaker, a Holocaust survivor, on his return to Poland. *Shtetl* does not feature Marzynski's story, though: he is effectively a conduit — literally serving as a translator at times — for other personal narratives. In *Shtetl* Marzynski adopts the guise of detective, investigating what happened to the Jews in Poland, and the motivation for Poles to collaborate with Germans, or at the very least to be complicit in the liquidation of the Jewish population.

Traveling on trains, buses, or by car, Marzynski accompanies two men, Nathan Kaplan and Zbyszek Romaniuk, to points in Poland, Jerusalem, and the United States. Born and raised in Chicago, Kaplan is in search of his roots, a shtetl — Yiddish for "little town" — in the town of Bransk, Poland, close to the Russian border, 60 miles east of Warsaw. Romaniuk is an enthusiastic 29-year-old Bransk resident who is interested in Jewish history, and also Kaplan's penpal. Marzynski is the intermediary, through which their personal stories materialize, frequently conveying information to the spectator through voiceover. Early in the film he informs us that: "Nathan was 2 years old when his father died. 'I have no memory of my father,' he told me. 'It's only by going to Bransk that I can touch him, that I can understand who I am.'"

On a train bound for Bransk, Marzynski in voiceover reflects on his own biography,

> I was among the few survivors, a child hidden by Christians in Warsaw. My war began in a horse wagon. In 1942, I was smuggled from the Warsaw ghetto to the Christian side of the city. I was sitting in the carriage with a woman guide, her hand over my mouth as I struggled to scream, "I want to go back to the ghetto. I want to go back to Mummy."

In a re-enactment, we witness Marzynski's mother taking him to the courtyard of a Christian charity, and as Marzynski's voiceover continues to explain, placing "a cardboard sign around my neck, 'My name is Marys. My parents are dead.'" Marzynski's post-war experience is embittered:

In the 25 years I lived in Poland after the war, I returned only once to Leczyca, in 1969. But when I started asking questions about those in my family who were killed and those who betrayed them, I couldn't take it. I decided never to return to my shtetl. I left for America with the image of shtetl life frozen in time. It smelled of death.

It is through this experience that Marzynski's encounters and interactions with Kaplan and Romaniuk in the film are framed.

Like *Shoah*, absence is also present in *Shtetl*. Not a single Jew remains in Bransk, and the shtetl that once flourished there has effectively been erased; 2,500 Jews were deported from Bransk and exterminated at Treblinka. Marzynski's voyage is filtered through Kaplan's:

I find a way to enter this haunted world of my ancestors. My friend from Chicago is searching for his Jewish roots. It's easier for him. He was born in America. He never lived in Poland. I feel secure with him leading the way. I will be his translator.

In this way Marzynski can negotiate his own experience through the lens of another; it somehow places a buffer between him and his deeply felt anguish.

Prior to his trip to Bransk, Kaplan had developed an intense letter-writing relationship with Romaniuk, who himself was fascinated with Polish Jewish history and in the film is instrumental in helping to navigate the two travelers. In fact, Romaniuk has amassed something of a small personal archive of material — old photographs, segments from a Torah discovered in a house that was being remodeled — and it is his selfless efforts that make Kaplan's experience as rich as it is.

Kaplan in his journey is able to connect with his past, to somehow make it tangible. Kaplan inspires Marzynski, but he becomes increasingly interested in Romaniuk, who is a wellspring of information; very few Poles share his enthusiasm for a subject that is for practical purposes a Polish taboo. In fact we learn that Romaniuk's interest in Jewish history in Bransk makes him subject to ridicule and suspicion among the townspeople — he is called a "Jew," a Star of David is scratched into the door of his family's home. The local Poles become anxious when Romaniuk tours curious Jews around town — pointing out and snapping pictures of this or that house which used to be a Jewish home — the locals assume that these tourists intend to reclaim property that was stolen from them.

In order to erase all trace of Jews in Bransk, the Germans ordered that the headstones in the Jewish graveyard be used as pavers on the roads and sidewalks. Romaniuk, Marzynski, and Kaplan go to the Catholic parish in Bransk, and ask permission to dig up some of the pavers. The priest obliges them, but asks, conveyed in Marzynski's voiceover narration, "'But I have one request,' says the priest. 'When you show this film, make sure in your commentary that it is clear that the Germans did this, not the Poles.'" The archeological dig reveals, indeed, that the pavers are Jewish headstones. At another location, on a farm another headstone is found; the farmer, a woman old enough to remember the Jews in Bransk, recalls, "We saw Jews floating in the river. People took their gold and dumped them in the water. And I saw Jews tied with rope, carried to the Germans." It is revealed that Romaniuk and his friends have been finding headstones and returning them to the old Jewish graveyard, collecting over 175 in total. Marzynski is profoundly moved by this. "Zbyszek [Romaniuk] calls it a 'lapidarium', a museum of stones. For Nathan and me, these stones are alive. This is a roll call of the dead — for the Kaplans, the Rubins, the Edels, the Finkelsteins, the Tykockis. When World War II started, there were 2,500 of them in this town."

The tone of the documentary then changes from a road movie into a detective narrative as Polish betrayal, or collaboration with Germans to root out Jews, suddenly becomes the focus of the film. Marzynski in his questioning of elderly Poles channels Claude Lanzmann. "From the pages of survivors' testimonies certain names stand out," Marzynski says, "like the brothers Hrycz, who would receive Jews, grab their belongings, bludgeon them to death and throw their bodies in the river. I learn from Zbyszek that one of the brothers Hrycz is still alive." When Marzynski arrives at Hrycz's farm, he greets the elderly man, "I've heard a lot about you. You are one of the oldest people in this village. You remember the war. The times were hard?" Like Lanzmann, Marzynski presses him hard as the diminutive man averts his eyes, and his hand trembles as he repeats the refrain, "Death already sits on my nose."

Kaplan is stupefied by the contradictory information that he receives; on the one hand, Poles were sympathetic to the Jewish plight, and on the other hand instrumental in their destruction. As Kaplan wrestles with this issue, for Marzynski the matter is clear as day: the Poles are in the best case guilty of indifference, and in the worst case complicit; this position is made abundantly clear by the conclusion of the film. In the latter moments of the film, we learn that Romaniuk has been elected vice-mayor of Bransk, and is charged with organizing the celebration of the 500-year anniversary of the town's founding. Marzynski invites himself to one of the town meetings in preparation for the town celebration. There, he unfairly torpedoes Romaniuk in a public forum, by challenging the young public official to incorporate Jewish history into the program. "'So they were here for 430 years', I say. 'Don't you believe that their contribution to this town deserves public recognition?'" Romaniuk agrees, "Yes, but I believe it is a delicate subject." Marzynski continues, "I am saying that in 1939, 65 percent of people here were Jewish, so in a five-minute speech about Bransk, can you spend a minute on the Jews or is it too much?"[13] Certainly, the questions are legitimate, but Marzynski's vitriol does not serve him well, as he attacks the one Pole who exhibits sympathy, even enthusiastic interest in Jewish history in Poland. Marzynski adds fodder to that Polish refrain often tinged with anti-Semitism: "We were victims too." Although the two are frequently compared, Marzynski is no Claude Lanzmann. And Romaniuk is not Franz Suchomel.[14] At the end of the day, Romaniuk is correct when he says, "This film is your vision of events," because in fact that is precisely what *Shtetl* is. Although Marzynski frames himself as a neutral conduit for other personal narratives, in actuality, like *Return to Poland*, *Shtetl* is a personal campaign to hold Poles accountable.[15]

Chapter Thirteen

Holocaust Documentaries IV: The Poetic Documentary

INTRODUCTION

Incongruity and radical juxtaposition are trademarks of the poetic documentary. At the core, then, of the poetic Holocaust documentary are comparative strategies to measure temporal differences, generational differences, and moral/ethical dispositions, by drawing analogies, or combining elements of documentary and narrative fiction. Kees Hin and Hans Fels's 1995 short 12-minute documentary *Auschwitz-Birkenau 1940-1945-1995* considers the contemporary with the historical, negotiating temporal differences; Alain Resnais's 1955 film *Night and Fog* weighs the moral cost of the Holocaust by positing questions; and Errol Morris's 1999 documentary, *Mr. Death: The Rise and Fall of Fred A. Leuchter, Jr.* relies heavily on (visual) analogies for rhetorical purposes.

On some occasions the poetic documentary invites mediation on form; while the content might be focused on the Holocaust, there is a propensity to reflect on the process of representing. This latter trope of the poetic begins to overlap with what Bill Nichols identifies as the reflexive mode,[1] which he categorizes as distinct and separate from the poetic mode. The example of Peter Forgács's films offers a look into these two documentary paradigms, as his poetic documentaries exhibit a fascination with the material of film itself: amateur/home movies. As he crafts his films from old home movies, the texture of the material itself, which Forgács goes to great length to emphasize, butts up against the characteristics of the reflexive documentary. "Reflexive texts are self-conscious not only about form and style, as poetic ones are," Nichols says, "but also about strategy, structure, conventions, expectations, and effects."[2] Because of the affinities between the poetic and the reflexive mode this chapter will examine them together.

Poetic documentaries — or poetic elements in a documentary — emphasize the aesthetics of the film, be it in the form of rhythm, tone, composition or any combination of these. There is frequently a predisposition for visual analogies or metaphoric imagery, and rhetorical cohesion might give way to radical juxtapositions, or (sometimes quite loose) associative imagery, ideas, or themes. While working with the historical material of the Holocaust (or related subject), the poetic documentary typically reconfigures the imagery into something else, usually ascribing it with, or at least pointing towards some sort of "meaning" — inhumanity, victimization, cruelty and the like.

Holocaust documentaries that utilize the reflexive mode are not only concerned with the subject but also in the ways which the content is represented, as Nichols posits, "the reflexive mode addresses the question of *how* we talk about the historical world."[3] Additionally, reflexive documentaries tend to place how they are made on exhibit, rather than concealing the filmmaker's crafting. When Claude Lanzmann cuts between the van monitoring the covert videotaping of SS Unterstürmfuhrer, Franz Suchomel, and the resulting grainy black and white interview, this gestures towards the reflexive mode — exhibiting the very construction of the interview — but the overriding concern of *Shoah* remains *what* Suchomel says, not in *how* Lanzmann constructs the scene. Despite the explicit display of its own constitution, *Shoah* is not strictly speaking a reflexive documentary.

While films like Alain Resnais's film *Night and Fog* (a subject of later discussion) are now considered as central to the canon of Holocaust visual culture, these poetic ventures into the Holocaust are not without their critics. *Night and Fog*, for instance, does not contextualize the Holocaust as a uniquely Jewish event, but rather as a human event, and the poetic rhetoric of the film advances this more universal reading. Some might consider the poetic documentary to be an affront to the history of the Holocaust, based on the conservative tradition of its representation summed up in Theodor Adorno's dictum: "To write poetry after Auschwitz is barbaric."[4] The inherent fear in this position — not necessarily shared by Adorno; he was more concerned with the ethics of profiting from suffering, his dictum nonetheless underscores this conservative position — is that poetic discourse might in some fashion distort or manipulate the event. And invariably the poetic documentary must plead guilty to this charge; the question that should be posed, though, is whether or not a poetic treatment of Holocaust history is *inherently malicious*? To my mind, the answer is an emphatic "no." For instance, Eyal Sivan's 1999 documentary *The Specialist: The Portrait of a Modern Criminal*, co-written with Rony Brauman, exhibits certain poetic elements in its audio design, *adding* non-diegetic sound elements to the trial of Adolf Eichmann. The raw material of the court proceedings, aside from their enormous historical significance, might be considered quite banal. The basic facts regarding the crimes against Jews and Eichmann's role in the implementation of the Final Solution might excise the horror of the crimes. Sivan's non-diegetic sound design, however, which shares certain affinities with the horror genre, *adds to* what the numbers, raw data, and judicial decorum cannot accommodate: the overwhelming *feelings* of abject horror in the face of the industrialization of death that Eichmann oversaw. Sivan's poetic audio design does not *take away* from the truth of the history, but instead *adds* to it.

The conservative position that demands absolute fidelity to the history of the Holocaust is always already problematic; it assumes that a transparent window onto the past is a viable strategy. As shown in the previous chapters, there are innumerable problems with such an assumption; objectivity — whatever that might constitute — itself is a red herring. In addition, the poetic documentary opens up great possibilities in the representational strategies of the Holocaust, namely, the sensual. While expository documentaries — and to a certain degree interactive and observational documentaries — seek to convey information, to argue a particular position, the poetic documentary on the other hand harbors the potential not only to engage with content but to explore the ways in which that content makes us feel.

Kees Hin and Hans Fels's 1995 short (12-minute) documentary *Auschwitz-Birkenau 1940–1945–1995* utilizes many poetic strategies; it is exquisitely shot, full of voluptuous color, replete with beautifully choreographed cinematography, and startling juxtapositions. The film begins with an iris shot of a single barb on a barbwire fence; a dissolve of this to a shot of the full moon establishes a graphic pattern, where the iris shot echoes the contours of the moon. This poetic rhythm of graphic form continues in the succeeding shot of a spotlight (a flashlight?), its roughly circular beam of light trained on the snowy ground, with bits of grass peeking through. The camera follows as the circular pool of light moves upward to illuminate a brick wall. The ambient sound track is broken by the scream of a little girl. The graphic pattern — which is composed of relatively tight close-ups or medium close-ups, shot in beautiful color, all contemporaneous (mid-1990s) — is also broken with a flash pan to frame an establishing shot, revealing the site to be Auschwitz. The subsequent shots are taken from archival material, archival images of corpses, and the waste of the concentration camp.

Highly choreographed crane shots move from the historical photographs that are posted throughout what is now the Memorial and Museum Auschwitz-Birkenau, to reveal the concentration camp in its current state.[5] These highly stylized shots that revel in movement are reminiscent of Resnais's *Night and Fog*, perhaps the single most important film that utilizes the poetic documentary form. Resnais provides a glimpse of what lies beyond the boundary of the barbwire fences, his camera, though, quickly moves inward; the opening shot of *Night and Fog* withdraws from the farm fields tracking methodically ever further into the interior of the camp. *Auschwitz-Birkenau 1940–1945–1995* also goes outside the perimeter of the barbwire fence, but far beyond what Resnais's camera reveals. The filmmakers venture into the surrounding town of Oświęcim (the Polish name for the town, what the Germans would rename "Auschwitz").[6]

Resituating the film in the town of Oświęcim, *Auschwitz-Birkenau 1940–1945–1995* adopts the poetic strategy of incongruity, assembling radical juxtapositions between archival material and the contemporary moment. A shot of a fashionable nightclub with live musicians playing swanky jazz is edited with an image of an orchestra playing in Auschwitz, showing the profoundly cynical ritual of internee-musicians playing for camp laborers leaving in the morning for work detail, and re-entering the camp after a day's work. Similarly, the camera in *Auschwitz-Birkenau 1940–1945–1995* tracks along mountains of hair as it is exhibited in the contemporary museum (similar shots are found in *The Last Stage* and *Night and Fog*), which is then juxtaposed with a sweeping crane shot that moves from an exterior shot of an Oświęcim street lined with shops to finally peer through the window of a beauty salon where a woman is having her hair cut. An Oświęcim elementary school, filled with boisterous children, is edited together with the shot of the newly liberated children from Auschwitz — lifting their sleeves to reveal their tattooed numbers.

Ambient sound from each of the shots is woven together with a babble of voices speaking a compendium of names, giving the audio design a poetic texture. The last shot of the film echoes the choreography of the opening shot of *Night and Fog*, but in reverse; a crane shot moves from inside the camp to the outside where an old man driving a horse-pulled cart urges the beast of burden on, "Ja, ja!" down the road. The contrast between the history of the Auschwitz concentration camp, set against the everydayness of Oświęcim, of life that simply goes on, makes for a somewhat uneasy comparison, a tension between historical moments — 1940, 1945, 1995. In many respects *Auschwitz-Birkenau 1940–1945–1995* makes use of the full arsenal of poetic strategies. What follows is a discussion of other films that avail themselves of the poetic device.

POETIC RUPTURES

The idea that we know about the world, we know about our history, through the things that history has cast off, whether it's pieces of evidence, documents, the testimony of people who have lived through those times. If you think about it for a moment, there is that really sad realization that it could all be lost. It's not like science, where the world replicates itself again and again. History comes by only once, and the residue of history can be lost.

– Errol Morris[7]

Errol Morris's 1999 documentary, *Mr. Death: The Rise and Fall of Fred A. Leuchter, Jr.*, makes extensive use of visual analogies and metaphors for rhetorical purposes. These poetic elements tend to be orchestrated in hyper-stylized cinematography, which calls attention to its own construction, thus gesturing towards one of the critical tropes of the reflexive documentary. *Mr. Death* exhibits *moments* of poetic rupture in an otherwise fairly conventional talking-heads interview documentary.

Morris presents the portrait of Fred Leuchter, an execution device consultant, contracted by State penitentiaries to build, repair, or refurbish aging instruments of capital punishment — electric chairs, lethal injection systems, gallows.

He gained public notoriety after the publication of, "The Leuchter Report," which claimed to prove that gas chambers at Auschwitz did not exist. Hired as an "expert" witness in the defense of Ernst Zündel, who was being charged with publishing "false history" in Canada, Leuchter was commissioned by Zündel's defense team to go to Auschwitz to retrieve samples from the walls of the gas chambers, and to render an opinion — based on his experience as a consultant — whether the structures from an engineering standpoint had the capacity to kill. As a product of Leuchter's deeply flawed methodology, and willful disregard of significant evidence, the report issued by the chemical laboratory analyzing the samples concluded that there was no significant residue of cyanide.

Like Claude Lanzmann, Morris stages scenes for dramatic and rhetorical purposes, and despite the fact that Morris "contrives" scenes this does not mean, as Janet Walker notes, that he "subtract[s] truth." Quite to the contrary, "Morris uses contrivance to develop critical consciousness about past events and about the means of its representations."[8] While the film is marked by elements of the poetic it unfolds in more or less the expository mode — a fairly conventional "portrait documentary" in many respects — a series of interviews with Leuchter and others are strung together, interlaced with re-enactments, archival material, and periodically punctuated with a black slug clearly indicating cuts. This last attribute, so indicative of Morris's work, could potentially be characterized as a reflexive element because it calls attention to its construction.[9] The general structure of the film is governed according to the principles of biographical chronology as Morris charts the trajectory of Leuchter's professional career as a consultant and eventual downfall spawned by his naiveté and vanity.

Innumerable documentary filmmakers have availed themselves of Leni Riefenstahl's 1935 film *Triumph of the Will*, and Morris is no exception to this. The difference, however, materializes in the use of this appropriated material. Typically, *Triumph of the Will* is used to illustrate the power of the Nazi state, and its love of pageantry, more often than not used in the most generic sense, shorn from its source altogether. Morris, on the other hand, draws from *Triumph of the Will* in a very specific way, and directly engages with its historical content and its place in cinematic history.

Triumph of the Will documents "the Reich Party Day" of 1934, a National Socialist Party political rally held in Nuremberg. It begins with Hitler's arrival in an airplane, followed by his procession through the city, which eventually leads to the main event, a series of parades and speeches outlining the party's agenda. The opening shots of the film, which have garnered a good deal of critical attention, are notable for their "divine-like" qualities. They are taken from Hitler's airplane as it makes its way to Nuremberg; the plane soars through the air amid majestic clouds hovering above the German landscape (fig. 13.1). These tranquil shots are set to a musical score, which complements them with placid strings ever so slightly evoking the melody of "Deutschland, Deutschland Über Alles," and suggests that Hitler is an angel who has descended from the heavens as Germany's savior.

Figure 13.1

　　Morris is mindful of cinematic history and relates the figure of Leuchter to Hitler vis-à-vis Riefenstahl's film. Zündel in fact characterizes Leuchter as a kind of savior, and neo-Nazis and revisionist historians see him in a similar light; he is the angelic figure that is going to "save" Germany from the history of the Holocaust. Utilizing poetic juxtaposition — cutting between Leuchter and *Triumph of the Will* — Morris illustrates this frightening transformation. Cutting between footage from Leuchter's original trip to Poland for the Zündel case, to re-enactments (or set pieces) depicting an image of a crossword puzzle entitled "Allusive," alongside a pen branded "Fred A. Leuchter Associates, Inc. Execution Equipment" (fig. 13.2) set on an airplane seat-tray, to finally the infamous opening shots taken from Hitler's airplane, Morris constructs a comparison between "Hitler the savior," and the diminutive Leuchter.[10] Not only in the engagement with the specifics of the appropriated material but the wider body of Riefenstahl's film, Morris here is situating Leuchter and his portrayal of him in a specific (cinematic) history. The poetic analogy of "Germany's savior" is constructed through the juxtaposition of material.

Figure 13.2

　　In another exemplary poetic moment James Roth, the chemist that analyzed Leuchter's cyanide samples, explains the process of identifying traces of cyanide and his role in the Zündel case, set to highly stylized re-enactments. "He [Leuchter] presented us with rock samples," Roth explains, anywhere from the size of your thumb, up to half the size of your fist. We broke them up with a hammer so that we could get a sub-sample. Place it in a flask, add concentrated sulfuric acid, and it undergoes a reaction. It produces a red-colored solution. It is the intensity of this red color that we can relate with cyanide concentration.

Close-ups of swirling flasks, and extreme close-ups of small concrete samples being pulverized by a hammer accompany this statement (fig. 13.3; fig. 13.4). The re-enactments do not correspond to the temporal or spatial continuity of the interview. Roth is interviewed in a nondescript black room, looking straight on and framed in a tight close-up, and describing past events. This is contrasted with the aesthetic character of the re-enactments that serve the rhetorical argument, but with no pretense whatsoever to illustrate, what Nichols would call, the historical world.[11]

Figure 13.3

Figure 13.4

The re-enactments in *Mr. Death* tend to be dramatically lit, and certain elements of these scenes — blown-out whites, reflective surfaces, beams of light — vibrate with intensity. Some shots are canted, or shot from odd angles, and frequently presented in a slightly slower speed than normal. Shot with a long focal length lens, the edges of the frame tend to fall out of focus, drawing attention to a centrally framed action or an object — a cupped hand with samples of concrete for instance (fig. 13.5). Morris also exhibits a taste for extreme close-ups, and put altogether — lighting, composition — at times the objects on-screen become nearly unrecognizable. When Leuchter discusses his addiction to coffee and cigarettes, for example, a series of lavish shots of a percolator brewing coffee disintegrates into abstraction (fig 13.6).

Figure 13.5

Figure 13.6

Irrespective of Leuchter's spurious methodology, neo-Nazis and historical revisionists champion him, and his supposed proof that the gas chambers did not exist. As a result of his newfound "celebrity," Leuchter is invited to conferences and rallies, where he speaks to enthusiastic crowds, all feeding into his timid disposition. Leuchter is ultimately torn down as a result of his popularity as a spokesperson for Holocaust-deniers. Prison contractors beat a hasty retreat and terminate deals with the execution consultant, his wife divorces him, and he is left in financial ruin.

During one of Morris's staged re-enactments we see Leuchter in what appears to be the ruins of one of the gas chambers in Auschwitz. Leuchter is poised over a small pool of water (fig. 13.7), and the historian Robert Jan Van Pelt, in voiceover, says:

> Holocaust-denial is a story about vanity. It's a way to get into the limelight, to be noticed, to be someone, maybe to be loved. I have sympathy for Fred who is lost in Auschwitz, because I think he's lost. But not any more with the Fred who appears at these conferences.

Again the imagery corresponds to the rhetoric of the scene but in no way corresponds to the spatial/temporal realities of Van Pelt's commentary. As

Van Pelt discusses Leuchter's "vanity," Morris's visual imagery alludes to the myth of Narcissus, who, taken by his own image reflected in a pond, falls into the water and drowns. In the pool of water we see Leuchter reflected upside down, suggestive of his distorted or backwards perspective. As we hear Van Pelt say, "Holocaust-denial is a story about vanity," a drop of water, presumably coming from the piece of debris that Leuchter has picked out from the pool of water, hits the surface of the pool on the word "vanity." The drop of water creates a ripple effect immediately distorting Leuchter's reflected image, as Van Pelt continues his voiceover, and Leuchter's deformed image undulates in the succeeding waves of water. The visual analogy — Leuchter as Narcissus — corresponds to the rhetorical thrust of the entire film.

Figure 13.7

Through the poetic staging and composition of the scene Morris adroitly delivers the thesis of the film: Leuchter is driven by narcissism. There is no ethical transgression here, Morris's multiple forays into history vis-à-vis individuals (e.g., Leuchter and Robert McNamara) in no way jeopardizes historical "truth"; with his staging, visual metaphors and analogies and outright manipulation, he does not subtract from historical discourse; rather, he adds to it by creating documentaries that are visually and narratively compelling. This kind of metaphorical visual imagery is central to the nuance of Morris's filmmaking and a mark of his careful craftsmanship and penchant for poetic imagery.

In an interview in *Cineaste* Morris reflects on *Mr. Death*, saying,

> There are so many visual metaphors in the film. No one ever writes about this — I think the movie gets so overwhelmed by questions of what it must be about or how it must function that the actual movie gets lost. I think in a way it's the most visually sophisticated thing that I have ever done.[12]

Janet Walker comments on this scene as well:

> Some images are so abstract that one cannot be sure they were actually shot on location. The slow-motion shots of a hammer hitting the head of a chisel and expelling rock fragments may not have been (and probably were not) shot at Auschwitz at all. At one point the film cuts from the video of Leuchter scraping up a handful of

pebbles from the bottom of a shallow pool of water on the chamber floor to a film image of concentric ripples created by a stone being dropped into a pool. There would have been no need to shoot this on location. In fact, better control of lighting and art direction could be achieved elsewhere. And are those really van Pelt's hands we see leafing through documents in the Auschwitz archive?[13]

Indeed, whether they are re-enactments of documentation of real events — Van Pelt visiting the archives at Auschwitz — really is of no consequence. Expository documentaries avail themselves of archival material without regard for the specifics of the event, but commonly use the archival material for rhetorical purposes. For Morris the same is true, but more particularly the elements of the poetic are artifacts of rhetorical — not spatial/temporal continuity.

INCANTATION

The constant idea was to not make a monument to the dead, turned to the past. If this existed, it could happen again; it exists now in another form.

—Alain Resnais[14]

The documentary genre (typically) seeks to convey "unadulterated reality," or "truthfulness" through the use of such cinematic conventions as the long take, archival photographs, archival documents, eyewitness testimony and expert testimony. These conventions are misleading, though, because they only connote "reality." Editing, stylized compositions, and other cinematic devices imply choice, and thus interpretation, manipulation, or deformity, challenging the integrity of the presumed allegiance between "pure history" and documentary film. Films that dispense with conventional modes of documentary are viewed as suspicious. Alain Resnais's 1955 Night and Fog straddles both sides of this debate. On the one hand, Resnais utilizes the standard conventions of the documentary genre, but at the same time in certain instances he adopts stylized cinematography and rhetoric issuing a subtle critique of the genre, which in the process makes for a powerful documentary about the Holocaust. "Night and Fog" as Elizabeth Cowie puts it, "is a documentary in the tradition of the 'creative treatment of actuality,' impassioned and personal."[15]

The influence of Night and Fog is far reaching. Not only has the film been viewed perhaps more widely than any other Holocaust documentary, but also it has been referenced in a number of subsequent films that address the Holocaust. As discussed earlier, in Kitty: Return to Auschwitz (1979) Peter Morely utilizes a haunting tracking shot of toilets in Auschwitz, a clear reference to a shot in Night and Fog.[16]

While conforming to many of the conventions of the documentary genre, Night and Fog at the same time destabilizes the very discourse that it employs through the use of ambiguity. This is witnessed through the subtle mixing of categories, and the blurring of genres. The film opens and closes with long takes scanning the ruins of Auschwitz. The opening shots in particular are quite unsettling. Resnais begins with a pastoral setting, a vast uninterrupted stretch of farm fields, where the upper two-thirds of the frame is filled with sky and dotted with clouds. In the same shot, the camera slowly cranes downward to reveal a barbwire fence, and the voiceover narrative begins by confirming what we see, "Even a peaceful landscape, even a meadow in harvest, with crows circling overhead and grass fires." The second shot also presents a farm field where crows fly across the screen left to right and, in a stylized manner, tracks backward to reveal a barbwire fence. These tracking shots are indicative of Resnais's style.

These images at first appear to be incongruous with the Holocaust. However, it becomes clear that Resnais appears to draw on our cultural knowledge of Van Gogh's "Crows in a Wheat-field" (1890).[17] The crows in Van Gogh's painting, which hang over the field, have subsequently been read as an ominous sign, pointing to the painter's pending fate; on July 27, 1890, Van Gogh shot himself, and as a result he died two days later. Given the mythos that surrounds Van Gogh's "Crows in a Wheat-field," and its connotations of suffering and death, perhaps Resnais is priming the spectator, prefiguring what is about to unfold. The camera's movements seem to confirm this subtle visual strategy; from this pastoral imagery and the voiceover narrative that references "crows circling overhead," the camera moves into the interior of the camp, the site of death and suffering.

In these first two introductory shots, Resnais establishes something of a troubling motif: mixing beauty with horror, where somewhere between the banalities of everyday life "even a road where cars and peasants and couples pass, even a resort village with a steeple and country fair can lead to a concentration camp." These two shots stay well within the bounds of the documentary genre — drawing on conventions such as voiceover narrative and long takes — but at the same time, the stylized elements used (tracking and crane shots, the self-conscious composition) are more commonly associated with standard narrative (fiction) film. This mixing of genres subtly unfastens our expectations regarding the genre of documentary film. Resnais ever so slightly then unnerves the spectator by introducing a degree of ambiguity through the mixing of beauty and horror, and genres. This ambiguity embodies the abject and sets the stage for the conclusion of the film, which attempts to locate culpability, suggesting that responsibility for the catastrophic events of the Holocaust is not limited to the perpetrators, to the guards and officers who ran the camps, but is to one degree or another the responsibility of all humanity (a conclusion for which it has been criticized).

As the film progresses the voiceover introduces a degree of reflexivity: "The only visitor to the blocks now is the camera. A strange grass covers the paths once trod by inmates. No current runs through the wires. No footstep is heard but our own." This is set to the last in a series of tracking shots before shots from *Triumph of the Will* are inserted. Coupled with the tracking shots — which in themselves already signify artifice — the voiceover breaks down the fourth wall, revealing its own construction.

When first presented with the idea of making a film about the Holocaust Resnais initially declined, and it was not until Jean Cayrol agreed to join the project that he decided to make *Night and Fog*. Resnais, although drafted in 1945 and stationed in Allied-occupied Germany and Austria, had no direct relation or experience with the German death camps. Thus, his initial refusal to Argos Films and the Historical Committee of the Second World War,[18] who proposed that he make a documentary about the concentration camps. Recounting how the project finally came about, the director notes, "To make a film about the concentration camps, it seemed to me you had to have been an inmate, or deported for political reasons . . . I accepted only on the condition that the commentary would be written by Jean Cayrol because he was himself a survivor."[19] Jean-Raphaël-Marie-Noël Cayrol, a Catholic poet, joined the French Resistance during the Second World War, and would eventually be deported to Mauthausen. While interned in the concentration camp Cayrol composed poems, and he would continue to do so after the war; in 1946 he published a collection of his poems, *Poèmes de la nuit et du brouillard* (*Poems of the Night and of the Fog*). Cayrol, given his firsthand experience, in a sense gave Resnais license to make the film. While, on the one hand, Cayrol's narrative provides an "authentic" accounting of the events, it nevertheless delivers stoic and horrific facts through his poetic incantation. Resnais's camera in a sense follows Cayrol's lead here; the film employs long takes, uses archival still photographs and stock footage, all of which suggests an "unmediated" view typifying the documentary genre. However, along with these typical tropes of the documentary genre Resnais also employs his signature and highly stylized tracking shots. Smoothly and gently Resnais's tracking camera repeatedly punctures the boundary of the concentration camp, drawing us further and further into the belly of the beast. While Cayrol's more stoic discourse (e.g., listing a litany of horrific facts) corresponds to Resnais's conventional documentary elements (e.g., long takes, use of archival material), Cayrol's more poetic reflections correspond to Resnais's more stylized cinematography.

William Rothman in his *Documentary Film Classics* argues that Resnais's camera is closely related to the perpetrators of the Holocaust. Rothman, who is taking his lead from Jay Cantor,[20] argues that Resnais's cinematic artistry in some fashion is performative, and in this performativity is enacting the Nazis' masterful artistry of death; to further his argument he cites that, "the camera most often belongs not to Resnais at all, but to the builders and operators of the camps."[21] This is not exactly true. A good deal of the footage seen in *Night and Fog*, and particularly the footage that Rothman cites as German footage, is from Allied forces that liberated the camps. True, there is some footage of Jewish deportations, one photograph that was surreptitiously taken by one of the Sonderkommando, and a couple of stills from executions at the hands of the Einsatzgruppen (a military attachment that followed the regular German military and whose duty it was to execute Jews),[22] but there is very little footage that exists of a concentration camp *in operation*, as Rothman seems to suggest. There are also in *Night and Fog* excerpts from Leni Riefenstahl's *Triumph of the*

Will. While certainly emblematic of the regime's ideology, none of the footage in Riefenstahl's film, of course, depicts concentration camps. For the most part, and this is especially true of some of the most disturbing images in *Night and Fog*, the film largely relies on footage from Allied sources.

Quite interestingly, the film also features two short clips taken from Wanda Jakubowska's 1947 film *The Last Stage*. (Rothman perhaps mistakenly takes this material from *The Last Stage* as Nazi footage.) In one of these shots Resnais renders non-contiguous space as contiguous, by cutting between archival material depicting a train deportation and the ominous arrival of the train in *The Last Stage* at Auschwitz-Birkenau. The train in the archival material travels right to left across the screen, which matches Jakubowska's shot of the train slowing to a stop inside the camp. The dramatic lighting of *The Last Stage*, the composition of the train and a line of German soldiers on the ramp leading into the distance towards the vanishing point, highlighted by fog and darkness, adds to the tension of the scene. The rhetorical coherence of the voiceover also ties these two shots together, irrespective of the origin of the visual material. As the train in the archival material disappears into the distance the voiceover narrates, "A message flutters to the ground. Will it be found? Death makes its first cut." The succeeding images from *The Last Stage* continue the discourse on deportation, "Its second is made on arrival in the night and fog." Death makes its second cut, as deportees are about to disembark the train that has just arrived in Auschwitz-Birkenau. The poetics of movement (of the trains) and the voiceover establish continuity between the two shots.

There is a second critical scene in *The Last Stage* that Resnais appropriates. A group of female internees are loaded onto trucks inside the Birkenau camp and led down a road leading to the crematoria at the far end. In the distance, black smoke bellows out from one of the chimneys. What is of particular interest in this clip, and it is not evident from just watching *Night and Fog*, is that the women in the trucks begin to sing the French national anthem, "La Marseillaise." The women on the trucks all know their fate is sealed, but this is a small gesture of resistance nonetheless, a refusal in the face of imminent death to surrender one's pride and dignity. Replacing the audio track from *The Last Stage* with the *Night and Fog* voiceover transforms the "meaning" of the imagery; where in Jakubowska's film the shot illustrates the transport of particular characters to their death, in Resnais's film it becomes a generic substitute for transports in general. The fact, though, that Resnais elects to use this particular clip, intimately related to the French, is probably no small coincidence.

At the conclusion of *Night and Fog* a series of individuals, including German officers and kapos, testify, each denying their culpability in the crimes committed. Jean Cayrol, the narrator of *Night and Fog*, retorts, "Then who is responsible?" Immediately following this question, Resnais cuts to Allied footage of a pile of emaciated corpses, first in a medium long shot, then a medium shot, the vertebrae of some figures clearly visible, some with their skin split open, allowing the question to linger over these horrific images. Rothman, in discussing this sequence, says:

What this passage is saying — what all of *Night and Fog* is saying — is that the Kapo and the officer are responsible — as the victim is not, as we are not — for building and operating these cities of death, for the "endless fear" that was their "true dimension." But responsibility for liberating the camps — condemning the executioners, laying the dead to rest, welcoming the survivors into our midst, freeing ourselves and our world — is in our hands, the hands of all us survivors.[23]

In this rhetorical turn of phrase, Rothman groups us all under the category of "survivor," and, at the same time, figures perpetrators of the Holocaust as agents of utter evil. This Manichaean arrangement — where "we" are positioned on the side of "good," and "they" are positioned on the side of "evil" — reduces Resnais's richly nuanced film into a formulaic and tawdry documentary, and indeed, propaganda. Rothman wants to let us — the spectators — off the hook too quickly; and although he says that *Night and Fog* is really a condemnation of the perpetrators, and an exultation of the survivors (to which we have been given honorary membership), Resnais's film *is not* a simple renunciation of the Nazis and their criminality.

Rothman is correct insofar as Resnais places the Holocaust "in our hands," but Resnais does this not so much to appease the viewer or commend us for our triumph over evil. He places the Holocaust "in our hands" as an admonishment. In the closing moments of the film Resnais makes this clear. As a matter of pattern or habit the camera tracks left to right, and in the closing moments of the film as the camera tracks left to right over the ruins of Auschwitz, the voiceover says: "The crematoria are no longer used. The Nazis' cunning is but child's play today. Nine million dead haunt this countryside. Who among us keeps watch from this strange watchtower, to warn of the arrival of our new executioners? Are their faces really different from our own?" Whereas Rothman wants to situate *Night and Fog* as a triumph of good over evil, or as he says, "condemning the executioners, laying the dead to rest, welcoming the survivors into our midst, freeing ourselves and our world," *Night and Fog* is hardly so simple. Quite contrary to Rothman's Manichaean arrangement, the closing moments of *Night and Fog* encourage us not to simply condemn but to do something far more painful, far more horrific, to see a little bit of ourselves in the faces of the executioners.

When the film first screened at the 1956 Cannes Film Festival, the German government issued a formal complaint, commenting that the film would generate anti-German hatred, and the French, likewise, demanded that one of the photographic images in the film be removed before it could be authorized for screening in France. Resnais had violated an unspoken taboo by including a photograph depicting French collaboration in the network of deportations to concentration camps; "only after Resnais masked the kèpi on a French gendarme in a photo of the Pithiviers camp where French prisoners awaited deportation," could the film be screened, because of course the photograph would "have reminded viewers of Vichy complicity in deportations"[24] (fig. 13.8; fig. 13.9). In post-war France the role of the resistance has been romanticized, while the accounts of sympathizers and collaborators with the German regime have been quietly hidden. (This is the overarching theme of Marcel Ophüls's 1969 documentary *The Sorrow and the Pity*.) Resnais notes in a radio interview that a compromise had to be reached regarding this sensitive topic "because there were buyers waiting to bring it out in the theaters, which was really surprising. So we compromised on this incredible detail by painting in a beam that obscured the policeman's cap."[25]

Figure 13.8

Figure 13.9

The artistry of the film is in its ability to stare abjection in the face, and Resnais does this both through the form (e.g., long takes in a tracking shot) and the content of the film (e.g., the photograph of French collaboration). When watching *Night and Fog*, as François Truffaut insists, we must drop the pretense of being a "moviegoer" and be involved in the film "as human beings who have to open our eyes and question ourselves."[26]

In the film, Resnais examines a number of the "practical" problems of mass murder: what to do with material possessions of the concentration camp detainees: combs, eyeglasses, or even women's hair. The camera tends to float, scanning across the "by-products" of murder, and in some cases illustrates the "creative solutions" for the "by-products" of manufactured death; for example, as the camera scans across a vast accumulation of human hair, the following shot shows rolls of fabric interwoven with hair.

Likewise when the narrator says, "From the bones . . . fertilizer," an oven door in one of the crematoriums opens to reveal skeletal remains, followed immediately by a shot of human bones, and once again the "creative solution" for the by-product of mass murder is shown. In this case bones become fertilizer and subsequently we are presented with a shot of a farm field full of cabbages. This shot, in a sense a reversal of the opening sequences, is taken from a farm field with the concentration camp off in the distance, one of the guard towers jutting up above the horizon.

Much of *Night and Fog* up to this point has kept violence and death within the boundaries of the camp. In the opening shots of the film the camera tracks inward, moving from the pastoral exterior of the camp into the hypocenter of death. In addition, prior to this exterior shot in the cabbage field, what we have seen is the movement of deportees into the camp, again in maintaining the distinction between inside and outside the camp, which — within the film — operates as something like a centrifuge, containing within its center horrific violence and death. What this exterior shot from the farm field does is begin to break down the barriers between inside and outside, between life and death, between the monstrous acts of the Nazis and the mundane world beyond the camp's perimeter. This exterior shot illustrates that the boundaries between inside and outside the camp are not as clearly defined as we might imagine; even the opening shots suggest this in the manner in which the camera seemingly penetrates the porous boundary partitioning the camp from the "ordinary" world outside. In addition, there is an even more disturbing breakdown of boundaries; in fields fertilized with human bones, life consumes death. This exterior shot then introduces, in a literal and figurative way, one of the most fundamental prohibitions: cannibalism, the most vile breakdown of boundaries between the living the dead. Concentration camps are not just sites of violence and death; this is where humanity consumes itself.

Resnais is calling attention to the dimensions of abjection in *Night and Fog*, not just in its content but also in its form. As discussed earlier, there is a degree of ambiguity in the mixing of beauty and horror, and the mixing of genres. The tracking shots that are so characteristic of Resnais's work seem to run counter to the content. The smooth tracking camera connotes tranquility, and although Resnais films the camps long after the war, the violence that impregnates the ground is still there; these sites are charged with catastrophic history. The tracking shots that Resnais utilizes, then, are quite uncanny insofar as they resemble the penetrating movement of the cattle-cars into the concentration camp. In this performative gesture the spectator is positioned as a deportee (perhaps in this regard echoing Rothman's argument). There is in fact some similarity between Resnais's strategy and Lanzmann's; recall that when filming at Auschwitz Lanzmann says, "I pushed the dolly myself,"[27] admitting that he was compelled to one degree or another to "relive" the experience.

Perhaps more than Lanzmann's film, *Night and Fog* shares affinities with Pier Paolo Pasolini's *Salò, or the 120 Days of Sodom*, where both films go out of their way to mix beauty and horror. *Night and Fog* has long tracking/crane shots, which appear to emulate Western landscape paintings and, likewise, *Salò's mise en scène* bursts with high modernist architecture, paintings, décor, and furnishing. Despite this, drawing from sophisticated Western traditions of art, their content appears incongruous, illustrative of an abject lining of culture. This is what Horkheimer and Adorno called the dialectic of Enlightenment, the parallel trajectory of humanity and barbarism. Both films also emphasize the distinction between inside and outside, those who were trapped inside the concentration camps (or the Château de Silling in *Salò*), and the rest of the world outside. They carefully navigate the spectator inside the sight/site of horror, and situate — to one degree or another — culpability with the spectator. Filmmaker and Pasolini's longtime collaborator Jean-Claude Biette in the making of documentary *Salò: Yesterday and Today* (Amaury Voslion, 2002)[28] is cited as saying, "Anyone interested in civics must see *Night and Fog* and *Salò.*"

In *Night and Fog*, Resnais coaxes the spectator inside the concentration camp through his artful tracking and crane shots. In the erasure of clearly defined lines between inside and outside, however, Resnais asks us to identify less with the concentration camp interns, and more with the perpetrators, the technicians, the community just adjacent to the camps. Much of the film's power is this abject revelation about culture's complicity, and *Salò* does much the same in its constant insistence on the spectator's identification with the libertines. Neither film simply condemns the monstrosity of the Nazi genocidal program but, rather, both emphasize the potential failure within culture. The horrors of the Second World War are not an anomaly, but rather a looming threat that might happen again.

The act of murder, of genocide, is horrific in its own right, but what makes the concentration camps so utterly abject is that "culture" — science, architecture, engineering, creative problem solving — was employed for the purposes of mass murder. Seen from this perspective, the Holocaust is not a product of monsters, but rather a human endeavor, an "achievement" of human "ingenuity." In the narrative, and in the visual rhetoric, Resnais seems to be breaking down the boundaries between "us" and "them"; temporal moments are collapsed; archival footage mixes freely with the material he films. Resnais wants us to own the Holocaust in the contemporary moment. The concentration camps were not a product of the German imagination, of a monstrous imagination, of an anomalous history, but of an all too human imagination. The Holocaust is not a "German problem," it is a human problem.

Chapter Fourteen

Experimental Films I: Rituals of Memory

INTRODUCTION

The following two chapters focus on experimental films that use innovative formal strategies to negotiate the Holocaust. Experimental film, or often what is referred to as avant-garde cinema, is generally concerned with what narrative and documentary film disavow. Experimental works push representational boundaries, and they place a premium on aesthetic and formal pursuits above narrative ends. This is not to say that experimental films completely abandon narrative or content. Rather, what experimental films narrate does not easily conform to the conventions of linear narrative practices (including those found in the documentary genre). "How does one speak the unspeakable," Jeffrey Skoller says, contemplating the nature of experimental film, "make clear what is opaque, understand what is not understandable, when the limits of linguistic and representational forms are the only thing that *is* clear? It is here that the search for adequate strategies that could take into account the aporias of such an event become necessary."[1] The aporias — the holes, the gaps in the visual record, the abyss of abject horror, the impasse of representational limits — these elements are precisely what conventional narrative and documentary film disavow: concealed behind the cloak of narrative coherence, or fixating on what is visible as a displacement for what is invisible (e.g., the use of archival material in documentaries).

"Artists for whom taking into account the aporias in an event like the Shoah," Skoller notes of them that it is imperative to "start from the position of silence and incomprehension and work within it rather than trying to overcome it. Their work raises more questions than it answers."[2] Claude Lanzmann's *Shoah*, an unconventional documentary which utilizes these experimental tactics, does this in the cutaways to concentration camps; there is no denial of absence, rather there is an abundance of it. Documentaries often obsessively conceal the holes in our (visual) knowledge of the Holocaust with archival material, testimony (the witness functions as an index of the event), or re-enactments, whereas experimental films exhibit a tendency to meditate on absence. Skoller cites Ernie Gehr's 1982–85 film *Signal — Germany on the Air*, as an example of this. In it, a number of shots of an ordinary Berlin street intersection finally give way to the realization of the historical charge associated with the space: a billboard in three languages reads, "This was the site of a Gestapo torture chamber." As with *Shoah*, "empty" spaces evoke something else altogether, signifying what is absent, and what has no visible evidence.

This chapter focuses on the ritualistic treatment of memory as distinct from the formal strategies of using found footage and assemblage techniques, discussed in the following chapter. Many of the films discussed in this and the succeeding chapter resonate deeply with themes covered elsewhere in this book, as indeed the Holocaust as a subject poses a unique challenge to representation and often filmmakers use an array of strategies to approach it.

The work of Péter Forgács, for instance, is very clearly about the fragility of memory, and its ritualistic reconstruction in celluloid. I have elected, however, to contextualize his work in the discussion of found footage and assemblage, because so much of it depends on the formal qualities that materialize in the tactile reworking of amateur films or home movies. The films featured in this chapter, through their carefully crafted tones and rhythms, look at the rituals of memory and invite comparisons to prayer. Specifically, they are *From the East*, *The Trap*, *Silent Song*, *The Ties That Bind*, *The March*, and *run/dig*. Furthermore, many also exhibit the qualities associated with personal, poetic, and/or reflexive documentaries. In many instances very modest productions, perhaps the work of a single individual, they possess intimate and thus highly idiosyncratic sign systems. This chapter then surveys a range of experimental strategies, from animation and installation, that address the Holocaust.

NEGOTIATING ABSENCE

Negotiating absence, as already established, is one of the most common tropes of experimental Holocaust films, and this invites, if not necessitates, poetic strategies. Experimental works might negotiate phantom memories — memories that are not properly belonging to the filmmaker, or the subject of the filmmaker, but nonetheless experienced. "The amputated are left only with phantom pains," Nadine Fresco writes, "but who can say that the pain felt in a hand that one no longer has is not pain. These latter-day Jews are like people who have had a hand amputated that they never had."[3] Experimental films as a strategy might look to exhibit some of the characteristics of "phantom pains," those things that are physically absent but physically present.

Jay Rosenblatt's 2005 film *Phantom Limb* is not a Holocaust film that looks literally at the event; instead, it deals with it obliquely, through the death of the filmmaker's younger brother as a child, and meditates "on the guilt and suffering that have haunted family members since," Michael Renov observes. "It is a film that takes a terrible and inexpressible family secret as its founding condition and challenge. As a work of mourning, *Phantom Limb* is produced decades after the fact, a clue to the deferred or dislocated temporality that death and mourning can engender."[4] The relevance of Holocaust representations is clear here. Renov is speaking specifically about autobiographical films with regard to *Phantom Limb*; however, autobiographical film in its poetic incantations often adopts experimental strategies.

> It [*Phantom Limb*] is a haunting meditation that, in addition to its aesthetic value, may have some therapeutic power as well. But it also offers a chastening message — that autobiographical films, like all art, can never hope to wholly displace or heal the secrets and traumas they disclose. Yet we remain drawn to these meditative vehicles, perhaps for their purgative powers, perhaps for the mysteries of the heart which they momentarily expose.[5]

Julia Kristeva asks a related question in *Black Sun*, "Painting as a substitute for prayer?"[6] Indeed, if it is artistic practice that shoulders the burdens once the sole domain of organized religion, it is no wonder that experimental films evoke something of an incantation, a personal prayer, frequently displaying a ritualistic sensibility for its purgative potential to negotiate the trauma of the Holocaust.

René Girard's book *Violence and the Sacred* is a discourse on the nature and function of ritual: "Violence is the heart and secret soul of the sacred."[7] It is ritual, or its counterpart the aesthetic experience, evoked through artistic practices, that releases us from the horrifying grip of violence. "Ritual," Girard comments, "is nothing more than the regular exercise of 'good' violence."[8] There are examples of this in art history, such as Hermann Nitsch,[9] whose performances were exactly that, an exorcising of "good violence" designed to channel violent energy, to sublimate it; others might include Christian Boltanski and his altar-like pieces, or Anselm Kiefer and his performance-oriented work giving the Nazi salute in the context of historically charged sites, confronting Germany with its own history. "The function of ritual is to 'purify' violence,"[10] and it is through ritualistic practices, according to Girard, that tempers violence by allowing it to surface in a proscribed manner. Most of the experimental works, such as *Phantom Limb*, do not explicitly rely on ritualized practices, but rather engender ritual in the process of excavating traumatic memories, memories scarred by the violence of the Holocaust.

Joshua Hirsch discusses the materialization of Holocaust trauma through the post-traumatic flashback in cinema in his *After Image: Film, Trauma and the Holocaust*. Hirsch refers to post-traumatic flashbacks (or a return to something which is no longer present) as a cinematic device that cleaves narrative cohesion, breaking or impeding narrative progression. He posits that avant-garde films — having pushed the boundaries of narrative structure — have made the post-traumatic flashback acceptable to mainstream American audiences. "Situated in the avant-garde of mainstream American film, . . . [Sidney Lumet's 1964 film] *The Pawnbroker*, was able to borrow the posttraumatic flashback from [Alain Resnais's 1959 film] *Hiroshima mon amour* and import it into American film culture in such a way as to deliver a formal shock to a mass audience."[11] The whole of Chantal Akerman's 1993 film *From the East* might be conceived of as a post-traumatic flashback, a dream that returns to a haunted landscape.

From the East exhibits some of the characteristics of the personal documentary. Akerman "returns" to Eastern Europe, a "'back to my roots,' kind of film,"[12] as she puts it, where her parents — Polish Jews who emigrated to Belgium in the 1930s — lived prior to the outbreak of the Second World War. The film is effectively a series of long takes — many static shots, and other long dolly shots — depicting the everydayness of Poland, (East) Germany, and the Soviet Union shot on three different trips between 1992 and 1993. *From the East* exhibits some differences with the personal documentary form, though. For instance, there is no narration, no interlocutors, no labeling or title cards contextualizing what's on-screen. Indeed, there is no narrative as such; instead, simply a series of meditative, enigmatic shots. Additionally, Akerman, as Alisa Lebow observes,

> never specifies any personal markers or indicates her investment in the terrain. She eschews iconographic Jewish images (no synagogues, no cemeteries, no crematoria) and avoids interviews and narration that might concretize her position. She even bypasses the specific town from which her family came. Akerman seems convinced of the impossibility of finding any meaningful remnants of the past.[13]

The presumed Western viewer does not see the banalities of everyday life in the East, but rather *projects* the weight of history onto "vacant" places and faces. "The effect for Ashkenazi Jews of Eastern European descent," Lebow argues, "is that 'the old country' becomes a sign without referent, an imaginary construct with no actual geographical correlate."[14] The landscapes and the people that populate the film do not signify what is seen but instead what is absent.

The uncanny specter that haunts the landscape transforms the ordinary into the horrific. Images of men and women marching through the snow evoke "a historical imaginary," as Lebow calls it, "redirecting our attention away from these contemporary specificities towards the collective memory of prior (forced) frozen marches."[15] The film, as Kristine Butler notes, "is ostensibly 'about' the fall of the Eastern bloc, [and] renounces the authoritative voice of the documentary, eliminating the voiceover and narrative structure which would typically weave through and connect the various moments."[16] We are encouraged, if not obliged, though, to read the imagery differently without a voiceover or narrative structure. The end of the Soviet era is evident, but the Holocaust haunts the vacant sites (especially the Polish landscape). Cut loose from the moorings of specificity, the spectator is free to project onto the images *from the east*.

But let's be frank here, there is an orientalist sensibility in the film. "The Orient is not only adjacent to Europe," Edward Said posits, but it is the recurring "other" in the Western imagination, that has "helped to define Europe (or the West), as its contrasting image, idea, personality, experience."[17] There is at once something profoundly familiar in Akerman's images, and at the same time deeply disturbing, an uncanny quality, something scary as Lanzmann suggests. These feelings, though, come from without, not from within the images. The people that populate the film are simply going about their lives, indifferent and impassive. The spectator (and the filmmaker), on the other hand, projects the collective history of the Holocaust onto those Eastern landscapes. And perhaps, as students of film, and specifically Holocaust films, the incessant use of dolly shots in Akerman's film — unconsciously even — call to mind Alain Resnais's use of tracking shots in *Night and Fog*, and Lanzmann's compulsion to relive the Holocaust experience, where he says, for instance, that "the tracking shot into Auschwitz, I push the dolly myself. If the film is a resurrection, it's because of how I was compelled to do it."[18] In form (tracking shots) and content (the East) perhaps unfairly, then, Akerman renders the East as oriental — robbed of specificity, and hollowed out of localized meaning — serving merely as a screen where we are given license to project the history of the Holocaust. In which case, then, perhaps it's not the filmmaker who bears the responsibility for this orientalist sensibility so much as the spectator.

(RE)ANIMATION

Orly Yadin and Sylvie Bringas's 1998 short animated film *Silence* is a beautiful mediation on Tana Ross's personal memories. When Ross first approached Yadin in 1996 to make a film about her Holocaust experience the filmmaker refused, citing the abundance of documentaries already on the subject. Interned at Theresienstadt as a small child, Ross was born in Berlin in 1940. "By some miraculous coincidence," Yadin recounts, "her grandmother had been sent separately to the same camp, found her and kept her hidden until liberation."[19] As with many Theresienstadt internees, Ross's mother was transported to Auschwitz where she was murdered; however, Ross did not learn of this until much later in life. While the filmmakers use live-action archival footage to establish historical and geographical context in the narrative, they freely manipulate the material, and use animation to enter the subjective space of personal memory.

Thinking about how to represent Ross's story posed a series of challenges. "The only visual documentation that Tana had of her childhood was a couple of photographs and three letters," Yadin recalls. "Apart from the Nazi propaganda film made of Theresienstadt, there was no footage that I knew of that could help illuminate her story."[20] Uninterested in adding to the abundance of interview-based documentaries on the Holocaust experience, Yadin continued to rebuff Ross. "One day, however," Yadin recalls, "I had a flash of inspiration and realized that if we could animate her childhood experiences and enter the realm of imagination that way, then the film could work for us."[21] Yadin insists that the animated documentary is more "honest," because it is all too easy — for spectators and filmmakers alike — to assume that the photographic/filmic record is a transparent window onto the past. "The honesty of animation lies in the fact that the filmmaker is completely upfront about his or her intervention with the subject and if we believe the film to be true it is because we believe the intention was true."[22] As with many expository documentaries, there frequently is a reliance on archival material for rhetorical purposes, without regard for spatial/ temporal continuity within the diegesis. All too often scenes of deportation or liberation footage are used for generic purposes irrespective of the specific event they depict. Documentary filmmakers, as Yadin correctly observes, "might even resort to using the 'wrong' footage in desperation!" Animated documentaries inherently yield to the limits of representing reality, "what you are seeing is not a photographic record but it is nonetheless a true re-presentation of a reality."[23]

One of the animators for *Silence* specifically cites animation's capacity to utilize poetic discourse. "Animation's access to the language of metaphor and transformation allowed," animator Ruth Lingford reflects,

> a subtler and more concentrated portrayal of the situation than would have been possible using live-action drama. Images such as the one where the children transform into cockroaches and are swept away with a giant broom have [fig. 14.1], I think, an effect that is both visceral and thought-provoking. Using animation makes it clear that this is a subjective account.[24]

Figure 14.1

Detached from the presumptions of realism, or mimesis — the photographic/ filmic medium always already infers a privileged access to reality — animation is readily accepted as subjective, and perfectly suited not only to re-present historical events, but the personal perception of those events. Where the photographic medium is presumed to be shackled to realist conventions, and the historical world, animation has unbridled access to the full range of visual poetics — drawing visual analogies, metaphors, symbolism, and the like — free of any expectations that the animated film is constrained by assumed fidelity to reality.

The use of animation has a number of distinct advantages, as I have begun to illustrate, but "It also points to the limitations of traditional documentary methods in adequately revealing the survivors' (or other personal) experiences."[25] The photographic/filmic Holocaust record is finite, as evident in the habitual recycling of archival material seen again and again (e.g., the Bergen-Belsen liberation footage, the children at Auschwitz who roll up their sleeves to reveal their tattooed numbers). "Animation can show us an un-filmed past and can enter the depths of human emotions."[26] The inherent difficulties of representing the past is further complicated in the effort to express the feelings and emotions of a young child. As discussed in an earlier chapter, Lydia Chagoll's 1979 short expository documentary *They Came From Far Away* does this by incorporating illustrations done by children at Theresienstadt. *Silence* goes a step further. While Chagoll's film *tells us* about the experience of children in the concentration camp, and shows us the evidentiary artifacts, *Silence* creates "a child's world through animated images."[27] Although the filmmakers insist that *Silence* is a documentary, its formal techniques are perhaps more aligned with narrative fiction; as Yadin reveals, "our hope was that telling the story in this way would enable us to recreate the little girl's point of view and help the audience to identify with the central character."[28]

Among the advantages of exploiting the animation form is that the filmmaker has complete control of what materializes on-screen. The use of archival material — especially some of the more horrific imagery — runs up against a number of problems including the potential of trivializing, generalizing, and anesthetizing spectator sensitivity to the true horrors of the Holocaust. The filmmakers for *Silence* decided, as animator Ruth Lingford recalls, "early on not to be too grim, [and] not to use horrific images." Lingford continues, "So my job was to evoke the misery of Tana's situation without resorting to scenes of obvious horror."[29] Thus, the filmmakers were able to use "strong harsh images without repelling and alienating the audience."[30] There is no need for bulldozers pushing heaps of corpses into pits, there is no need to repeat the wasteland imagery of Bergen-Belsen, but rather the animator is free to create highly nuanced on-screen imagery that is at once emotive and contemplative.

Amy Kravitz's 1998 five-minute black lithographic crayon-on-paper animated film *The Trap* is based on a citation from Elie Wiesel's book *Souls on Fire*, "I try to imagine my grandfather in the train that carried him away."[31] The film is a complete abstraction; shifting shades, tones, vague forms and shapes recede into blackness or are consumed by light, evoking movement, and yet — although paradoxically — confinement, paralysis, the feeling of being *trapped* (in a cattle-car). The audio design, also abstract, is perhaps the most suggestive of the film's originating premise; the ghostly acoustics are reminiscent of the "clickity-clack" of railroad tracks, train whistles, and the clap of a cattle-car door latch.

Enigmatic and innately fragmentary in form, the film is in a sense infinitely more faithful than any documentary or narrative film that represents the experience of deportation. In some respects its abyss of abstraction is similar to Claude Lanzmann's barren landscapes that show "nothing." While narrative and documentary films often disavow the fragmentary nature of historical knowledge, by plugging in the fissures in the visual record with existing archival material, re-enactments, and computer animation, *The Trap* is precisely interested in these gaping fissures in the visual record. The spectator tries to identify forms and sounds, and grasps at the semblance of something "meaningful," but there are only vague traces of events that have no indexical referent (fig. 14.2).

Figure 14.2

Unlike *Silence*, there is no pretense of documenting any one specific event or individual experience; in fact, there is no effort to represent anything literally. The film *derives* from, rather than *represents*, the Wiesel citation. It is an abstraction of the concept of deportation and, more accurately, is a representation of the *feeling* of deportation: the motion, and acrid charcoal black of a train that has taken a loved one away.

RELIVING, RETELLING, RE-PRESENTING . . .

Su Friedrich's 1985 film *The Ties That Bind* in part explores her mother's experience of growing up in Nazi Germany.[32] Friedrich's mother, Lore Friedrich, prompted by questions posed by her daughter/filmmaker, examines her life under the Nazi regime, life in occupied Germany, and finally life after marrying an American soldier whom she met while working in the de-Nazification program.[33] Assembled together with a myriad of sources, Friedrich's film both intones the theme of memory examined in this chapter, as well as adopting the practice of assemblage discussed in the following chapter. The visual material that she presents frequently functions according to associative links, and is not directly representative of her mother's reflections.

The Ties That Bind, Patrical Hampl observes, "is not 'seeking a self' as the cliché sell-line of contemporary memoirs so often promise. She is not even seeking her mother's life as she intercuts interview segments with period footage and film from her own contemporary visits to Ulm, her mother's hometown."[34] While experimental films — or even personal, or poetic documentaries — have the potential of indulging exercises in self-absorption, *The Ties That Bind* never does. Rather, the film seeks to locate "a shard of the historical puzzle, a small but essential fragment she feels capable of placing in the abiding mystery and misery of that war. The story may be 'personal,' but it is autobiographical more in the service of history than psychology."[35]

Although Friedrich recorded both her questions, and her mother's responses on audiotape, she has edited herself out of the audio narrative. On occasion we notice Friedrich's presence — an audible gasp, for instance, when her mother describes the bombing of Stuttgart, which killed three-quarters of the population. In the place of the filmmaker's audible voice, the questions are posed word by word, scratched directly on to film[36] (fig. 14.3). This strategy of presenting her voice has received contrasting interpretations. While Scott MacDonald views this as a universalizing agent, offering an entry point for viewers, removed from the specificity of Friedrich's voice, Hampl, on the other hand, sees it as an individual expression. The filmmaker's voice materializes on-screen, for Hampl, in the

carefully calibrated [scrawl] to suggest levels of emotion. The presentation is jerky, even frantic as the subject gets desperate. The technique is particularly effective when Friedrich is trying to elicit information about her German mother's awareness of the treatment of the Jews and the existence of the death camps during the war years.[37]

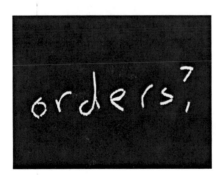

Figure 14.3

And perhaps these positions are not mutually exclusive. Writing the questions, as opposed to speaking them in the unique texture of her own voice, invites the spectator's inner voice to recite the question (if only in their head), and at the same time, the character of the writing is expressionistic, with an undeniable kinetic quality that corresponds to the sense of urgency in each respective question.

The imagery that appears in the film is frequently not representative, but associative. "Friedrich's painstaking editing creates a complex sensuous weave which continually articulates meaning," Scott MacDonald observes. "A range of suggestive intersections between various strands in the weave are developed. In some instances, these intersections are poignant and/or amusing."[38] For instance, as Lore discusses the absurdity of warfare, and her adamant anti-war position, this is juxtaposed with imagery of professional wrestling from a television screen (fig. 14.4). Similarly, when Lore describes her forced conscription into the Nazi machinery as a secretary at the Dornstadt airbase and she notes that she was "very, very cautious, and they were questioning me, and I would keep my mouth shut, because I thought, 'My God, I've already gotten into enough trouble'," Friedrich offers the images of a television commercial for a dental hygiene product (fig. 14.5).

Figure 14.4

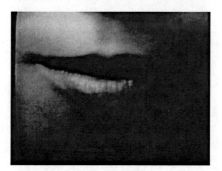

Figure 14.5

In contrast to these more "amusing" images, *The Ties That Bind* exhibits, as MacDonald characterizes it, there is poignant material as well. For instance, amid crushing economic depression, Lore explains, "people were very definitely looking for some way out of their total and utter misery. And, see, that is what I always find so striking in history in general, that there are times where when something good should happen, evil arises!" (fig. 14.6) This reflection is set to Super8 footage — enlarged to 16 mm — of what appears to be the snowbound mountains of Germany, a bird of prey soaring in the sky. The bird, at once evoking ideas of "freedom," as an angelic apparition, also summons to mind the opening of *Triumph of the Will*, or even some of Hitler's own home movies shot in his mountain villa. The associative value of the image of the bird is thus illustrative of how Germany viewed Hitler as its heavenly savior, but also evokes a menacing dread. The signifier vacillates, shifts from one signified to the other, creating a fascinating interplay between word and image.

Figure 14.6

Friedrich also uses archival material in several different ways. "At the very beginning of the film, for example," MacDonald notes,

> as Lore Bucher [Friedrich] tells of first learning about the Nazis when she was a child, the photographed imagery is a subjective camera shot of someone coming out of a tunnel into the light — suggesting the young Bucher's growing consciousness of the larger world and the birth of the Reich, as well as Friedrich's coming out of the darkness about her past.[39]

While imagery such as this is indicative of a more associative strategy, Friedrich also utilizes some archival material in fairly conventional representational ways. For instance, in Lore's description of the Allied bombing campaign in Stuttgart, Friedrich comments in her scrawling written text, "I just cannot imagine it." Lore implores, "Oh, it is — I mean, it's inconceivable. It is inconceivable. Why do you think I'm so violently anti-war?" She continues in this vein, lambasting warmongers, as Friedrich continues to cycle through a series of archival photographs depicting the bombed-out shell of Stuttgart.

Lore's hometown of Ulm was also devastated by the war and her family home destroyed. Throughout the first half of the film, Friedrich returns to the staged image of a toy model German home. Early on the small model is taken out of box. Later its components are set in orderly fashion, then the model is seen in various states of construction, and when it is assembled a pair of jackboots smashes it (fig. 14.7). Finally, it is set ablaze (fig. 14.8) and its charred remains cleared away with a spatula (fig. 14.9). There is no pretense to representing reality; the toy model is quite clearly a substitute that corresponds to Lore's discourse on her wartime experience. It is also a creative strategy to represent — to reconstruct — something that no longer exists.

While Friedrich re-imagines, or re-presents her mother's experience, Robin Kandel in her video installations recreates not only the details of her father's story but spars with the periphery of his experiences by bridging the fissures in memory. She achieves this by filling in historical gaps, reaffirming the things she

Figure 14.7

Figure 14.8

Figure 14.9

knows, interrogating the things she thinks she knows, and imagining events she does not know.

In April 2002 Kandel learned of two audiotapes from a 1983 interview that recounts her father's childhood experiences in Berezno, Ukraine, and his story of survival. Kandel's experience as a child of a survivor is fairly typical; she recalls the experience of growing up and hearing vague bits of her father's story, who survived by hiding in the forest.[40] Prior to the discovery of the audiotapes, these episodes were only known in fragments, and as a child most of her father's experience remained veiled behind adult secrecy. Nevertheless, as Fred Kandel says, "I think a lot of it was carried over from the adults because as a kid you just feel what the atmosphere is around you."

The recreation of her father's experience, through her video installations, is a ritualistic act. While Fred Kandel's experience during the war was a matter of life and death through split second decisions, Kandel's video installations re-enact gestures that saved her father's life — digging and running for instance — to achieve a cathartic effect. The video installations have been presented on small flat-screen monitors, or projected on a wall, but regardless, though, the presentations are featured in a small dark room. The voice of Fred Kandel detailing his story typically accompanies the installation, but is only heard in a faint whisper. Kandel implicitly invites us to participate in this ritual by stepping into the environments she creates.

Rituals are always re-enactments of violence, as Girard attests, and the trace of violence persists in Kandel's three-part video installation: *story 1: run* (2002), *story 2: postola* (2003), and *run/dig* (2004). The power of her video installations is in part drawn from grim associations and a lingering fascination with the survivor narrative. But, the adrenaline-filled fear that is present in Kandel's work intends to function ultimately as a purgative experience. Kandel's installations, and perhaps other works like hers (Amy Kravitz's 1998 animated short *The Trap* is probably the closest), are not expressions of pathological morbidity but rather an exorcising of violence.

Kandel's 2002 video installation *story 1: run* embodies the experience of running for one's life. The video image, shot entirely from a point-of-view perspective, recreates the experience of running through the forest. Anxiety-provoking, and offering no respite, the work is a continuous long-take loop. The blur of trees, the high contrast of the black and white footage, creates a disorientating and chaotic sensory experience and simulates Fred Kandel's experience. Although clearly simulation, the video does not demonstrate what running is like; it *is* running (fig. 14.10). The video is remarkably similar to Jan Nemec's 1964 film *Diamonds of the Night* about survival, discussed in Chapter 4.

Kandel explores another dimension of her father's narrative in *story 2: postola*. Fred Kandel was only a child at the time and did not have the brawn to carry weapons, but everyone did their part, and one of his duties was *making shoes*. "The shoes are called postolas," he recalls.

> The peasants in the area had it to an art form. We just made crude versions. But when we were in an area that had birch trees we would cut one inch wide and very long strips from the bark. And whenever we had time we would weave shoes. They didn't last long.

The artist asked her father, "Do you still remember how to make them?" Sure enough he did, and the artist created *story 2: postola*, documenting her father 60 years after the fact fabricating a shoe from tree bark (fig. 14.11).

Figure 14.10

Figure 14.11

Shoes are a significant motif in Holocaust narratives, because in many cases they potentially meant the difference between living and dying. One of the most important literary texts reflecting on the Holocaust experience, Primo Levi's *Survival at Auschwitz*, discusses the significance of shoes. "And do not think that shoes form a factor of secondary importance in the life of the Lager. Death begins with the shoes; for most of us, they show themselves to be instruments of torture, which, after a few hours of marching, cause painful sores which become fatally infected."[41] Kitty Hart miraculously discovers a shoe in a darkened barracks in Peter Morley's 1980 documentary *Kitty: Return to Auschwitz*. Upon finding it she explains in an exasperated tone, "Oh, oh, god, oh my god that meant life or death for somebody, I can tell you."[42] Ilan Avisar observes, regarding *Diamonds of the Night*, that it emphasizes the experience of running and that "the protagonist is tortured by a hurting shoe, and director Jan Nemec often focuses on the foot and the shoe as silent emblems for the misery of those caught in the predicament of relentless persecution."[43] Shoes, feet, and running meant life and death, and Kandel's *story 2: postola* focuses on one very small precise detail — the hands of Kandel's elderly father crafting shoes from tree bark — to illustrate the associative link between shoes and existence itself.

Elida Schogt's 1999 film *Zyklon Portrait* — which is part of a trilogy of Holocaust films, including *The Walnut Tree* (2000), and *Silent Song* (2001) — exhibits similar performative elements as well. While half of the film is a personal reflection on the impact of the Holocaust on three generations of women in her family, the film also presents a clinical exposition on the systematic processes of extermination. Similar to the voiceover in Alain Resnais's 1955 film *Night and Fog* during Jean-Raphaël-Marie-Noël Cayrol's matter-of-fact discussion of what was done with human remains in the concentration camp, in Schogt's film the voiceover commentary explains, among other things, the effect that Zyklon B has on the human body. Using an x-ray image of lungs, the image begins to break down and Schogt introduces abstract patterns. Eventually, the visual field itself breaks apart with black leader. The visual field not only represents the ill effects of Zyklon B on the lungs, but it does the very thing that it is representing; literally the visual field falls apart. Zyklon B effectively causes the lungs to disintegrate, rendering them incapable of supplying oxygen to the bloodstream; subjects exposed to the gas frequently go into convulsions before finally succumbing to death, and Schogt's disintegrating imagery is "amongst the most unsettling examples" of the representation of the gas chambers, and calls attention to our viewing position.[44] There is no re-enactment of the gas chamber, no archival material, no effort to realistically detail the Holocaust, but nevertheless in the performative materiality of the film Schogt approaches it. And in this respect *Zyklon Portrait* finds affinities with the performative elements in Kandel's video installations and *Diamonds of the Night*.

Born in Walbrzych, Poland in 1947, experimental filmmaker Abraham Ravett spent a good part of his early childhood growing up in Israel (the family had moved there in 1950), before his family emigrated to the United States in 1955. Among his films that negotiate the experience of the Holocaust in some fashion, two in particular have attracted keen critical attention, *Everything's For You* (1989), and *The March* (1999). These films are very much in keeping with the genre of personal documentary, as particularly told from the perspective of a child of a survivor similar to Manfred Kirchheimer's 1986 film, *We Were So Beloved*, and Abby Jack Neidik and Irene Lilienheim Angelico's co-directed 1985 documentary *Dark Lullabies*. Ultimately, though, his films are very different in execution.

Everything's For You features Ravett's attempts to reconcile with his father, Chaim Ravett, a Holocaust survivor, and who remained by and large quiet about the past throughout his life. Chaim passed away in 1979, and Ravett pieces the film together using archival material, family photographs, animated re-enactments, interviews with his father between 1974 and 1977, as well as home movie material featuring Ravett's own family — his son, daughter and wife — shot between 1984 and 1989. In repeated refrains, Ravett attempts to crack his father's stoic silence, posing questions: "Pop, what about your family?" His father asks in return evasively, "What do you mean?" Ravett continues to press him, "The family that you had before the war." Resisting his adult son's inquiry, he says, "Nobody's here." Like Kandel, Ravett knows something of the truth of things, and so continues to press him, "What did you have? Did you have children?" Finally, Chaim relents, "I had childrens. Two childrens — boy and girl. The girl was eleven and the boy was eight. Until forty-five I lived with my family in the Lodz Ghetto." We eventually learn that in 1921 Chaim was married, and had two children, a son and a daughter (just like the filmmaker). After being deported to Auschwitz from the Lodz Ghetto, his wife and children were immediately gassed to death. This early exchange in the film — as with others — happens over a fragmented visual field, multiple frames within the screen over a black-matte, or even on some occasions simply a black screen. Many of the exchanges are in Yiddish, and translated text either appears as subtitling (although not necessarily in sync with the audio), or as text that appears in the black-matte adjacent an image. Although Ravett does pry information from his father, impossible fissures remain, and the film locates some of these ineffable elements in the visible gaps in the film, the holes, and the non-linear structure of the narrative.

In addition to the use of black space, and fractured framing, Ravett also uses archival material, sometimes exhibited frame by frame. "What did you do when they transported you out of the ghetto? What did your children wear? What did your wife say?" Ravett poses these questions off-screen over Holocaust era archival material featuring a group of Jews, apparently a work-detail, marching along an icy Lodz Ghetto street. "What did you do when they sent you out of Lodz? What did your children carry? What did your wife say?" The questions are repeated like the chorus of a song, or ritual, but also like a young child who incessantly asks questions and wants to know why.

As much as the film is about Chaim and his past, it is also about the film-maker himself (again very characteristic of the personal documentary genre). Childhood memories, for the most part, are presented in the form of animation. Ravett recalls a traumatic experience of being hit by his father. In simple illustration Chaim beats the young boy with a towel. Ravett's mother implores with her husband, who she calls Henyek, "Henyek control yourself!" Ravett asks, "Abba, where are you now? I want to talk to you. Pop, where are you? Where are you now, Pop?" And later, "Why did you hit me so hard? Tell me why!" The trauma of being hit in some fashion meets up with the trauma of the Holocaust. What provoked Chaim, was there something in his past that motivated such a violent response?

While *Everything's For You* focuses on Ravett's father, *The March* features the memories of Ravett's mother, Fela. The two films share similar formal qualities, but one of the key distinguishing tropes is that the repeated motifs that appear in

Fela's anecdotal accounts — such as trepches; blanket; Rivers: Odra, Nysa; bread; sardines; green blanket; walk quickly; wooden shoes — materialize on-screen in the black-matte opposite the framed image of Fela, some of this text is typeset, and others are written in her own hand. "Throughout *The March*," Jeffrey Skoller observes,

> Ravett introduces each new section by using different elements of the filmmaking process normally rendered invisible, such as head and tail leadering with handwriting on it, holes punched into the film stock, end-of-roll flares, and flash frames; often we see him setting up a shot, turning the camera on and off at the beginning and end of each shot.[45]

Although the formal qualities that Skoller associates with distinctive sections of *The March*, these techniques are not as delineated in *Everything's For You*; however, nearly all the techniques are evident. While certain movements are clearly evident in *Everything's For You*, *The March* is chronologically structured, each section marked with a title card giving the year, moving from one year to the next, which Skoller cites as a "kind of filmic cataloging [that] creates meaning from the accumulation of fragments of images and information through the repetition of the yearly interview format."[46] What accumulates, however, over the course of years is not an expanding or more detailed body of knowledge but an accretion of fissures.

Unlike Ravett's father, Fela would frequently recount experiences on the Auschwitz death march. In the spring of 1945 as the Soviet Army approached the camp internees were evacuated from Auschwitz, forced to walk for weeks on end. Shot between 1984 and 1997, the film documents not only Fela's recollections of the death march but also the deterioration of her physical body and eventually her mental capacities. The collection of anecdotal accounts spanning more than ten years — perhaps too casual to constitute testimony — rather than creating a coherent unified whole, does in fact just the opposite; wider gaps in the narrative open up, details are contradicted from year to year.[47]

In a 1986 interview, despite the fact that it is quite cold — and Fela mentions as much — she still entertains her son's wishes, and conducts the interview on the porch in the cold. She is bundled up in a heavy red coat with a blanket covering her legs, and Ravett begins by asking her questions in Yiddish, and he requests that she should respond in Yiddish, but she protests saying she is more comfortable speaking in English. "Everyone got a *whole* loaf of bread, a blanket, and a can of meat . . . whoever ate that meat probably died . . . I gave my can away and got a piece of margarine." Fela sees no point in conducting the interview outside in the cold, but there is something evocative about it in the context of Fela's story, replicating the experience of the march in sensation of being cold.

In a 1993 interview Ravett asks who gave them food after liberation. Puzzled, she asks, "Who, the Germans?" Ravett clarifies, "No, the Americans." Fela continues, "Maybe, they gave some, but who remembers? I want just one thing . . .

Abe don't ask me any more because I start feeling bad." The final interviews take place with Fela in failing health; she has had a stroke that has taken its toll on her cognitive and motor functions. In 1997 over a black screen we hear Ravett ask, "Do you remember anything about the march, do you remember anything?" Fela responds, "No, I don't want to talk about that. Enough, my son! You have enough there. They say in German, English . . . 'overdo.' To overdo. I just had a stroke — Do I have to remember? Think about it!" Ravett chuckles and says, "Okay, never mind." "What is so moving about Fela Ravett's testimony is that she is trying so hard," Skoller notes, "but each time she speaks, she has less and less to say."[48] In the end, in 1998, there is no visual material as such, and no audio track, just the scrawled words in Fela's own hand — visibly affected by the stroke, some almost unintelligible, some of these words include: "Olga & M Nysa; sardines; green koc; laufen." The loss of memory or the capacity to communicate memories is just as much the subject of the film as is the content of Fela's stories.

While narrative and documentary forms tend to conceal the inevitable fissures in historical knowledge, through the use of coherent linear narrative, experimental films include the ineffable qualities of the Holocaust as part of their subject. "*The March*, as well as Ravett's other films that take up his parents' experience in the Shoah," Skoller observes,

> use the presentational elements of the film's materiality to signify an outside or limit of what in their experience can be represented and what Ravett himself can ever know about his parents' past. These elements of filmic material are experienced as actual gaps in the process of trying to put the history of his family trauma into cinematic form.[49]

Ravett's 1985 film *Half Sister* deals with similar subject matter; when the filmmaker was 26 he discovered — and saw for the first time, ten years later — a photograph of his mother with a 6-year-old girl, Toncia. As it turns out, Fela, like his father, was also previously married and had a child, but they too were claimed by the Holocaust. Toncia would have been Ravett's half-sister. The experimental form allows the filmmaker to approach the fissures inherent to Holocaust narratives without disavowing the gaps.

Chapter Fifteen

Experimental Films II: Lost and Found (Footage)

INTRODUCTION: LOOK WHAT I FOUND

Found footage films are works that adopt a technique of assemblage to make meaning from images; that is, a strategy of collecting and editing together ephemeral material to fashion something entirely new. Found footage is distinct from archival material, which, Michael Zryd differentiates as, "an official institution that separates historical record from the outtake." When speaking of found footage, he continues that "much of the material used in experimental found footage films is *not* archived but from private collections, commercial stock shot agencies, junk stores, and garbage bins, or has literally been found in the street."[1] While archival material typically services existing historical narratives as illustrative examples (e.g., this is what a deportation looks like), the strategies of assemblage (which in some cases very well might use archival footage as source material) are frequently deployed to question or reconceptualize historical knowledge. "Found footage filmmaking is a metahistorical form commenting on the cultural discourses and narrative patterns behind history," Zryd says. "Whether picking through the detritus of the mass mediascape or refinding (through image processing and optical printing) the new in the familiar, the found footage artist critically investigates the history *behind* the image, discursively embedded within its history of production, circulation, and consumption."[2] Rather than act as a mouthpiece of history reiterating the standard historical narrative, found footage assemblage films tend to question the very project of historical narrative, much of which is engendered in the fact that the source material is ephemeral, or was not intended to be used in an official capacity, or indeed to have meaning beyond specific parameters. As we will see, the footage discussed here was certainly not intended to find its way into official narratives about the Holocaust, the Second World War, and the Nazi regime's systematized genocidal program.

The tradition of assemblage, especially as it is drawing from the history of art where it is sometimes dubbed junk art, is the collection of material that is then recontextualized in unexpected ways, creating a new set of meanings. Figures that have utilized this technique include: Bruce Conner, Edward Kienholz, Joseph Beuys, and Louise Nevelson. Bruce Conner bridges the gap between the practice of assemblage in the world of fine arts and filmmaking. Known in the art world for his junk art sculpture, Conner collects the detritus of culture and reassembles the disparate pieces into a unified whole. His films effectively do the same; famously known for his film *A Movie* (1958), Conner edits together unrelated shots from numerous sources — car races, pornography, and the like — and the result is a humorous juxtaposition of incongruent material that prompts one to interrogate the very notion of what *a movie* is. His other films function according to similar principles, including a 1978 music video for DEVO's "Mongoloid." In fact, filmmakers like Conner, as well as others like Kenneth Anger (addressed shortly), are the progenitors of the contemporary music video.

One of the single most important filmmakers who utilizes the assemblage technique to create moving personal narratives related to the Holocaust is Péter Forgács. Setting himself apart from conventional film practices, Forgács places himself instead within the tradition of assemblage artists, saying, "I prefer Kienholz, Duchamp, alchemy and psycho-archeology," than conventional documentary filmmaking practices.[3] Forgács collects personal home movies, personal photographs, and artifacts that official archives neglect to preserve, as they are created from personal, not institutional sources. Forgács, as Jeffrey Skoller says with respect to avant-garde film in general, "attempts to makes sense out of the fragmented, fractured, and decontextualized remains of the past by creating forms through which they might come to have meaning."[4] Treating home movies as excavation sites, Forgács reassembles past lives, what otherwise might have been lost to oblivion. "My archeology-archive is like an excavation to the hidden and forgotten past. It's not only my past; it's a common East-European past, with this suppressed, substitute past."[5] Living through an Orwellian nightmare, where people and events were written out of official records and history, Forgács brings the "unperson" back not only from the grips of fascist Europe, but also out from the shadow of Soviet oppression in the post-war era. "My works are the findings of the past by a substituted wonderer self in THE ARCHIVE," Forgács explains. "On the other hand, it was an avant-gardism, a gesture to create this archive, which is completely different from any other archives in Hungary. It is not the official representation of the Hungarian films and not the official OK photographs, but it's the *bad* photographs and the *banal* films."[6] The piecing together of unofficial material, the bad photographs, and the private films is in the best tradition of the practice of assemblage, and Forgács is masterful in his craftsmanship.

In distinction from the tradition of assemblage, the practice of appropriation typically draws on official material — be it archival material, existing (narrative) film, or official narratives — and then, like assemblage, recontextualizes the material to fashion new meanings. For example, Jay Rosenblatt's 1998 short experimental piece *Human Remains* is a biographical portrait of five of the world's most notorious twentieth-century tyrants: Hitler, Mussolini, Stalin, Franco, and Mao. The visual material is drawn from archival sources, but it is manipulated in two ways: first, alteration of the visual field, through experimentation with film speed, image reversal (positive-negative), framing, and film direction, and, second, fabrication of audio design, where first-person voiceover commentary is radically different from the image's "intended" or expected purpose. Comical at times, the Hitler episode includes a voiceover sequence on flatulence, "I have trouble with gas. I took some of Doctor Küster's anti-gas pills at each meal, and this helped me with my flatulence, though, not completely." As the first-person commentary confesses to this embarrassing problem, Hitler, Hermann Göring, and another figure wave their hands about as if to fan away an offending odor (fig. 15.1). Completely shorn from its origins, the audio commentary turns archival material into farce. "History does not reside, in a simplistic way, *in* the image," Zryd notes, "the capacity of the image to serve as historical evidence lies in the contextual framing of the image, what we have been told (or what we recognize) about the image."[7] Perhaps trivial and sophomoric, Rosenblatt's audio exercise illustrates the malleability of the image, and that history is not inherently inscribed "*in* the image," but rather is manufactured *in* the construction of narrative.

Figure 15.1

Thus we can differentiate found footage assemblage works, which use ephemeral material, from works of appropriation, which recontextualize "official" archival material, and often exhibit a satirical element, or use archival material as fodder for explicit political purposes. Charles A. Ridley's 1942 short film *Lambeth Walk — Nazi Style* is similar to *Human Remains* in its humorous approach and application of existing official footage. But perhaps even more so, Ridley's film, made during the war, was made explicitly to ridicule the Nazi regime. Appropriating material from Leni Riefenstahl's 1935 film *Triumph of the Will*, Ridley adds a popular tune with cheeky riffs on a cowbell, boisterous thumps on a kettledrum, and other impudent noises. Goose-stepping Nazis are played in forward and reverse, to make them appear to be dancing in step with the silly little musical number. Hitler and other party officials are treated in a similar fashion. Appropriating what was intended as a flamboyant exposition of the Nazi political platform, the material is turned on its head and deflated.

Experimental works that utilize appropriation strategies confront, or in some instances cross, ethical boundaries. Appropriating Holocaust material uncritically, grabbing bits and pieces as hyperbole, or radically ripping something out of context — whether in the form of experimental film or not — are genuine concerns. Likewise, filmmaking technology has made this process quite simple and easy and the act of appropriation has extended beyond the worlds of experimental cinema and has entered into the vernacular of popular culture.

Oliver Hirschbiegel's 2004 film *Downfall* has been appropriated many times over, in particular a scene where Hitler (played brilliantly by Bruno Ganz) in his Berlin bunker learns that the end is imminent and is sent into a rage. Appropriators have recontextualized this scene by leaving the German audio intact, but adding in their own English subtitled interpretations. In one version Hitler wants a Whopper, but Burger King is closed, in another, his car has been stolen, and in yet another Hitler is upset with the results of the MTV movie awards. In many respects the subtitling for the non-German speaker does precisely what the voiceover audio commentary does in *Human Remains*, illustrating the malleability of the image.

Online platforms such as YouTube (where all of the above works can be seen) are a venue in which the visual culture of the Holocaust materializes autonomously, and is presented outside "official" channels.[8] Indeed, with inexpensive digital filmmaking tools, the possibility for creative new experimental works is enormous. Individuals and small groups now have at their disposal the capacity to create works that expand the possibilities for unique combinations of image, sound, and text, and foster environments that are potentially more "interactive." These works rely less on an agent of authorial knowledge (e.g., film director, historian, museum curator) that dictates a particular prescribed (historical) narrative, and more on an inquisitive consumer-turned-producer. "In this respect," Anna Reading concludes, "the interactive and nonlinear narrative possibilities offered by digital formats using hypertext links allows for the history and stories of the Holocaust to be articulated in ways that are distinct from other visual forms."[9] Written nearly a decade ago, with the exponential growth of consumer digital media and online platforms, Reading's conclusions are more salient today than they ever were. It's a brave new world . . .

STRATEGIES OF APPROPRIATION

Pioneering avant-garde filmmaker Kenneth Anger's seminal 1964 film *Scorpio Rising* is an illustrative example of how the strategy of appropriation is able to reconfigure images to make new meanings. In particular, it is film that offers an idiosyncratic perspective on the Holocaust through American pop culture.

The film features the leader of a biker gang, Scorpio, who is at once an image of hetero-normative masculinity, and at the same time utterly consumed by homoeroticism. In the film he surrounds himself with images of masculinity and destruction — including pin-ups of James Dean, and a magazine clipping of Hubert Lanzinger's 1935 painting "The Standard Bearer," which depicts a horse-mounted Hitler in a suit of shining armor foisting the Nazi flag. Anger documents the queering of the hyper-masculine and hetero-normative iconography, in the images of James Dean, Marlon Brando, Jesus Christ, Adolf Hitler, as well as the symbols of Christianity and fascism. The film is part experimental montage and part documentary, following Scorpio, played by Bruce Byron, and his biker gang who are effectively playing themselves — true motorcycle enthusiasts.

Scorpio Rising, the film, doesn't in itself appropriate the hyper-masculinist iconography of Nazism — but rather it documents the ways in which Byron appropriates the imagery. Anger recalls that Byron

> had collected that stuff. Hitler and James Dean, which is an odd combination. He wasn't an intellectual. He just dug these swastikas and symbols — as a kind of disturbing, interesting thing. He certainly was unaware. I mean, you couldn't call him a neo-Nazi, but I saw how these symbols still worked in an emotional way on people and how somebody like this Bruce could be swept up by a leader in some very destructive kind of thing.[10]

Regardless of how much agency Byron had in the shaping of the character Scorpio, it is Anger who expressly illustrates the (homo)eroticism of Nazi paraphernalia, and how libidinal energy is channeled into the iconography of death and destruction. While setting the visual track to popular songs like "I will follow him," by Little Peggy March, Anger edits together images of idolatry — Jesus Christ, Marlon Brando in the role of Johnny Strabler in *The Wild One* (Laslo Benedek, 1953) — with that of Nazism, and it is through montage that Anger's film "is able to deconstruct what it cites; it alters language systems as it adopts them. In *Scorpio Rising*, montage specifically 'remakes' and 're-presents' heterosexist symbol systems in order to envision sustainable homosexual desire."[11]

The division between formal strategies of assemblage and appropriation and the rituals of memory is arbitrary, and *Scorpio Rising* is exemplary of how these strategies overlap. As compared to other experimental filmmakers, such as Maya Deren, "Anger's use of ritual is quite different," Carel Rowe observes, "his narrative model is constructed through a comparative analysis of myths, religions, and rituals and their associations external to their respective systems. His two works which give greatest evidence of this are *Inauguration of the Pleasure Dome* (1954–1966) and . . . *Scorpio Rising* (1964)."[12] What is particularly significant here, and this helps to distinguish *Scorpio Rising* from the work discussed in the previous chapter, is that Anger's film documents the ritualistic, as opposed to explicitly integrating it into the form of the film itself.[13] The images of Nazism, the leather gear, the Totenkopf, are fetishistic totems of masculine doom and destruction.[14]

Elida Schogt's short 2001 film *Silent Song* exhibits some of the characteristics of the reflexive documentary in its contemplation of the process of constructing Holocaust imagery. The film begins with Schogt asking, "Why this boy?" while a small image hovering in frame-in-frame over a black-matte reveals the face of an 11-year-old boy. As Schogt continues, the film cuts to a full frame revealing the youngster in medium shot playing the accordion.

> I happened upon his image, doing research that I was working on. I keep coming back this boy, because I know something of what has happened to him. But I don't know his name; I haven't even made an effort to find out. I've been thinking of him for a few years. Not really about him, about his image.

The very discussion of construction is at play here; through the interrogation of the filmmaker's own strange inexplicable fascination with the youngster. To emphasize the focus on the boy Schogt slows the film down, inviting the spectator to look and consider details that might otherwise go unnoticed through a contemplative gaze.

Schogt recognizes that her interest lies not in the boy himself — his biography, who he is, and what happened to him — it's not "really about him, [but rather] about his image," she says. It is the image that captivates Schogt's attention, and this — if only implicitly — delivers a subtle critique of the expository propensity to sacrifice individual and localized experience for rhetorical coherence. Schogt discloses that the superficial quality of the image is what gives her pause. But at what expense? The images of deportation, the reels of liberation footage, repeated *ad nauseam* in documentaries, typically sacrifice specificity and serve as generic signifiers of the Holocaust experience.

At the conclusion of the film Schogt reflects on the Holocaust-associated phrase, "never forget," about which she says, "I felt that it was a cliché about the Holocaust, 'never forget.' Remembering hasn't stopped us from continuing to commit genocide." The filmmaker though retracts from her initial cynicism, and notes that in fact the film is about not forgetting, and contemplates her fear of being forgotten. She doesn't want to be forgotten — and she has in fact submitted her films to the National Archive of Canada, offering her own film to the same kind of institution that she found the film's archival footage in. This final reflection on the filmmaker's own mortality is indicative of the rituals of memories, a turn inwards towards self-reflection, and like Chantal Akerman's film *From the East*, the images appropriated from beyond function as blank screens for the spectator/filmmaker to project their own anxieties or memories.[15]

While Schogt's work embodies the fear of forgetting, *Hitler: A Film From Germany* is arguably an exercise in trying to forget. Hans-Jürgen Syberberg's 1977 seven-and-a-half-hour theatrical epic (also sometimes given as *Our Hitler*) meditates on the representation of Hitler, Nazism, and Nazi-era Germany, and is set in a Wagner-inspired theatrical environment, with elements of Brechtian dramatic strategies.[16] The entire film is shot on a sound stage, and with no pretense for verisimilitude, it is sparsely set, sometimes simply relying on rear-projection backdrops. Similar to *Shoah*, Syberberg's estimation is that fascism is not representable as such — at least, in Syberberg's estimation of it fascism is not representable as a realist enterprise, and instead emphasizes the artifice of the film. Anton Kaes views *Shoah* as a corrective to Syberberg's film

> by drawing a sharp line between Nazi criminals and their victims. . . . Thus Lanzmann's work throws Syberberg's project in relief: although both filmmakers believe in the presence of the past (which explains, on the formal level, their shared disregard for chronological narratives and their sense of post-histoire, of "timelessness"), ultimately their projects differ radically.[17]

While Lanzmann and Syberberg generally agree where to locate accountability and the aesthetic limits of realism in representing the past, Syberberg's ambition to appropriate Germany's aesthetic tradition is a slippery slope.

Syberberg re-appropriates the Germanic aesthetic tradition, and tearing it free from the grips of its Nazi past, attempts to purge it. "Syberberg (not unlike Anselm Kiefer) . . . stages the myths of the Nazi past — not to glorify them, but to find some redemptive way back to the spiritual *Heimat* [homeland] of the Germans, which he believes has been lost to both fascism and postwar materialism."[18] Leaving the moorings of historical fidelity, namely the dirty business of the Holocaust, gives Syberberg the latitude he needs to explore one of the major themes of the film: that Hitler was a mere conduit through which German sentiments were expressed, a projection of desire, and more than this, the various "Hitlers" that appear on stage — multiple puppets, Charlie Chaplin, even a toy-stuffed dog with Hitler's likeness — are not indicative of the historical figure, but the Hitlers in each one of us (or so the film posits). A contentious position, no doubt. But this might also explain the generally negative critical response in Germany, which prefers to locate accountability for the Holocaust in history (read: the distant past), and in a specific handful of demonized historical figures. Syberberg insists that culpability be shared with the viewing subject; we are implicated linguistically with the use of linguistic shifters — "you," "we," "our." The various Hitlers in the film, especially in their more messianic form, have acted upon our behalf (or Germany's), enacting only what we (or the German people) secretly wanted.

At the conclusion of the film Hitler is ruled guilty, but the verdict is rendered not for implementing the systematic extermination of European Jewry, and not for plunging Germany into a disastrous war of aggression, but rather for forever poisoning the German well of culture. In a long monologue, the ruling is recited:

> You're responsible for the houses without a soul, with burnt out eyes, without tears, towns which cannot weep. Motor-landscapes without stillness, full of noise. You've

taken away the sunsets, sunsets by Kaspar David Friedrich. You're to blame that we can't see a cornfield without thinking of you. You've made kitsch of the old Germany, with your simplified crafts and peasant pictures.

Hitler's inquisitor continues, and laments for Germany's lost future, "because you've occupied everything else and poisoned it with your touch. Everything! Honor, loyalty, country life, rest of work, films, dignity, fatherland, pride, belief. You're the executioner of Western civilization." Without hope, there is in the end the ambition to start over, to wipe the slate completely clean, to begin from the very point of creation. "The longing for the apocalypse," Anton Kaes observes, "and the end of history may be provoked by the utopian hope to begin once more, to create a pure moment of origin that is not contaminated by history."[19] A moment, more specifically, that is not haunted by the specter of Auschwitz.

STRATEGIES OF ASSEMBLAGE

Péter Forgács's body of work, including *Private Hungary*, a 12-film series (1988–97),[20] reworks amateur film and home movies from the era prior, during and following the Second World War. In the early 1980s Forgács began to amass a collection of photographs and films, which he would later name the Private Film and Photo Archives, in Budapest. His work with the Cultural Research Institute and then with the Béla Balázs Studio in Budapest afforded him access to a wealth of material. "My terrain is the unofficial visual imprint of my culture," Forgács notes, "and I soon realized this image collection might represent something new and fill some of the gaps of the vast, destroyed, and lost past."[21] From this footage he has assembled numerous films including, *The Diary of Mr. N* (1990), *Free Fall* (1997), and *The Danube Exodus* (1998). The Private Film and Photo Archives have continued to grow, and as of 2002 he has catalogued 500 hours of private histories. In addition to the material that he has collected, Forgács also interviewed a number of the family members (or surviving relatives) featured in the films. All of Forgács's finished films are treated in his signature style: manipulation of tinting and film speed, utilization of freeze-frames, punctuating the narrative with audio and/or visual ellipses, superimposition of text and images, periodic voiceover narration, and hauntingly melodic scores.

Minimalist Hungarian composer Tibor Szemzö frequently writes the scores for the films (including all three films mentioned above), and his contribution to the films cannot be overstated. Szemzö, much in the same way that Philip Glass is integral to the success of the films of Errol Morris and Godfrey Reggio, establishes a poetic rhythm, an incantation of memory, and solemnity. Forgács and Szemzö collaborated in a minimalist music ensemble called Group 180 between 1978 and 1987 and he describes his experience as a

fruitful cooperation, as I never had a chance before to understand what music is about. Those years rehearsing and performing the pieces of Reich, Glass, or Rzewski — the contemporary US and Hungarian composers, not forgetting the composition by the members Group 180 — were a permanent revelation. This was a powerful period with the group: I learned how music structures time and what time-based art is.[22]

The melodic pacing of Forgács's films, the repetition of freeze-frames, and meditative slow motion, these all bear the hallmarks of minimalist scoring. And in fact, before Forgács fashioned proper films, he experimented with the material during performances: "In the arts scene, where I had had performances, from time to time I started to collaborate with Tibor Szemző. He performed the music (one may hear it in my films, as well) and I screened some of the home movie found footage on stage with improvised text."[23] Indeed, his first films were the culmination of these years of onstage experiments and archiving.

In certain instances Forgács thinks of the musical score as the protagonist's voice, calling from the past, or facilitating a degree of distance from the subject for meditative contemplation. And still on other occasions he thinks of the music as the driving force of the film, propelling the emotions of the story forward. "From the first day of editing," Forgács explains, "I use already-existing music (mainly Szemző, then Glass, Eno, or Monteverdi) to search and edit the silent cinema's rhythm and subconscious."[24] After a rough cut is ready, then, Forgács invites Szemző into the process to render a score based on the architecture of the rough cut. The final cut is subsequently tailored along with Szemző's score.[25] The music in conjunction with the manipulated images engenders a complex dynamic where "the musical image (sound-scape) is woven together with the filmic image in a fitting and contemplative way."[26] And ultimately it is the music that bridges the inherently fragmentary nature of the compiled images spanning the fissure between the past and the present. "I want to keep a minimalist attitude throughout the piece," Forgács explains. "I want the vision, the message on all its levels and in its appeal to all the senses, to move you, along with the music, text and image as well."[27] The objective of the *Private Hungary* series, according to Berber Hagedoorn, is "not to reminiscence, not to educate and not to inform, but to *create emotions*."[28]

It is perhaps not entirely accurate to say that the objective of the *Private Hungary* series is strictly to elicit emotions — it seems to me that this would render Forgács's films as a form of pornography, stimulating the body through human suffering. Rather, Forgács in his collisions of public and private history, and of the raw character of home movies and the careful crafting of aesthetic embellishments, creates histories that are evocative. Beyond emotional stimulation, we do in fact learn something, even if it is specific to one family's experience. In an interview with Bill Nichols, Forgács outlines a seven-point program that governs his filmmaking practice: (1) the work should not be expository; (2) the films should reveal "the magic of these unconscious home filmstrips, the magic of re-contextualizing, layer after layer to feel the graphic intensity of each frame"; (3) Forgács's films are made for his friends, offerings, which he presents by saying, "'Look what I've found for you,' while I peel the source material to its roots"; (4) his films "do not explain, or educate, but involve, engulf the viewer as much possible"; (5) his films "address the unconscious, the sensitive, unspeakable, touchable but mostly silent part of the viewer"; (6) his films "let the music orchestrate and rule the emotional story"; and (7) Forgács focuses on learning "how to hear my own low inner voice, the guide of creation" to filter out the noise and get to the essence of the film.[29] Forgács's rejection of exposition is not built around a rejection of educating his audience but towards the general tendency to didacticism in conventional documentary film. In fact, we learn a tremendous amount when watching Forgács's films. As is the case with the Hungarian Jewish Petö in *Free Fall*, that members were able to live a relatively normal life into the spring of 1944 before they were finally deported is astonishing. Forgács does not *tell us* this, rather it is conveyed in the ordinariness of György Petö cuddling his baby in contrast to the text that inform us of what is unfolding around them in the public sphere. All Forgács's films are personal diaristic accounts that, as Jaimey Fisher observes, "demonstrate and elaborate upon how diaries offer readers and viewers not indisputable facts, but instead a specifically configured relationship to time and history."[30]

In many ways, such as the case with the Petö family, Forgács acts as a spiritual medium; his films are a communing with the dead. A number of critics, rightly so, point to the similarities between Roland Barthes's *Camera Lucida*, a book ostensibly about photography, but in fact about his recently deceased mother, and Forgács's films. Indeed, in both cases there is a meditation on death; when contemplating Alexander Gardner's photograph of Lewis Payne (1865), who has been condemned to capital punishment, for instance, Barthes thinks to himself, "*he is going to die*. I read at the same time: *This will be* and *this has happened*; I observe with horror an anterior future of which death is the stake."[31] In many respects this is precisely how we receive the likeness of people long since dead in Forgács's films.

The voiceover narrations in the *Private Hungary* series do not correspond to the conventions of the voice-of-God found in many documentary films. The tone, for one, is more an incantation than a signifier of an embodied bearer of authorial knowledge. The markers of authority are undercut in the restrained, subdued, and self-consciously metered utterance in Forgács's films, owing no doubt to the filmmaker's engagement with minimalist music. The content of the voiceover typically conveys "mere facts," for instance the recitation of regulations pertaining to Jews. In *Free Fall* marriage laws, and related statutes that define who is and who is not a "Jew," are recited over images of a Hungarian labor camp. Where the voice-of-God in a conventional documentary provides commentary, in the case of Forgács's films we are instead given perspective. While the former insists that the viewer "see-it-my-way," as Bill Nichols notes, in the latter instance the spectator is offered an opportunity to "see-for-yourself."[32]

There are other ways in which Forgács's films shirk conventional documentary modes. "His films evoke the phenomenal world," Ernst Van Alphen observes. Forgács's films are effectively about real life, "they are about vitality, enjoyment, about activities such as dancing and playing. Whereas the archival mechanisms of objectification and categorization strip images of their singularity, Forgács's archival footage keeps insisting on the private and affective."[33] Indeed, as I have illustrated in previous chapters, while conventional documentaries tend to utilize archival material for generic purposes — deportation, suffering in concentration camps — with Forgács's films there is an insistence upon the specificity of individual people, places, and events. Forgács views the red-coated girl in Steven Spielberg's 1993 film *Schindler's List* in similar terms to the generic appropriation of archival material.

> The girl herself is there to illustrate a metaphor. In my films, *The Bartos Family*, for example, I'd say Mr. Bartos is a concrete Bartos for family use (in terms of the footage as home movies), on the one hand, and, for us, he represents a man who went through this and that in his own individual way without providing service as a symbol or metaphor, on the other hand. The story has a concrete and a substantial meaning at the same time.[34]

And this is the real genius in Forgács's films, at once preserving the integrity of the unique character of each family narrative, and at the same time locating universal points of entry that accommodate identification with the characters in the film.

Forgács compares the narrative strategy of his films to Hitchcock's rules for suspense. Unlike a surprise, which occurs without warning, with suspense the audience is fully aware of the perils that are looming, and we feel anxious on behalf of the characters on-screen who go about their business unaware.[35] "We know ahead of time that the innocent victim will fall into the hands of the killer," Forgács explains. "We want to warn her/him; watch out! And our palms are sweating. We can't help, and here — in my films — it anticipates real blood, real suffering, we always have that in mind even if we never see it in my films."[36] The suspense of Forgács's films, given our knowledge of the history of the Holocaust, is acute.

In terms of Forgács's Holocaust-related films *The Diary of Mr. N* (1990) is worth examining because the protagonists of the film, Mr. N's family, are ostensibly on the "wrong side."[37] Although the family's politics are never articulated, Mr. N and Ilona, his wife, work at a Hungarian munitions factory that will eventually supply the German war effort. Footage that Mr. N shoots during a visit by German officials who come to inspect the facility is incorporated into the film. Together the couple has eight children, four boys and four girls. Whatever their politics, the protagonists are likable; they're doting parents, in their younger years charmingly playful, and lovers of the outdoors (we see the couple on a number of rural excursions). Ordinary in just about every respect, this Gentile family appears to be simply getting on with life as history happens all around them.

We of course identify with the protagonists of the film, Mr. N and Ilona, and our sympathies for them remains throughout. It should be mentioned that this does not hold true of all the characters in Forgács's films (Arthur Seyss-Inquart, who I'll be speaking of shortly, in *The Maelstrom* for instance never really wins our wholehearted sympathy). There are nevertheless details in *The Diary of Mr. N* that remind us of the impending doom awaiting Mr. N's fellow citizens. On one of the couple's excursions to Kárpátaljàn, in the summer of 1939, Mr. N documents orthodox Jews living in the town (fig. 15.2), on the Hungarian/Polish border just weeks before the Germans and Soviets invade (fig. 15.3). The exterior of a Ukrainian concentration camp (or so it's called in the film) (fig. 15.4) and a graveyard for the victims of the First World War are also documented. All of these referents are invested with an uncanny charge, given what we know is about to happen, and what has already happened. On more than one occasion Forgács uses stormy weather (fig. 15.5) in *The Diary of Mr. N* to signify the blowing winds of history that are going to profoundly shape Hungary's course during the twentieth century; Forgács employs this poetic device in *The Maelstrom* as well.

Figure 15.2

Figure 15.3

Figure 15.4

Figure 15.5

The Maelstrom: A Family Chronicle (1997) features home movies shot between 1933 and 1942 by Max Peereboom, the eldest of three sons of the Jewish Dutch family. We are introduced to the family early in the film at the silver anniversary for Flora and Jozeph Peereboom, the patriarch of the family. At the celebration, a freeze-frame and superimposed text identifies each of the family members, Simon the youngest son, Louis the middle child, Max and his bride Annie. These home movies are set in juxtaposition with footage of Arthur Seyss-Inquart and his family. Hitler appointed Seyss-Inquart as the Reich Commissioner for the Netherlands (he was executed in 1946 following his conviction in the Nuremberg War Crimes trial). In keeping with Forgács's established style, *The Maelstrom* documents the intersection of the private lives of the Peereboom family with that of public history, and the gradual changes that impacted the Jewish family. The entire Peereboom family, save one, the youngest son, Simon, was murdered in Nazi concentration camps.

The English word "maelstrom" originates from the "early modern Dutch — *maelstrom* (now *maalstroom*)" meaning "whirlpool — *malen* to grind, to whirl round," and "*stroom* STREAM *n.*"[38] Appropriately, the film opens with green-tinted amateur footage of a stormy sea hammering the Dutch coastline, curious onlookers are pushed back from the seawall with each crashing wave; a single fishing vessel struggles to make it into port. The storm, which is a repeated motif in the film, signifies the pending maelstrom that is about to swallow up the Peereboom family, who we are introduced to in the following sequence. "Because we know what is coming," Berber Hagedoorn observes,

> the effect of the maelstrom is extremely poignant. The swirl of *The Maelstrom* is like a knot in your stomach, which Forgács keeps twisting and turning, increasingly tighter, until you cannot breathe any more. *The Maelstrom* never visually displays the atrocities of the Holocaust, but this public event is continually mixed in emotionally with the private experiences shown on the screen.[39]

The Maelstrom is largely composed of private home movie footage, and the storm motif comes to fill in the gaps of public history. In one case a poignant moment in the history of the Holocaust and the lives of the Peereboom family, "1 September 1939, German troops attack Poland" is emblazoned across the familiar images. This shot is effectively a poetic cutaway; in a conventional documentary a filmmaker at this juncture would typically cut to archival newsreel footage of German forces invading Poland, but Forgács resists the expository disposition.

Forgács does nevertheless include various historical events to indicate where the private world intersects with the public world. These historical moments are not expository, however — they do not speak directly to the Peereboom's situation, nor are they illustrative of historical events as such — they function as reference points. In another sequence, a radio broadcast from the 1936 Berlin Olympic Games, announcing that the Dutchman Osendarp has won the bronze medal in the 100-meter dash, is set to Peereboom footage documenting a sporting retreat for the young family. The Berlin Olympics say nothing about Annie's sporting club, but they contextualize the family's personal history within the larger pre-war history of 1936, and the accession of Nazi Germany. In January of 1937 Max documents the procession of the Dutch royal family on the occasion of the marriage of Crown Princess Juliana to Bernhard von Lippe-Biesterfeld. "That the family filmed these events can be read as symptomatic for their assimilation into Dutch culture," Ernst Van Alphen observes. "But the other insertions of history are by the hand of the director."[40] The Peereboom's Crown Princess Juliana footage offers a direct encounter between public and private history, but it is framed literally within the lens of a private perspective. This is different, but certainly related, as Van Alphen indicates, to historical material such as the radio broadcast that contextualizes a familial history into a national/historical discourse.

In addition to the various historical markers — the 1936 Berlin Olympics, for example — there are other uncanny specters of the pending storm. Forgács, for instance, includes 1935 amateur footage of the Dutch equivalent of the Hitler Youth, the Dutch National Socialist Youth Storm Camp (fig. 15.6). This is the closest that Forgács comes to exposition, through the blue-tinted amateur footage illustrative of the Dutch political/social environment. The coloring sets it apart from the core diegesis of the film, effectively commenting on the proper narrative. Regardless of its formal characteristics, the *pre-war* footage is a harbinger of the imminent storm. Max shot footage at a local carnival; a young Dutch boy, air-rifle in hand, takes aim at a shooting gallery, and Forgács adds in the sound of a real gun firing, heightening the emotive charge of what is otherwise an "innocent" image (fig. 15.7). In the context of a looming war, the image is invested with other meanings. Similarly a young boy watching a parade of Dutch Nazis gives the fascist salute (fig. 15.8). These small details of everyday Dutch life in the context of the film signify the growing threat and add to the narrative's suspense. We witness the Peereboom family going about their daily lives, as well as the details that signify the encroaching Nazi threat, and are helpless to warn them of their fate.

Figure 15.6

Figure 15.7

Figure 15.8

The suspense that builds is a product of the disparity of knowledge. Having the foreknowledge of history we know what looms in the future for the Peerebooms, all the while they march headlong into disaster seemingly without the slightest inkling of what awaits them; in fact, all the way up to the eve of their deportation to Auschwitz. "Through this suspense," Elizabeth Cowie observes, "the film's re-presenting of these fragments of family home movie enacts a 'remembering' that engages the viewer in coming to know of loss as an emotional experience summed up by the words 'if only.'"[41] This bifurcated temporality and knowledge — of the recorded historical moment in 1943, set in distinction to the present tense of watching the events that have been, and for which we know the outcome — contribute to the suspense, but they also structure the experience of watching Forgács's films as melodrama. One of the core tropes of the melodrama is "too late-ness," what Cowie identifies as the "if only," and, indeed, Forgács's films are "tinged with the melancholy of loss," as Linda Williams says regarding melodrama: our encounter with the characters "always take place too late, on death beds or over coffins."[42] But there is something unusual in this melodramatic structuring, because it is not characters within the diegesis that discover that it's "too late," but rather us, the spectator; Forgács's films are structured as an extra-diegetic melodrama. There are no deathbeds, no coffins in the film, but it is the film itself that signifies death. "It is a personal memory of loss," Cowie says, "even though we ourselves never knew the Peerebooms, which draws us into a work of mourning that is also a commemoration."[43]

One of the horrifying realizations in *The Maelstrom* is that Arthur Seyss-Inquart is not monstrous, but rather quite the opposite. In all outward appearances he seems utterly normal, living an idyllic family life (if a little bit too proper). On a formal level, there is ostensibly no difference between the Peereboom and Seyss-Inquart home movies, as Michael Renov recognizes. The films all bear the familiar trademarks of the home movie genre: recording the momentous occasions in life (weddings, birthdays, births), characters on-screen shooting smiles and waving towards the camera, the presentation of newborn children, or the parading of youngsters. What Forgács does with them, however, is singular. Setting associative imagery in dialectic conflict, we see a Peereboom ice skating outing in contradistinction to the Seyss-Inquart family ice skating. Seyss-Inquart hosts Reichsführer SS Heinrich Himmler and his wife at the palatial Clingendael estate and the two apparently take a break from official business to play a friendly match of tennis. This is immediately set in opposition to the Peereboom family, who, restricted by anti-Jewish laws, are obliged to spend their holiday on the roof of their home. The very kinetics of Himmler and Seyss-Inquart running from end to end of the tennis court, versus the static figures of the Peereboom family, confined to the space of their roof, is illustrative of the formal compositional and existential conflicts that are reaching a climax. And yet despite the "parallel construction" these families are, Renov says, "also on a collision course."[44] One of the other ways in which the footage from the two families is treated is that while the Peereboom material is generally tinted in sepia tone, the Seyss-Inquart material is in color or treated with a blue-green tint, calling to mind the repeated green-tinted stormy sea material.[45] The tonal affinities between the stormy sea material and the Seyss-Inquart footage, if only unconsciously, aligns the historical figure of Arthur Seyss-Inquart with the repeated poetic motif established in the film.

The noose slowly tightens in the years leading up to the family's deportation. Jews were forced to relocate to Amsterdam in preparation for their deportation to concentration camps and anti-Jewish laws further constricted daily life. The last material that Max shoots is of the family preparing for their deportation, over which Forgács includes the text: "4 September 1942, Franklin, Flora, Max, Annie and her stepmother are deported to Auschwitz." The final image of the film is a photograph of Simon and his new wife, Rees Beesemer, married on October 23, 1942. The camera zooms into a medium close-up of Simon, excising his wife from the frame, where new text is superimposed on the screen: "Simon Peereboom is freed from Buchenwald in 1945, he is the only one to survive the war."

Part 10 of the 12-part *Private Hungary* series, Forgács's 1997 film *Free Fall* chronicles the life of György Petö and his family. It echoes the experience of the Peereboom family, and documents approximately the same historical moment, roughly from the early 1930s until the spring of 1944. Like his Dutch counterpart Max Peereboom, György Petö, a wealthy Hungarian Jew, filmed most of the footage included in *Free Fall*. A photograph introduces us to "our hero and cameraman, György 'Gyuri' Petö in 1918," text that is superimposed on the image (fig. 15.9). The Petö family resides in Szeged, in southern Hungary, on the Tisza River. When György's father dies in 1936 he takes over the family business, the Petö Bank House and the lottery ticket shop. A bit of a playboy and extravagant, György talks up the "pretty girls in Szeged," (fig. 15.10) as they're labeled in the film, and enjoys taking his speedboat out on the Tisza.

Figure 15.9

Figure 15.10

Free Fall is perhaps the most intimate of Forgács's Holocaust-related films. Included in the film is an encounter between György and his lover, and soon-to-be wife, Éva Lengel; he records her as she disrobes, bathes, and retreats to bed where she seductively beckons for György, behind the camera, to "come hither" (fig. 15.11). Undeniably voyeuristic and sensual, this footage humanizes the victims of the Holocaust and positions them as normal people, filled with passion and sexual desire. The scene's audio, however, stands in marked contrast to this act of genuine intimacy, detailing Act IV of the anti-Jewish laws of 1939. By recognizing the sexuality in the characters on-screen, we lend them an important part of the human experience; they are just like us. Alvin Rosenfeld claims, for instance, that the concentration camp robbed internees of all traces of humanity, and in its place left just the constant gnawing of hunger. Further, that "one of the characteristics of Holocaust writings at their most authentic is that they are peculiarly and predominantly sexless."[46] Forgács returns human dignity to the victims of the Holocaust; by exhibiting sexuality, he returns precisely what has been taken from them. The material taps into the universal experience of the utmost act of human intimacy, the act of making love, and at the same time remains a distinctly unique recording of an encounter between two specific individuals in a specific historical instance.[47]

Figure 15.11

There are also reflexive moments in *Free Fall*. We see for instance, György Petö editing film he shot with his 8 mm camera, "he bought his 8 mm camera equipment in 1937" (fig. 15.12). Later in the film, we see Petö setting up his projector, and subsequently view a part of one of his shorts, *Shovels of Souvenir*, a document of conscripted Jewish labor service between 1940 and 1941 (fig. 15.13). Because

Figure 15.12

Figure 15.13

Jews were banned from serving in the Hungarian military, they were expected to fulfill their national service in labor camps. Bandi Kardos, György's compatriot, also served in the same labor service, and playfully goes about his work digging ditches. He poses for the camera, and in freeze-frame a superimposed text informs us that he is shot to death four years later. One of the Hungarian guards approaches the mugging Kardos, and pretends to strike him with a riding-crop, an uncanny specter of things to come.

Unlike *The Maelstrom* where the protagonists of the film are claimed by the Holocaust, György and Éva survive, but not unscathed. On June 24, 1944, while serving in his labor detail on the Russian front, György disappears, having been detained in a Soviet prison. Éva is eventually deported to a concentration camp, but survives. Their first child, Andris Petö, then dies in the Neukirchen concentration camp in November 1944 and most of György and Éva's relatives share Andris's fate. Against the odds, however, the pair are reunited and the film ends with text superimposed over manipulated footage of a rugged forest: "Kati, their daughter was born in November, 1946 . . . but that is another story . . ."

Notes

Chapter One: Introduction

1   Terrence Des Pres, "Holocaust *Laughter?*" in Berel Lang, ed., *Writing and the Holocaust* (New York: Holmes and Meier, 1988), 220.

2   Ibid., 217.

3   Millicent Marcus, *After Fellini: National Cinema in the Postmodern Age* (Baltimore: The John Hopkins University Press, 2002), 268. Marcus continues by noting that the use of the "term *fundamentalism*" is a deliberate strategy "implying that for such critics" who ascribe to the belief that the Holocaust can only be represented realistically, "the factual record stands as a sacred textual source that gives the Holocaust the status of a religious absolute any deviation from which amounts to heresy" (Marcus, 268–9).

4   Imre Kertész, "Who Owns Auschwitz?" Translated by John MacKay, *The Yale Journal of Criticism* vol. 14, no. 1 (Spring 2001): 269.

5   *Oxford English Dictionary*, s.v. "Holocaust."

6   Bruno Bettelheim, "The Holocaust — One Generation After," in Roger S. Gottlieb ed., *Thinking the Unthinkable: Meanings of the Holocaust* (New York: Paulist Press, 1990), 379.

7   Claude Lanzmann cited in Stuart Liebman, "Introduction," to Stuart Liebman ed., *Claude Lanzmann's Shoah: Key Essays* (New York: Oxford University Press, 2007), 7–8.

8   Frankly, the boundaries of what the Holocaust is are murky for me. Does the Holocaust exclusively apply to the death camps, or might we also include in this the labor camps, which would mean recognizing the suffering of political prisoners alongside the endeavor to eradicate European Jewry? Does the Holocaust include the mobilized Einsatzgruppen, or because these operations pre-date the initiation of the Final Solution, as dictated by Operation Reinhard in 1942, does this — although undeniably horrific — fall outside the parameters of what we call the Holocaust? What about the ghettos, do we characterize the establishment of ghettos as part of the Holocaust? To be a "Holocaust victim" must one have been exterminated in a systematic way — mobile gas van, gas chamber — what then of those that succumbed to hunger, or disease? What about resistance fighters — irrespective of those that died, were injured, or survived, fought in urban landscapes, or the forest — do they fall under the umbrella of the Holocaust?

9   Judith Peterson makes the same observation in her "A Little-Known Classic: *Night and Fog* in Britain," in Ewout van der Knaap ed., *Uncovering the Holocaust: The International Reception of* Night and Fog (New York: Wallflower Press, 2006), 109. In the introduction to this volume, Ewout van der Knaap adds, "In the film the Jewish and political victims were seen as one and the same. A significant portion of the genocide was Judeocide, but the film does not make this explicit" (van der Knaap, 18).

10 Hayden White, "Historical Emplotment and the Problem of Truth," in Saul Friedlander ed., *Probing the Limits of Representation: Nazism and the "Final Solution"* (Cambridge: Harvard University Press, 1992), 41.

11 See, for example, Kobi Niv's book-length essay, *Life Is Beautiful, but Not for Jews: Another View of the Film by Benigni.* Translated by Jonathan Beyrak Lev. (Lanham, MD: The Scarecrow Press, Inc., 2003).

12 Hilene Flanzbaum, "'But Wasn't It Terrific?': A Defense of Liking *Life Is Beautiful*," *The Yale Journal of Criticism* vol. 14, no. 1 (Spring 2001): 284. Earlier in the text Flanzbaum writes, "The past twenty years have given rise to a growing number of professional critics who cling to this notion of authenticity above all else. In the reception of the mini-series *Holocaust*, of popular films such as *Schindler's List* and *Life is Beautiful*, and of dozens of other popular representations of the Holocaust, one question eclipses all others: how close did it come to documenting the atrocity of the actual event? The answer, of course, is always 'not close enough,' for to claim otherwise is not only an obvious falsehood, but also a transgression of Holocaust etiquette's cardinal rule. How could a non-survivor say anything else? Yes, the critic would report, *this* movie does wholly and completely render the Holocaust exactly as it was. Sensibly, the critic falls back on the safer position: No, he says, every time, not close enough. But that negation, too, has become an intellectually hollow position, a tired refrain that both obscures more specific and noteworthy details of a particular piece, and places the critic in a straitjacket of good intentions. By insisting that verisimilitude be the ultimate goal of Holocaust representation, the critic has confined himself to an intellectual and political bind from which escape appears impossible" (Flanzbaum, 274).

13 Elie Wiesel is a Holocaust survivor, and one of the most well known figures in the field, publishing extensively on the subject, including his memoir *Night*. The psychologist Bruno Bettelheim, also a Holocaust survivor, wrote on emotional distress — especially with respect to children — but also wrote critical essays on film.

14 Theodor Adorno, *Prisms*. Translated by Samuel and Shierry Weber (London: Neville Spearman, 1967), 34.

15 Theodor Adorno, *Negative Dialectics*. Translated by E. B. Ashton (New York: The Seabury Press, 1973), 362.

16 American censorship imposed between 1945 and 1952 also necessitated "alternative" narrative strategies. No information regarding the atomic bomb could be published or screened without explicit permission from the occupational authority. Not even medical information could be released without prior approval.

17 Naomi Mandel, "Rethinking 'After Auschwitz': Against a Rhetoric of the Unspeakable in Holocaust Writing," *Boundary 2* vol. 28, no. 2 (2001): 209–10.

18 Ibid., 223–4. Mandel concludes her article by arguing: "The unspeakable, I urge, must be spoken. Complicity needs to be confronted, not avoided. Unlike language, complicity has no limits; unlike rhetorical performance, ethical practice cannot reasonably gesture toward its own inefficacy. Only by speaking the unspeakable, confronting the fact of complicity and assuming our own, can we effectively delineate the complexity of the victims' experience, confront the presence of the Holocaust in our past, and, perhaps, reach a more responsible understanding of what 'after Auschwitz' really means" (Mandel, 228).

19 Ibid., 219.

20 Günter Grass observes, "We cannot get around Auschwitz. And no matter how greatly we want to, we should not attempt to get around it, because Auschwitz belongs to us,

is a permanent stigma of our history — and is a positive gain! It has made possible this insight: Finally we know ourselves." Günter Grass, *Two States — One Nation?* Translated by Krishna Winston and A. S. Wensinger (San Diego: Harcourt Brace Jovanovich, 1990), 123.

21 Alvin H. Rosenfeld, *A Double Dying: Reflections on Holocaust Literature* (Bloomington: Indiana University Press, 1980), 154.

22 Kertész, "Who Owns Auschwitz?", 267.

23 Flanzbaum, "'But Wasn't It Terrific?'", 274.

24 Bill Nichols, *Representing Reality: Issues and Concepts in Documentary* (Bloomington: Indiana University Press, 1991), 178.

25 Ibid., 35.

Chapter Two: The Realistic Imperative

1 Imre Kertész, "Who Owns Auschwitz?" Translated by John MacKay, *The Yale Journal of Criticism* vol. 14, no. 1 (Spring 2001): 269–70.

2 Hilene Flanzbaum, "'But Wasn't It Terrific?': A Defense of Liking *Life Is Beautiful,*" *The Yale Journal of Criticism* vol. 14, no. 1 (Spring 2001): 274.

3 Annette Insdorf, *Indelible Shadows: Film and the Holocaust* (second edn) (Cambridge: Cambridge University Press, 1990), xv.

4 Ibid., xix.

5 This underlying fear regarding the revisionist agenda governs many critical assessments of Holocaust films, and compels some to stringently police representational strategies. Alvin Rosenfeld argues, for instance that: "The lines that separate fact from fiction need to be scrupulously observed, therefore, lest the tendency to reject the Holocaust, already strong, be encouraged by reducing it altogether to the realm of the fictive." Alvin H. Rosenfeld, *A Double Dying: Reflections on Holocaust Literature* (Bloomington: Indiana University Press, 1980), 161.

6 Here are just a couple of samples illustrating Insdorf's application of "authenticity" as the criterion on which to access the quality of a film: Despite all of its narrative excess Insdorf views Luchino Visconti's 1969 film *The Damned* with its "numerous scenes of murder and sexual perversion (rape, incest, pedophilia, transvestism)" as a "historically *faithful* tapestry of the rise of Nazism" (Insdorf, 138–9). Emphasis added. This propensity for the authentic is also evident in the third edition of *Indelible Shadows.* For instance in her discussion of "Rediscoveries," Insdorf says that "Aleksander Ford's magnificent Holocaust drama [*Border Street*] renders Jewish life with *authenticity* and reverence (for example, the last Sabbath meal a family will enjoy together before being taken to the Warsaw Ghetto)." Annette Insdorf, *Indelible Shadows: Film and the Holocaust* (third edn) (Cambridge: Cambridge University Press, 2003), 254. Emphasis added. Ilan Avisar utilizes "authenticity" as a measure of quality as well; when discussing *The Great Dictator* of all things, he too feels compelled to contextualize Charles Chaplin's 1940 parody of Hitler and the Nazi regime in the authentic. Avisar insists that, "the wild comic gag, like other slapstick moments in *The Great Dictator*, never obscures the *realistic* background. The pictures of the admiring adherents which immediately follow are based on *authentic* photographs from *Triumph of the Will*, including the greeting by a little flower girl and the dictator's posing with a baby. In Chaplin's versions, the baby, to be sure, fails to show proper respect, wetting the disgusted dictator." Ilan Avisar, *Screening the Holocaust: Cinema's Images of the Unimaginable* (Bloomington: Indiana University Press, 1988), 137. Emphasis added.

7 See Roland Barthes, "The Reality Effect," in *The Rustle of Language.* Translated by Richard Howard (Berkeley: University of California Press, 1989), 141–8.

8 Barthes, *The Rustle of Language*, 148.

9   Ibid., 132.

10 Barbara Mruklik, "Wiernosc sobie. Rozmowa z Wanda Jakubowska," *Kino* vol. 6 (1985): 7. Jakubowska would make two more films that were set within the concentration camp: *The End of Our World* (*Koniec naszego swiata*), Wanda Jakubowska, 1964; and *The Invitation* (*Zaproszenie*), Wanda Jakubowska, 1986.

11 Insdorf hails the success of Jakubowska's film, again premised on its "authenticity." She writes: "The 1948 Polish production [of *The Last Stop*], from a script by Jakubowska and Gerda Schneider, is also one of the most powerful and historically accurate feature films made about (and in) Auschwitz." Insdorf continues, "*The Last Stop* has tremendous authenticity because the film was made *where* it happened; by and with people *to whom* it happened; and in the native languages." She adds that all the characters speak their respective languages — which runs counter especially to many American films — and that the filmmaker herself "was . . . imprisoned in Auschwitz" (Insdorf, *Indelible Shadows*, 152–3). Ewa Mazierska observes that "The recent production of large numbers of films in the newly democratic Poland have made both critics and ordinary viewers there more aware that all films, not only those which are crude propaganda (as Jakubowska's films were often perceived), are representations, rather than presentations of the world as it really is." Ewa Mazierska, "Wanda Jakubowska's Cinema of Commitment," *European Journal of Women's Studies* vol. 8, no. 2 (May 2001): 222.

12 Béla Balázs cited in Hanno Loewy, "The Mother of All Holocaust Films?: Wanda Jakubowska's Auschwitz trilogy," *Historical Journal of Film, Radio and Television* vol. 24, no. 2 (2004): 179.

13 Loewy, "The Mother of All Holocaust Films?", 179.

14 Ibid., 197.

15 Mazierska, "Wanda Jakubowska's Cinema of Commitment," 224.

16 Ibid., 223.

17 See Hanno Loewy's "The Mother of All Holocaust Films?" where among other things he discusses the pre-production planning for *The Last Stage* and how the narrative was shaped into its final version. "Jakubowska added the elements of dramatic narration she was asked for and a month later Wazik was pleased that now the 'bestialities are better to take' and the narrative would now develop from 'a martyrium, that is imposed on the figures, to a conscious fight'" (Loewy, 181).

18 Jiri Cieslar, "*Daleká Cesta/Distant Journey*," in Peter Hames ed., *The Cinema of Central Europe* (New York: Wallflower Press, 2004), 45.

19 Describing his upbringing in rural Southern Bohemia, Alfréd Radok explains, "At that time my perception of rural life was intense: both Christian and Jewish holidays were celebrated rigorously. At Christmas the Christ Child brought the Christmas tree, and a servant blew the horn on the village green; at Easter we followed the Resurrection Service by going to my grandfather's for the seder." Alfréd Radok in Antonín J. Liehm, *Closely Watched Films: The Czechoslovak Experience* (White Planes, NY: International Arts and Sciences Press, Inc., 1974), 37.

20 Ilan Avisar offers a slightly different take on the relationship between Hana and Tonik: "Tony, her boyfriend, gives her the opportunity to be even more belonging to her Gentile society. He offers to marry her, hoping that as a Gentile's wife she will not have to suffer the same ordeals as the other Jews." Ilan Avisar, *Screening the Holocaust: Cinema's Images of the Unimaginable* (Bloomington: Indiana University Press, 1988), 56. While this position is not without merit, it seems to me that Tonik is genuinely in love with Hana, and in no respect treats her as a "charity case."

21 Cieslar, "*Daleká Cesta/Distant Journey*," 50.

22 Ibid., 45.

23 Ibid., 46.

24 Ibid., 49.

25 Avisar cites Robert Hughes's written text, which lends credence to Radok's expressionist and imaginative venture into representing the Holocaust: "The event which

revealed that painting could no longer deal cathartically with modern horrors was the Holocaust . . . after Auschwitz, Expressionist distortion of the human body in art seemed to many sensitive minds to have no future — in fact, to be little more than an impertinence or an intrusion, a gloss on what the Nazis had done, on a vast industrial scale, to real bodies. Reality had so far outstripped art that painting was speechless. What could rival the testimony of the photograph?" (Robert Hughes cited in Avisar, *Screening the Holocaust*, 62). See Robert Hughes, *The Shock of the New* (New York: Alfred A. Knopf, 1981), 299.

26 André Bazin, "Le Ghetto Concentrationnaire," *Cahiers du Cinema* vol. 2, no. 9 (February 1952): 59. This passage also appears in Avisar's *Screening the Holocaust*, on page 63.

27 Bazin, "Le Ghetto Concentrationnaire," 59.

28 "The suicide scene" Avisar similarly observes, "ends with a match cut from the blowing curtains to the SS flags and pictures of Himmler and concentration camps" (Avisar, *Screening the Holocaust*, 60).

29 Micheal Stevenson, "*The Pianist* and its Contexts: Polanski's Narration of Holocaust Evasion and Survival," in John Orr and Elzbieta Ostrowska, eds., *The Cinema of Roman Polanski: Dark Spaces of the World* (New York: Wallflower Press, 2006), 147.

30 Ewa Mazierska, "Double Memory: the Holocaust in Polish Film," in Toby Haggith and Joanna Newman, eds., *Holocaust and the Moving Image: Representations in Film and Television Since 1933* (New York: Wallflower Press, 2005), 233.

31 Lawrence Baron, *Projecting the Holocaust into the Present: The Changing Focus of Contemporary Holocaust Cinema* (New York: Rowman and Littlefield Publishers, Inc., 2005), 155.

32 Sander Gilman writes this about the origins of Becker's work: "The biographical origins of the film are not especially in Becker's own memories of the Lodz ghetto. He claims that in the 1960s he had few such memories. He seems to have been inspired by his father, Max Becker, whose views of his own adult experiences in Lodz and Auschwitz shaped his son's vision. Max wanted Jurek to write of the bravery of the Jews in the ghetto, specifically the tale of a man who hid a radio and was the source of inspiration to his friends. Jurek decided to do exactly the opposite. His father's response was: 'You can tell the stupid Germans what it was like in the Ghetto; you can't tell me, I was there. I was a witness. You cannot tell me silly stories. I know that it was different.'" For the audience in the GDR (and the rest of the world) Becker's film was an appropriate (read: comic) response to the Shoah, but not necessarily for his father (whose death in 1972 precluded him actually seeing the final film). Indeed, Becker noted, his father did not speak to him for a year after the novel was published. Sander L. Gilman, "Is Life Beautiful? Can the Shoah Be Funny? Some Thoughts on Recent and Older Films," *Critical Inquiry* vol. 26, no. 2 (Winter 2000): 298.

33 Elie Wiesel, "Trivializing the Holocaust: Semi-Fact and Semi-Fiction," *New York Times* (April 16, 1978).

34 Alan L. Mintz, *Popular Culture and the Shaping of Holocaust Memory in America* (Seattle: University of Washington Press, 2001), 23. Mark Anderson recounts, "On May 1 [1978] of that year, two weeks after the program had aired on national television, President Jimmy Carter stood in the Rose Garden with the Israeli ambassador to mark the thirtieth anniversary of the founding of the State of Israel and announced plans for a Holocaust memorial to commemorate the death of six million Jews. Whereas in 1964 the parks commissioner of New York City had rejected plans for a memorial to the victims of the Warsaw ghetto because city monuments must 'be limited to events of American history,' Carter's plan, which was supported by all three subsequent presidents, led to the creation of the Holocaust Museum in Washington in 1993. The museum is now one of the capital's most popular tourist venues, adjacent to the Mall and in symbolic proximity to the Lincoln Memorial and the Washington Monument."

Mark M. Anderson, "The Child Victim as Witness to the Holocaust: An American Story?" *Jewish Social Studies: History, Culture, Society* vol. 14, no. 1 (Fall 2007): 2.

35 Jeffrey Shandler similarly notes, "the response to its broadcast in the United States and abroad arguably proved to be a more noteworthy cultural landmark than the miniseries itself." Jeffrey Shandler, *While America Watches: Televising the Holocaust* (New York: Oxford University Press, 1999), 159.

36 Avisar, *Screening the Holocaust*, 130.

37 Cited in Avisar, *Screening the Holocaust*, 130.

38 Ibid., 130.

39 Insdorf, *Indelible Shadows* (third edn), 3.

40 Paddy Chayefsky, cited in Insdorf, *Indelible Shadows* (third edn), 3. In an interview, filmmaker Hans-Jürgen Syberberg comments on the television miniseries: "The same people: Jews who perhaps lost members of their family now make money out of the ashes of Auschwitz. How Goebbels would laugh!" Hans-Jürgen Syberberg, "Interview with Hans-Jürgen Syberberg," *The Threepenny Review* 2 (Summer 1980): 5.

41 Claude Lanzmann, "From the Holocaust to 'Holocaust,'" in Stuart Liebman ed., *Claude Lanzmann's Shoah: Key Essays* (New York: Oxford University Press, 2007), 30.

Chapter Three: The Holocaust as Dramatic Spectacle

1 Judith Doneson, "The Jew as a Female Figure in the Holocaust Film," *Shoah: a Review of Holocaust Studies and Commemorations* vol. 1, no. 1 (1978): 11. Elsewhere Doneson speaks directly to *Schindler's List*: "there are *no* references to resistance and organization within the ghetto, the Jews remain the perfect victims — weak, ineffectual, incapable of helping themselves — the stereotype of women. If someone strong, fearless, and virile — an Oskar Schindler — does not act on their behalf, they are doomed." Judith E. Doneson, "The Image Lingers: The Feminization of the Jew in *Schindler's List*," in Yosefa Loshitzky ed., *Spielberg's Holocaust: Critical Perspectives on Schindler's List* (Bloomington: Indiana University Press, 1997), 145.

2 Concurring with this assessment, Doneson says, "They consummate their relationship when Stern readily shares a drink with Schindler." Judith E. Doneson, "The Image Lingers: The Feminization of the Jew in *Schindler's List*," in Yosefa Loshitzky ed., *Spielberg's Holocaust: Critical Perspectives on Schindler's List* (Bloomington: Indiana University Press, 1997), 146.

3 Steve Neale, "Melodrama and Tears," *Screen* vol. 26, no. 6 (November–December 1986): 11–12.

4 Costa-Gavras's 2002 film *Amen* also conforms to the Jew-as-victim motif, so clearly illustrated in *Schindler's List*. Once again it is the Gentile's mission to save hapless Jews. The transformation of Gentiles also happens in Alan J. Pakula's 1982 film *Sophie's Choice* and Stephen Daldry's 2008 film *The Reader*. *The Reader* is *Sophie's Choice* in reverse. Where Stingo, the principal male character in Pakula's film, undergoes a transformative process — namely, a sexual coming of age — via a victim of the Holocaust, Sophie, in *The Reader* Berg undergoes an analogous transformation via a perpetrator of the Holocaust.

5 Adam's character and his fate are premised on Attila Petschauer, who was a Hungarian fencing champion, and who was beaten to death in a labor camp. Susan Rubin Suleiman, "Jewish Assimilation in Hungary, the Holocaust, and Epic Film: Reflections on István Szabó's *Sunshine*," *The Yale Journal of Criticism* vol. 14, no. 1 (Spring 2001): 236.

6 See, for example, Claudia Eppert, "Entertaining History: (Un)Heroic Identifications, Apt Pupils, and an Ethical Imagination," *New German Critique: An Interdisciplinary Journal of German Studies* 86 (Spring–Summer 2002): 71–101.

7   Helena Frenkil Schlam, "Contemporary Scribes: Jewish American Cartoonists," *Shofar: An Interdisciplinary Journal of Jewish Studies* vol. 20, no. 1 (Fall 2001): 101.

8   "I think, beneath the costumes, and the spectacle, the fighting, and the fun, there's an underlying philosophy about prejudice, about feeling outcast, fear of the unknown, trying to find your place in the world," Bryan Singer says in an interview, "very universal concepts that people have been attracted to . . ." Bryan Singer interviewed by Charlie Rose, *The Charlie Rose Show*, PBS, included on the *X-Men* DVD extras. "Unlike those who insist on the uniqueness of the Holocaust," Baron Lawrence echoes the comments expressed during the Charlie Rose interview, "Singer employs the Holocaust as a metaphor for the vulnerability of any minority group." Lawrence Baron, "X-Men as J Men: The Jewish Subtext of a Comic Book Movie," *Shofar: An Interdisciplinary Journal of Jewish Studies* vol. 22, no. 1 (Fall 2003): 51. Lawrence cites Stephen T. Katz's, *The Holocaust in Historical Context, Volume 1 The Holocaust and Mass Death Before the Modern Age* (Oxford University Press: New York, 1994), as an example of a critic that insists upon the uniqueness of the Holocaust.

9   Thomas Elsaesser, "Subject Positions, Speaking Positions: From *Holocaust, Our Hitler*, and *Heimat* to *Shoah* and *Schindler's List*," in Vivian Sobchack, ed., *The Persistence of History: Cinema, Television, and the Modern Event* (New York and London: Routledge, 1996), 151–2. Also see Saul Friedlander, *Reflections of Nazism: An Essay on Kitsch and Death*. Translated by Thomas Weyr (Bloomington: Indiana University Press, 1993).

10   Libby Saxton, *Haunted Images: Film, Ethics, Testimony and the Holocaust* (New York: Wallflower Press, 2008), 71.

11   Ibid., 73. Saxton notes on the same page, "Windows in general and spyholes in particular are amongst the oldest motifs in film and film theory. At once aperture and frame, the window simultaneously facilitates and limits our vision; in this respect at least it might be understood as an allegory of cinema."

12   The peephole motif in Holocaust films share points in common with feminist film theory where the female form is typically negotiated in one of two ways: either, (1) it is fetishized, or (2) it is subject to the punishing sadistic gaze, where "pleasure lies in ascertaining guilt," as Laura Mulvey argues, "asserting control and subjugating the guilty person through punishment or forgiveness." Laura Mulvey, *Visual and Other Pleasures* (Bloomington: Indiana University Press, 1989), 21–2. With respect to not breaking the narrative diegesis Mulvey says: "the device of the show-girl allows for the two looks to be unified technically without any apparent break in the diegesis. A woman performs within the narrative; the gaze of the spectator and that of the male characters in the film are neatly combined without breaking narrative verisimilitude" (Mulvey, *Visual and Other Pleasures*, 19).

13   Survivor Jolana Roth recounts seeing female SS guards at Auschwitz, noting that you never saw many, "But the ones you did see — they were worse than the men. I will never forget the one who would stand at the peephole of the gas chamber just because she wanted to." Jolana Roth cited in Claudia Koonz, *Mothers in the Fatherland: Women, the Family, and Nazi Politics* (New York: St. Martin's Press, 1987), 404–5.

14   Caroline Joan Kay S. Picart and David A. Frank, *Frames of Evil: The Holocaust as Horror in American Film* (Carbondale: Southern Illinois University Press, 2006), 19.

15   Ibid., 19–20.

16   Ibid.

17   This is similar to the Yehiel Dinur's 1955 novella, *The House of Dolls*, which he published under the pseudonym Ka-Tzetnik 135633, where the principal character discovers his sister conscripted into a Joy Division — a concentration camp brothel. Also the description of the brothel in *House of Dolls* matches quite closely with what we see in *The Pawnbroker*.

18   Sara Horowitz in stronger terms also sees a pattern: "The appeal to the audience's voyeurism is repeated in the shower scene at Auschwitz, a scene pornographic both

for its depiction of terrified, naked Jewish women and for its use of the gas chamber to provoke the viewer's sense of suspense." Sara R. Horowitz, "But Is It Good for the Jews? Spielberg's Schindler and the Aesthetics of Atrocity," in Yosefa Loshitzky ed., *Spielberg's Holocaust: Critical Perspectives on Schindler's List* (Bloomington: Indiana University Press, 1997), 128. Horowitz also speaks to literary forms and other films that exhibit similar motifs of mixing eros and violence: "As the film enacts the progress of genocidal brutality acted out on the bodies of women it evokes a common trope of Holocaust films, the eroticized woman victim. Figured in an unproblematized manner in such films as *Sophie's Choice* and *The Night Porter*, and critiqued in films such as *Angry Harvest*, the trope reaches its most extreme form in pornographic paperback novels [the Stalag genre] which utilize the camp setting and the relationship between Nazis and female inmates as the occasion for the playing out of sadomasochistic fantasies" (Horowitz, "But Is It Good for the Jews?", 127). This pornographic sensibility is discussed in Chapter 8.

19 Ibid., 127–8.

20 Lawrence Kramer suggests that Roman Polanski's 2002 film *The Pianist* is in part a response to this scene: "His response, taking a pianist as protagonist, turns Spielberg's scene against itself: if this music is not the foe of such atrocity, what is?" Lawrence Kramer, "Melodic Trains: Music in Polanski's *The Pianist*," in Daniel Goldmark et al., eds, *Beyond the Soundtrack: Representing Music in Cinema* (Berkeley: University of California Press, 2007), 67–8.

21 There are a number of cinematic references at play in this climatic scene. First, the Nordic figure in the final sequence alludes to Hans-Jürgen Syberberg's 1977 film *Hitler: A Film From Germany*. Syberberg also emphasizes "staginess," and the operatic, specifically evoking Wagner, attempting to reclaim Germany's romantic heritage, and cleanse it of its Nazi taint. Second, the air raid is achieved by using stock footage cutaways, characters simply looking upwards beyond the frame, and audio cues, precisely in the same way that Wanda Jakubowska does in her 1947 film *The Last Stage*. And, just as with *Kornblumenblau*, the very sight of Allied bombers sends the SS running for cover. In addition, the French national anthem also figures significantly in *The Last Stage*; as a group of women are loaded onto trucks to be sent to the gas chamber — and the women know as much — they break into "La Marseillaise." This shot from *The Last Stage* is used in Alain Resnais's 1955 *Night and Fog*. Lastly, the use of the "Ninth Symphony" is no small accident, as it is also used in Stanley Kubrick's 1971 film *A Clockwork Orange*, which features the "Ninth Symphony," a film that likewise aims to critique the spectacle of violence. It is interesting to note as well that the "Ninth" has been taken as the anthem for the European Union.

22 Libby Saxton similarly observes, "There are competing demands on Tadeusz's attention: his gaze, represented by the subjective camera, flits back and forth between the condemned men, the raw onion he is ravenously munching and the white petticoat intermittently visible beneath the skirt of one of the women. In this sequence an array of incompatible looks intersects with out own on the gallows, reflecting, respectively, the satisfaction of the officials, the voyeuristic curiosity of the women, Tadeusz's conflicting sensations of terror, hunger and desire and, finally, the agony of dying" (Saxton, *Haunted Images*, 68).

23 Saxton argues that this scene situates the spectator as complicit: "In positioning us, by turns, as unseeing victim and as voyeuristic persecutor, this sequence implicates us in its violence, deprives us of any innocent perspective and foregrounds our complicity in the spectacle" (Saxton, *Haunted Images*, 69).

24 In both *Amen* and the NBC miniseries *Holocaust*, the spectator is taken right up to the gas chamber door, and characters gaze through the peephole, but in both cases the films never cut to the subjective view; leaving the spectator right at the threshold. A trailer for a yet-to-released Uwe Boll film, on the other hand, takes us from the peephole straight into the gas chamber during a gassing.

25 This title is taken from Robin Wood's seminal essays "Return of the Repressed," *Film Comment* vol. 14, no. 4 (July–August 1978): 25–32; and "Gods and Monsters," *Film Comment* vol. 14, no. 5 (September–October 1978): 19–25.

26 Stuart Klawans, "*Scream 4*: The Holocaust?" *Nation* vol. 267, no. 14 (November 2, 1998): 34.

27 Bryan Singer cited in Picart and Frank, *Frames of Evil*, 99.

28 Interestingly, the homosexual subtext of the film led to "real world" consequences. As reported in *The Advocate*, "a group of six teenage boys and their parents sued Singer, Phoenix Pictures, and others involved in the production, alleging that the boys [who played Todd's classmates] were forced to strip naked for a shower scene against their will and without the permission of their parents." The lawyers for the plaintiffs characterized Singer and the film as "homosexual pedophiles. . . . Marty Rub, who represents two of the six boys, denies that his side saw the filmmakers as an easy target because several people involved in the production are gay. 'The boys and their families didn't want to sue,' Rub insists. 'We wanted to see the film [of the shower scene] destroyed and the pictures destroyed. Phoenix just said the boys were lying.'" *Advocate*, "Hollywood Gay Baiting," (March 3, 1998), 24. The uproar regarding this scene is illustrative of the rampant inequities within our culture. The scene is easily comparable to the opening in Brian De Palma's 1976 classic *Carrie*. The difference of course is that viewer takes the young female body as the object of visual pleasure in *Carrie*, whereas *Apt Pupil* erotically engages the young *and* elderly male body.

29 Picart and Frank, *Frames of Evil*, 102.

30 This scene — with its eroticism and the putting on of a costume — might have certain affinities with Luchino Visconti's 1969 film *The Damned*, Liliana Cavani's 1974 film *The Night Porter*, and Elijiah Moshinsky's 1993 comedy *Genghis Cohn*.

31 Picart and Frank, *Frames of Evil*, 120.

32 Ibid., 123–4.

Chapter Four: Defiance and Resistance

1 Member of the Jewish Council in the NBC miniseries *Holocaust* (Marvin Chomsky, 1978).

2 Bruno Bettelheim, *The Informed Heart: Autonomy in a Mass Age* (Glecoe, IL: Free Press, 1961), 264–5.

3 Judith Doneson, "The Jew as a Female Figure in the Holocaust Film," *Shoah: a Review of Holocaust Studies and Commemorations* vol. 1, no. 1 (1978): 12.

4 Ibid.

5 Ibid., 13.

6 Ibid., 18.

7 Annette Insdorf, *Indelible Shadows: Film and the Holocaust Second Edition* (Cambridge: Cambridge University Press, 1990), 182.

8 Joshua Newton's *Iron Cross* stars Helmut Berger, who plays a haggard elderly man, a far cry from his young nubile self in the 1970s. In the 1970s Berger starred in a number of different films including *The Damned*, and *Salon Kitty*, playing a sharp but twisted SS officer; in *The Garden of the Finzi-Continis*, though, he plays Alberto the sickly and queer-coded Jew. Berger had an amazing capacity to straddle the line between waif-dandy and the archetype of the supposed Aryan master race, between decadence and strident exemplar of the Nazi subject.

9 Judith E. Doneson, "The Image Lingers: The Feminization of the Jew in *Schindler's List*," in Yosefa Loshitzky, *Spielberg's Holocaust: Critical Perspectives on Schindler's List* (Bloomington: Indiana University Press, 1997), 140.

10   There are some possible exceptions to this trope of Jew-as-victim; in fact there are films
     where Jews literally step into the ring to fight their oppressor. In Peter Solan's 1963
     film *The Boxer and Death* the principal character, Jan Kominek, earns a reprieve from
     the gas chamber when the camp commandant, Kraft, sees him as a potential worthy
     opponent in the boxing ring. While on the one hand Kominek entertains Kraft's
     desires, at the same time Kominek uses his so-called opportunity for the good of all.
     By comparison Robert Young's 1989 film *Triumph of the Spirit* also features a boxer —
     premised on the real-life experiences of Salamo Arusch — but unlike Solan's theme
     of political solidarity the latter film falls more in line with the American sensibility of
     individual fortitude, and the motif of "love conquers all."

11   Gene Moskowitz, "The Uneasy East," *Sight and Sound* vol. 27, no. 3 (Winter 1957):
     137.

12   Ilan Avisar, *Screening the Holocaust: Cinema's Images of the Unimaginable* (Bloomington:
     Indiana University Press, 1988), 39.

13   Stuart Liebman, "The Art of Memory: Andrzej Wajda's War Trilogy," *Cineaste* vol. 32,
     no. 1 (Winter 2006): 42.

14   Insdorf, *Indelible Shadows*, 163.

15   Arnost Lustig, *Darkness Casts No Shadows*. Translated by Jeanne Nemocova (Evanston,
     IL.: Northwestern University Press, 1985); this is also published as Arnost Lustig,
     Diamonds of the Night. Translated by Jeanne Nemocova (Evanston, IL.: Northwestern
     University Press, 1986).

16   Avisar similarly comments, "Nemec's style is outstanding, for he dispenses with some
     basic elements of conventional dramatic action" (Avisar, *Screening the Holocaust*, 76).
     Antonin Novak, though, finds the stylized cinematography gimmicky: "Nemec is trying
     to make us share the very anxiety and loneliness tormenting the minds of the two boys.
     The connection is broken only where, intoxicated with his opportunities or overdoing
     his efforts to achieve the deserved effect, he too blatantly reveals the mechaniques of
     his methods and arousing mere curiosity." Antonin Novak, *Films and Filmmakers in
     Czechoslovakia*. Translated by George Theiner (Prague: Orbis, 1968), 59.

17   Stuart Liebman and Leonard Quart, "Czech Films of the Holocaust," *Cineaste* vol. 22,
     no. 1 (April 1996): no pagination.

18   Ibid.

19   Avisar arrives at the same conclusion; see Avisar, *Screening the Holocaust*, 78–9.

20   Janet Ward, "Holocaust Film in the Post-9/11 Era: New Directions in Staging and
     Emplotment," *Pacific Coast Philology* vol. 39 (2004): 34.

21   Axel Bangert, "Changing Narratives and Images of the Holocaust: Tim Blake Nelson's
     film *The Grey Zone* (2001)," *New Cinemas: Journal of Contemporary Film* vol. 6, no. 1
     (2008): 17.

22   See Arun Kumar's 1996 documentary, *The Bielsky Brothers: The Unknown Partisans*,
     for an unflinching examination of the Bielsky brothers and their group.

23   Jakubowska returns to the subject of Auschwitz in two other films: *The End of Our
     World* in 1964 and *The Invitation* in 1986.

24   Insdorf, *Indelible Shadows*, 156.

25   Doneson, "The Image Lingers," 142.

26   Ibid.

27   On October 14, 1943, the largest and most successful insurrection was mounted at
     Sobibor, a death camp located at Poland's eastern border. Jack Gold's 1987 made-for-
     television movie *Escape from Sobibor* dramatizes this event. Also, originally recorded
     for his documentary *Shoah*, Claude Lanzmann interviews one of the Sobibor survivors
     in his 2001 documentary *Sobibór, 14 octobre 1943, 16 heures*.

28   Liebman and Quart, "Czech Films of the Holocaust," no pagination.

29   At least two other documentaries have employed footage from *The Last Stage*: Leo
     Hurwitz's 1956 film *The Museum of Fury*, and Allan Holzman's 1996 *Survivors of the
     Holocaust*.

30   Jaromil Jires's 1972 film *Give My Love to the Swallows* shares certain affinities with *The Last Stage*. It features Maruska Kuderíková, a saintly female figure, working in the resistance, and like Martha, sentenced to die. While the politics of *Give My Love to the Swallows* is just as strident as *The Last Stage*, the execution of Jires's film is far more modest; a beautiful film. Also similar to *The Last Stage*, Frank Beyer's 1963 film *Naked Among Wolves* is a story of solidarity, compassion, and the survival of innocence. A group of Buchenwald internees shelter a small boy who arrives on a transport from Auschwitz. The plot might be read as a predecessor to *The Grey Zone*, where the Sonderkommando shelter an adolescent girl who miraculously survives the gas chamber.

31   Zbynek Brynych also made the 1965 film *The Fifth Horsemen Is Fear*. Its principal character, Braun, a former doctor, becomes a reluctant accomplice to the resistance.

32   Avisar, *Screening the Holocaust*, 67. Avisar goes on to discuss resistance in *Transport from Paradise* further; see Avisar, ibid., 69.

33   Addressing sexuality Alvin Rosenfeld states, "In the camps themselves, as virtually all survivor accounts indicate, the central, most frustrated, and hence most abiding appetite was for food. Other passions were secondary and, it seems, for most were held in abeyance. As a result, one of the characteristics of Holocaust writings at their most authentic is that they are peculiarly and predominantly sexless." Alvin H. Rosenfeld, *A Double Dying: Reflections on Holocaust Literature* (Bloomington: Indiana University Press, 1980), 164.

34   Alexander Stein suggests that Szpilman's musical disposition fostered his capacity to survive his ordeal; see Stein, "Music and Trauma in Polanski's *The Pianist* (2002)," *Psychoanalytic Inquiry* vol. 27, no. 4 (September 2007): 449.

35   Lawrence Kramer, "Melodic Trains: Music in Polanski's *The Pianist*," in Daniel Goldmark et al., eds., *Beyond the Soundtrack: Representing Music in Cinema* (Berkeley: University of California Press, 2007), 67. Daniel Mann's 1980 made-for-television movie *Playing for Time* also utilizes music, if not as a form of a resistance, then as a defense.

36   Kramer, although quite critical of the film, does in fact seem to concur with these sentiments; see Kramer, "Melodic Trains," 67.

37   See Janet Ward, "Holocaust Film in the Post-9/11 Era: New Directions in Staging and Emplotment," *Pacific Coast Philology* vol. 39 (2004): 32–3.

38   Alan Starski was the production designer for this film, and did an amazing job. Interestingly, many of the films discussed here relied on Starski's craftsmanship and design skills: *Escape from Sobibor* (Jack Gold, 1987), *Europa Europa* (Agnieszka Holland, 1990), and *Schindler's List* (Steven Spielberg, 1993).

39   In fact, Szpilman played Chopin's "Nocturne in C-Sharp Minor." A number of scholars have addressed this scene: Celia Applegate, "Saving Music: Enduring Experiences of Culture." *History & Memory* vol. 17, no. 1/2 (Spring/Summer 2005): 236 n. 23; Stein, "Music and Trauma," 451; Kramer, "Melodic Trains," 79. Szpilman in his memoir explains that he was terribly frightened and out of practice. "The glassy, tinkling sound of the untuned strings rang through the empty flat and the stairway, floated through the ruins of the villa on the other side of the street and returned as a muted, melancholy echo. When I finished, the silence seemed even gloomier and more eerie than before." Wladyslaw Szpilman, *The Pianist: The Extraordinary True Story of One Man's Survival in Warsaw 1939–1945*. Translated by Anteha Bell (New York: Picador, 1999), 177–8.

40   Kramer finds the lighting dangerously kitschy; see Kramer, "Melodic Trains," 79.

41   Stein, "Music and Trauma," 452.

42   Ibid.

43   Kramer, "Melodic Trains," 73.

44   Michel Chion, "Mute Music: Polanski's *The Pianist* and Campion's *The Piano*," translated by Claudia Gorbman, in Daniel Goldmark et al. eds., *Beyond the Soundtrack: Representing Music in Cinema* (Berkeley: University of California Press, 2007), 91.

45 Interestingly, Eli Roth apparently directed the faux-movie *Nation's Pride*. Roth plays an important part in the intersection between the horror genre and the visual culture of the Holocaust; he also directed *Hostel* and *Hostel: Part II*, both of which are laced with Holocaust imagery.

46 Eyal Peretz illuminated this point at the 2010 annual Society for Cinema and Media Studies (March 17–21, 2010). Peretz's presentation on *Inglourious Basterds* was excellent and I expect that it will be published in the near future.

47 Laurent Bouzereau addresses the use of violence in Tarantino's films; see Bouzereau, *Ultraviolent Movies: from Sam Peckinpah to Quentin Tarantino* (Secaucus, NJ: Citadel Press, 1996) 74; 83.

48 David Denby, "Americans in Paris: *Inglourious Basterds* and *Julie & Julia*," *New Yorker* (August 24, 2009): 82.

49 Ibid., 83.

50 Ibid., 82.

Chapter Five: Holocaust Comedies?

1 Omer Bartov concurs, noting: "*Life Is Beautiful* may not be as successful as *Jakob the Liar*, but to assert, as some have, that it is false (as well as flippant and irresponsible) is to say that the only manner to represent the Holocaust is by depicting it 'as it really was,' as if that were either possible or desirable. Ultimately, the film's [*Life Is Beautiful*] authenticity lies not in the conditions it recreates, but in its insistence on the power of love to transform reality." Omer Bartov, *The "Jew" in Cinema: From The Golem to Don't Touch My Holocaust* (Bloomington: Indiana University Press, 2005), 123.

2 David A. Brenner, "Laughter Amid Catastrophe: *Train of Life* and Tragicomic Holocaust Cinema," in David Bathrick et al., eds., *Visualizing the Holocaust: Documents, Aesthetics, Memory* (Rochester: Camden House, 2008), 261.

3 Ethical concerns probably ensured that Jerry Lewis's film *The Day the Clown Cried* (1972) never saw the light of day. Officially, Lewis's film collapsed due to financial reasons, but its premise certainly made some nervous. Lewis plays a clown that entertains children and ultimately leads them into the gas chamber. This film — like *Jakob the Liar* and *Life Is Beautiful* — is about telling lies to "protect" children from the horrific realities of the Holocaust. The rudiments of this plot materialize in Karel Kachyna's 1991 film *The Last Butterfly*, but set within the conventional confines of dramatic narrative. See Walter C. Metz, "'Show Me the Shoah!': Generic Experience and Spectatorship in Popular Representations of the Holocaust," *Shofar: An Interdisciplinary Journal of Jewish Studies* vol. 27, no. 1 (Fall 2008): 24–5.

4 Steve Lipman, *Laughter in Hell: The Use of Humor during the Holocaust* (Norhvale, NJ: Jason Aronson, Inc., 1991), 8–9. Also see Alan Dundes and Thomas Hauschild, "Auschwitz Jokes," *Western Folklore* vol. 42, no. 4 (October 1983): 249–60; and Alan Dundes and Uli Linke, "More on Auschwitz Jokes," *Folklore* vol. 99, no. 1 (1988): 3–10.

5 David Brenner makes a similar observation, "Those who resist representation seem to act out of concern that the Holocaust will be forgotten, that it will be denied, or both." David A. Brenner, "Laughter Amid Catastrophe: *Train of Life* and Tragicomic Holocaust Cinema," in David Bathrick et al., eds., *Visualizing the Holocaust: Documents, Aesthetics, Memory* (Rochester: Camden House, 2008), 265.

6 Bartov, *The "Jew" in Cinema*, 123.

7 Radu Mihaileanu in Annette Insdorf, *Indelible Shadows: Film and Holocaust* (3rd edn) (Cambridge: Cambridge University Press, 2003), 285–6.

8 This echoes one of the most famous lines in Ernst Lubitsch's 1942 film *To Be or Not to Be*, Joseph Tura (disguised as a Nazi) asks a (real) fellow Nazi if he happened to see

Tura's performance in Shakespeare's *Hamlet*, to which the Nazi says, "What he did to Shakespeare we are now doing to Poland."

9   See the following for further discussion of this Seinfeld episode: Metz, "'Show Me the Shoah!'," 24. There are other comedic television programs that have evoked the Holocaust: Comedian Sarah Silverman jokes about the Holocaust and Nazis in her stand-up routine and her Comedy Central series *The Sarah Silverman Program*. In the episode, "Wowschwitz" (2010), Sarah competes with her sister to create the best Holocaust memorial at the Valley Village Jewish retirement center. Using Nazi gold, Laura Silverman creates a plaque, while her sister has a large sculpture of a "Jewish nose." Also see Ian Harris and Jamison Reeve's 2010 short *Kenny Kountry Kitchen* (available online).

10   See Michael D. Richardson, "'Heil Myself!': Impersonation and Identity in Comedic Representations of Hitler," in David Bathrick et al., eds., *Visualizing the Holocaust: Documents, Aesthetics, Memory* (Rochester: Camden House, 2008), 279.

11   Slavoj Zizek, "Camp Comedy," *Sight and Sound* vol. 10, no. 4 (April, 2000): 27.

12   Ibid. Zizek continues by warning against placing the Holocaust into a special category that can be accessed and expressed in a very narrow perspective.

13   Terrence Des Pres, "Holocaust *Laughter*?" in Berel Lang, ed., *Writing and the Holocaust* (New York: Holmes and Meier, 1988), 219.

14   "As comic works of art, or works of art including a comic element, they afford us laughter's benefit without betraying convictions. In these ways they foster resilience and are life-reclaiming" (Des Pres, "Holocaust *Laughter*?", 232). Here Des Pres is specifically addressing three literary works — Tadeusz Borowski's *This Way for the Gas, Ladies and Gentlemen*, Leslie Epstein's *King of the Jews*, and Art Spiegelman's *Maus* — but no doubt he'd give license to other cinematic examples.

15   One might also include a film like John Sturges's 1963 film *The Great Escape*, but the concern here is the comedic genre.

16   Charles Chaplin, *My Auto-Biography* (New York: Simon and Schuster, 1964), 392–3.

17   Another YouTube sensation is the appropriation of Gloria Gaynor's disco hit, "I Will Survive," which is set of Holocaust survivors (and their grandchildren) dancing at Holocaust sites – e.g., Auschwitz, the Lodz Ghetto Memorial.

18   Richardson, "'Heil Myself!'," 277. Chaplin himself recalls in his autobiography: "Halfway through making *The Great Dictator* I began receiving alarming messages from United Artists. They had been advised by the Hays Office that I would run into censorship trouble. Also the English office was very concerned about an anti-Hitler picture and doubted whether it could be shown in Britain. But I was determined to go ahead, for Hitler must be laughed at" (Chaplin, *My Auto-Biography*, 392).

19   See Lewis Jacobs, "World War II and the American Film," *Cinema Journal* vol. 7 (Winter, 1967–68): 1–21.

20   Among the films that use the Faustian theme include: István Szabó's work, including his 1981 film *Mephisto*, and Luchino Visconti's 1969 film *The Damned*.

21   Theodor Adorno, "On Commitment." Translated by Francis McDonagh, *Performing Arts Journal* vol. 3, no. 2 (Autumn 1978): 10–11.

22   Richardson, "'Heil Myself!'," 284.

23   Other animated films include Clyde Geronimi's 1943 ten-minute short, *Education for Death: The Making of A Nazi*, which asks how a German becomes a Nazi? The *mise en scène* — the lighting, the décor — as well as the composition, are clearly drawn from the German Expressionist tradition, specifically Robert Wiene's 1920 classic *The Cabinet of Doctor Caligari*. While *Education for Death* strikes a serious tone the short also includes a number of Hitler gags that make it funny.

24   Zizek, "Camp Comedy," 29.

25   Ibid. Similarly, Sander Gilman says this about *Life Is Beautiful*: "Benigni's promise is that there are no accidents, that at the end of the comedy the gods in the machine will arrive to resolve the action and rescue those in danger." Sander L. Gilman, "Is Life

Beautiful? Can the Shoah Be Funny? Some Thoughts on Recent and Older Films," *Critical Inquiry* vol. 26, no. 2 (Winter 2000): 304.

26 There are some distinct similarities between *Jacob the Liar* and *Life Is Beautiful*, not least of which is premised on the primary character disseminating lies about what's unfolding. Additionally, both films feature children, protected from the realities of the Holocaust by paternal figures. Jacob facilitates Lina's flights of fancy by furnishing make-believe stories, allowing her to escape into her imagination, while Guido transforms the suffering of intolerance and the concentration camp into a game for Giosué in *Life Is Beautiful*.

27 Lawrence Baron, *Projecting the Holocaust Into the Present: The Changing Focus of Contemporary Holocaust Cinema* (New York: Rowman and Littlefield Publishers, Inc., 2005), 156.

28 There are certain affinities with Hans-Jürgen Syberberg's 1977 seven-and-a-half-hour theatrical epic *Hitler: A Film From Germany*, which plays with the staginess of Nazi politics and also utilizes the cabaret and ventriloquists manipulating Hitler puppets.

29 It is rumored that Benigni was actually offered the leading role, and sent a script for *Train of Life*, but turned it down; Benigni denies this.

30 Radu Mihaileanu interviewed by Stefan Steinberg, "An Interview with Radu Mihaileanu, the Director of *Train of Life*: 'We have to learn to articulate these deep emotions,'" *World Socialist* website (March 31, 2000): no pagination. Available at: http://www.wsws.org.

31 Baron, *Projecting the Holocaust Into the Present*, 153. The unspoken rule of preference given to those that have first-hand or even second-hand (via familial relations) knowledge of the Holocaust is a shortsighted strategy.

32 Mihaileanu, "An Interview with Radu Mihaileanu," no pagination.

33 David Denby, "In the Eye of the Beholder," *The New Yorker* (March 15, 1999): 96–9.

34 Ibid.

35 Alessandra Stanley, "The Funniest Italian You've Probably Never Heard Of," *New York Times Magazine* (October 11, 1998): 44.

36 Roberto Benigni cited in Stanley, ibid., 44.

37 Regarding saving innocence Bartov says, "if [Volker Schlöndorff's 1996 film] *The Ogre* is a Wagnerian drama about a soul-snatcher, *Life Is Beautiful* is a heart-warming comedy about a soul-savior." Omer Bartov, *The "Jew" in Cinema: From The Golem to Don't Touch My Holocaust* (Bloomington: Indiana University Press, 2005), 123.

38 Carlo Celli, "The Representation of Evil in Roberto Benigni's *Life Is Beautiful*," *Journal of Popular Film & Television* vol. 28, no. 2 (Summer 2000): 78.

39 Millicent Marcus, *After Fellini: National Cinema in the Postmodern Age* (Baltimore: The John Hopkins University, 2002), 275.

40 Marcus views this scene as a comedic rendition of a scene in Gillo Pontecorvo's 1959 film *Kapò*, "in which a concentration camp inmate, Thérèse, is required to translate to her fellow prisoners the SS rationale for executing one of their group. In an act of resistance, Thérèse refuses to continue with the translation process, thus rejecting her role as liaison between Nazi law enforcers and their subjects. Because translation is such an integral part of the German apparatus of control, Thérèse's recalcitrance is seen as a serious breach of authority, earning her three months of solitary confinement on one-half rations" (Marcus, *After Fellini*, 276).

41 Marcus concurs with this assessment of Guido's revision of the camp rules, "In Guido's translation, the German system of oppression turns into a system of play, the regime of forced obedience becomes one of voluntary adherence, the imposition of arbitrary punishment gives way to the reassurance of familiar behavior guidelines, and the audience of victims becomes a team of possible winners" (Marcus, *After Fellini*, 276).

42 Ibid., 283.

43 This logic, devoid of ethics, also materializes in the banter around the table at Rodolfo and Dora's engagement party earlier in the film. One of the dinner guests, the principal

of Dora's school, explains to Dora and Rodolfo that even in the countryside third grade students in Germany can solve complicated arithmetic questions. The example that the principal provides is an economic question about the cost savings of exterminating the infirm, relative to the cost of continued health care. The fascist mentality only sees the pure economics of it, but is completely blind to the inhumanity of the content. Divorced of any ethical concern, people are reduced to numerical figures, no different than counting apples in a basket.

Chapter Six: Sadism and Sexual Deviance

1   Some of the scholars that have assessed Sade's work in light of Nazism and the Holocaust include Max Horkheimer and Theodor Adorno's, "Juliette or Enlightenment and Morality," in *Dialectic of Enlightenment*. Translated by John Cumming (New York: Continuum, 1996), 81–119. Also see Pierre Klossowski, *Sade My Neighbour*. Translated by Alphonso Lingis (London: Quartet Books Limited, 1992); Jacques Lacan, "Kant avec Sade." Translated by James B. Swenson, Jr. *October* 51 (Winter, 1989): 55–104; this essay has been subsequently 're-read' by Slavoj Zizek twice, "Much Ado about a Thing," in *For they know not what they do: Enjoyment as a Political Factor* (New York: Verso, 1991), 229–77; and "Kant with (or against) Sade," in Elizabeth Wright and Edmond Wright eds., *The Zizek Reader* (Oxford: Blackwell, 1999), 283–301.

2   Zizek, *The Zizek Reader*, 285.

3   Bruno Bettelheim, *Surviving and Other Essays* (New York: Alfred Knopf, 1979), 256.

4   Annette Insdorf, *Indelible Shadows: Film and the Holocaust* (second edn) (Cambridge: Cambridge University Press, 1990), 45.

5   Geoffrey Nowell-Smith, *Luchino Visconti* (New York: The Viking Press, 1973), 185.

6   Luchino Visconti said regarding *The Damned*, "I want to ask this picture where lay the responsibility for the Nazi in Germany. The most grave responsibility was with the bourgeoisie and the industrialists, because if Hitler had not had their help he would never have arrived to real power. Books say that the Krupps paid Hitler, so I don't invent." Cited in Claretta Micheletti Tonetti, *Luchino Visconti* (New York: Twayne Publishers, 1997), 129.

7   *The Damned* is not a Holocaust film necessarily, but rather more about the rise of Nazism in Germany. The Holocaust is visited upon Thallman and his family, though: Thallman is the "conscience" of the film, an anti-fascist and is set up for the murder of Joachim Von Essenbeck. His wife and two children are sent to Dauchau. Herbert goes into hiding, but decides to give himself up to the Gestapo; in exchange his daughters are set free, but it's too late for his wife, Elisabeth Thallman — she died in the death camp.

8   Unfortunately, and to the detriment of the film, the familial politics reduce the film to soap opera. Others have called it melodrama: "*The Damned* is not a film on Nazism, it is not a film on the great capital, but it is — and maybe this time more than ever — a great melodrama" (Lino Miccichè cited in Tonetti, *Luchino Visconti*, 132).

9   Critical of the film, Nowell-Smith says, "The characters, as characters, have become irrelevant, but their value as emblems of social forces has been undermined and the film ends on a void, expressionism with nothing to express" (Nowell-Smith, 189).

10   Ibid., 187.

11   Tonetti, *Luchino Visconti*, 130.

12   Nowell-Smith, *Luchino Visconti*, 186.

13   Ibid., 186.

14   Tonetti, *Luchino Visconti*, 134.

15   Richard Schickel cited in Tonetti, ibid., 138.

16   Bernardo Bertolucci's 1970 film *The Conformist* also trades heavily in the supposed
      parity between fascism and sexual depravity. And just like Visconti's *The Damned*
      this film conflates male homosexuality with pedophilia, which in turn is associated
      with the taint of fascism. Bertolucci employs the overwrought equation of sexuality
      and fascism, and sees a *single* homosexual experience as establishing the roots of
      future depraved behavior in the principal male character Marcello Clerici, including
      becoming a fascist. Tonetti draws similar conclusions about the equation of sexuality
      and fascism: "The choice of a homosexual seduction as a seminal primal scene in *The
      Conformist* results from the fact that in portraying Marcello, Bertolucci is focusing
      on his protagonist's latent homosexuality, which, together with his cruelty and fascist
      conditioning, constitutes the triptych pattern recurring throughout the film" (Tonetti,
      Luchino Visconti, 101).
17   An Italian court indicted the filmmaker, Liliana Cavani, and the two actors play-
      ing the principal characters, Dirk Bogarde and Charlotte Rampling, on charges of
      obscenity.
18   For a discussion on the sadomasochistic relationship in *The Night Porter* see Eugenie
      Brinkema, "Pleasure in/and Perversity: Plaisagir in Liliana Cavani's *Il portiere di notte*,"
      The Dalhouse Review vol. 84, no. 3 (2004): 430–1.
19   Marguerite Waller, "Signifying the Holocaust: Liliana Cavani's *Portiere di Notte*,"
      in Maria Ornella Marotti, ed., *Italian Women Writers from the Renaissance to the
      Present: Revisiting the Canon* (University Park, Pennsylvania: The Pennsylvania State
      University Press, 1996), 268. Also see Brinkema, "Pleasure in/and Perversity," 425.
      Cathy S. Gelbin insists that *The Night Porter* must be read through the context of
      feminist and queer politics of the 1970s; see her discussion on the subject in, "Double
      Visions: Queer Femininity and Holocaust Film from *Ostatni Etap* to *Aimée & Jaguar*,"
      Women in German Yearbook: Feminist Studies in German Literature & Culture vol. 23
      (2007): 187.
20   According to biblical lore Salome, daughter of Herodias and stepdaughter of Herod
      Antipas, is instrumental in the execution of John the Baptist. "And she came in
      straightway with haste unto the king, and asked, saying, I will that thou give me by
      and by in a charger the head of John the Baptist." (Mark 6.25)
21   Recall too that Max's first encounter with Lucia is from behind a film camera, which
      perhaps then draws parallels between Max and the deranged Mark Lewis in Michael
      Powell's 1960 thriller, *Peeping Tom*, who literally turns his camera into a weapon.
      Interestingly, too, in *The Serpent's Egg* when Dr. Vergerus commits suicide he studies
      his own face as death closes in, a mirror in one hand, and holding a lamp in another;
      this has certain affinities with Mark's suicide in *Peeping Tom*.
22   Marga Cottino-Jones, "What Kind of Memory? Liliana Cavani's *Night Porter*,"
      Contention vol. 5, no. 1 (Fall 1995): 110.
23   Teresa de Lauretis, "Cavani's *Night Porter*: A Woman's Film?" *Film Quarterly*, vol. 30,
      no. 2 (Winter 1976–77): 35–6. Chiara Bassi similarly argues, "The traumatic shock
      value responsible for the movie's reception is that it is possible to read *The Night Porter*
      as a perfect allegory of the condition of women." Chiara Bassi, "Fathers and Daughters
      in the Camp: *The Night Porter* by Liliana Cavani," in Laura Benedetti, Julia Hairston,
      and Silvia M. Ross, eds., *Gendered Contexts: New Perspectives in Italian Cultural Studies*
      (New York: Peter Lang, 1996), 165.
24   Marguerite Waller, "Signifying the Holocaust: Liliana Cavani's *Portiere di Notte*," in
      Maria Ornella Marotti, ed., *Italian Women Writers from the Renaissance to the Present:
      Revisiting the Canon* (University Park, Pennsylvania: The Pennsylvania State University
      Press, 1996), 261. Waller cites specifically Primo Levi and Bruno Bettelheim.
25   Waller, ibid., 269.
26   The ways in which torture has been justified, especially by the George W. Bush
      administration, bear the marks of clinical sadism. The euphemisms that the Nazis
      employed, to evacuate any sort of sentimentally "special treatment," for instance,

comes uncomfortably close to Donald Rumsfeld's instance that the United States does not torture, but rather employs "enhanced interrogation" techniques.

27 Susan Buck-Morss, "The City as Dreamworld and Catastrophe," *October* vol. 73 (Summer 1995): 3.

28 In fact, in the opening credits Pasolini cites five French critics and their work on Sade: Roland Barthes's *Sade/Fourier/Loyola*; Maurice Blanchot's *Lautréamont and Sade*; Simone De Beauvoir's "Must We Burn Sade?"; Pierre Klossowski's *Sade My Neighbor*, and *The Philosopher-Villain*; and Philippe Sollers's *Writing and the Experience of Limits*. Pasolini was seemingly unaware of Horkheimer and Adorno's "Juliette or Enlightenment and Morality," although out of all the scholarship listed in the credits, the film shares more in common with this piece of critical literature.

29 Roland Barthes, "Sade — Pasolini," in Beverly Allen ed., *Pier Paolo Pasolini: The Poetics of Heresy* (Saratoga, CA: ANMA LIBRI, 1982), 100–3.

30 Marquis de Sade, *The 120 Days of Sodom and Other Writing*. Translated by Austryn Wainhouse and Richard Seaver (New York: Grove Weidenfeld, 1987), 224.

31 Ibid., 225.

32 Ibid.

33 Ibid. As with many episodes in *Salò* Pasolini directly adapts Sade's tale; here Sade describes the rejection of a young girl: "One, lovely as the day, was weeded out because one of her teeth grew a shade higher from the gum than the rest" (ibid.).

34 It also seems that in Sade's historical context he is mocking the democratic values of the revolutionaries, who justified sending thousands to the guillotine to advance the Republican agenda, whilst espousing freedom and democratic principles.

35 Primo Levi, *Survival in Auschwitz*. Translated by Stuart Woolf (New York: Collier Books, 1961), n. 80.

36 Ibid., 82.

37 Sade, *The 120 Days of Sodom*, 236.

38 See Charles Delzell, *Mussolini's Enemies: the Anti-Fascist Resistance* (Princeton: Princeton University Press, 1961).

39 In his commentary on Sade's infamous novel, and *Salò*, "Sade is Within Us," Italo Calvino finds the inclusion of this sequence particularly disturbing. "It greatly displeased me," he notes, "to see appear on a street sign the name of the town where a terrible massacre actually took place, Marzabotto. The evocation of the Nazi occupation can only reawaken a depth of emotions that is the complete opposite of the paradoxical ruthlessness that Sade poses as the first rule of the game not only to his characters but to his readers as well." Italo Calvino, "Sade is Within Us," in Beverly Allen ed., *Pier Paolo Pasolini: The Poetics of Heresy* (Saratoga, CA: ANMA LIBRI, 1982), 109.

40 See for example Omer Bartov, "Spielberg's Oskar: Hollywood Tries Evil," in Yosefa Loshitzky ed., *Spielberg's Holocaust: Critical Perspectives on Schindler's List* (Bloomington: Indiana University Press, 1997). Bartov says: "there exists an inherent tension between exposure to the sheer brutality of the event and its trivialization, between complete ignorance of its course and scope and the dangers of partial or distorted knowledge, between a total distancing which breeds indifference and false objectivity, and a false familiarity which breeds an erroneous sense of understanding, between the abhorrence evoked by human degradation and suffering, and a perverse, pornographic curiosity about the limits of human depravity (as manifest, for instance, in Pasolini's *Salò*)" (Bartov, 52).

41 Sade, *The 120 Days of Sodom*, 237–8.

42 The *mise en scène* was intended to suggest that the château and the things in it are the vestiges of confiscated loot from rich deported Jews.

43 Spectator identification with the cinematic apparatus, or the camera, not the character(s) per se has been discussed by a number of film theorists including: Daniel

Dayan, "The Tudor-Code of Classical Cinema," in Bill Nichols, ed., *Movie and Methods volume I* (Berkeley: University of California Press, 1976), 438–51.

44 Gelbin arrives at a similar conclusion: "When Cavani's SS men film and observe Lucia, or Pasolini's 'nazifascist' murderers observe each other for visual pleasure, these films locate themselves within the problem of Nazi spectacle and expose the sadistic potential of all visual consumption of the Holocaust" (Gelbin, "Double Visions," 189).

Chapter Seven: Body Genres I: Melodramatic Holocaust Films

1 Linda Williams, "Film Bodies: Gender, Genre, and Excess," *Film Quarterly* vol. 44, no. 4 (Summer 1991): 3.

2 Ibid., 4.

3 Ibid.

4 Ibid., 5.

5 Ibid. See James Twitchell, *Dreadful Pleasures: An Anatomy of Modern Horror* (New York: Oxford University Press, 1985), 10. The OED traces the etymological origins of "horror" to the Latin, "horre," which is defined as: "to stand on end (as hair), to bristle, to be rough; to shake, tremble, shiver, shudder, quake; to shudder at, dread, loathe." *Oxford English Dictionary*, s.v. "horror"; "horre."

6 Geoffrey Nowell-Smith, "Minnelli and Melodrama," in Christine Gledhill ed., *Home Is Where the Heart Is: Studies in Melodrama and the Woman's Film* (London: BFI Publishing, 1994), 70.

7 Williams, "Film Bodies: Gender, Genre, and Excess," 11. See Franco Moretti, "Kindergarte," in *Signs Taken for Wonders: Essays in the Sociology of Literary Forms.* Translated by Susan Fischer, et al. (London: Verso, 1983), 179.

8 Williams, "Film Bodies: Gender, Genre, and Excess," 12.

9 Ilan Avisar, *Screening the Holocaust: Cinema's Images of the Unimaginable* (Bloomington: Indiana University Press, 1988), 69.

10 André Bazin, *What Is Cinema Volume II.* Translated by Hugh Gray (Berkeley: University of California Press, 1972), 21.

11 Gillo Pontecorvo discusses the transformation of Edith into Nicole: "The best scene I have ever done in film is that in *Kapò* when the doctor, long accustomed to the sadness and sorrow of the camp, transforms the girl through hardness and efficiency. He changes her from someone outside of the world of the camp into a person able to survive it. He gives her a triangle to wear, rather than the required yellow star, signifying that she is a political prisoner. He cuts her hair and instructs her to pay 'attention to the kapò,' like someone with very few minutes remaining. Outside, she sees her naked mother and father going to the 'showers.' The music at this moment is a series of chords separated one from the other with great tension. Then the door is opened. You realize, because of the sounds outside, that she is being thrown into the concentration camp universe: you hear the command, '*Links! Links! Links!*' (Left, Left, Left), and this little baby is thrust outside. I think it is beautiful." Gillo Pontecorvo cited in Joan Mellen, *Filmguide to* The Battle of Algiers (Bloomington: Indiana University Press, 1973), 11–12.

12 Dave Kehr's *New York Times* review of the newly released *Criterion Collection* DVD of *Kapò* calls the film an "anti-Anne" film; that is, setting it in opposition to *The Diary of Anne Frank.* "Starring Susan Strasberg, who played Anne Frank onstage but not in the film, *Kapò* seems almost sadistically determined to express all the horror that had been left out of *Diary.* Where the Stevens film has only one brief shot set in a concentration camp (when Millie Perkins's Anne strains to imagine the fate of a friend), *Kapò* depicts a full range of atrocities, from camp guards raping prisoners to bodies heaped in lime pits." Dave Kehr, "Lessons in 20th-Century History," *New York Times* (April 18, 2010).

13 Mellen, *Filmguide*, 11.

14 Avisar, 46.

15 Williams, "Film Bodies: Gender, Genre, and Excess," 4. Walter Metz also speaks about Williams's body genres in relationship to Holocaust narratives: "Defending the melodramatic nature of *Life is Beautiful* is one necessary project for expanding our definition of how the Holocaust may be meaningfully represented beyond the devices of classical realism and modernism, but I believe it is only one in a larger terrain that needs to attend to what Charles Affron terms the politics of affect. Useful in this regard is Linda Williams' essay on what she terms body genres, namely horror films, melodrama, and pornography. Williams is interested in how these genre films are seen by an elite intellectual culture as suspicious because they are designed to appeal to the body, not to reason: melodrama makes you cry, pornography makes you aroused, and horror films make you scream. Significantly, the one body genre that Williams does not discuss in detail is the comedy, even though it fits her definition as a form that elicits a bodily response, laughter." Metz, Walter C. "'Show Me the Shoah!': Generic Experience and Spectatorship in Popular Representations of the Holocaust," *Shofar: An Interdisciplinary Journal of Jewish Studies* vol. 27, no. 1 (Fall 2008): 23. In fact Williams does speak about comedy and laughter; however, she argues that comedy encourages us to *laugh at*, rather than share or empathize with, the character on-screen. It is precisely for this reason I have situated the comedy chapter in this book in the section on narrative film, rather than the section on body genres. As for the reference to Charles Affron see his, *Cinema and Sentiment* (Chicago: University of Chicago Press, 1982).

16 Williams, "Film Bodies: Gender, Genre, and Excess," 4. Williams later goes to specifically address films of the genre: "In the woman's film a well-known classic is the long-suffering mother of the two early versions of *Stella Dallas* [Henry King, 1925; and King Vidor, 1937] who sacrifices herself for her daughter's upward mobility. Contemporary film-goers could recently see Bette Midler going through the same sacrifice and loss in the film *Stella* [John Erman, 1990]. Debra Winger in *Terms of Endearment* [James L. Brooks, 1983] is another familiar example of this maternal pathos" (Williams, ibid., 5).

17 Ibid., 11. Franco Moretti, *Signs Taken for Wonders: Essays in the Sociology of Literary Forms*. Translated by Susan Fischer, et al. (London: Verso, 1983). Pakula observes that many men probably have fantasies of *saving someone*, and this is theme that interested the filmmaker. "The whole idea of being in love and thinking you can save somebody. For me the tragedy is when you can't and you have to realize the limits of your power." Alan Pakula cited in Jared Brown, *Alan J. Pakula: His Films and His Life* (New York: Back Stage Books, 2005), 240.

18 Brown, *Alan J. Pakula*, 266.

19 Phyllis Deutsch, "*Sophie's Choice* Undeserved Guilt," *Jump Cut*, 29 (February 1984): no pagination.

20 Alvin H. Rosenfeld, *A Double Dying: Reflections on Holocaust Literature* (Bloomington: Indiana University Press, 1980), 164.

21 Indeed the film with close scrutiny has very little to do with the Holocaust, and in fact has more to do with Stingo than it does Nathan or Sophie. "More than anything else," Alvin Rosenfeld agrees, "[the novel] *Sophie's Choice* is given over to exorcising Stingo's sexual demon, a feat constantly sought, forever delayed, and finally achieved at the expense, once more, of suffering Sophie" (Rosenfeld, *A Double Dying*, 164).

22 Katharina Von Kellenbach, "God's Love and Women's Love: Prison Chaplains Counsel the Wives of Nazi Perpetrators," *Journal of Feminist Studies in Religion* vol. 20, no. 2 (Fall 2004): 24.

23 Ibid., 7–24.

24 Susan Napier, *Anime: From Akira to Princess Mononoke Experiencing Contemporary Japanese Animation* (New York: Palgrave, 2001), 161–2.

25 Ibid., 162.
26 George Stevens was personally acquainted with the Holocaust; working as a camera-man he shot concentration camps.
27 Here are 18 examples of Anne Frank films: *The Diary of Anne Frank*, George Stevens, 1959; *Dnevnik Ane Frank*, Mirjana Samardzic, 1959; *Ein Tagebuch für Anne Frank*, Joachim Hellwig, 1959; *The Diary of Anne Frank*, Axel Segal, 1967; *The Diary of Anne Frank*, Boris Sagal, 1980; *Het dagboek van Anne Frank*, Hank Onrust, 1985; *The Diary of Anne Frank*, a BBC production, 1987; *The Attic: The Hiding of Anne Frank*, John Erman, 1988; *Laatste zeven maanden van Anne Frank*, Willy Lindwer, 1988; *Anne Frank Remembered*, Jon Blair, 1995; *Anne no nikki*, Akinori Nagaoka, 1995; *El diari d'Anna Frank*, Tamzin Townsend, 1996; *Forget Me Not: The Anne Frank Story*, Fred Holmes, 1996; *Remembering Anne Frank*, Wouter van der Sluis, 1998; *Het korte leven van Anne Frank*, Gerrit Netten, 2001; *Classmates of Anne Frank*, Eyal Boers, 2008; *The Diary of Anne Frank*, Jon Jones, 2009; *Memories of Anne Frank*, Alberto Negrin, 2010.
28 Geoffrey Nowell-Smith, "Minnelli and Melodrama," in Christine Gledhill ed., *Home Is Where the Heart Is: Studies in Melodrama and the Woman's Film* (London: BFI Publishing, 1994), 73.

Chapter Eight: Body Genres II: Pornography and Exploitation

1 Susan Sontag, *Under the Sign of Saturn* (New York: Farrar, Straus and Giroux, 1980), 99.
2 Sontag says, "SS uniforms were tight, heavy, stiff and included gloves to confine the hands and boots that made legs and feet feel heavy, encased, obliging their wearer to stand up straight" (Sontag, *Under the Sign of Saturn*, 99).
3 Ibid., 103.
4 See Cathy S. Gelbin's "Double Visions: Queer Femininity and Holocaust Film from *Ostatni Etap* to *Aimée & Jaguar*," specifically for a discourse of representations of lesbianism and its link to both victimhood and the "perversion" of Nazism, published in *Women in German Yearbook: Feminist Studies in German Literature & Culture* vol. 23 (2007): 179–204.
5 The author's original family name was Feiner, but as Omer Bartov notes, "changed his name to Dinur, or 'of fire' in Aramaic (the name may also be associated with the Hebrew word 'din,' which can mean trial, justice, and punishment, and especially with the Dinur river mentioned in the Book of Daniel and interpreted by the Kabbalah as 'a river of fire in the upper reaches of hell that descends upon the evil after their death to purify them'). For the next four decades [following the war] he devoted himself to writing on his own experience in the camps, on the fate of his parents, siblings, and wife, who all died in the Holocaust, and on his post-Auschwitz life in Israel and his struggle to build a new identity while remaining totally obsessed with the genocide he had survived." Omer Bartov, "Kitsch and Sadism in Ka-Tzetnik's Other Planet: Israeli Youth Imagine the Holocaust," *Jewish Social Studies: History, Culture, and Society* vol. 3, no. 2 (Winter 1997): 43. Dinur testified at Eichmann's trial, and collapsed after revealing that he was Ka-Tzetnik. Bartov recounts the exchange between the novelist and the presiding judge: "'Why did you hide behind the pen-name Ka-Tzetnik?' To which he replied; 'This is not a pen-name. I do not see myself as an author who writes literature. This is a chronicle from the planet of Auschwitz, whose inhabitants had no names, they were neither born nor bore any children; they were neither alive nor dead. They breathed according to different laws of nature. Every fraction of a minute there revolved on a different time scale. They were called Ka-Tzetnik, they were skeletons with numbers'" (Bartov, "Kitsch and Sadism in Ka-Tzetnik's Other

Planet," 54). Dragan Kujundzic describes Dinur's famous courtroom collapse in this way: "After repeated insistence by the prosecutor to tell what he saw, the 'katzetnik', who was not particularly old, or ill, fell prostrate on the ground and almost died of stroke in the court. His inability to testify actually testified, better than any words, to the Holocaust, particularly in the very inability to testify, to produce a narrative which would have meaning." Dragan Kujundzic, "*Archigraphia*: On the Future of Testimony and the Archive to Come," in Charles Merewether, ed., *The Archive* (Cambridge: The MIT Press, 2006), 174. Dinur also appears in a *60 Minutes* feature on Eichmann, "The Devil Is a Gentleman."

6 Bartov, "Kitsch and Sadism in Ka-Tzetnik's Other Planet," 49.

7 Patrice Rhomm's 1977 film *Fraulein Kitty* (aka *Elsa Fräulein SS*) shares some of these rather confused characteristics.

8 Clement Greenberg, "Avant-Garde and Kitsch," in Francis Frascina, ed., *Pollock and After: The Critical Debate* (New York: Harper and Row, Publishers, 1986), 25.

9 Mikel J. Koven takes issue, noting: "[Omayra] Cruz identifies *Il portiere di notte* (*The Night Porter*, Italy, 1974, Liliana Cavani) as the first of these films [that touches off the Naziploitation genre]. Or rather, that based on this one film's success, a cycle emerged which quickly degenerated into exploitation fare. But in his [sic] consideration of these films, Cruz neglects *Salò o le 120 giornate di Sodoma* (*Salò*, Italy, 1975, Pier Paolo Pasolini) as being another 'high-art' precursor, particularly in its depiction of Sadean sexuality, a theme that is picked up in many of these later films." Mikel J. Koven, "'The Film You Are About to See Is Based on Fact': Italian Nazi Sexploitation Cinema," in Ernest Mathijs and Xavier Mendik, eds. *Alternative Europe: Eurotrash and Exploitation Cinema Since 1945* (New York: Wallflower Press, 2004), 20. In fact, Omayra Cruz and I were classmates at the University of Leeds, and we had many very spirited debates about the ethics of "profiting" from representations of the Holocaust, and *Salò* was frequently the focus of our discussion. *She* is most certainly aware of Pasolini's film, but is correct in arguing that Cavani's film functions as something of a catalyst for the phenomena of Naziploitation films in the mid-70s.

10 Koven, "'The Film You Are About to See Is Based on Fact'," 20.

11 Ibid., 22–3. Also see Saul Friedlander, *Reflections of Nazism: An Essay on Kitsch and Death*. Translated by Thomas Weyr (Bloomington: Indiana University Press, 1993).

12 This narrative pattern — with respect to the treatment of female and male victims — is very similar to the pattern found in the slasher genre. Whereas women are made to suffer in slasher films, as Carol Clover argues, "The death of a male is always swift; even if the victim grasps what is happening to him, he has no time to react or register terror. He is dispatched and the camera moves on. The death of a male is moreover more likely than the death of a female to be viewed from a distance, or viewed only dimly (because of darkness or fog, for example), or indeed to happen offscreen and not be viewed at all. The murders of women, on the other hand, are filmed at closer range, in more graphic detail, and at greater length." Carol Clover, "Her Body, Himself: Gender in the Slasher Film," *Representations* vol. 20 (Autumn 1987): 200–1.

13 Koven, "'The Film You Are About to See Is Based on Fact'," 23.

14 David Friedman, interestingly, "developed his filmmaking skills as a member of the US Army Signal Corps during World War II." John McCarty, *The Sleaze Merchants: Adventures in Exploitation Filmmaking* (New York: St. Martin's Griffin, 1995), 55.

15 Alexandra Przyrembel also notes that the West German press dubbed Ilse Koch: "'lamp-shade Ilse' or the 'red-headed green-eyed witch of Buchenwald'"; Alexandra Przyrembel, "Transfixed by an Image: Ilse Koch, the 'Kommandeuse of Buchenwald'." Translated by Pamela Selwyn, *German History* vol. 19, no. 3 (October 2001): 396.

16 Archival footage (without sound) from Ilse Koch's war crimes tribunal are available through archive.org at: http://www.archive.org/details/1948-10-28_Ilse_Lock_war_crimes_trial

17 Przyrembel, "Transfixed by an Image," 369.

18 See Przyrembel, ibid., 378.

19 Ibid., 382–3.

20 Linda Williams, "Film Bodies: Gender, Genre, and Excess," *Film Quarterly* vol. 44, no. 4 (Summer 1991): 4.

21 Lynn Rapaport arrives at a similar conclusion; however, her argumentation is not particularly well-nuanced. Lynn Rapaport, "Holocaust Pornography: Profaning the Sacred in *Ilsa: She-Wolf of the SS*," *Shofar: An Interdisciplinary Journal of Jewish Studies* vol. 22, no. 1 (Fall 2003): 53–79.

22 Przyrembel, "Transfixed by an Image," 387.

23 See Barbara Creed's *The Monstrous-Feminine: Film, Feminism, Psychoanalysis* (New York: Routledge, 1993) for a discussion of the castrating woman. See specifically her discussion of *I Spit on Your Grave* (Meir Zarchi, 1978), in her chapter, "The Femme Castratrice: *I Spit on Your Grave, Sisters*."

24 Marc Lanval cited in Elizabeth D. Heineman, "Sexuality and Nazism: The Doubly Unspeakable?" *Journal of the History of Sexuality* vol. 11, no. 1 and no. 2 (January/April 2002): 63. Originally in Marc Lanval, "Ilse Koch — Sex Terrorist," *Sexology* vol. 19, no. 1 (1951): 30–6.

25 Williams, "Film Bodies: Gender, Genre, and Excess," 6.

26 Ibid., 8. Williams draws on discussions of fantasy that illustrate how this oscillation between sadism and masochism, between active and passive, function: "In their classic essay 'Fantasy and the Origins of Sexuality,' Jean Laplanche and J. B. Pontalis (1968) argue that fantasy is not so much a narrative that enacts the quest for an object of desire as it is a setting for desire, a place where conscious and unconscious, self and other, part and whole meet. Fantasy is the place where 'desubjectified' subjectivities oscillate between self and other occupying no fixed place in the scenario." (Williams, 10); see Jean Laplanche and J. B. Pontalis, "Fantasy and the Origins of Sexuality," *The International Journal of Psycho-Analysis* 49 (1968): 16. Interestingly, Caroline Joan S. Picart and Jason Grant McKahan also read Bryan Singer's 1998 film *Apt Pupil* through this lens, employing Williams's ideas about the oscillation between sadism and masochism. See Caroline Joan S. Picart, and Jason Grant McKahan, "*Apt Pupil's* Misogyny, Homoeroticism and Homophobia: Sadomasochism and the Holocaust Film," *Jump Cut: A Review of Contemporary Cinema* vol. 45 (2002): available at http://www.ejumpcut.org/archive/jc45.2002/picart/index.html.

27 Rikke Schubart, *Super Bitches and Action Babes: The Female Hero in Popular Cinema, 1970–2006* (Jefferson, North Carolina: McFarland & Company, Inc., 2007), 81.

28 Ibid., 227.

29 Alvin H. Rosenfeld, *A Double Dying: Reflections on Holocaust Literature* (Bloomington: Indiana University Press, 1980), 166.

30 Joe D'Amato's 1995 *Operation Sex* dispenses with expository narrative altogether and cuts straight to explicit sexual material. Similar to *The Joy Club*, *Operation Sex* features many of the same actors and actresses, and adopts many of the same scenarios found in *The Joy Club*. In fact it is entirely possible, if not quite probable, that the two films are assembled from the same shoot.

31 Susan Sontag, *Under the Sign of Saturn* (New York: Farrar, Straus and Giroux, 1980), 99.

32 Alan Pakula cited in Jared Brown, *Alan J. Pakula: His Films and His Life* (New York: Back Stage Books, 2005), 276.

33 David Denby, "Out of Darkness," in Stuart Liebman, ed., *Claude Lanzmann's Shoah: Key Essays* (New York: Oxford University Press, 2007), 75.

34 Bartov, "Kitsch and Sadism in Ka-Tzetnik's Other Planet," 65. Bartov continues later: "And since fantasies of horror tend to find an audience, it is reasonable to assume that some of those who rushed to buy the book [i.e., Dinur's] were curious to read precisely those 'thick' [i.e., abject] descriptions of atrocities that, they had been told, were so much more 'powerful' and 'gripping' than the laborious interpretations of conventional

historians. *This* is a disturbing thought, because it implies that what is most marketable about the Jewish Holocaust is its horror, and hence that the more one concentrates on horror the more one is likely to appear to be engaged in a sincere attempt to expose 'what actually happened,' and at the same time to achieve commercial success. Which of course should not come as a great surprise to any Hollywood producer who has made his millions through blockbuster horror films" (Bartov, "Kitsch and Sadism in Ka-Tzetnik's Other Planet," 65–6).

Chapter Nine: Body Genres III: *The Horror Genre and the Holocaust*

1   Caroline Joan Kay S. Picart and David A. Frank, *Frames of Evil: the Holocaust as Horror in American Film* (Carbondale: Southern Illinois University Press, 2006), 19.

2   I would like to acknowledge my colleague Julian Hoxter who pointed out the possible connection between Cronenberg and Nazi medical experimentation. Elana Gomel and Stephen Weninger say the following regarding Cronenberg's *Dead Ringers*: the film "reveals the intrinsic entanglement of their positions [i.e., victim and perpetrator], rooted in the intransigent commonality of the flesh. The twin gynecologists [in *Dead Ringers*] are simultaneously lords of life and death, loftily exercising the absolute power they have as physicians over the 'mutant' bodies of their patients, and monsters or mutants themselves. In a sense, they are at once avatars of both Mengele and his victims." Gomel and Weninger, "Cronenberg, Greenaway and the Ideologies of Twinship," *Body and Soul* vol. 9, no. 3 (2003): 30.

3   This motif is also used in the *X-Files*; see Linda Badley, "The Rebirth of the Clinic" in David Lavery et al., eds., *"Deny All Knowledge: Reading the X-Files* (New York: Syracuse University Press, 1996), 163; 158, n. 4. The Mengele motif appears in a number of different films including Bryan Singers' 2000 film *X-men*; see Lawrence Baron, *Projecting the Holocaust Into the Present: The Changing Focus of Contemporary Holocaust Cinema* (New York: Rowman and Littlefield Publishers, Inc., 2005), 260.

4   Joan Hawkins, *Cutting Edge: Art-Horror and the Horrific Avant-garde* (Minneapolis: University of Minnesota Press, 2000), 87.

5   Zombies allow for representations of Holocaust victims as the living-dead, or conversely as Nazis embodied as nearly indestructible automatons. Tommy Wirkola's 2009 film *Dead Snow* envisions the latter scenario. Scotty Barker's 2008 film, *The Diary of Anne Frank the Dead* is a short zombie film that expands on the Anne Frank story.

6   Based on the novel *The Dance of Genghis Cohn* by Romain Gary, Elijiah Moshinsky's 1993 adaptation, *Genghis Cohn*, takes a comedic approach to the dybbuk narrative. A Jewish comedian is shot and killed in Dachau, and he returns to haunt his executioner (see Chapter 5).

7   Lester Friedman says that "dybbuk" is Hebrew for "holding fast." See his, "'Canyons of Nightmare': The Jewish Horror Film," in Barry Keith Grant and Christopher Sharrett eds., *Planks of Reason: Essays on the Horror Film* (Lanham, Maryland: Scarecrow Press, 2004), 90.

8   S. Morris Engel's introduction to Shloyme-Zanvl ben Aaron Hacohen Rappaport (aka Solomon An-Ski), *The Dybbuk: Between Two Worlds*, trans. S. Morris Engel (South Bend, Indiana: Regnery/Gateway, 1979), 23–4.

9   Ira Konigsberg, "'The Only 'I' in the World': Religion, Psychoanalysis, and *The Dybbuk*," *Cinema Journal* vol. 36, no. 4 (Summer, 1997): 29.

10   The dybbuk is hardly benign, though, and Nathan Schnaper and H. William Schnaper associate our word "devil," with "dybbuk." They write: "*Dybbuk* is the Yiddish word for 'devil,' but comes from the Hebrew root word, *dawvak*, (to cling to, to attach, to glue). This dybbuk, male and/or female, is the wicked wandering soul of some dead person seeking purification in the body of another. It may have to go through many hosts,

plants, animals, or human beings. It can be exorcised only by some good and great man steeped in the Kabbalah." Nathan Schnaper and H. William Schnaper, "A few kind words for the Devil," *Journal of Religion and Health* vol. 8, no. 2 (April 1969): 114.

11 Konigsberg, "'The Only 'I' in the World'," 30.

12 Chanan goes on later to extol to his fellow Yeshiva student: "Which sin is the strongest, which the hardest to conquer? It is the sin of lust for a woman, isn't it? When this sin has been cleansed in a powerful flame it then becomes the greatest holiness, it becomes the *Song of Songs!*"

13 The same might be said of Paul Wegener's 1920 film *The Golem*. Konigsberg comments on this issue as well, see Konigsberg, "'The Only 'I' in the World'," 25.

14 Ibid., 33.

15 With regard to the genre of mainstream American horror, *The Unborn*, in addition to having certain historical antecedents in *The Exorcist*, also might be placed in a genealogy of films where a child is figured as the spawn of Satan, for example, Richard Donner's 1976 film *The Omen*, and Roman Polanski's 1968 film *Rosemary's Baby*.

16 Some of the slasher film conventions originate in the Italian filmmaker Mario Bava; for example, his 1971 film *Bay of Blood* (*Reazione a catena*), but for American audiences their first introduction came in the form of films like Bob Clark's 1974 film, *Black Christmas*, followed by John Carpenter's *Halloween* in 1978, and the 1980 film *Friday the 13th*, directed by Sean Cunningham.

17 For more on the "final girl" and the slasher genre see Carol Clover, *Men, Women, and Chainsaws: Gender in the Modern Horror Film* (Princeton: Princeton University Press, 1992). See specifically her chapter, "Her Body, Himself," this chapter also appears in Carol Clover, "Her Body, Himself: Gender in the Slasher Film," *Representations* 20 (Autumn 1987): 187–228.

18 Friedman, "'Canyons of Nightmare'," 93. For a discussion of Dr. Joseph Mengele and his experiments see the chapter "The Man Who Collected Blue Eyes," in Simon Wiesenthal's memoir, *The Murderers Among Us*, Joseph Wechsberg, ed. (New York: McGraw-Hill Book Company, 1967).

19 Barbara Creed, *The Monstrous-Feminine: Film, Feminism, Psychoanalysis* (New York: Routledge, 1993), 43.

20 Ibid.

21 Ka Tzetnik 135633 (aka Yehiel Dinur), *The House of Dolls*. Translated by Moshe M. Kohn (London: Frederick Muller, Ltd., 1965), 68.

22 For a discussion of the dybbuk and the female body see Konigsberg, "'The Only 'I' in the World'," 29–30.

23 This rhetorical strategy is part of a renewed interest in Holocaust scholarship, generations removed from the event, to locate affinities in representing the catastrophic or traumatic experience (e.g., the post-colonial experience). This is evident in, for example, the seminar series *Research Project Concentrationary Memories* at the University of Leeds, organized by Griselda Pollock and Max Silverman. See for example Max Silverman's work, "Interconnected Histories: Holocaust and Empire in the Cultural Imaginary," where he writes regarding this new trend in research: "It is . . . an attempt to unearth an overlapping vocabulary, lexicon, imagery, aesthetic and, ultimately, history, shared by representations of colonialism and the Holocaust." Max Silverman, "Interconnected Histories: Holocaust and Empire in the Cultural Imaginary," *French Studies* vol. 62, no. 4 (October 2008): 420.

24 Brian Price, "Pain and the Limits of Representation," *Framework: the Journal of Cinema and Media* vol. 47, no. 2 (Fall 2006): 22.

25 See for instance Jason Middleton, "The Subject of Torture: Regarding the Pain of Americans in *Hostel*." *Cinema Journal* vol. 49, no. 4 (Summer 2010): 1–24.

26 Hayden White, "Historical Emplotment and the Problem of Truth," in Saul Friedlander, ed., *Probing the Limits of Representation: Nazism and the "Final Solution"* (Cambridge: Harvard University Press, 1992), 41.

27 In a discussion between Paul A. Taylor and Srecko Horvat, the former suggests that *Hostel* is in effect a return of the repressed; see Paul A. Taylor, interview by Srecko Horvat, *International Journal of Zizek Studies* vol. 1 (2007): 5.

28 Kim Newman, "Torture Garden," *Sight & Sound* vol. 16, no. 6 (June 2006): 30.

29 In the second film, *Hostel: Part II*, victims are auctioned off to the highest bidder.

30 In Eli Roth's 2007 film *Hostel II* Whitney pleads, "What did I do wrong?"

31 In Eli Roth's 2007 follow-up to this film, *Hostel: Part II*, Ruggero Deodato plays an Italian cannibal; Deodato directed the infamous *Cannibal Holocaust* (1980).

32 The character biography listed on imdb.com.

33 There are certain elements of Szell's character that are also reminiscent of other former Nazis, particularly Klaus Barbie, the Butcher of Lyon, who in the aftermath of the war was on the United States's payroll working as an agent (the US Army's Counter Intelligence Corps, the CIC) against the communist threat. Barbie under an alias hid in South America, and probably was involved with paramilitary operations, perhaps even being instrumental in the killing of Che Guevara. Marcel Ophüls's 1988 film *Hotel Terminus* goes to great length detailing Barbie's clandestine operations during and after the war.

34 See Elaine Scarry, *The Body in Pain: the Making and Unmaking of the World* (New York: Oxford University Press, 1985), 41.

35 Ibid.

36 Szell too has real-life counterparts, as Scarry notes, "Reports of torture from prisoners in the Philippines include references to 'unwanted dental work.' . . . In Brazil, there were forms of torture called 'the mad dentist' and 'the operating table.'" The topsy-turvy world where medicine is employed for the purposes of torture was the *modus operandi* of the concentration camp. See (Scarry, *The Body in Pain*, 42).

37 Ibid., 41.

38 David Edelstein, "Audience is Loser in Haneke's Unfunny 'Games,'" *Fresh Air*, (March 14, 2008) available at: http://www.npr.org/templates/story/story.php?storyId=88230619

39 Silverman, "Interconnected Histories," 427, n. 29.

40 This should come as no surprise, in the "The *Sight and Sound* Top Ten Poll of 2002," Haneke ranks Pasolini's *Salò* fourth on his list of top films. Haneke explains that at the age of 20 he saw *Salò* for the first time, "I was completely destroyed. I was sick, destabilized for two weeks." Anthony Lane, "Happy Haneke," *The New Yorker* (October 5, 2009): 65.

41 Haneke cited in Nick James, "Darkness Falls," *Sight & Sound* vol. 13, no. 10 (October 2003): 17.

42 Lane, "Happy Haneke," 66. Ingmar Bergman's 1977 film *The Serpent's Egg* could be read as a companion piece to *The White Ribbon*. Bergman's film is set in Germany in the wake of the First World War, and Hans Vergerus — a proto-type of Dr. Josef Mengele — is conducting human medical experiments; setting the stage for what's to come.

43 Lane, "Happy Haneke," 66.

Chapter Ten: Holocaust Documentaries I: Telling Like It Really It Was

1 Bill Nichols, *Representing Reality: Issues and Concepts in Documentary* (Bloomington: Indiana University Press, 1991), 34.

2 Ibid.

3 Ibid., 35.

4 There are at least two other documentaries on Chiune Sugihara and the Jews that are settled in the Shanghai Ghetto: *Sugihara: Conspiracy of Kindness* (Robert Kirk, 2000), and *Shanghai Ghetto* (Dana Janklowicz-Mann and Amir Mann, 2002). Chris

Tashima's 1997 film *Visas and Virtue* is a short dramatization of this. China witnessed some of the strangest confluences of Second World War history; Florian Gallenberger's 2009 film *John Rabe* is a narrative feature film about the historical figure John Rabe, a German businessman and Nazi Party member, who sheltered Chinese from the Imperial Japanese Army. He ran the Siemens plant in Nanking, the site of the infamous wholesale slaughter of Chinese by Japanese forces. Many reviewers of the film note that in one scene Chinese shelter under a giant *Nazi flag*, to protect themselves from a Japanese air-raid, assuming the Japanese would not bomb a site associated with Germany.

5   Nichols, *Representing Reality*, 37.

6   Ibid., 38.

7   Ibid., 40.

8   Similarly, the unacknowledged and non-responsive filmmaker in the observational mode, Nichols says, "clears the way for the dynamics of empathetic identification, poetic immersion, or voyeuristic pleasure" (Nichols, 44).

9   Ibid., 43–4.

10   Ibid., 44.

11   Ibid., 47.

12   Ibid., 48. Nichols is actually addressing Emile de Antonio's 1968 film *In the Year of the Pig* here, and the pronoun "his," is a reference to de Antonio.

13   The reflexive mode, Nichols cites, "is the most self-aware mode; it uses many of the same devices as other documentaries but sets them on edge so that the viewer's attention is drawn to the device as well as the effect" (Nichols, *Representing Reality*, 33).

14   Annette Insdorf, *Indelible Shadows: Film and the Holocaust Second Edition* (New York: Cambridge University Press, 1990), 228.

15   About 1000 Jewish refugees were settled in the colony and could live without fear, but such an effort was a mere drop in the bucket relative to the urgent needs of European Jewry. For more information on the Sosua colony see Richard Symanski and Nancy Burley, "The Jewish Colony of Sosua," *Annals of the Association of American Geographers* vol. 63, no. 3 (September 1973): 366–78.

16   This tragic journey is dramatized in the film *Voyage of the Damned* (Stuart Rosenberg, 1976).

17   Insdorf, *Indelible Shadows*, 228.

18   Mary Ann Doane observes that, "In the history of the documentary, this voice has been for the most part that of the male, and its power resides in the possession of knowledge and in the privileged, unquestioned activity of interpretation. This function of the voice-over has been appropriated by the television documentary and television news programs, in which sound carries the burden of 'information' while the impoverished image simply fills the screen. Even when the major voice is explicitly linked with a body (that of the anchorman in television news), this body, in its turn, is situated in the non-space of the studio." Mary Ann Doane, "The Voice in the Cinema: The Articulation of Body and Space," *Yale French Studies* vol. 60 (1980): 42.

19   Nichols, *Representing Reality*, 35.

20   This was actually the second attempt to create a propaganda film in Theresienstadt; a screenwriting competition was held in the camp and Irena Dodalova won, but the Nazi leadership was unhappy with the result, and Gerron was subsequently brought in to develop the film that we have today. For more information see Karel Margry, "The First Theresienstadt Film (1942)," *Historical Journal of Film, Radio, and Television* vol. 19, no. 3 (1999): 309–37. Yael Hersonski's 2010 film *A Film Unfinished* similarly reconstructs recently discovered propaganda footage shot in the Warsaw Ghetto.

21   "Deportations to Auschwitz further decimated the camp population. In all, between 1941 and 1945, 141,000 Jews were sent to Theresienstadt; 33,430 died there; and 88,000 were shipped to death camps in the east (of which only 3,500 survived)" (Margry, "The

First Theresienstadt Film (1942)," no pagination). The experience of "cultured Jews" being sent to Theresienstadt is dramatized in the NBC *Holocaust* miniseries as well.

22   For more regarding the camp beautification project and the Red Cross visit see Margry, "The First Theresienstadt Film (1942)". Also see Claude Lanzmann's 1997 *A Visitor From the Living*; Lanzmann interviews a Red Cross official, Maurice Rossel, about the Theresienstadt inspection.

23   Lutz Becker notes, "The discovery of the concentration camps, particularly the liberation of the Auschwitz extermination camp in January 1945, had revealed for all the world to see the true nature of 'the Final Solution.' Historical facts finally defused the propagandistic power of the film and made it redundant." Lutz Becker, "Film Documents of Theresienstadt," in Toby Haggith and Joanna Newman eds., *Holocaust and the Moving Image: Representations in Film and Television Since 1933* (New York: Wallflower Press, 2005), 96.

24   For information on Fritz Hippler, and his film work, see Roel Vande Winkel's succinct article, "Nazi Germany's Fritz Hippler, 1909–2002," *Historical Journal of Film, Radio and Television* vol. 23, no. 2 (2003): 91–9.

25   Among the other notable figures referenced in Hippler's *The Eternal Jew* is Peter Lorre, whose character in Fritz Lang's 1931 film *M* is utilized as, Joan Clinefelter observes, as supposed "documentary proof of Jewish criminality and immortality . . ." see Clinefelter, "A Cinematic Construction of Nazi Anti-Semitism: The Documentary *Der ewige Jude*," Robert C. Reimer, ed., *Cultural History Through a National Socialist Lens: Essays on the Cinema of the Third Reich* (Rochester, NY: Camden House, 2002), 146.

26   Elizabeth Cowie, "Seeing and Hearing for Ourselves: the Spectacle of Reality in the Holocaust Documentary," in Toby Haggith and Joanna Newman, eds., *Holocaust and the Moving Image: Representations in Film and Television Since 1933* (New York: Wallflower Press, 2005), 182.

27   After recounting Susan Sontag's famous recollection of seeing these horrific images when she was 12 years old, which Sontag conveys as something of a traumatic encounter, Elizabeth Cowie posits this concern in the following way: "Seeing with one's own eyes is clearly, then, not a matter of simple objectivity but also of affect, of an emotional response and with it, perhaps, a defensive reaction of denial, or even anger at the victims for the anguish horror they have aroused" (Cowie, "Seeing and Hearing for Ourselves," 183). For Sontag's discussion of seeing these images for the first time see her book, *On Photography* (New York: Farrar, Straus and Giroux, 1978), 19–20.

28   For more information see Kay Gladstone, "Separate Intentions: the Allied Screening of Concentration Camp Documentaries in Defeated Germany in 1945–46: *Death Mills* and *Memory of the Camps*," in Toby Haggith and Joanna Newman, eds., *Holocaust and the Moving Image: Representations in Film and Television Since 1933* (New York: Wallflower Press, 2005).

29   Toby Haggith, "Filming the Liberation of Bergen-Belsen," in Toby Haggith and Joanna Newman, eds., *Holocaust and the Moving Image: Representations in Film and Television Since 1933* (New York: Wallflower Press, 2005), 33.

30   Ibid., 34.

31   Presumably the reference to Ilse Koch was pulled from the film because a test audience responded so poorly to this material.

32   Assembled from earlier circulated Allied newsreels *Death Mills* was, despite its attribution, based on the treatment submitted by Lieutenant Hans Burger.

33   This film is available online at archive.org: http://www.archive.org/details/DeathMills

34   Gladstone, "Separate Intentions," 56.

35   Ibid.

36   Haggith similarly notes, "As well as panning and shooting in long- and mid-shot to give a sense of the great numbers that had suffered, the cameramen filmed many details in

forensic close-up: arms tattooed with prison numbers; portraits of dead faces; mouths gaping open" (Haggith, "Filming the Liberation of Bergen-Belsen," 39).

37 Seeming to contradict his earlier wariness for "tricky editing," "Tanner also recalls Hitchcock suggesting the sequence in the final reel covering the possessions of the dead at Auschwitz, the harrowing montage of hair, wedding rings, spectacles and toothbrushes" (Gladstone, "Separate Intentions," 56).

38 Ibid.

39 Haggith, "Filming the Liberation of Bergen-Belsen," 42.

40 Ibid.

41 Ibid., 45.

Chapter Eleven: Holocaust Documentaries II: Testimonials

1 See http://www.library.yale.edu/testimonies/index.html

2 UCS Shoah Foundation Institute for Visual History and Education, "Interviewer Guidelines," (2007), 3. This document is available in PDF format through the Shoah Foundation website: http://www.usc.edu/vhi

3 Ibid.

4 Ibid.

5 Ibid., 10.

6 Ibid., 13.

7 Claude Lanzmann, "Site and Speech: An Interview with Claude Lanzmann about *Shoah*," in Stuart Liebman ed., *Claude Lanzmann's Shoah: Key Essays* (New York: Oxford University Press, 2007), 38.

8 See the Shoah Foundation website for information: http://college.usc.edu/vhi/scholarship/archival_access/accessing/

9 The "Videographer Guidelines" notes that the composition should "Always choose a location that allows for depth, with a glimpse of the survivor's home in the background. **NEVER** position a survivor against a flat wall." Other guidelines indicate that, "To achieve a more 'portrait' look, use a longer lens at a wide open F-stop, softening the background." UCS Shoah Foundation Institute for Visual History and Education, "Videographer Guidelines," (2007), 5; bold text is original.

10 Ibid., 7. Also see "Interviewer Guidelines," 11.

11 "Videographer Guidelines," 7. At the end of the testimonial account if any objects, photographs, or documents needed to be recorded they are shot according to strict guidelines: "**Be sure to shoot beyond all four edges of the photograph and then move in if necessary for details.** Since the photographs will also be part of the archive, they must be established as being complete, unedited, untrimmed documents" ("Videographer Guidelines," 8); bold text in the original.

12 Jean Epstein, "Magnification and Other Writings." Translated by Stuart Liebman, *October* vol. 3 (Spring 1977): 13. For more on close-ups see Mary Ann Doane's succinct study, "The Close-Up: Scale and Detail in the Cinema," *Differences: A Journal of Feminist Cultural Studies* vol. 14, no. 3 (2003): 89–111.

13 Ernst Van Alphen warns of the potential pitfalls of archives and implicitly the issues of subjectivity; while video archives are conceived of as depositories of living knowledge, at the same time, they are — once committed to tape — no longer embodiments of lived-experiences, but rather objects, raw material that has use-value. See Ernst Van Alphen, "Visual Archives as Preposterous History," *Art History* vol. 30, no. 3 (June 2007): 379. For interesting counter-strategies to this "ethnographic" tactic see Andrzej Brzozowski's short (15-minute) 1967 documentary *Archeologia*, which dispenses with conventional documentary shooting strategies altogether. There is effectively an inversion of conventional documentary shooting patterns; specifically the film

exhibits an abundance of close-ups and limits the use of medium or long shots. The film documents an excavation at Auschwitz.

14   Lanzmann, "Site and Speech," 45.

15   "Interviewer Guidelines," 10. Elsewhere Lanzmann says, "memories are full of holes. But if you re-create the scene in concrete conditions, you get not just memory but a re-living." Lanzmann cited in Insdorf, *Indelible Shadows: Film and the Holocaust Second Edition* (New York: Cambridge University Press, 1990), 254.

16   Marcel Ophüls cited in Insdorf, *Indelible Shadows*, 252.

17   Nichols, *Representing Reality*, 45.

18   Ibid. 264.

19   Ibid.

20   This same footage is used elsewhere, including in Alain Resnais's 1955 film *Night and Fog*.

21   Ophüls cited in Insdorf, *Indelible Shadows*, 243; 245. Although this is cited in Insdorf's book, Ophüls's statement is at odds with her assessment of his films: "Despite the obvious sympathies of the filmmakers, there is *fairness of presentation toward all the subjects*. Whether consciously or unconsciously, they reveal themselves to the camera, which maintains the *same objective angle* for 'heroes' and 'villains' alike — usually a medium close-up — and presents them in their own environments" (Insdorf, *Indelible Shadows*, 239). Emphasis added. Insdorf aspires to group "good" Holocaust films under the rubric of the authentic, and thus reads the consistent use of the standard documentary convention of the talking-head as "the same objective angle."

22   Lanzmann, "Site and Speech," 44. Although he did not use it, Lanzmann did interview Reinhard Wiener, a German soldier and amateur cinematographer, who shot in 1941 an 8 mm film lasting little more than a minute, depicting the summary execution of Jews in Liepaja, Latvia. Depending on how one contextualizes it this might be the only known moving image archival material documenting any sort of systematized killing of Jews. Lanzmann is supremely sensitive to "re-victimization" of those murdered: "Lanzmann on occasion indicated that Adorno's proscriptions had an impact on his thinking, and from the outset he seems to have followed Adorno's lead in rejecting them [i.e., archival images] as well. Depicting the atrocities in graphic detail, he believed, were not necessary for remembering or memorializing the horrors." Stuart Liebman, "Introduction," to Stuart Liebman, ed., *Claude Lanzmann's Shoah: Key Essays* (New York: Oxford University Press, 2007), 13.

23   From the remaining approximately 340 hours of footage not used in *Shoah*, Lanzmann has since gone back and created other shorter films including his 1997 film *A Visitor from the Living*, and the 2001 film *Sobibor, October 14 1943, at 4:00 pm*.

24   *Shoah* received enthusiastic reviews worldwide, but one notable exception is Pauline Kael's review in the *New Yorker* (December 1985); she was apparently strained by the film's length. For many years *Shoah* remained the most profitable documentary in the United States. (Liebman, "Introduction," 5). Simone De Beauvoir says of the film: "I should add that I would never have imagined such a combination of beauty and horror. True, the one does not help to conceal the other. It is not a question of estheticism: rather, it highlights the horror with such inventiveness and austerity that we know we are watching a great oeuvre. A sheer masterpiece." Simone De Beauvoir, "*Shoah*," preface to Claude Lanzmann, *Shoah: An Oral History of the Holocaust* (New York: Pantheon Books, 1985), x. Documentary filmmaker Marcel Ophüls, who has made a number of films about the Holocaust including *The Sorrow and the Pity* (1969), says of Lanzmann's film: "I consider *Shoah* to be the greatest film I've ever seen about the Holocaust." Marcel Ophüls, "Closely Watched Trains," in Stuart Liebman ed., *Claude Lanzmann's Shoah: Key Essays* (New York: Oxford University Press, 2007), 78.

25   Lanzmann says in an article responding to *Schindler's List* and his disappointment at Spielberg's reconstruction of the extermination of Jews, "If I had stumbled on a real SS film — a secret film, because filming was strictly forbidden — that showed how

3,000 Jewish men, women and children were gassed in Auschwitz's crematorium 2, not only would I not have shown it but I would have destroyed it. I cannot say why. It just goes without saying." Claude Lanzmann, "Why Spielberg has distorted the truth," *The Guardian Weekly* (April 3, 1994): 14.

26 Stuart Liebman contends that, "Perhaps even more significant is the fact that no filmmaker before Lanzmann had devoted so much time to reflecting not only on *what* to represent in a film about the Holocaust, but also on *how* to do so" (Liebman, "Introduction," 6).

27 Nichols, *Representing Reality*, 44.

28 Lanzmann, "Site and Speech," 39.

29 Ibid. "For all the stunning details he elicits," Stuart Liebman notes, "and despite the solidity of the historical framework underlying the film's complex narrative weave, Lanzmann does *not* attempt to provide a complete history of the Holocaust" (Liebman, "Introduction," 11). Lanzmann also says of films such as *Schindler's List* and the NBC miniseries *Holocaust* that "Images kill the imagination and make it possible for people to identify comfortably with Schindler, who is a highly debatable 'hero." Lanzmann, "Why Spielberg has distorted the truth," *The Guardian Weekly* (April 3, 1994): 14.

30 Liebman laments the exploitation of the Holocaust as a mere "background for senti-mental stories of rescue and deliverance" (Liebman, "Introduction," 6).

31 Lanzmann, "From the Holocaust to 'Holocaust,'" in Stuart Liebman ed., *Claude Lanzmann's Shoah: Key Essays* (New York: Oxford University Press, 2007), 35. Regarding chronology Lanzmann says elsewhere, "The chronological account that would begin with the boycott [of Jewish businesses] in April 1933 and culminated naturally in the gas chambers of Auschwitz or Treblinka would not be false, strictly speaking, but it would be miserably shallow and one-dimensional. No, in creating a work of art, one deals with another logic, another way of telling the story" (Lanzmann, "From the Holocaust to 'Holocaust,'" 34). Simone De Beauvoir observes that *Shoah* "does not follow a chronological order. I should say it is a poetical construction, if I may use the word in connection with such a subject." De Beauvoir, "*Shoah*," in Stuart Liebman ed., *Claude Lanzmann's Shoah: Key Essays* (New York: Oxford University Press, 2007), 65.

32 Lanzmann, "Site and Speech," 39.

33 Lanzmann describes the film as having a circular pattern, which is "derived from the obsessional character of my questions, my personal obsessions: the cold, the fear of the East (the West for me is human; the East scares the hell out of me). I became aware that I asked everyone these questions: about the cold, always the cold, the idea that these people waited for death in this passageway, that they drove them on with lashes of the whip" (Lanzmann, "Site and Speech," 43–4). Elsewhere, when thinking about the prospects of breaking the film up into parts, or keeping it a unified 9-hour whole Lanzmann says: "No, the film is round, a circular film, and it must end as it began" (Lanzmann, "Site and Speech," 46).

34 Lanzmann, "Site and Speech," 41.

35 Ibid., 45. Müller's account is also published in a memoir *Eyewitness Auschwitz: Three Years in the Gas Chamber*, trans. Susanne Flatauer (Chicago: Ivan R. Dee; the United States Holocaust Memorial Museum, 1979).

36 Lanzmann, "Site and Speech," 45.

37 Ibid., 38.

38 Shoshana Felman, "The Return of the Voice: Claude Lanzmann's *Shoah*," in Shoshana Felman and Dori Laub eds., *Testimony: Crises of Witnessing in Literature, Psychoanalysis, and History* (New York: Routledge, 1992), 251.

39 Lanzmann, *Shoah: An Oral History of the Holocaust* (New York: Pantheon Books, 1985), 54.

40 Lanzmann cited in Insdorf, *Indelible Shadows*, 253.

41 Ophüls, "Closely Watched Trains," 84.

42   Insdorf, *Indelible Shadows*, 254.

43   Lanzmann cited in Insdorf, *Indelible Shadows*, 252.

44   Liebman, "Introduction," 16.

45   Daniel Listoe makes a similar argument about *Shoah* and the representation of a *lack* of visible evidence. See Daniel Listoe, "Seeing Nothing: Allegory and the Holocaust's Absent Dead," *SubStance* vol. 35, no. 2 (2006): 51–70.

46   Jay Cantor describes these sequences differently: "Lanzmann is stupefyingly literal minded. Everything must be shown." Cantor, "Death and the Image," in Charles Warren, ed., *Beyond Document: Essays on Nonfiction Film* (Hanover: Wesleyan University Press; University Press of New England, 1996), 31–2.

47   Lanzmann, "Site and Speech," 39.

48   De Beauvoir, "*Shoah*," vii.

49   Liebman, "Introduction," 14.

50   Lanzmann, "Site and Speech," 41.

51   Ibid., 43.

52   I showed this sequence to my MFA class, and one student, visibly moved, said that the Bomba sequence was *the* single most powerful piece of film she had ever seen. Indeed, it is doubtful that anyone could go unmoved by this sequence.

53   Claude Lanzmann, "Seminar with Claude Lanzmann 11 April 1990," *Yale French Studies: Literature and the Ethical Question*, vol. 79 (1991): 95.

54   Ibid.

55   Lanzmann, "Site and Speech," 41.

56   Ibid.

57   It is naïve, if not dishonest, to think that historians do not rely on similar devices (e.g., allusions, comparisons, metaphor) in order to convey a historical narrative. See Wolfgang Ernst, "Distory: Cinema and Historical Discourse," *Journal of Contemporary History* vol. 18, no. 3, (July 1983): 408.

58   Lanzmann cited in Annette Insdorf, *Indelible Shadows*, 254.

59   In Hayden White's essay, "Historical Text as Literary Artifact," he suggests that, "one mark of a good professional historian is the consistency with which he reminds his [sic] readers of the purely provisional nature of his characterization of events, agents, and agencies found in always incomplete historical record." in Robert Canary and Henry Kozicki eds., *The Writing of History* (Madison: University of Wisconsin Press, 1978), 42.

60   Lanzmann, "Seminar with Claude Lanzmann 11 April 1990," 92.

Chapter Twelwe: Holocaust Documentaries III: Personal Documentaries

1   Bill Nichols, *Representing Reality: Issues and Concepts in Documentary* (Bloomington: Indiana University Press, 1991), 44. Exemplary of this voyeuristic gaze, the filmmaker and subject of *Shtetl* (1996), Marian Marzynski, comments on a Polish Gentile, Zbyszek Romaniuk, who has an enthusiastic interest in Jewish history in Poland: "After our first experience, I feel like a voyeur. I am watching Zbyszek as he trespasses into a foreign territory, just as I did during the war when I lived among Christians in Poland. I watch him entering a world he could only imagine until now."

2   Maureen Turim in her book on flashbacks observes that: "The historian tries to imagine the past as the lived experience of individuals or groups and treats documents and artifacts as fragments of a hypothetical memory to be reconstructed. There is an implicit analogy between the project of writing history and a phenomenological view of the functioning of personal memory." Maureen Turim, *Flashbacks in Film: Memory and History* (New York: Routledge, 1989), 104–5. There are some affinities between the ways in which the historian works in the reconstruction of memory and how the

documentarian effectively turns images — be they cutaways, or archival footage — into representatives of subjective memory.

3   This latter film, Jonas Mekas's 1971 film *Reminiscences of a Journey to Lithuania*, is a personal account, adopting the diarist strategy. Mekas narrates a documented voyage to his homeland, and reflects on his past: his collaboration with the resistance and detention in a Nazi labor camp. Like many films of the personal genre, *Reminiscences* is also about a return. What sets Mekas's film apart is that instead of a conventional shooting strategy and coherent linear narrative, *Reminiscences* exhibits a certain "amateur" quality, profoundly personal in content and form. Another "diarist" film that touches on the Holocaust is *First Person Plural: The Electronic Diaries of Lynn Hershman: 1984–1996*, released in 1996; Hershman's piece is a series of confessional video-diaries negotiating the filmmaker's own anxieties brought on by divorce, her subsequent retreat into cycles of binge eating, all the while haunted by traumatic physical and sexual abuse suffered as a child. This trauma is connected to the Holocaust.

4   Robert Satloff is the director of the Washington Institute for Near East Policy, and is the "central character" of William Cran's 2010 documentary *Among the Righteous: Lost Stories From the Holocaust in Arab Lands*. Satloff is our veritable Sherlock Holmes, in the pursuit of a mystery. The film posits a simple question: "Did any Arabs save Jews during the Holocaust?" and goes in search for clues to solve this mystery. The video is available online, along with additional material, at: http://www.pbs.org/newshour/among-the-righteous/

5   Peter Morley cited in Annette Insdorf, *Indelible Shadows: Film and the Holocaust* (second edition) (Cambridge: Cambridge University Press, 1990), 235. On the night before arriving at the Auschwitz-Birkenau main gate, Morley consulted with Hart and her son over dinner, "Kitty then told me that she was worried because she was very uncertain about how she would react on seeing the camp again. I crossed my fingers." Peter Morley, "*Kitty — Return to Auschwitz*," in Toby Haggith and Joanna Newman, eds., *Holocaust and the Moving Image: Representations in Film and Television Since 1933* (New York: Wallflower Press, 2005), 156.

6   See the "Corruption," episode of *Auschwitz: Inside the Nazi State* (2005) documentary series, which details the systematic looting by the SS.

7   Morley, "*Kitty — Return to Auschwitz*," 156.

8   Ibid., 159.

9   Ilan Avisar, *Screening the Holocaust: Cinema's Images of the Unimaginable* (Bloomington: Indiana University Press, 1988), 88.

10 For more information on second-generation trauma see: Joshua Hirsch's *Afterimage: Film, Trauma, and the Holocaust* (Philadelphia: Temple University Press, 2004); Janet Walker's *Trauma Cinema: Documenting Incest and the Holocaust.* (Berkeley: University of California Press, 2005); and Marianne Hirsch's, "Projected Memory: Holocaust Photographs in Personal and Public Fantasy," in Mieke Bal et al., eds., *Acts of Memory: Cultural Recall in the Present* (Hanover, NH: University Press of New England, 1999) 2–23. Other films that negotiate second-generation trauma include Pier Marton's 1984 film *Say I'm a Jew*, and Joshua Hirsch's 1995 video *Second Generation Video.*

11 Vincent Canby comments on this scene in his review of the film for the *New York Times*, "It's also a singular moment in *We Were So Beloved* and, apparently, a controversial one, at least to those who believe we should lay claim to heroism, even theoretically and with hindsight. That's too easy. The elder Mr. Kirchheimer's statement — it is not an admission — is that of a man who continues to think and feel. His profound doubt is one of the film's most moving, most humane expressions of what the Holocaust still means to those who outlived it." Vincent Canby, review, *We Were So Beloved*, *New York Times* (August 27, 1986): no pagination.

12 Harald Lüders along with his co-director, Pavel Schnabel, made an interesting film about German denial, *Now . . . After All These Years* in 1981 focusing on the town of Rhina, Germany.

13 Romaniuk wrote a letter to Marzynski taking him to task on a number of different points, including the size of the Jewish population in Bransk: "The history of the Jews in Bransk encompasses approximately 60 years (1880–1942), when they were the majority in the town. Your movie creates an impression that Jews were dominating for 500 years. Sometimes you've got wrong numbers: between 1897 and 1921 there was 58% of Jews (the highest number was 58%). Later on this percentage diminished to reach 50% in 1939. At the end of the movie, when we talk in the conference room: 65%!!!" Zbyszek Romaniuk to Marian Marzynski (February 14, 1996): http://www. pbs.org/wgbh/pages/frontline/shtetl/reactions/zbyszeklett.html

14 As discussed in the previous chapter the reader will recall that Claude Lanzmann openly lies to former SS Unterscharfüher, Franz Suchomel, who was stationed at Treblinka.

15 Menachem Daum and Oren Rudavsky's 2004 observational documentary *Hiding and Seeking: Faith and Tolerance After the Holocaust* is a perfect counterbalance to Marzynski's vitriol; like *Shtetl* it is also a return to Poland.

Chapter Thirteen: Holocaust Documentaries IV: The Poetic Documentary

1 Michael Renov also observes the tendency for the poetic documentary to turn towards metacriticism. See Michael Renov, "Toward a Poetics of Documentary," in Michael Renov, ed., *Theorizing Documentary* (New York: Routledge, 1993), 12–36.

2 Bill Nichols, *Representing Reality: Issues and Concepts in Documentary* (Bloomington: Indiana University Press, 1991), 57.

3 Ibid.

4 Theodor Adorno, *Prisms*. Translated by Samuel and Shierry Weber (London: Neville Spearman, 1967), 34.

5 Note that most of the shots in *Auschwitz-Birkenau 1940–1945–1995* are taken in Auschwitz I.

6 Oświęcim is approximately a 5-minute car ride away from the main camp.

7 Errol Morris interview by Roy Grundmann and Cynthia Rockwell, "The Truth Is Not Subjective: An Interview with Errol Morris," *Cineaste*, vol. 25, no. 3 (2000): 7.

8 Janet Walker, *Trauma Cinema: Documenting Incest and the Holocaust* (Berkeley: University of California Press, 2005), 187.

9 Zoë Druick says this about the punctuating black in Morris's work: "Eschewing the ethos of *cinéma vérité*, Morris punctuates these interviews with jarring stretches of black leader and makes liberal use of dramatic music. The film-maker repeatedly draws our attention to the construct of the film itself as both aesthetic experience and inadequate guarantor of truth." Zoë Druick, "Documenting False History: Errol Morris and *Mr. Death*," *Studies in Documentary Film* vol. 1, no. 3 (2007): 212.

10 Note that the lighting of the shot depicting the crossword puzzle is clearly indicative of Morris's style, as is the use of longer focal length lens; the edges of the frame go out of focus. In addition Zoë Druick makes an interesting observation regarding the contrast of form between the videotaped documentation of the Zündel defense team relative to Morris's work: "It is significant for Morris that the neo-Nazi's film-making style is cinema vérité. By contrast, the highly constructed nature of his own film, using dramatically lit re-enactments of Leuchter at Auschwitz, for example, asserts by comparison its moral grounding through its storytelling rather than relying on some false notion of technical objectivity" (Druick, "Documenting False History," 213).

11 Much has been made of Morris's interview style; he uses what he dubbed the "Interrotron," which is a device that is specifically designed to give the appearance that interviewee is directly addressing the spectator; the Interrotron is "Essentially a series of modified teleprompters . . . [that] bounces a live image of Morris onto a glass

plate in front of the interviewee, just as the director — 'off in a booth somewhere, like the Wizard of Oz' — addresses a video image of his subject. In the same way, interviewees respond to an image of Morris that floats directly in line with the camera." Shawn Rosenheim, "Interrotroning History: Errol Morris and the Documentary of the Future," in Vivian Sobchack, ed., *The Persistence of History: Cinema, Television, and the Modern Event* (New York and London: Routledge, 1996), 221. For more on the ethics of this interview technique see: Alex Gerbaz, "Direct Address, Ethical Imagination, and Errol Morris's Interrotron," *Film-Philosophy* vol. 12, no. 2 (September 2008): 17–29. Also see Heather Nunn, "Errol Morris: Documentary as Psychic Drama," *Screen* vol. 45, no. 4 (2004): 416.

12 Morris, "The Truth Is Not Subjective," 8.

13 Walker, *Trauma Cinema*, 186–7.

14 Alain Resnais cited in Annette Insdorf, *Indelible Shadows: Film and the Holocaust* (second edn) (Cambridge: Cambridge University Press, 1990), xix.

15 Elizabeth Cowie, "Seeing and Hearing for Ourselves: the Spectacle of Reality in the Holocaust Documentary," in Toby Haggith and Joanna Newman eds., *Holocaust and the Moving Image: Representations in Film and Television Since 1933* (New York: Wallflower Press, 2005), 184.

16 Peter Morley insists that his film, *Kitty: Return to Auschwitz* (1979) does not stage anything: "Nothing was staged. I just followed her, and didn't even know — when the taxi arrived at Auschwitz — whether she'd turn right back and leave." Morley interviewed by Insdorf, *Indelible Shadows*, 235. My question is, though, is there anything more staged than a tracking shot?

17 This is probably no coincidence; in 1948 Resnais released his Oscar-winning film *Van Gogh*.

18 See http://www.ihtp.cnrs.fr/cih2gm/

19 Resnais cited in Insdorf, *Indelible Shadows*, 213.

20 Jay Cantor, "Death and the Image," in Charles Warren, ed., *Beyond Document: Essays on Nonfiction Film* (Hanover: Wesleyan University Press; University Press of New England, 1996), 23–49.

21 William Rothman, *Documentary Film Classics* (Cambridge: Cambridge University Press, 1997), 52. In François Truffaut's brief commentary on *Night and Fog*, he says that the film is haunting because: "Are we not all 'deporters'? Or couldn't we be, at least by complicity?" François Truffaut, *The Films In My Life*. Translated by Leonard Mayhew (New York: Simon and Schuster, 1978), 303.

22 For a very brief discussion of the Einsatzgruppen see Leni Yahil, *The Holocaust: The Fate of European Jewry, 1932–1945*. Translated by Ina Friedman and Haya Galai (New York: Oxford University Press, 1990), 255–8. For further discussion, examining a specific Einsatzgruppen team, see Christopher R. Browning, *Ordinary Men: Reserve Police Battalion 101 and the Final Solution in Poland* (New York: Harper Collins, 1992).

23 Rothman, *Documentary Film Classics*, 62.

24 Donald Reid, "Germaine Tillion and Resistance to the Vichy Syndrome," *History & Memory* vol. 15, no. 2 (Fall–Winter 2003): 43. Judy Meisel in the film *Tak for Alt: Survival of a Human Spirit* (Laura Bialis et al., 1999) similarly concludes that everyone is responsible, as Janet Walker suggests, Meisel "evokes a vision of collective action for justice rather than a vision of atomized individuals" (Insdorf, *Indelible Shadows*, 155). The newest Criterion DVD release of *Night and Fog* includes this image unmasked. Also, the extras on this DVD include excerpts from a radio interview with Resnais speaking about the film. It was thought that the film would never see a theatrical release because of the violence within it. The radio interview adds, "And the French policeman in Pitiviers." Resnais then responds, "No, that hadn't even occurred to us yet. That's a good story, but it would take ten minutes to tell. It was absolutely amazing. We never even noticed that policeman." The radio interviewer then adds, "We should point out that the camp in Pitiviers was a kind of pre-deportation camp for

those later destined for Germany, and it was guarded by French policemen." Resnais continues, "Yes, and in fact on the back of that photograph there was the German Eagle authorized by the Kommandantur, or something like that. It was fantastic. And France would not allow anything that had been authorized by the Nazis. There are plenty of anecdotes about the French Control Commission."

25   Resnais, interview on *Les étoiles du cinema*, 1994. An excerpt from this radio interview is included on the Criterion *Night and Fog* DVD.

26   Truffaut, *The Films in My Life*, 304. Similarly, James Roy MacBean notes: "And where Resnais's *Nuit et brouillard* [*Night and Fog*] can be 'read' — and passed off — as one man's very personal appeal to our conscience, *Le chagrin et la pitié* [*The Sorrow and the Pity*, Marcel Ophüls, 1969] reads as a self-incriminating revelation by the French people themselves! Moreover, Resnais's collapsing of past and present is carried out in a way that points to the future. The tone of *Nuit et brouillard* is prophetic. It is the oracular tone of the artist-priest. As in Greek tragedy, the message is chilling but the medium is so exhilarating that the effect is cathartic." James Roy MacBean, "*The Sorrow and the Pity*: France and Her Political Myths," in Alan Rosenthal, ed., *New Challenges for Documentary* (Berkeley: University of California Press, 1988), 478.

27   Lanzmann cited in Insdorf, *Indelible Shadows*, 252.

28   This is available on the Criterion Collection two DVD set of Pier Paolo Pasolini's 1975 film *Salò, or the 120 Days of Sodom*.

Chapter Fourteen: Experimental Films I: Rituals of Memory

1   Jeffrey Skoller, *Shadow, Specters, Shards: Making History in Avant-Garde Film* (Minneapolis: University of Minnesota Press, 2005), 110.

2   Ibid.

3   Nadine Fresco, "Remembering the Unknown," *International Review of Psycho-Analysis* 11 (1984): 421. Joshua Hirsch says of Fresco's article that it is "one of the best pieces of writing on the second generation — suggest that second-generation memory can be thought of as a postmodern phenomenon because it functions as a kind of simulacrum, the memory of an event that was never witnessed." Joshua Hirsch, *Afterimage: Film, Trauma, and the Holocaust* (Philadelphia: Temple University Press, 2004), 150.

4   Michael Renov, "Family Secrets: Alan Berliner's *Nobody's Business* and the (American) Jewish Autobiographical Film," *Framework: The Journal of Cinema and Media* vol. 49, no. 1 (Spring 2008): 64.

5   Ibid.

6   Julia Kristeva, *Black Sun: Depression and Melancholia*. Translated by Leon S. Roudiez (New York: Columbia University Press, 1989), 138.

7   René Girard, *Violence and the Sacred*. Translated by Patrick Gregory (Baltimore: The John Hopkins University Press, 1989), 31.

8   Ibid. 37.

9   Hermann Nitsch is an Austrian performance artist and painter. He was a founding member of the Aktionismus group (the Viennese Actionists) in 1964. Nitsch's performance work incorporated the use of animal carcasses and animal blood. He would also use animal blood as paint. Through these works Nitsch ritualistically exercised violence, attempting to arrive at catharsis — a purging of the innate violence inhabiting the human body. The associates of blood, the human body, and violence are hard — if not impossible — to read outside the history of the Holocaust.

10   Girard, *Violence and the Sacred*, 36.

11   Hirsch, *Afterimage*, 110.

12   Chantal Akerman, "On *D'Est*," in Kathy Halbreich and Bruce Jenkins, eds., *Bordering on Fiction: Chantal Akerman's D'Est* (Minneapolis: The Walker Arts Center, 1995), 22.

13 Alisa Lebow, "Memory Once Removed: Indirect Memory and Transitive Autobiography in Chantal Akerman's *D'Est*," *Camera Obscura* vol. 18, no. 1 (2003): 36. Elsewhere Lebow speaks of the surface of the image in terms of temporality: "There is no attempt to probe under the facade; the film accepts, as it were, at face value, the conditions of the present. There is the conspicuous absence of archival footage that would aspire to literalize the past, anchoring it to definite imagery and lending it an illusory presence. Yet even without any attempt to penetrate the contemporary facade or to put a historical face on the memories of the past through the use of archival footage, there still seems to be no way to see this present represented outside of, or independently from, the past that echoes within it" (Lebow, 48–9).

14 Ibid., 36.

15 Ibid., 49.

16 Kristine Butler, "Bordering on Fiction: Chantal Akerman's *D'Est*," *Postmodern Culture* vol. 6, no. 1 (1995): no pagination.

17 Edward Said, *Orientalism* (New York: Vintage Books, 1994), 1–2.

18 Cited in Annette Insdorf, *Indelible Shadows: Film and the Holocaust* (second edn) (Cambridge: Cambridge University Press, 1990), 252.

19 Orly Yadin, "But Is It Documentary?" in Toby Haggith and Joanna Newman, eds., *Holocaust and the Moving Image: Representations in Film and Television Since 1933* (New York: Wallflower Press, 2005), 168.

20 Ibid.

21 Ibid., 169.

22 Ibid.

23 Ibid. Yadin says elsewhere, "It contains no archival images of the Holocaust, no interviews with survivors, experts or eyewitnesses, no shots of the locations where these events took place, and yet it is a documentary and a true story." She continues to explain that, "all forms of documentary are merely *representations* of reality and in that sense, an animation film is no different from any other film style" (Yadin, "But Is It Documentary?" 168).

24 Ruth Lingford and Tim Webb, "*Silence*: The Role of the Animators," in Toby Haggith and Joanna Newman, eds., *Holocaust and the Moving Image: Representations in Film and Television Since 1933* (New York: Wallflower Press, 2005), 173. Stylistically, Czekala Ryszard's 1971 eight-minute animated short *Apel* is somewhere between the Lingford's contribution to *Silence*, and the work of South African artist William Kentridge; *Apel* is another example of an animated film negotiating the Holocaust.

25 Yadin, "But Is It Documentary?" 169.

26 Ibid.

27 Ibid., 170.

28 Ibid.

29 Lingford and Webb, "*Silence*: The Role of the Animators," 173.

30 Ibid.

31 Elie Wiesel, *Souls on Fire: Portraits and Legends of Hasidic Masters*. Translated by Marion Wiesel (New York: Simon and Schuster, 1972), 167.

32 What might be considered a companion piece, *Sink or Swim* (1990), reflects on her estranged father, a former American soldier.

33 Scott MacDonald contextualizes this technique in a history of other films: "The basic situation of the daughter/filmmaker talking with her mother about their shared background is reminiscent of a group of films made during the early to mid-1970s — Martha Coolidge's *David: Off and On* (1973), Claudia Weill's *Joyce at 34* (1973), Amalie Rothschild's *Nana, Mom and Me* (1974), Ed Pincus's *Diaries* (1976) — in which the domestic life of the filmmaker (and the effects of the camera's intrusion into this environment for a purpose other than mythifying it in conventional home movies) is the object of investigation." Scott MacDonald, "Su Friedrich: Reappropriations," *Film Quarterly* vol. 41, no. 2 (Winter, 1987–88): 35.

34   Patricia Hampl, "Memory's Movies," in Charles Warren, ed., *Beyond Document: Essays on Nonfiction Film* (Hanover, NH: Wesleyan University Press, 1996), 57.

35   Ibid.

36   Scott MacDonald also contextualizes this technique in a history of other films: "Because they are scratched, they give the film a handcrafted, personal feel (an effect familiar from the history of filmic uses of scratches as imagery: Brakhage's titles and 'by Brakhage,' for example, and Len Lye's *Free Radicals*, Carolee Schneemann's *Fuses* and *Plumb Line*, Diana Barrie's *Letters from China* and *Magic Explained*). And because of Friedrich's one-word-at-a-time presentation, and her skillful timing, they have considerable graphic and narrative power" (MacDonald, "Su Friedrich: Reappropriations," 36).

37   Hampl, "Memory's Movies," 75. Speaking of *Sink or Swim*, but certainly applicable to *The Ties That Bind*, Hampl says that, "Friedrich does not approach her own voice. Her 'voice' is all over the image of the film. The place where image makes itself distinct from voice is less clear in her work — or perhaps the two are more harmoniously united. The 'sound' of words cast on the screen is the sound the viewer's inner voice makes upon reading them rather than the literal sound of the filmmaker's voice" (Hampl, 75).

38   MacDonald, "Su Friedrich: Reappropriations," 40.

39   Ibid., 36.

40   See the catalogue entry for Robin Kandel in Aaron Kerner, *Reconstructing Memories*, exhibition catalogue (Honolulu: University of Hawaii Art Gallery, 2006), 36–9.

41   Primo Levi, *Survival in Auschwitz*. Transated by Stuart Woolf (New York: Collier Books, 1961), 29. This passage is also cited by Ilan Avisar in his *Screening the Holocaust: Cinema's Images of the Unimaginable* (Bloomington: Indiana University Press, 1988), 61.

42   Peter Morley discusses the discovery of the shoe: "As she walked out into daylight caressing this battered object I whispered to the cameraman that no one would believe this. I had seen a mountain of many thousands of similar shoes in the Auschwitz museum. What was a single one doing in this pitch-dark block? How did it get there? Had it languished there since 1945 when the Russians liberated the camps?" During postproduction, Morley had to consider how to cut the film and continues, "I had to think twice whether to include this sequence in the final cut. If someone thought that I had planted that shoe in advance for the sake of 'good television' might it not undermine the honesty of the whole film?" In a footnote Morley goes on to state that the source of the shoe was never determined and remains a mystery. Peter Morley, "*Kitty — Return to Auschwitz*," in Toby Haggith and Joanna Newman, eds., *Holocaust and the Moving Image: Representations in Film and Television Since 1933* (New York: Wallflower Press, 2005), 158.

43   Avisar, *Screening the Holocaust*, 61.

44   Libby Saxton, *Haunted Images: Film, Ethics, Testimony and the Holocaust* (New York: Wallflower Press, 2008), 71.

45   Skoller, *Shadow, Specters, Shards*, 141.

46   Ibid.

47   Skoller describes the accounts in this way: "Always speaking anecdotally, rather than descriptively, she is never able to give her telling a coherent narrative with a linear progression. Despite the suggestions that Ravett makes off camera at interpreting her memories to make the anecdotes cohere, they never do. The gaps become too big, and the repetitions too frequent. The memories are out of time, and there is never a clear sense of the temporal order of her narrative" (Skoller, *Shadow, Specters, Shards*, 143).

48   Ibid.

49   Ibid., 141.

Chapter Fifteen: Experimental Films II: Lost and Found (Footage)

1   Michael Zryd, "Found Footage Film as Discursive Metahistory: Craig Baldwin's *Tribulation 99*," *The Moving Image* vol. 3, no. 2 (Fall 2003): 41.

2   Ibid., 42.

3   Péter Forgács interviewed by Bill Nichols, "The Memory of Loss: Péter Forgács's Saga of Family Life and Social Hell," *Film Quarterly* vol. 56, no. 4 (Summer 2003): 7.

4   Jeffrey Skoller, *Shadows, Specters, Shards: Making History in Avant-Garde Film* (Minneapolis: University of Minnesota Press, 2005), xviii.

5   Péter Forgács interviewed by Sven Spieker, "At the Center of Mitteleuropa: A Conversation with Péter Forgács," *Art Margins* (Monday 20, 2002): no pagination. Available online at: http://www.artmargins.com.

6   Forgács "At the Center of Mitteleuropa," no pagination.

7   Zryd, "Found Footage Film as Discursive Metahistory," 47.

8   Examples of this might include fan-made music videos; for example, the group Death in June flirts (with some nuance) with Nazi iconography — including a slightly modified Totenkopf for the band's moniker, and the name of the band itself is a reference to the Night of Long Knives (June 30–July 2, 1934). Many of the fan-made music videos for songs like "Heaven Street" use existing film, archival film, or photographic stills from various sources (e.g., tourist snap shots, archival photographs). While some pieces are skillfully made, others are offensive and uninspired, pointing to the ethical limits of appropriative strategies.

9   Anna Reading, "Clicking on Hitler: The Virtual Holocaust @Home," in Barbie Zelizer ed., *Visual Culture and the Holocaust* (New Brunswick, NJ: Rutgers University Press, 2001), 336.

10 Kenneth Anger interviewed by Kate Haug, *Wide Angle* vol. 18, no. 4 (1996): 81.

11 Patrick S. Brennan, "Cutting through Narcissism: Queering Visibility in *Scorpio Rising*," *Genders* vol. 36 (2002): no pagination.

12 Carel Rowe, "Illuminating Lucifer," *Film Quarterly* vol. 27, no. 4 (Summer 1974): 26.

13 Carel Rowe disagrees with this position, at least concerning Kenneth Anger's other work: "To date, all of his films have been evocations or invocations, attempting to conjure primal forces which, once visually released, are designed to have the effect of 'casting a spell' on the audience. The Magick in the film is related to the Magickal effect of the film *on* the audience" (Rowe, "Illuminating Lucifer," 26; also see 36).

14 See Cathy S. Gelbin regarding queering of Nazi imagery, "Double Visions: Queer Femininity and Holocaust Film from *Ostatni Etap* to *Aimée & Jaguar*," *Women in German Yearbook: Feminist Studies in German Literature & Culture* vol. 23 (2007): 186.

15 The appropriation of Holocaust imagery for the purposes of self-reflection is also used in *First Person Plural: The Electronic Diaries of Lynn Hershman: 1984–1996*, released in 1996. This film is a series of confessional video-diaries negotiating the filmmaker's own anxieties brought on by divorce, her subsequent retreat into cycles of binge eating, all the while haunted by traumatic physical and sexual abuse suffered as a child. Short sections of the 75-minute video make associative links between personal trauma, and the trauma of the Holocaust.

16 Syberberg began as one of Brecht's disciple — working for him in 1952–53, filming his productions in Eastern Germany. Such a pairing — Wagner and Brecht — is a contradiction in terms; Susan Sontag reconciles this in the following way: "According to Syberberg, his work comes from 'the duality Brecht/Wagner'; that is the 'aesthetic scandal' he claims to have 'sought.' In interviews he invariably cites both as his artistic fathers, partly (it may be supposed) to neutralize the politics of one by the politics of the other and place himself beyond issues of left and right; partly to appear more

evenhanded than he is." Susan Sontag, "Syberberg's Hitler," *Under the Sign of Saturn* (New York: Farrar, Straus, Giroux, 1980), 156.

17 Anton Kaes, "Holocaust and the End of History: Postmodern Historiography in Cinema," in Saul Friedlander, ed., *Probing the Limits of Representation: Nazism and the "Final Solution"* (Cambridge: Harvard University Press, 1992), 221. Also see Kaes, "Holocaust and the End of History," 319-20.

18 Kaes, "Holocaust and the End of History," 221.

19 Ibid., 222. In defense of Syberberg, Susan Sontag observes that: "Hitler is depicted through examining our relation to Hitler (the theme is 'our Hitler' and 'Hitler-in-us'), as the rightly unassimilable horrors of the Nazi era are represented in Syberberg's film as images or signs. (Its title isn't *Hitler* but, precisely, *Hitler, a Film . . .*)" (Sontag, "Syberberg's Hitler," 139).

20 The *Private Hungary* series includes the following films: *The Bartos Family* (Private Hungary 1, 1988), *Dusi & Jenő* (Private Hungary 2, 1989), *Either–Or* (Private Hungary 3, 1989), *The Diary of Mr. N.* (Private Hungary 4, 1990), *D-film* (Private Hungary 5, 1991), *Photographed by László Dudás* (Private Hungary 6, 1991), *Bourgeoisie Dictionary* (Private Hungary 7, 1992), *Notes of a Lady* (Private Hungary No 8, 1994), *The Land of Nothing* (Private Hungary No. 9, 1996), *Free Fall* (Private Hungary 10, 1997), *Class Lot* (Private Hungary 11, 1997), *Kadar's Kiss* (Private Hungary 12, 1997).

21 Forgács, "At the Center of Mitteleuropa," no pagination.

22 Ibid. Tibor Szemzo also wrote the score for Rob Epstein and Jeffrey Friedman's 2000 documentary *Paragraph 175*, about homosexuals in Nazi Germany subject to the penal code of 1871, paragraph 175, which criminalized homosexuality.

23 Forgács, "At the Center of Mitteleuropa."

24 Forgács, "The Memory of Loss," 9.

25 See Forgács, "The Memory of Loss," 9.

26 Forgács, "At the Center of Mitteleuropa."

27 Forgács, "The Memory of Loss," 10.

28 Berber Hagedoorn, "'Look What I Found!': (Re-)Crossing Boundaries between Public/Private History and Biography/Autobiography in Péter Forgács' *The Maelstrom*," *Studies in Documentary Film* vol. 3, no. 2 (2009): 184.

29 Forgács, "The Memory of Loss," 7.

30 Jaimey Fisher, "Home-Movies, Film-Diaries, and Mass Bodies: Péter Forgács's *Free Fall* into the Holocaust," David Bathrick et al., eds, *Visualizing the Holocaust: Documents, Aesthetics, Memory* (Rochester, NY: Camden House, 2008), 241.

31 Roland Barthes, *Camera Lucida: Reflections on Photography*. Translated by Richard Howard (New York: Hill and Wang, 1993), 96.

32 For a discussion regarding the difference between commentary and perspective see Bill Nichols, *Representing Reality: Issues and Concepts in Documentary* (Bloomington: Indiana University Press, 1991), 126-30.

33 Ernst Van Alphen, "Visual Archives as Preposterous History," *Art History* vol. 30, no. 3 (June 2007): 379.

34 Forgács, "The Memory of Loss," 10.

35 In a famous interview with François Truffaut, Hitchcock explains the difference between surprise and suspense: "Let us suppose that there is a bomb underneath this table between us. Nothing happens, and then all of a sudden, 'Boom!' There is an explosion. The public is surprised, but prior to this surprise, it has seen an absolutely ordinary scene, of no special consequence. Now, let us take a suspense situation. The bomb is underneath the table, and the public knows it, probably because they have seen the anarchist place it there. The public is aware that the bomb is going to explode at one o'clock and there is a clock in the décor. The public can see that it is a quarter to one. In these conditions this same innocuous conversation becomes fascinating because the public is participating in the scene." François Truffaut, *Hitchcock* (New York: A Touchstone Book; Simon and Schuster, 1985), 73.

36 Forgács, "The Memory of Loss," 9.

37 In this respect Forgács's 1998 film *The Danube Exodus* might be comparable to *The Diary of Mr. N*, because it offers visions of both Jewish and German perspectives. The film features amateur film shot in 1939 by Nándor Andrásovite, captain of the ship the *Queen Elizabeth* (Erzsebet királyné). Aron Grünhut, the president of the Bratislava Orthodox Jewish Community, hires the *Queen Elizabeth*, and another vessel, to transport Jews down the Danube to the Black Sea, with the ambition of securing a ship to Palestine. The *Queen Elizabeth* is charted with 608 passengers. On the return voyage up the Danube, the Nazi government charters the *Queen Elizabeth* to transport the Germanic population of Bessarabia (what is now Ukraine and Moldova) following Soviet annexation of the territory. The German government intends to "re-settle" the Bessarabian Germans in Poland, in an effort to "aryanize" the Polish frontier.

38 *Oxford English Dictionary*, s.v., "maelstrom." The definition is given as: "A powerful whirlpool, originally (usu. Maelstrom) one in the Arctic Ocean off the west coast of Norway, which was formerly supposed to suck in and destroy all vessels within a wide radius."

39 Hagedoorn, "'Look What I Found!'," 181.

40 Van Alphen, "Visual Archives as Preposterous History," 378. Also see Van Alphen, 379.

41 Elizabeth Cowie, "Seeing and Hearing for Ourselves: the Spectacle of Reality in the Holocaust Documentary," in Toby Haggith and Joanna Newman eds., *Holocaust and the Moving Image: Representations in Film and Television Since 1933* (New York: Wallflower Press, 2005), 187.

42 Linda Williams, "Film Bodies: Gender, Genre, and Excess," *Film Quarterly* vol. 44, no. 4 (Summer 1991): 11. This is based on Steve Neale, "Melodrama and Tears," *Screen* vol. 27, no. 6 (November–December 1986): 6–22.

43 Cowie, "Seeing and Hearing for Ourselves," 186–7.

44 Michael Renov, "Historische Diskurse des Unvorstellbaren: Péter Forgács's *The Maelstrom*," *Montage/av* vol. 11, no. 1 (2002): 36. Also see Elizabeth Cowie, "Seeing and Hearing for Ourselves," 188, n. 12.

45 See Hagedoorn, "'Look What I Found!'," 182.

46 Alvin H. Rosenfeld, *A Double Dying: Reflections on Holocaust Literature*, (Bloomington: Indiana University Press, 1980), 164.

47 Jaimey Fisher offers a similar reading of this scene. Fisher makes quite a convincing case for the body politics of this scene set in distinction to the "perpetrator's gaze," which materializes in both the Nazi propaganda and Spielberg's shower scene in *Schindler's List*; see Fisher, "Home-Movies, Film-Diaries, and Mass Bodies," 254–6.

Filmography

25 Fireman's Street (*Tüzoltó utca 25*), István Szabó, 1973, 97 min.
81ˢᵗ Blow, The (*Ha-Makah Hashmonim V'Echad*), David Bergman, Jacques Ehrlich, and Haim Gouri, 1974, 115 min.
A Clockwork Orange, Stanley Kubrick, 1971, 136 min.
A Film Unfinished, Yael Hersonski, 2010, 88 min.
A Generation (*Pokolenie*), Andrzej Wajda, 1955, 83 min.
A Generation Apart, Jack Fisher, 1984, 56 min.
A Movie, Bruce Conner, 1958, 12 min.
Addiction, The, Abel Ferrara, 1995, 82 min.
Address Unknown, William Cameron Menzies, 1944, 75 min.
After the Truth (*Nichts als die Wahrheit*), Roland Suso Richter, 1999, 128 min.
Akira, Katsuhiro Otomo, 1988, 124 min.
Among the Righteous: Lost Stories From the Holocaust in Arab Lands, William Cran, 2010, 60 min.
And Along come Tourists (*Am Ende kommen Touristen*), Robert Thalheim, 2007, 85 min.
Anne no nikki, Akinori Nagaoka, 1995, 102 min.
Apel, Czekala Ryszard, 1971 8 min.
Apt Pupil, Bryan Singer, 1998, 118 min.
Archeologia, Andrzej Brzozowski, 1967, 15 min.
As if It Were Yesterday (*Comme si c'était hier*), Myriam Abramowicz and Esther Hoffenberg, 1980, 85 min.
Ashes and Diamonds (*Popiól i diament*), Andrzej Wajda, 1958, 103 min.
Auschwitz: Inside the Nazi State, 2005, 285 min.
Auschwitz-Birkenau 1940–1945–1995, Kees Hin and Hans Fels, 1995, 12 min.
Bad Luck (*Zezowate szczescie*), Andrzej Munk, 1960, 92 min.
Barefoot Gen (*Hadashi no Gen*), Mori Masaki, 1983, 83 min.
Because of That War (*B'Glal Hamilhamah Hahi*), Orna Ben-Dor Niv, 1988, 90 min.
Benny's Video, Michael Haneke, 1992, 105 min.
Bent, Sean Mathias, 1997, 105 min.
Bielsky Brothers, The: The Unknown Partisans, Arun Kumar, 1996, 53 min.
Big Red One, The, Samuel Fuller, 1980, 113 min.
Birds, The Alfred Hitchcock, 1963, 119 min.
Black Thursday (*Les guichets du Louvre*), Michel Mitrani, 1974, 92 min.
Blitzkrieg: Escape from Stalag 69, Keith J. Crocker, 2008, 120 min.
Blue Angel, The (*Der blaue Engel*), Josef von Sternberg, 1930, 124 min.
Border Street (*Ulica Graniczna*), Aleksander Ford, 1948.
Boxer and Death, The (*Boxer a smrt*), Peter Solan, 1963, 120 min.

Boy in the Striped Pyjamas, The, Mark Herman, 2008, 94 min.
Boys from Brazil, The, Franklin Schaffner, 1978, 125 min.
Boys of Buchenwald, The, Audrey Mehler, 2002, 47 min.
Breaking the Silence: The Generation After the Holocaust, Edward A. Mason, 1984, 58 min.
Cabaret, Bob Fosse, 1972, 124 min.
Cabinet of Doctor Caligari, The, Robert Wiene, 1920, 71 min.
Captive Women II: Orgies of the Damned (Lager SSadis Kastrat Kommandantur), Sergio Garrone, 1976, 91 min.
Captive Women 4 (Elsa Fräulein SS), Patrice Rhomm, 1977, 81 min.
Captive Women 5: Mistresses of the 3rd Reich (Train spécial pour SS), Alain Payet, 1977, 75 min.
Carrie, Brian De Palma, 1976, 98 min.
Chicken Run, Peter Lord and Nick Park, 2000, 84 min.
Condemned of Altona, The (I sequestrati di Altona), Vittorio De Sica, 1962, 114 min.
Confidence (Bizalom), István Szabó, 1980, 105 min.
Conformist, The (Il conformista), Bernardo Bertolucci, 1970, 111 min.
Cremator, The (Spalovac mrtvol), Juraj Herz, 1969, 95 min.
Damned, The (La caduta degli dei), Luchino Visconti, 1969, 156 min.
Danube Exodus, The, Péter Forgács, 1998, 60 min.
Dark Lullabies, Irene Lilienheim Angelico and Abby Jack Neidik, 1985, 82 min.
Day the Clown Cried, The Jerry Lewis, 1972.
Dead Ringers, David Cronenberg, 1988, 116 min.
Dead Snow (Død snø), Tommy Wirkola, 2009, 91 min.
Death in Love, Boaz Yakin, 2008, 97 min.
Death Mills, Billy Wilder, 1945, 22 min.
Defiance, Edward Zwick, 2008, 137 min.
Der Fuehrer's Face, Jack Kinney, 1942, 8 min.
Diamonds of the Night (Démanty noci), Jan Nemec, 1964, 63 min.
Diary of Anne Frank, The, George Stevens, 1959, 180 min.
Diary of Mr. N, The, Péter Forgács, 1990, 51 min.
Distant Journey (Daleká cesta aka The Long Journey), Alfréd Radok, 1950, 108 min.
Divided We Fall (Musíme si pomáhat), Jan Hrebejk, 2000, 120 min.
Don't Touch My Holocaust (Al Tigu Le B'Shoah), Asher Tlalim, 1994, 140 min.
Downfall (Der Untergang), Oliver Hirschbiegel, 2004, 156 min.
Dybbuk, The, Michal Waszynski, 1937, 121 min.
Eagle Has Landed, The, John Sturges, 1976, 135 min.
Education for Death: The Making of a Nazi, Clyde Geronimi, 1943, 10 min.
End of Our World, The (Koniec naszego swiata), Wanda Jakubowska, 1964, 138 min.
Eroica, Andrzej Munk, 1958, 87 min.
Escape from Sobibor, Jack Gold, 1987, 120 min.
Eternal Jew, The (Der ewige Jude; aka The Wandering Jew), Fritz Hippler, 1940, 62 min.
Europa Europa, Agnieszka Holland, 1990, 112 min.
Everything Is Illuminated, Liev Schreiber, 2005, 106 min.
Everything's For You, Abraham Ravett, 1989, 58 min.
Exorcist, The, William Friedkin, 1973, 122 min.
Experiments of the S.S. Last Days (La bestia in calore), Luigi Batzella, 1977, 86 min.
Falkenau, the Impossible: Samuel Fuller Bears Witness, Emil Weiss, 1988, 52 min.
Fifth Horsemen Is Fear, The (. . . a páty jezdec je Strach), Zbynek Brynych, 1965, 100 min.
First Person Plural: The Electronic Diaries of Lynn Hershman: 1984–1996, Lynn Hershman, 1996, 75 min.
Flame and Citron (Flammen & Citronen), Ole Christian Madsen, 2008, 130 min.
Forrest Gump, Robert Zemecki, 1994, 142 min.
Fraulein Kitty (aka Elsa Fräulein SS), Patrice Rhomm, 1977, 90 min.
Free Fall (Az örvény), Péter Forgács, 1997, 75 min.

Friday the 13th, Sean S. Cunningham, 1980, 95 min.

From the East (D'Est), Chantal Akerman, 1993, 107 min.

Fuhrer Gives a City to the Jews, The (or *Theresienstadt; Der Fuhrer Schenkt den Juden Eine Stadt*), Kurt Gerron, 1944, 25 min.

Funny Games, Michael Haneke, 1997, 106 min.

Funny Games, Michael Haneke, 2007, 111 min.

Garden of the Finzi-Contintis, The (Il Giardino del Finzi-Contini), Vittorio De Sica, 1970, 90 min.

Genghis Cohn, Elijiah Moshinsky, 1993, 79 min.

Gentleman's Agreement, The, Elia Kazan, 1947, 118 min.

Germany Year Zero (Germania anno zero), Roberto Rossellini, 1948, 78 min.

Gestapo's Last Orgy (L'ultima orgia del III Reich), Cesare Canevari, 1977, 81 min.

Give My Love to the Swallows (. . . a pozdravuji vlastovky), Jaromil Jires, 1972, 86 min.

Gold of Romé (L'oro di Roma), Carlo Lizzani, 1961, 110 min.

Golem, The (Der Golem), Carl Boese and Paul Wegener, 1920, 91 min.

Good, Vicente Amorim, 2008, 96 min.

Goodbye, Children (Au revoir les enfants), Louis Malle, 1987, 104 min.

Grave of the Fireflies (Hotaru no haka), Isao Takahata, 1988, 89 min.

Great Dictator, The, Charles Chaplin, 1940, 125 min.

Great Escape, The, John Sturges, 1963, 172 min.

Grey Zone, The, Tim Blake Nelson, 2001, 108 min.

Haven, John Gray, 2001, 180 min.

Hidden (Cache), Michael Haneke, 2005, 117 min.

Hiding and Seeking: Faith and Tolerance After the Holocaust, Menachem Daum and Oren Rudavsky, 2004, 85 min.

Hiding Place, The, James F. Collier, 1975, 148 min.

High Street (Rue haute), André Ernotte, 1976, 94 min.

History of the Third Reich, The, Liliana Cavani, 1962, 240 min.

Hitler: A Film from Germany (Hitler — ein Film aus Deutschland, aka *Our Hitler)*, Hans-Jürgen Syberberg, 1977, 442 min.

Holocaust: The Story of the Family Weiss, Marvin Chomsky, 1978, 475 min.

Holocaust 2 (Holocaust parte seconda: i ricordi, i deliri, la vendetta), Angelo Pannacciò, 1980, 76 min.

Hostel, Eli Roth, 2005, 94 min.

Hostel: Part II, Eli Roth, 2007, 93 min.

Hotel Terminus: The Life and Times of Klaus Barbie, Marcel Ophüls, 1988, 267 min.

How Much to Remember: One Family's Conversation with History, Nina Koocher, 2007, 57 min.

Human Remains, Jay Rosenblatt, 1998, 30 min.

I Have Never Forgotten You: The Life and Legacy of Simon Wiesenthal, Richard Trank, 2007, 105 min.

I, Justice (Já, spravedlnost), Zbynek Brynych, 1967, 88 min.

Illyria: A Journey of Resistance, Myriam Abramowicz, 2009, 123 min.

Ilsa: Harem Keeper of the Oil Sheiks, Don Edmonds, 1976, 87 min.

Ilsa: She-Wolf of the SS, Don Edmonds, 1975, 96 min.

Ilsa: the Tigress of Siberia, Jean LaFleur, 1977, 88 min.

Ilsa, the Wicked Warden (Greta — Haus ohne Männer), Jesus Franco, 1977, 90 min.

Imaginary Witness: Hollywood and the Holocaust, Daniel Anker, 2004, 92 min.

In Dark Places: Remembering the Holocaust, Gina Blumenfeld, 1978, 60 min.

In the Year of the Pig, Emile de Antonio, 1968, 103 min.

Inglourious Basterds, Quentin Tarantino, 2009, 153 min.

Inheritance, James Moll, 2006, 75 min.

Inheritors, The (Die Siebtelbauern), Stefan Ruzowitzky, 1998, 95 min.

Invitation, The (Zaproszenie), Wanda Jakubowska, 1986, 92 min.

Jacob the Liar (*Jakob, der Lügner*), Frank Beyer, 1975, 100 min.
Jakob the Liar, Peter Kassovitz, 1999, 120 min.
Joe Smith, American, Richard Thorpe, 1942, 63 min.
John Rabe, Florian Gallenberger, 2009, 134 min.
Joy Club, The, Joe D'Amato, 1996, 100 min.
Judgment at Nuremberg, Stanley Kramer, 1961, 186 min.
Just a Gigolo (*Schöner Gigolo, armer Gigolo*), David Hemmings, 1978, 147 min.
Kaddish, Steve Brand, 1984, 92 min.
Kanal, Andrzej Wajda, 1957, 91 min.
Kapò, Gillo Pontecorvo, 1959, 116 min.
Katyn, Andrzej Wajda, 2007, 118 min.
Keep, The, Michael Mann, 1983, 96 min.
Kitty: Return to Auschwitz, Peter Morley, 1979, 82 min.
Kornblumenblau, Leszek Wosiewicz, 1989, 88 min.
Kurt Gerrons Karussell, Ilona Ziok, 1999, 70 min.
Lacombe Lucien, Louis Malle, 1974, 138 min.
Lambeth Walk — Nazi Style, The, Charles A. Ridley, 1942, 2 min.
Last Butterfly, The (*Poslední motyl*), Karel Kachyna, 1991, 106 min.
Last Days, The, James Moll, 1998, 87 min.
Last Metro, The (*Le dernier métro*), François Truffaut, 1980, 131 min.
Last Stage, The (*Ostatni Etap*; aka *The Last Stop*), Wanda Jakubowska, 1947, 81 min.
Lebensborn, David Stephens, 1997, 98 min.
Lebensborn, Werner Klinger, 1961, 91 min.
Liebes Lager, Lorenzo Gicca Palli, 1976, 103 min.
Life Is Beautiful (*La vita è bella*), Roberto Benigni, 1997, 116 min.
Lili Marleen, Rainer Werner Fassbinder, 1981, 120 min.
Long is the Road (*Lang ist der Weg*), Herbert B. Fredersdorf and Marek Goldstein, 1948, 77 min.
Love Camp (*Frauen im Liebeslager*), Jesus Franco, 1977, 71 min.
Love Camp 7, Lee Frost, 1969, 96 min.
Maelstrom, The: A Family Chronicle, Péter Forgács, 1997, 60 min.
Man in the Glass Booth, The, Arthur Hiller, 1975, 117 min.
Man Who Captured Eichmann, The, William A. Graham, 1996, 96 min.
Marathon Man, John Schlesinger, 1976, 125 min.
March, The, Abraham Ravett, 1999, 25 min.
Memory of Justice, The, Marcel Ophüls, 1976, 278 min.
Memory of the Camps, Sidney Bernstein (producer), 1985, 56 min.
Mephisto, István Szabó, 1981, 144 min.
Modern Times, Charles Chaplin, 1936, 87 min.
Mortal Storm, Frank Borzage, 1940, 100 min.
Mr. Death: The Rise and Fall of Fred A. Leuchter, Jr., Errol Morris, 1999, 91 min.
Murderers Are Among Us, The (*Die Möerder Sind Unter Uns*), Wolfgang Staudte, 1946, 81 min.
Museum of Fury, The Leo Hurwitz, 1956, 56 min.
Music Box, Costa-Gavras, 1989, 124 min.
My Enemy's Enemy, Kevin Macdonald, 2007, 87 min.
Naked Among Wolves (*Nackt unter Wölfen*), Frank Beyer, 1963, 116 min.
Nathalie: Escape from Hell (*Nathalie rescapée de l'enfer*), Alain Payet, 1978, 100 min.
Nazi Designers of Death, Mike Rossiter, 1995, 55 min.
Nazi Hunter: The Beate Klarsfeld Story, Michael Lindsay-Hogg, 1986, 120 min.
Nazis Designers of Death, Mike Rossiter, 1995, 55 min.
Night and Fog (*Nuit et brouillard*), Alain Resnais, 1955, 32 min.
Night Porter, The (*Il portiere di notte*), Liliana Cavani, 1974, 118 min.

Now . . . After All These Years (*Jetzt — Nach so vielen Jahren*), Harald Lüders and Pavel Schnabel, 1981, 60 min.

Odessa File, The, Ronald Neame, 1974, 130 min.

Omen, The, Richard Donner, 1976, 111 min.

One Man's War (*La guerre d'un seul homme*), Edgardo Cozarinsky, 1982, 105 min.

OSS 117: Lost in Rio (*OSS 117: Rio ne repond plus*), Michel Hazanavicius, 2009, 101 min.

Paragraph 175, Rob Epstein and Jeffrey Friedman, 2000, 81 min.

Partisans of Vilna, Joshua Waletzky, 1986, 130 min.

Passenger, The (*Pasazerka*), Andrzej Munk, 1963, 62 min.

Pawnbroker, The, Sidney Lumet, 1964, 116 min.

Phantom Limb, Jay Rosenblatt, 2005, 28 min.

Pianist, The, Roman Polanski, 2002, 143 min.

Playing for Time, Daniel Mann, 1980, 150 min.

Prisoner of Paradise (aka *Nazi Love Island*), Bob Chinn and Gail Palmer, 1980, 75 min.

Prisoner of Paradise, Malcolm Clarke and Stuart Sender, 2002, 96 min.

Producers, The, Mel Brooks, 1968, 88 min.

Psycho, Alfred Hitchcock, 1960, 109 min.

Psychology of Neo-Nazism, The: Another Journey by Train to Auschwitz, Mark Cousins and Mark Forrest, 1993, 52 min.

Raiders of the Lost Ark, Steven Spielberg, 1981, 115 min.

Rape of Europa, The, Richard Berge, Bonni Cohen, and Nicole Newnham, 2007, 116 min.

Rat Race, Jerry Zucker, 2001, 112 min.

Reader, The, Stephen Daldry, 2008, 124 min.

Red Cherry (*Hong ying tao*), Daying Ye, 1995, 120 min.

Red Nights of the Gestapo, The (*Le lunghe notti della Gestapo*), Fabio De Agostini, 1977, 103 min.

Reminiscences of a Journey to Lithuania, Jonas Mekas, 1971, 88 min.

Rescuers, The: Heroes of the Holocaust, Michael King, 2009, 300 min.

Return to Poland, Marian Marzynski, 1981, 58 min.

River of Death, Steve Carver, 1989, 107 min.

Rome, Open City, Roberto Rossellini, 1945, 102 min.

Rope, Alfred Hitchcock, 1948, 80 min.

Rosemary's Baby, Roman Polanski, 1968, 136 min.

run/dig, Robin Kandel, 2004, 5 min.

S.S. Extermination Love Camp (*KZ9 — Lager di Sterminio*), Bruno Mattei, 1977, 97 min.

Salò, or the 120 Days of Sodom (*Salò o le 120 giornate di Sodoma*), Pier Paolo Pasolini, 1975, 116 min.

Salon Kitty, Tinto Brass, 1976, 110 min.

Sandra of a Thousand Delights (*Vaghe stelle dell'Orsa . . .*), Luchino Visconti, 1965, 105 min.

Saw, James Wan, 2004, 103 min.

Say I'm a Jew, Pier Marton, 1984, 28 min.

Schindler's List, Steven Spielberg, 1993, 195 min.

Scorpio Rising, Kennth Anger, 1964, 28 min.

Second Generation Video, Joshua Hirsch, 1995, 25 min.

Secrets of the Nazi Criminals (*Krigsförbrytare*), Tore Sjöberg, 1956, 82 min.

Serpent's Egg, The, Ingmar Bergman, 1977, 119 min.

Seven Beauties (*Pasqualino Settebellezze*), Lina Wertmüller, 1975, 115 min.

Shadow of Doubt (*Een schijn van twijfel*), Rolf Orthel, 1975, 53 min.

Shanghai Ghetto, Dana Janklowicz-Mann and Amir Mann, 2002, 96 min.

Shoah, Claude Lanzmann, 1985, 503 min.

Shock of the New, The, David Richardson, 1982, 60 min.

Shop on Main Street, The (*Obchod na korze*), Ján Kadár and Elmar Klos, 1965, 128 min.

Shtetl, Marian Marzynski, 1996, 236 min.

Silence, Orly Yadin and Sylvie Bringas, 1998, 10 min.

Silent Song, Elida Schogt, 2001, 6 min.

So Many Miracles, Kartherine Smalley and Vic Sarin, 1987, 48 min.

Sobibor, October 14, 1943, at 4:00pm (Sobibór, 14 octobre 1943, 16 heures), Claude Lanzmann, 2001, 95 min.

Sophie Scholl: The Final Days (Sophie Scholl: Die Letzten Tage), Marc Rothemund, 2005, 120 min.

Sophie's Choice, Alan J. Pakula, 1982, 150 min.

Sorrow and the Pity, The (Le Chagrin et la Pitie), Marcel Ophüls, 1969, 264 min.

Sound of Music, The, Robert Wise, 1965, 174 min.

Special Section (Section spéciale), Costa-Gavras, 1975, 110 min.

Specialist, The, Eyal Sivan, 1999, 128 min.

Spring of Life (Pramen zivota), Milan Cieslar, 2000, 107 min.

Stalag 17, Billy Wilder, 1953, 120 min.

Stalags, Ari Libsker, 2008, 63 min.

Stars (Sterne), Konrad Wolf, 1959, 103 min.

story 1: run, Robin Kandel, 2002, 5 min.

story 2: postola, Robin Kandel, 2003, 5 min.

Sugihara: Conspiracy of Kindness, Robert Kirk, 2000, 103 min.

Sunshine, István Szabó, 1999, 181 min.

Survivors of the Holocaust, Allan Holzman, 1996, 70 min.

Sweet Light in a Dark Room (Romeo, Julia a tma), Jirí Weiss, 1960, 92 min.

Tak for Alt: Survival of a Human Spirit, Laura Bialis et al., 1999, 61 min.

Taking Sides, István Szabó, 2001, 108 min.

Tel Aviv-Berlin, Tzipi Trope, 1987, 90 min.

They Came From Far Away (Zij kwamen van ver), Lydia Chagoll, 1979, 27 min.

Third Part of the Night, The (Trzecia czesc nocy), Andrzej Zulawski, 1971, 105 min.

Ties That Bind, The, Su Friedrich, 1985, 55 min.

To Be or Not to Be, Alan Johnson, 1983, 107 min.

To Be or Not to Be, Ernst Lubitsch, 1942, 99 min.

Top Secret Trial of the Third Reich (Geheime Reichssache), Jochen Bauer, 1979, 110 min.

Train of Life (Train de vie), Radu Mihaileanu, 1998, 103 min.

Transport from Paradise (Transport z raje), Zbynek Brynych, 1962, 93 min.

Triumph of the Spirit, Robert M. Young, 1989, 120 min.

Triumph of the Will (Triumph des Willens), Leni Riefenstahl, 1935, 114 min.

Truce, The (La tregua), Francesco Rosi, 1997, 125 min.

Unborn, The, David S. Goyer, 2009, 88 min.

Under the World (Debajo del mundo), Beda Docampo Feijóo, 1987, 100 min.

Untouchables, The Brian De Palma, 1987, 119 min.

Valkyrie, Bryan Singer, 2008, 121 min.

Visas and Virtue, Chris Tashima, 1997, 26 min.

Voyage of the Damned, Stuart Rosenberg, 1976, 182 min.

Walk on Water, Eytan Fox, 2004, 103 min.

Walnut Tree, The, Elida Schogt, 2000, 11 min.

We Were So Beloved, Manfred Kirchheimer, 1986, 145 min.

Weapons of the Spirit, Pierre Sauvage, 1988, 118 min.

When I Was Fourteen: A Survivor Remembers, Marlene Booth and Jameson C. Goldner, 1995, 58 min.

White Ribbon, The (Das Weisse Band), Michael Haneke, 2009, 144 min.

Who Shall Live and Who Shall Die? Laurence Jarvik, 1982, 90 min.

Wild One, The Laslo Benedek, 1953, 79 min.

Witnesses, The (The Time of the Ghetto; Le temps du ghetto), Frédéric Rossif, 1961, 90 min.

X-Men, Bryan Singer, 2000, 104 min.

You Nazty Spy! Jules White, 1940, 20 min.

Zyklon Portrait, Elida Schogt, 1999, 13 min.

Bibliography

Aaron, Frieda W. "Yiddish and Polish Poetry in the Ghettos and Camps." *Modern Language Studies* vol. 19, no. 1 (Winter 1989): 72–87.

Adorno, Theodor. *Prisms*. Translated by Samuel and Shierry Weber. London: Neville Spearman, 1967.

—*Negative Dialectics*. Translated by E. B. Ashton. New York: The Seabury Press, 1973.

—"On Commitment." Translated by Francis McDonagh. *Performing Arts Journal* vol. 3, no. 2 (Autumn 1978): 3–11.

—*Can One Live After Auschwitz? A Philosophical Reader*. Edited by Rolf Tiedmann. Translated by Rodney Livingstone, et al. Stanford: Stanford University Press, 2003.

Affron, Charles. *Cinema and Sentiment*. Chicago: University of Chicago Press, 1982.

Agamben, Giorgio. *Remnants of Auschwitz: The Witness and the Archive*. Translated by Daniel Heller-Roazan. New York: Zone Books, 1999.

Allan, Seán and Sandford, John, eds. *DEFA: East German Cinema, 1946–1992*. New York: Berghahn Books, 2003.

Allen, Beverly. *Pier Paolo Pasolini: The Poetics of Heresy*. Saratoga, CA: ANMA LIBRI, 1982.

Anderson, Mark M. "The Child Victim as Witness to the Holocaust: An American Story?" *Jewish Social Studies: History, Culture, Society* vol. 14, no. 1 (Fall 2007): 1–22.

Anger, Kenneth. Interviewed by Kate Haug. *Wide Angle* vol. 18, no. 4 (1996): 74–92.

Applegate, Celia. "Saving Music: Enduring Experiences of Culture." *History & Memory* vol. 17, no. 1/2 (Spring/Summer 2005): 217–37.

Arendt, Hannah. *Eichmann in Jerusalem: A Report on the Banality of Evil*. New York: Penguin, 1994.

Avisar, Ilan. *Screening the Holocaust: Cinema's Images of the Unimaginable*. Bloomington: Indiana University Press, 1988.

Baer, Elizabeth R. and Goldenberg, Myrna. *Experience and Expression: Women, the Nazis, and the Holocaust*. Detroit: Wayne State University Press, 2003.

Bal, Mieke et al. eds. *Acts of Memory: Cultural Recall in the Present*. Hanover, NH: University Press of New England, 1999.

Bangert, Axel. "Changing Narratives and Images of the Holocaust: Tim Blake Nelson's film *The Grey Zone* (2001)." *New Cinemas: Journal of Contemporary Film* vol. 6, no. 1 (2008): 17–32.

Barker, Clive. *Clive Barker's A–Z of Horror*. Compiled by Stephen Jones. New York: HarperPrism, 1997.

Baron, Anne-Marie. *The Shoah On-Screen: Representing Crimes Against Humanity Volume I*. Strasbourg: Council of Europe Publishing, 2006.

Baron, Jaimie. "Contemporary Documentary Film and 'Archive Fever': History, the Fragment, the Joke." *The Velvet Light Trap* vol. 60 (Fall 2007): 13–24.

Baron, Lawrence. "X-Men as J Men: The Jewish Subtext of a Comic Book Movie." *Shofar: An Interdisciplinary Journal of Jewish Studies* vol. 22, no. 1 (Fall 2003): 44–52.

—*Projecting the Holocaust into the Present: The Changing Focus of Contemporary Holocaust Cinema*. New York: Rowman and Littlefield Publishers, Inc., 2005.

Barthes, Roland. *The Rustle of Language*. Translated by Richard Howard. Berkeley: University of California Press, 1989.

—*Camera Lucida: Reflections on Photography*. Translated by Richard Howard. New York: Hill and Wang, 1993.

Bartov, Omer. "Kitsch and Sadism in Ka-Tzetnik's Other Planet: Israeli Youth Imagine the Holocaust." *Jewish Social Studies: History, Culture, and Society* vol. 3, no. 2 (Winter 1997): 42–76.

—*The "Jew" in Cinema: From* The Golem *to* Don't Touch My Holocaust. Bloomington: Indiana University Press, 2005.

Basilico, Lawrence. *Cut: Film as Found Object in Contemporary Video*. Milwaukee: Mikwaukee Art Museum, 2004.

Bathrick, David; Prager, Brad; and Richardson, Michael D. eds. *Visualizing the Holocaust: Documents, Aesthetics, Memory*. Rochester, NY: Camden House, 2008.

Bazin, André. "Le Ghetto Concentrationnaire." *Cahiers du Cinema* vol. 2, no. 9 (February 1952): 58-60.

—*What Is Cinema Volume II*. Translated by Hugh Gray. Berkeley: University of California Press, 1971.

Benedetti, Laura; Hairston, Julia; and Ross, Silvia M., eds. *Gendered Contexts: New Perspectives in Italian Cultural Studies*. New York: Peter Lang, 1996.

Bernard-Donals, Michael and Glejzer, Richard, eds. *Witnessing the Disaster: Essays on Representation and the Holocaust*. Madison: The University of Wisconsin Press, 2003.

Bettelheim, Bruno. "Violence: A Neglected Mode of Behavior." *Annals of the American Academy of Political and Social Science* vol. 364 (March 1966): 50-9.

—*The Informed Heart: Autonomy in a Mass Age*. Glencoe, IL: The Free Press, 1961.

—*Surviving and Other Essays*. New York: Alfred Knopf, 1979.

Bogart, Anne. "Stepping out of Inertia." *The Drama Review*, vol. 27, no. 4 (Winter 1983): 26-8.

Borowski, Tadeusz. *This Way for the Gas, Ladies and Gentlemen*. New York: Viking Penguin, 1967.

Bouzereau, Laurent. *Ultraviolent Movies: from Sam Peckinpah to Quentin Tarantino*. Secaucus, NJ: Citadel Press, 1996.

Bratton, Jacky et al., eds. *Melodrama: Stage, Picture, Screen*. London: BFI Publishing, 1994.

Brennan, Patrick S. "Cutting through Narcissism: Queering Visibility in *Scorpio Rising*." *Genders* vol. 36 (2002): no pagination.

Brinkema, Eugenie. "Pleasure in/and Perversity: Plaisagir in Liliana Cavani's *Il portiere di notte*." *The Dalhouse Review* vol. 84, no. 3 (2004): 419–39.

Brockmann, Stephen. "Syberberg's Germany." *The German Quarterly* vol. 69, no. 1 (Winter 1996): 48-62.

Brooks, Peter. *The Melodramatic Imagination: Balzac, Henry James, Melodrama, and the Mode of Excess*. New Haven: Yale University Press, 1976.

Brown, Jared. *Alan J. Pakula: His Films and His Life*. New York: Back Stage Books, 2005.

Browning, Christopher R. *Ordinary Men: Reserve Police Battalion 101 and the Final Solution in Poland*. New York: Harper Collins, 1992.

Buchar, Robert. *Czech New Wave Filmmakers in Interviews*. Jefferson, NC: McFarland, 2004.

Buck-Morss, Susan. "The City as Dreamworld and Catastrophe." *October* vol. 73 (Summer 1995): 3–26.

Butler, Kristine. "Bordering on Fiction: Chantal Akerman's *D'Est*." *Postmodern Culture* vol. 6, no. 1 (1995): no pagination.

Byg, Barton. "Cinema in the German Democratic Republic." *Monatshefte* vol. 82, no. 3 (Fall 1990): 286–93.

Canary, Robert and Kozicki, Henry, eds. *The Writing of History*. Madison: University of Wisconsin Press, 1978.

Canby, Vincent. Review, *We Were So Beloved*. *New York Times*. August 27, 1986: no pagination.

Carmody, Todd. "The Banality of the Document: Charles Reznikoff's 'Holocaust' and Ineloquent Empathy." *Journal of Modern Literature* vol. 32, no. 1 (Fall 2008): 86–110.

Cayrol, Jean. *Poèmes de la nuit et du brouillard* (*Poems of the Night and of the Fog*). Editions Pierre Seghers, 1946.

Celli, Carlo. "The Representation of Evil in Roberto Benigni's *Life Is Beautiful*." *Journal of Popular Film & Television* vol. 28, no. 2 (Summer 2000): 74–9.

Chaouat, Bruno. "In the Image of Auschwitz." *Diacritics* vol. 36, no. 1 (Spring 2006): 86–96.

Chaplin, Charles. *My Auto-Biography*. New York: Simon and Schuster, 1964.

Cherry, Robert D. and Orla-Bukowska, Annamaria, eds. *Rethinking Poles and Jews: Troubled Past, Brighter Future*. Lanham, MA: Rowan and Littlefield, 2007.

Clendinnen, Inga. *Reading the Holocaust*. Melbourne: The Text Publishing Company, 2000.

Clover, Carol. "Her Body, Himself: Gender in the Slasher Film." *Representations* vol. 20 (Autumn 1987): 187–228.

—*Men, Women, and Chainsaws: Gender in the Modern Horror Film*. Princeton: Princeton University Press, 1992.

Cottino-Jones, Marga. "What Kind of Memory? Liliana Cavani's *Night Porter*," *Contention* vol. 5, no. 1 (Fall 1995): 105–11.

Coulteray, George de. *Sadism in the Movies*. Translated by Steve Hult. New York: Medical Press, 1965.

Creed, Barbara. *The Monstrous-Feminine: Film, Feminism, Psychoanalysis*. New York: Routledge, 1993.

Crnkovic, Gordana P. "From the Eye to the Hand: The Victim's Double Vision in the Films of Roman Polanski." *Kinoeye* vol. 4, no. 5 (November 2004): no pagination.

Cronin, Paul, ed. *Roman Polanski: Interviews*. Jasckson: University Press of Mississippi, 2005.

Dargis, Manohla. "Mengele, the Holocaust and Horror Movie Staples." *New York Times*, January 9, 2009: 16.

Davis, Whitney. "The World Rewound: Peter Forgács's *Wittgenstein Tractatus*." *Journal of Aesthetics and Art Criticism* vol. 64, no. 1 (Winter 2006): 199–211.

de Lauretis, Teresa. "Cavani's *Night Porter*: A Woman's Film?" *Film Quarterly*, vol. 30, no. 2 (Winter 1976–77): 35–8.

Dean, Carolyn J. "Empathy, Pornography, and Suffering." *Differences: a Journal of Feminist Cultural Studies* vol. 14, no. 1 (Spring 2003): 88–124.

Delzell, Charles. *Mussolini's Enemies: the Anti-Fascist Resistance*. Princeton: Princeton University Press, 1961.

Denby, David. "In the Eye of the Beholder." *The New Yorker*. March 15, 1999: 96–9.

—"Americans in Paris: *Inglourious Basterds* and *Julie & Julia*." *New Yorker*. August 24, 2009: 82–3.

Deutsch, Phyllis. "*Sophie's Choice* Undeserved Guilt," *Jump Cut* vol. 29 (February 1984): 9–10.

Diederichsen, Diedrich. "Spiritual Reactionaries after German Reunification: Syberberg, Foucault, and Others." Translated by Peter Chametzky. *October* vol. 62 (Autumn 1992): 65–83.

Dixon, Wheeler Winston and Foster, Gwendolyn Audrey, eds. *Experimental Cinema: The Film Reader*. New York: Routledge, 2002.

Doane, Mary Ann. "The Voice in the Cinema: The Articulation of Body and Space." *Yale French Studies* vol. 60 (1980): 33–50.

——"The Close-Up: Scale and Detail in the Cinema." *Differences: A Journal of Feminist Cultural Studies* vol. 14, no. 3 (2003): 89–111.

Doneson, Judith. "The Jew as a Female Figure in the Holocaust Film." *Shoah: a Review of Holocaust Studies and Commemorations* vol. 1, no. 1 (1978): 11–13; 18.

——*The Holocaust in American Film, Second Edition*. New York: Syracuse University Press, 2002.

Drescher, Ruth Lieberman. Review of *We Were So Beloved: The German Jews of Washington Heights*, directed by Manfred Kirchheimer. *The Oral History Review* vol. 17, no. 1 (Spring 1989): 149–51.

Druick, Zoë. "Documenting False History: Errol Morris and *Mr. Death*." *Studies in Documentary Film* vol. 1, no. 3 (2007): 207–19.

Dundes, Alan and Hauschild, Thomas. "Auschwitz Jokes." *Western Folklore* vol. 42, no. 4 (October 1983): 249–60.

Dundes, Alan and Linke, Uli. "More on Auschwitz Jokes." *Folklore* vol. 99, no. 1 (1988): 3–10.

Edelstein, David. "Now Playing at Your Local Multiplex: Torture Porn." *New York Magazine* vol. 39, no. 4 (2006): 63–4.

——"Audience is Loser in Haneke's Unfunny 'Games'," *Fresh Air*. (March 14, 2008) Available at: http://www.npr.org/templates/story/story.php?storyId=88230619

Elsaesser, Thomas. "Myth as the Phantas-magoria of History: H. J. Syberberg, Cinema and Representation." *New German Critique* vol. 24–25 (Fall/Winter 1981/1982): 108–54.

——*New German Cinema: A History*. New Brunswick, NJ: Rutgers University Press, 1989.

Engel, S. Morris. *The Dybbuk: Between Two Worlds*. Translated by S. Morris Engel. South Bend, IN: Regnery/Gateway, 1979.

Eppert, Claudia. "Entertaining History: (Un)Heroic Identifications, Apt Pupils, and an Ethical Imagination." *New German Critique: An Interdisciplinary Journal of German Studies* vol. 86 (Spring–Summer 2002): 71–101.

Epstein, Jean. "Magnification and Other Writings." Translated by Stuart Liebman. *October* vol. 3 (Spring 1977): 9–25.

Epstein, Leslie. *King of the Jews*. New York, London: W.W. Norton, 1979.

Ernst, Wolfgang. "Distory: Cinema and Historical Discourse." *Journal of Contemporary History* vol. 18, no. 3 (July 1983): 397–409.

Ezrahi, Sidra De Koven. "After Such Knowledge, What Laughter?" *The Yale Journal of Criticism* vol. 14, no. 1 (Spring 2001): 287–313.

Feinstein, Stephen. "Art from the Concentration Camps: Gallows Humor and Satirical Wit." *Journal of Jewish Identities* no. 2 (July 2008): 53–75.

Felman, Shoshana. "In an Era of Testimony: Claude Lanzmann's Shoah." *Yale French Studies: Literature and the Ethical Question* vol. 79 (1991): 39–81.

Felman, Shoshana and Laub, Dori eds. *Testimony: Crises of Witnessing in Literature, Psychoanalysis, and History*. New York: Routledge, 1992.

Ferlita, Ernest and May, John R. *The Parables of Lina Wertmüller*. New York: Paulist Press, 1977.

Flanzbaum, Hilene. "'But Wasn't It Terrific?': A Defense of Liking *Life Is Beautiful*." *The Yale Journal of Criticism* vol. 14, no. 1 (Spring 2001): 273–86.

Forgács, Péter. Interviewed by Sven Spieker. "At the Center of Mitteleuropa: A Conversation with Péter Forgács." *Art Margins* (Monday 20, 2002): no pagination.

——Interviewed by Bill Nichols. "The Memory of Loss: Peter Forgács's Saga of Family Life and Social Hell." *Film Quarterly* vol. 56, no. 4 (Summer 2003): 2–12.

Foucault, Michel. *The Archaeology of Knowledge: and the Discourse of Language*. Translated by A. M. Sheridan Smith. New York: Pantheon Books, 1972.

Francis, Richard Lee. "Beyond Narrative: Filmmaking in the Eighties: Recent Cinematic Developments." *Pacific Coast Philology* vol. 19, no. 1 and no. 2 (November 1984): 108–15.

Frascina, Francis, ed., *Pollock and After: The Critical Debate*. New York: Harper and Row, Publishers, 1986.

Fresco, Nadine. "Remembering the Unknown." *International Review of Psycho-Analysis* vol. 11 (1984): 417–27.

Friedlander, Saul. *Reflections of Nazism: An Essay on Kitsch and Death*. Translated by Thomas Weyr. Bloomington: Indiana University Press, 1993.

—"History, Memory, and the Historian: Dilemmas and Responsibilities." *New German Critique* 80 (Spring–Summer 2000): 3–15.

Friedlander, Saul, ed. *Probing the Limits of Representation: Nazism and the "Final Solution"*. Cambridge: Harvard University Press, 1992.

Friedman, David F. *A Youth in Babylon: Confessions of a Trash-Film King*. Buffalo, NY: Prometheus Books, 1990.

Friedman, R. M. "Exorcising the Past: Jewish Figures in Contemporary Films." *Journal of Contemporary History* vol. 19, no. 3 (July 1984): 511–27.

—"The Double Legacy of *Arbeit Macht Frei*." *Prooftexts* vol. 22, no. 1 and no. 2 (Winter/ Spring 2002): 200–20.

Friling, Tuvia. "A Blatant Oversight?: The Right-Wing in Israeli Holocaust Historiography." *Israel Studies* vol. 14, no. 1 (Spring 2009): 123–69.

Gary, Romain. *The Dance of Genghis Cohn*. Translated by Romain Gary with the assistance of Camilla Sykes. New York: World Publishing Co., 1968.

Gelbin, Cathy S. "Double Visions: Queer Femininity and Holocaust Film from *Ostatni Etap* to *Aimée & Jaguar*." *Women in German Yearbook: Feminist Studies in German Literature & Culture* vol. 23 (2007): 179–204.

Gemünden, Gerd. "Space out of Joint: Ernst Lubitsch's *To Be or Not to Be*," *New German Critique* vol. 89 (Spring–Summer 2003): 59–80.

Gerbaz, Alex. "Direct Address, Ethical Imagination, and Errol Morris's Interrotron." *Film-Philosophy* vol. 12, no. 2 (September 2008): 17–29.

Gilman, Sander L. "Is Life Beautiful? Can the Shoah Be Funny? Some Thoughts on Recent and Older Films." *Critical Inquiry* vol. 26, no. 2 (Winter 2000): 279–308.

Ginsparg, Sylvia Levine. "Humor and the Holocaust: Turning Comedians Into Victims to End the Millennium." *Psychoanalytic Psychology* vol. 20, no. 4 (Fall 2003): 710–16.

Girard, René. *Violence and the Sacred*. Translated by Patrick Gregory. Baltimore: The John Hopkins University Press, 1989.

Glasner-Heled, Galia. "Reader, Writer, and Holocaust Literature: The Case of Ka-Tzetnik." *Israel Studies* vol. 12, no. 3 (Fall 2007): 109–33.

Gledhill, Christine, ed. *Home Is Where the Heart Is: Studies in Melodrama and the Woman's Film*. London: BFI Publishing, 1994.

Goldmark, Daniel et al., eds. *Beyond the Soundtrack: Representing Music in Cinema*. Berkeley: University of California Press, 2007.

Gomel, Elana and Weninger, Stephen. "Cronenberg, Greenaway and the Ideologies of Twinship." *Body and Soul* vol. 9, no. 3 (2003): 19–35.

Gottlieb, Roger S., ed. *Thinking the Unthinkable: Meanings of the Holocaust*. New York: Paulist Press, 1990.

Grant, Barry Keith and Sharrett, Christopher, eds. *Planks of Reason: Essays on the Horror Film*. Lanham, Maryland: Scarecrow Press, 2004.

Grass, Günter. *Two States — One Nation?* Translated by Krishna Winston and A. S. Wensinger. San Diego: Harcourt Brace Jovanovich, 1990.

Gross, Sheryl W. "Guilt and Innocence in *Marathon Man*." *Literature Film Quarterly* vol. 8, no. 1 (1980): 52–68.

Grundmann, Roy and Rockwell, Cynthia. "The Truth Is Not Subjective: An Interview with Errol Morris," *Cineaste*, vol. 25, no. 3 (2000): 7.

Hagedoorn, Berber. "'Look What I Found!': (Re-)Crossing Boundaries between Public/ Private History and Biography/Autobiography in Péter Forgács' *The Maelstrom*." *Studies in Documentary Film* vol. 3, no. 2 (2009): 177–92.

Haggith, Toby and Newman, Joanna, eds. *Holocaust and the Moving Image: Representations in Film and Television Since 1933*. New York: Wallflower Press, 2005.

Halbreich, Kathy and Jenkins, Bruce, eds. *Bordering on Fiction: Chantal Akerman's D'Est*. Minneapolis: The Walker Arts Center, 1995.

Hames, Peter, ed. *The Cinema of Central Europe*. New York: Wallflower Press, 2004.

Haneke, Michael. Interview by Nick James. *Sight & Sound*, vol. 13, no. 10 (October 2003): 17–18.

Hareven, Tamara, ed. *Anonymous Americans: Explorations in Nineteenth-Century Social History*. Englewood Cliffs, NJ: Prentice-Hall, 1971.

Hart, Kitty. *I Am Alive*. New York: Abelard-Schuman, 1961.

Haug, Kate. Interview with Kenneth Anger. *Wide Angle* vol. 18, no. 4 (1996): 81.

Hawkins, Joan. *Cutting Edge: Art-Horror and the Horrific Avant-garde*. Minneapolis: University of Minnesota Press, 2000.

Hazlett, Allan. "Possible Evils." *Ratio* vol. 19, no. 2 (June 2006): 191–8.

Heineman, Elizabeth D. "Sexuality and Nazism: The Doubly Unspeakable?" *Journal of the History of Sexuality* vol. 11, no. 1 and no. 2 (January/April 2002): 22–66.

Henry, Patrick. "The Gray Zone." *Philosophy and Literature* vol. 33, no. 1 (April 2009): 150–66.

Hilberg, Raul. *The Destruction of the European Jews*. New York: Harper Colophon Books, 1979.

—*The Destruction of the European Jews*. New York: Holmes and Meier, 1985.

Hirsch, Joshua. *Afterimage: Film, Trauma, and the Holocaust*. Philadelphia: Temple University Press, 2004.

Hirsch, Marianne and Kacandes, Irene, eds. *Teaching the Representation of the Holocaust*. New York: The Modern Language Association of America, 2004.

Hoberman, J. *Bridge of Light: Yiddish Film Between Two Worlds*. New York: Museum of Modern Art; Schocken Books, 1991.

Horkheimer, Max and Theodor Adorno. *The Dialectic of Enlightenment*. Trans. John Cumming. New York: Continuum, 1996.

Horvat, Srecko. Interview with Paul A. Taylor. *International Journal of Zizek Studies* vol. 1 (2007): 5.

Hughes, Robert. *The Shock of the New*. New York: Alfred A. Knopf, 1981.

Huyssen, Andreas. "The Politics of Identification: *Holocaust* and the West German Drama." *New German Critique* vol. 19 (Winter 1980): 117–36.

—"Adorno in Reverse: From Hollywood to Richard Wagner." *New German Critique* vol. 29 (Spring–Summer 1983): 8–38.

—*After the Great Divide: Modernism, Mass Culture, Postmodernism*. Bloomington: Indiana University Press, 1986.

Insdorf, Annette. *Indelible Shadows: Film and the Holocaust* (second edn). Cambridge: Cambridge University Press, 1990.

—*Indelible Shadows: Film and Holocaust* (third edn). Cambridge: Cambridge University Press, 2003.

Iordanova, Dina. *Cinema of the Other Europe: The Industry and Artistry of East Central European Film*. New York: Wallflower Press, 2003.

Ishizuka, Karen L. and Zimmermann, Patricia Rodden, eds. *Mining the Home Movie: Excavations in Histories and Memories*. Berkeley: University of California Press, 2008.

Jacobs, Lewis. "World War II and the American Film." *Cinema Journal* vol. 7 (Winter 1967–68): 1–21.

James, David E., ed. *To Free the Cinema: Jonas Mekas and the New York Underground*. Princeton: Princeton University Press, 1992.

James, Nick. "Darkness Falls." *Sight & Sound* vol. 13, no. 10 (October 2003): 16–19.

Jameson, Fredric. "'In the Destructive Element Immerse': Hans-Jürgen Syberberg and Cultural Revolution." *October* vol. 17 (Summer 1981): 99–118.

Ka Tzetnik 135633. *The House of Dolls*. Translated by Moshe M. Kohn. London: Frederick Muller, Ltd., 1965.

Kaplan, Brett Ashley. "'The Bitter Residue of Death': Jorge Semprun and the Aesthetics of Holocaust Memory." *Comparative Literature* vol. 55, no. 4 (Autumn 2003): 320–37.

Katz, Stephen T. *The Holocaust in Historical Context, Volume 1 The Holocaust and Mass Death Before the Modern Age*. New York: Oxford University Press, 1994.

Kaufhold, Roland. "Documents Pertinent to the History of Psychoanalysis and Psychoanalytic Pedagogy: The Correspondence between Bruno Bettelheim and Ernst Federn." *Psychoanalytic Review* vol. 95, no. 6 (December 2008): 887–928.

Kehr, Dave. "Lessons in 20th-Century History." *New York Times*. April 18, 2010: AR12.

Kepley, Vance and Swender, Rebecca. "Claiming the Found: Archive Footage and Documentary Practice." *The Velvet Light Trap* vol. 64 (Fall 2009): 3–10.

Kerner, Aaron. *Reconstructing Memories*. Exhibition catalogue. Honolulu: University of Hawaii Art Gallery, 2006.

Kertész, Imre. "Who Owns Auschwitz?" Translated by John MacKay. *The Yale Journal of Criticism* vol. 14, no. 1 (Spring 2001): 267–72.

Kift, Roy. "Comedy in the Holocaust: The Theresienstadt Cabaret." *New Theatre Quarterly* vol. 48, no. 12 (1996): 299–308.

Klawans, Stuart. "*Scream 4*: The Holocaust?" *Nation* vol. 267, no. 14 (November 2, 1998): 34–5.

Klein Halevi, Yossi. *Memoirs of a Jewish Extremist: An American Story*. New York: Little, Brown and Company, 1995.

Klein, Yifat. "Situations of Horror: A Comparative Study of Works by Kafka, Fogel and Ka-tzetnik." *FACS: Florida Atlantic Comparative Studies* no. 7 (2004–05): 29–41.

Klossowski, Pierre. *Sade My Neighbour*. Translated by Alphonso Lingis. London: Quartet Books Limited, 1992.

Konigsberg, Ira. "'The Only 'I' in the World': Religion, Psychoanalysis, and *The Dybbuk*." *Cinema Journal* vol. 36, no. 4 (Summer 1997): 22–42.

—"Our Children and the Limits of Cinema: Early Jewish Responses to the Holocaust." *Film Quarterly* vol. 52, no. 1 (Autumn 1998): 7–19.

Koonz, Claudia. *Mothers in the Fatherland: Women, the Family, and Nazi Politics*. New York: St. Martin's Press, 1987.

Kossc, Wojtek. "Weirdness through Simplicity: Roman Polanski's *The Pianist* (2002)." *Kinoeye* vol. 2, no. 20 (December 2002): no pagination.

Kowal, Kristopher. "Krzysztof Kieslowski *Dekalog 8*: Narrating Jewish–Polish Reconciliation." *European Legacy* vol. 4, no. 4 (August 1999): 58–76.

Kristeva, Julia. *Powers of Horror: An Essay on Abjection*. Translated by Leon S. Roudiez. New York: Columbia University Press, 1982.

—*Black Sun: Depression and Melancholia*. Translated by Leon S. Roudiez. New York: Columbia University Press, 1989.

Kulavkova, Kata, ed. *Interpretations: European Research Project for Poetics & Hermeneutics, Volume I: Violence & Art*. Skopje, Macedonia: Macedonian Academy of Sciences and Arts, 2007.

Kushner, Tony. "Holocaust Testimony, Ethics, and the Problem of Representation." *Poetics Today* vol. 27, no. 2 (Summer 2006): 275–95.

Lacan, Jacques. "Kant avec Sade." Translated by James B. Swenson, Jr. *October* 51 (Winter 1989): 55–104.

Lane, Anthony. "Recurring Nightmare." *The New Yorker* (March 17, 2008).

—"Happy Haneke." *The New Yorker* (October 5, 2009): 60–7.

Lane, Jim. *The Autobiographical Documentary in America*. Madison: University of Wisconsin Press, 2002.

Lang, Berel, ed. *Writing and the Holocaust*. New York: Holmes and Meier, 1988.

Lanval, Marc. "Ilse Koch — Sex Terrorist." *Sexology* vol. 19, no. 1 (1951): 30–6.

Lanzmann, Claude. *Shoah: An Oral History of the Holocaust*. New York: Pantheon Books, 1985.

—"Seminar with Claude Lanzmann 11 April 1990." *Yale French Studies: Literature and the Ethical Question* vol. 79 (1991): 82–99.

—"Why Spielberg has distorted the truth." *The Guardian Weekly* (April 3, 1994): 14.

Laplanche, Jean and Pontalis, J. B. "Fantasy and the Origins of Sexuality." *The International Journal of Psycho-Analysis* vol. 49 (1968): 1–18.

Lavery, David et al., eds. *"Deny All Knowledge": Reading the X-Files*. New York: Syracuse University Press, 1996.

Le Grice, Malcolm. *Experimental Cinema in the Digital Age*. London: British Film Institute, 2001.

Lebow, Alisa. "Memory Once Removed: Indirect Memory and Transitive Autobiography in Chantal Akerman's *D'Est*." *Camera Obscura* vol. 18, no. 1 (2003): 35–83.

Lee, Loyd E., ed. *World War II in Asia and the Pacific and the War's Aftermath, with General Themes: A Handbook of Literature and Research*. Westport, CT: Greenwood Press, 1998.

Leger, Grindon. "Q & A: Poetics of the Documentary Film Interview." *Velvet Light Trap* no. 60 (Fall 2007): 4–12.

Levi, Niel and Rothberg, Michael, eds. *The Holocaust: Theoretical Readings*. New Brunswick, NJ: Rutgers University Press, 2003.

Levi, Primo. *Survival in Auschwitz*. Translated by Stuart Woolf. New York: Collier Books, 1961.

—*The Drowned and the Saved*. New York: Vintage, 1989.

Lichtner, Giacomo. *Film and the Shoah in France and Italy*. Portland, OR: Vallentine Mitchell, 2008.

Liebman, Stuart. "*If this Be a Man . . .* Eichmann on Trial in *The Specialist*." *Cineaste* vol. 27, no. 2 (Spring 2002): 40–2.

—"The Art of Memory: Andrzej Wajda's War Trilogy." *Cineaste* vol. 32, no. 1 (Winter 2006): 42–7.

—"*Man on the Tracks/Eroica/Bad Luck/Passenger*." *Cineaste* vol. 32, no. 2 (Spring 2007): 62–5.

—"*Verdict on Auschwitz*." *Cineaste* vol. 32, no. 4 (Fall 2007): 59–61.

Liebman, Stuart, ed. *Claude Lanzmann's Shoah: Key Essays*. New York: Oxford University Press, 2007.

Liebman, Stuart and Quart, Leonard. "Czech Films of the Holocaust." *Cineaste* vol. 22, no. 1 (April 1996): 49–51.

— "Lost and Found." *Cineaste* vol. 22, no. 4 (March 1997): 43–6.

Liehm, Antonín J. *Closely Watched Films: The Czechoslovak Experience*. White Planes, NY: International Arts and Sciences Press, Inc., 1974.

Lipman, Steve. *Laughter in Hell: The Use of Humor during the Holocaust*. Norhvale, NJ: Jason Aronson, Inc., 1991.

Listoe, Daniel. "Seeing Nothing: Allegory and the Holocaust's Absent Dead." *SubStance* vol. 35, no. 2 (2006): 51–70.

Loewy, Hanno. "The Mother of All Holocaust Films?: Wanda Jakubowska's Auschwitz trilogy." *Historical Journal of Film, Radio and Television* vol. 24, no. 2 (2004): 179–204.

Loshitzky, Yosefa, ed. *Spielberg's Holocaust: Critical Perspectives on Schindler's List*. Bloomington: Indiana University Press, 1997.

Losson, Nicolas. "Notes on the Images of the Camps." Translated by Annette Michelson. *October* vol. 90 (Autumn 1999): 25–35.

Lustig, Arnost. *Darkness Casts No Shadows*. Translated by Jeanne Nemocova. Evanston, IL: Northwestern University Press, 1985.

—*Diamonds of the Night*. Translated by Jeanne Nemocova. Evanston, IL: Northwestern University Press, 1986.

Ma, Sheng-mei. "*The Great Dictator* and *Maus*: 'The Comical' Before and After the Holocaust." *Proteus* vol. 12, no. 2 (1995): 47–50.

MacDonald, Scott. "Lost Lost Lost over *Lost Lost Lost*." *Cinema Journal* vol. 25, no. 2 (Winter 1986): 20–34.

—"Su Friedrich: Reappropriations." *Film Quarterly* vol. 41, no. 2 (Winter 1987–88): 34–43.

—*A Critical Cinema 4: Interviews with Independent Filmmakers*. Berkeley: University of California Press, 2005.

Manchel, Frank. "A Reel Witness: Steven Spielberg's Representation of the Holocaust in *Schindler's List*." *The Journal of Modern History* vol. 67, no. 1 (March 1995): 83–100.

Mandel, Naomi. "Rethinking 'After Auschwitz': Against a Rhetoric of the Unspeakable in Holocaust Writing." *Boundary 2* vol. 28, no. 2 (2001): 203–28.

Marcus, Millicent. *After Fellini: National Cinema in the Postmodern Age*. Baltimore: The John Hopkins University Press, 2002.

Margry, Karel. "*Theresienstadt* (1944–1945): The Nazi Propaganda Film Depicting the Concentration Camp as Paradise," *Historical Journal of Film, Radio & Television* vol. 12, no. 2 (June 1992): 145–63.

—"The First Theresienstadt Film (1942)," *Historical Journal of Film, Radio, and Television* vol. 19, no. 3 (1999): 309–37.

Marotti, Maria Ornella, ed. *Italian Women Writers from the Renaissance to the Present: Revisiting the Canon*. University Park, Pennsylvania: The Pennsylvania State University Press, 1996.

Marquis de Sade. *The 120 Days of Sodom and Other Writing*. Translated by Austryn Wainhouse and Richard Seaver. New York: Grove Weidenfeld, 1987.

Mason, Ann L. "Nazism and Postwar German Literary Style." *Contemporary Literature* vol. 17, no. 1 (Winter 1976): 63–83.

Mathijs, Ernest and Mendik, Xavier, eds. *Alternative Europe: Eurotrash and Exploitation Cinema Since 1945*. New York: Wallflower Press, 2004.

Mazierska, Ewa. "Wanda Jakubowska's Cinema of Commitment." *European Journal of Women's Studies* vol. 8, no. 2 (May 2001): 221–38.

—"Multifunctional Chopin: the Representation of Fryderyk Chopin in Polish Films." *Historical Journal of Film, Radio and Television* vol. 2 (June 2004): 253–68.

McCarty, John. *The Sleaze Merchants: Adventures in Exploitation Filmmaking*. New York: St. Martin's Griffin, 1995.

Mellen, Joan. *Filmguide to* The Battel of Algiers. Bloomington: Indiana University Press, 1973.

Merewether, Charles, ed. *The Archive*. Cambridge: The MIT Press, 2006.

Metz, Walter C. "'Show Me the Shoah!': Generic Experience and Spectatorship in Popular Representations of the Holocaust." *Shofar: An Interdisciplinary Journal of Jewish Studies* vol. 27, no. 1 (Fall 2008): 16–35.

Middleton, Jason. "The Subject of Torture: Regarding the Pain of Americans in *Hostel*." *Cinema Journal* vol. 49, no. 4 (Summer 2010): 1–24.

Miller, Cynthia J. "The 'B' Movie Goes to War in *Hitler, Beast of Berlin* (1939)." *Film & History: An Interdisciplinary Journal of Film and Television Studies* vol. 36, no. 1 (2006): 58–64.

Miller, Judith. *One, by One, by One: Facing the Holocaust*. New York: Simon and Schuster, 1990.

Milner, Iris. "The 'Gray Zone' Revisited: The Concentrationary Universe in Ka. Tzetnik's Literary Testimony." *Jewish Social Studies: History, Culture, and Society* vol. 14, no. 2 (Winter 2008): 113–55.

Milton, Sybil. "The Camera as Weapon: Documentary Photography and the Holocaust." *Simon Wiesenthal Center Annual* vol. 1 (1984): 45–68.

Mintz, Alan L. *Popular Culture and the Shaping of Holocaust Memory in America*. Seattle: University of Washington Press, 2001.

Moretti, Franco. *Signs Taken for Wonders: Essays in the Sociology of Literary Forms.* Translated by Susan Fischer, et al. London: Verso, 1983.

Morris, Errol Interview by Roy Grundmann and Cynthia Rockwell. "The Truth Is Not Subjective: An Interview with Errol Morris." *Cineaste* vol. 25, no. 3 (2000): 4–9.

Morris, Marla. *Curriculum and the Holocaust: Competing Sites of Memory and Representation.* Mahwah, NJ: Lawrence Erlbaum Associates, 2001.

Moskowitz, Gene. "The Uneasy East." *Sight and Sound* vol. 27, no. 3 (Winter 1957): 136–40.

Mruklik, Barbara. "Wiernosc sobie. Rozmowa z Wanda Jakubowska." *Kino* vol. 6 (1985): 5–9, 20–21.

Müller, Filip. *Eyewitness Auschwitz: Three Years in the Gas Chamber.* Tranlated by Susanne Flatauer. Chicago: Ivan R. Dee; the United States Holocaust Memorial Museum, 1979.

Mulvey, Laura. *Visual and Other Pleasures.* Bloomington: Indiana University Press, 1989.

Murray, Bruce A. and Wickham, Christopher J., eds. *From the Past: The Historiography of German Cinema and Television.* Carbondale: Southern Illinois University Press, 1992.

Myers, D. G. "Jews without Memory: *Sophie's Choice* and the Ideology of Liberal Anti-Judaism." *American Literary History* vol. 13, no. 3 (Autumn 2001): 499–529.

Napier, Susan. *Anime: From Akira to Princess Mononoke Experiencing Contemporary Japanese Animation.* New York: Palgrave, 2001.

Neale, Steve. "Melodrama and Tears." *Screen* vol. 26, no. 6 (November–December 1986): 6–22.

Newman, Kim. "The Keep." *Monthly Film Bulletin* vol. 52, no. 615 (April 1985): 127–8.

—"Torture Garden." *Sight & Sound* vol. 16, no. 6 (June 2006): 28–31.

Nichols, Bill. *Representing Reality: Issues and Concepts in Documentary.* Bloomington: Indiana University Press, 1991.

—"The Memory of Loss: Péter Forgács's Saga of Family Life and Social Hell." *Film Quarterly* vol. 56, no. 4 (2003): 2–12.

Nichols, Bill, ed. *Movie and Methods volume I.* Berkeley: University of California Press, 1976.

Niv, Kobi. *Life Is Beautiful, but Not for Jews: Another View of the Film by Benigni.* Translated by Jonathan Beyrak Lev. Lanham, MD: The Scarecrow Press Inc., 2003.

Novak, Antonin. *Films and Filmmakers in Czechoslovakia.* Translated by George Theiner. Prague: Orbis, 1968.

Nowell-Smith, Geoffrey. *Luchino Visconti.* New York: The Viking Press, 1973.

Nunn, Heather. "Errol Morris: Documentary as Psychic Drama." *Screen* vol. 45, no. 4 (Winter 2004): 413–22.

Nyiszli, Miklos. *Auschwitz: A Doctor's Eyewitness Account.* Translated by Tibère Kremer and Richard Seaver. New York: Frederick Fell Inc., 1960.

O'Pray, Michael. "From Dada to Junk: Bruce Conner and the Found-Footage Film." *Monthly Film Bulletin* (October 1987): 315–19.

Oesterreich, T. K. *Die Bessessenheit.* English ed. as *Possession: Demoniacal and Other among Primitive Races, in Antiquity, the Middle Ages, and Modern Times.* Translated by D. Ibberson. New Hyde Park, NY: University Books, 1966.

Ofer, Dalia and Weitzman, Lenore J., eds. *Women in the Holocaust.* New Haven, CT: Yale University Press, 1998.

Orr, John and Ostrowska, Elzbieta, eds. *The Cinema of Roman Polanski: Dark Spaces of the World.* New York: Wallflower Press, 2006.

Padover, Saul K. "The Ilse Koch Case." *The Nation* vol. 167, no. 19 (November 6, 1948): 519–20.

Phillips, Gene. "Exile in Hollywood: John Schlesinger." *Literature Film Quarterly* vol. 5, no. 2 (Spring 1977): 98–104.

Picart, Caroline Joan Kay S. and Frank, David A. *Frames of Evil: the Holocaust as Horror in American Film.* Carbondale: Southern Illinois University Press, 2006.

Picart, Caroline Joan Kay S. and McKahan, Jason Grant. "*Apt Pupil*'s Misogyny, Homoeroticism and Homophobia: Sadomasochism and the Holocaust Film." *Jump Cut: A Review of Contemporary Cinema* vol. 45 (2002): available at http://www.ejumpcut.org/archive/jc45.2002/picart/index.html.

Polt, Harriet R. "Notes on the New Stylization." *Film Quarterly* vol. 19, no. 3 (Spring 1966): 25–9.

Popkin, Jeremy D. "Ka-Tzetnik 135633: The Survivor as Pseudonym." *New Literary History: A Journal of Theory and Interpretation* vol. 33, no. 2 (Spring 2002): 343–55.

Price, Brian. "Pain and the Limits of Representation." *Framework: the Journal of Cinema and Media* vol. 47, no. 2 (Fall 2006): 22–9.

Prince, Stephen, ed. *Screening Violence.* New Brunswick, NJ: Rutgers University Press, 2000.

Przyrembel, Alexandra. "Transfixed by an Image: Ilse Koch, the 'Kommandeuse of Buchenwald.'" Translated by Pamela Selwyn. *German History* vol. 19, no. 3 (October 2001): 369–99.

Rapaport, Lynn. "Holocaust Pornography: Profaning the Sacred in *Ilsa, She-Wolf of the SS*." *Shofar: An Interdisciplinary Journal of Jewish Studies* vol. 22, no. 1 (Fall 2003): 53–79.

Rappaport, Shloyme Zanvl (aka An-Ski, Solomon.), *The Dybbuk: Between Two Worlds.* Translated by S. Morris Engel. South Bend, IN: Regnery/Gateway, 1979.

Reid, Donald. "Germaine Tillion and Resistance to the Vichy Syndrome." *History & Memory* vol. 15, no. 2 (Fall–Winter 2003): 36–63.

Reimer, Robert C., ed. *Cultural History Through a National Socialist Lens: Essays on the Cinema of the Third Reich.* Rochester, NY: Camden House, 2002.

Renov, Michael. "Historische Diskurse des Unvorstellbaren: Péter Forgács's *The Maelstrom*." *Montage/av* vol. 11, no. 1 (2002): 26–40.

—"Family Secrets: Alan Berliner's *Nobody's Business* and the (American) Jewish Autobiographical Film." *Framework: The Journal of Cinema and Media* vol. 49, no. 1 (Spring 2008): 55–65.

Renov, Michael, ed. *Theorizing Documentary.* New York: Routledge, 1993.

Renov, Michael and Suderburg, Erika, eds. *Resolutions: Contemporary Video Practices.* Minneapolis: The University of Minnesota Press, 1997.

Riding, Alan. "Images of Unspeakable Horror Stir Voices to Debate." *New York Times*, March 14, 2001, E 2.

Ringelheim, Joan Miriam. "The Unethical and the Unspeakable: Women and the Holocaust." *Simon Wiesenthal Center Annual* vol. 1 (1984): 69–87.

Rittner, Carol and Roth, John K., eds. *Different Voices: Women and the Holocaust.* St. Paul, MN: Paragon House, 1993.

Rosenfeld, Alvin H. *A Double Dying: Reflections on Holocaust Literature.* Bloomington: Indiana University Press, 1980.

Rosenthal, Alan, ed. *New Challenges for Documentary.* Berkeley: University of California Press, 1988.

Rothberg, Michael. "Between Auschwitz and Algeria: Multidirectional Memory and the Counterpublic Witness." *Critical Inquiry* vol. 33, no. 1 (Autumn 2006): 158–84.

Rothenberg, Michael. *Traumatic Realism: The Demands of Holocaust Representation.* Minneapolis: University of Minnesota Press, 2000.

Rothman, William. *Documentary Film Classics.* Cambridge: Cambridge University Press, 1997.

Rowe, Carel. "Illuminating Lucifer." *Film Quarterly* vol. 27, no. 4 (Summer 1974): 24–33.

Ruoff, Jeffrey K. "Home Movies of the Avant-Garde: Jonas Mekas and the New York Art World." *Cinema Journal* vol. 30, no. 3 (Spring 1991): 6–28.

Rutsky, R. L. and Macdonald, Bradley J., eds. *Strategies for Theory: From Marx to Madonna.* New York: State University of New York Press, 2003.

Rybin, Steven. *The Cinema of Michael Mann.* Lanham: Lexington Books, 2007.

Said, Edward. *Orientalism*. New York: Vintage Books, 1994.

Samberg, Joel. *Reel Jewish*. Middle Village, NY: Jonathan David Publishers, 2000.

Santer, Eric. "The Trouble with Hitler: Postwar German Aesthetics and the Legacy of Fascism." *New German Critique* 57 (Autumn 1992): 5–24.

Saxton, Libby. *Haunted Images: Film, Ethics, Testimony and the Holocaust*. New York: Wallflower Press, 2008.

Scarry, Elaine. *The Body in Pain: the Making and Unmaking of the World*. New York: Oxford University Press, 1985.

Schlam, Helena Frenkil. "Contemporary Scribes: Jewish American Cartoonists." *Shofar: An Interdisciplinary Journal of Jewish Studies* vol. 20, no. 1 (Fall 2001): 94–112.

Schnaper, Nathan and Schnaper, H. William. "A few kind words for the Devil." *Journal of Religion and Health* vol. 8, no. 2 (April 1969): 107–22.

Schubart, Rikke. *Super Bitches and Action Babes: The Female Hero in Popular Cinema, 1970–2006*. Jefferson, NC: McFarland & Company Inc., 2007.

Schulman, Peter and Lubich, Frederick A., eds. *The Marketing of Eros: Performance, Sexuality, Consumer Culture*. Essen, Germany: Blaue Eule, 2003.

Shandler, Jeffrey. *While America Watches: Televising the Holocaust*. New York: Oxford University Press, 1999.

Sicher, Efraim, ed. *Holocaust Novelists*. Detroit: Gale, 2004.

Silverman, Kaja. *Flesh of My Flesh*. Stanford: Stanford University Press, 2009.

Silverman, Max. "Interconnected Histories: Holocaust and Empire in the Cultural Imaginary." *French Studies* vol. 62, no. 4 (October 2008): 417–28.

Skloot, Robert. "'We Will Never Die': The Success and Failure of a Holocaust Pageant." *Theatre Journal* vol. 37, no. 2 (May 1985): 167–80.

Skoller, Jeffrey. *Shadow, Specters, Shards: Making History in Avant-Garde Film*. Minneapolis: University of Minnesota Press, 2005.

Sobchack, Vivian, ed. *The Persistence of History: Cinema, Television, and the Modern Event*. New York and London: Routledge, 1996.

Sontag, Susan. *On Photography*. New York: Farrar, Straus and Giroux, 1978.

—*Under the Sign of Saturn*. New York: Farrar, Straus, Giroux, 1980.

Spiegelman, Art. *Maus: A Survivor's Tale: My Father Bleeds History Volume I*. New York: Pantheon Books, 1986.

—*Maus: A Survivor's Tale: And Here My Troubles Began Volume II*. New York: Pantheon Books, 1991.

Spieker, Sven. "At the Center of Mitteleuropa: A Conversation with Péter Forgács," *Art Margins*. Monday 20, 2002: no pagination. Available online at: http://www.artmargins. com

Stanley, Alessandra. "The Funniest Italian You've Probably Never Heard Of." *New York Times Magazine*. October 11, 1998: 44

Stastny, Peter. "From Exploitation to Self-Reflection: Representing Persons with Psychiatric Disabilities in Documentary Film." *Literature and Medicine* vol. 17, no. 1 (Spring 1998): 68–90.

Stein, Alexander. "Music and Trauma in Polanski's *The Pianist* (2002)." *Psychoanalytic Inquiry* vol. 27, no. 4 (September 2007): 440–54.

—"The Sound of Memory: Music and Acoustic Origins." *American Imago* vol. 64, no. 1 (Spring 2007): 59–85.

Steinberg, Stefan. "An Interview with Radu Mihaileanu, the Director of *Train of Life*: 'We have to learn to articulate these deep emotions,'" World Socialist webSite (March 31, 2000): no pagination. Available at: http://www.wsws.org.

Strub, Whitney. "The Clearly Obscene and the Queerly Obscene: Heteronormativity and Obscenity in Cold War Los Angeles." *American Quarterly* vol. 60, no. 2 (June 2008): 373–98.

Suárez, Juan. "Kenneth Anger's *Scorpio Rising*: Avant-Garde Textuality and Social Performance." *Cinefocus* vol. 2, no. 2 (1992): 20–31.

Suhl, Yuri, ed. *They Fought Back: The Story of the Jewish Resistance in Nazi Europe*. New York: Crown Publishers Inc., 1967.

Suleiman, Susan Rubin. "Jewish Assimilation in Hungary, the Holocaust, and Epic Film: Reflections on István Szabó's *Sunshine*." *The Yale Journal of Criticism* vol. 14, no. 1 (Spring 2001): 233–52.

Sullivan, K. E. "Ed Gein and the Figure of the Transgendered Serial Killer," *Jump Cut* vol. 43 (July 2000): 38–47.

Syberberg, Hans-Jürgen. "Interview with Hans-Jürgen Syberberg." *The Threepenny Review* 2 (Summer 1980): 4–6.

Syberberg, Hans-Jürgen, et al. "Interview: Our Hitler as Visual Politics." *Performing Arts Journal* vol. 4, no. 3 (1980): 50–8.

Symanski, Richard and Burley, Nancy. "The Jewish Colony of Sosua." *Annals of the Association of American Geographers* vol. 63, no. 3 (September 1973): 366–78.

Szeintuch, Yechiel. "The Myth of the Salamander in the Work of Ka-Tzetnik." *Partial Answers: Journal of Literature and the History of Ideas* vol. 3, no. 1 (January 2005): 101–32.

Szpilman, Wladyslaw. *The Pianist: The Extraordinary True Story of One Man's Survival in Warsaw 1939–1945*. Translated by Anteha Bell. New York: Picador, 1999.

Taylor, Paul A. Interview by Srecko Horvat. *International Journal of Žižek Studies* vol. 1 (2007): 1–7.

Temple, Michael et al., eds. *For Ever Godard*. London: Black Dog Publishing, 2004.

Testaferri, Ada, ed. *Donna: Women in Italian Culture*. Ottawa: University of Toronto Italian Studies; Dovehouse Editions, 1989.

Tonetti, Claretta Micheletti. *Bernardo Bertolucci: The Cinema of Ambiguity*. New York: Twayne Publishers, 1995.

—*Luchino Visconti*. New York: Twayne Publishers, 1997.

Trommler, Frank. "Germany's Past as an Artifact." *The Journal of Modern History* vol. 61, no. 4 (December 1989): 724–35.

Truffaut, François. *The Films In My Life*. Translated by Leonard Mayhew. New York: Simon and Schuster, 1978.

—*Hitchcock*. New York: A Touchstone Book; Simon and Schuster, 1985.

Tsiolkas, Christos. "The Atheist's Shoah: Roman Polanski's *The Pianist*." *Senses of Cinema* vol. 26 (May–June 2003): no pagination.

Turim, Maureen. *Flashbacks in Film: Memory and History*. New York: Routledge, 1989.

Twitchell, James. *Dreadful Pleasures: An Anatomy of Modern Horror*. New York: Oxford University Press, 1985.

UCS Shoah Foundation Institute for Visual History and Education. "Interviewer Guidelines." (2007). Available from http://www.usc.edu/vhi

Van Alphen, Ernst. "Visual Archives as Preposterous History." *Art History* vol. 30, no. 3 (June 2007): 364–83.

Van der Knaap, Ewout, ed. *Uncovering the Holocaust: The International Reception of Night and Fog*. New York: Wallflower Press, 2006.

Vande Winkel, Roel. "Nazi Germany's Fritz Hippler, 1909–2002," *Historical Journal of Film, Radio and Television* vol. 23, no. 2 (2003): 91–9.

Viano, Maurizio. "*Life Is Beautiful*: Reception, Allegory, and Holocaust Laughter." *Film Quarterly* vol. 53, no. 1 (Autumn 1999): 26–34.

Vicari, Justin. "Fragments of Utopia: A Meditation on Fassbinder's Treatment of Anti-Semitism and the Third Reich," *Postmodern Culture* vol. 16, no. 2 (January 2006): no pagination.

Von Kellenbach, Katharina. "God's Love and Women's Love: Prison Chaplains Counsel the Wives of Nazi Perpetrators." *Journal of Feminist Studies in Religion* vol. 20, no. 2 (Fall 2004): 7–24.

Walker, Janet. "The Traumatic Paradox: Documentary Films, Historical Fictions, and Cataclysmic Past Events." *Signs* vol. 22, no. 4 (Summer 1997): 803–25.

—*Trauma Cinema: Documenting Incest and the Holocaust*. Berkeley: University of California Press, 2005.

Walsh, Russell. "Obscenities Offstage: Melbourne's Gay Saunas and the Limits of Representation." PhD diss., Victoria University, 2007.

Ward, Janet. "Holocaust Film in the Post-9/11 Era: New Directions in Staging and Emplotment." *Pacific Coast Philology* vol. 39 (2004): 29–41.

Warren, Charles, ed. *Beyond Document: Essays on Nonfiction Film*. Hanover, NH: Wesleyan University Press, 1996.

Wasserman, Steve and Syberberg, Hans-Jürgen. "Interview with Hans-Jürgen Syberberg." *The Threepenny Review* vol. 2 (Summer 1980): 4–6.

White, Hayden. *The Content of the Form: Narrative Discourse and Historical Representation*. Baltimore: The John Hopkins University Press, 1987.

Wiesel, Elie. *Souls on Fire: Portraits and Legends of Hasidic Masters*. Translated by Marion Wiesel. New York: Simon and Schuster, 1972.

—"Trivializing the Holocaust: Semi-Fact and Semi-Fiction." *New York Times*, April 16, 1978.

Wiesenthal, Simon. *The Murderers Among Us*. Edited by Joseph Wechsberg. New York: McGraw-Hill Book Company, 1967.

Williams, Linda. "Film Bodies: Gender, Genre, and Excess," *Film Quarterly* vol. 44, no. 4 (Summer 1991): 2–13.

Wood, Robin. "Return of the Repressed." *Film Comment* vol. 14, no. 4 (July–August 1978): 25–32.

—"Gods and Monsters." *Film Comment* vol. 14, no. 5 (September–October 1978): 19–25.

Wright, Elizabeth and Wright, Edmond, eds. *The Zizek Reader*. Oxford: Blackwell, 1999.

Yahil, Leni. *The Holocaust: The Fate of European Jewry, 1932–1945*. Translated by Ina Friedman and Haya Galai. New York: Oxford University Press, 1990.

Zelizer, Barbie, ed. *Visual Culture and the Holocaust*. New Brunswick, NJ: Rutgers University Press, 2001.

Zizek, Slavoj. "Much Ado about a Thing," in *For They Know Not What They Do: Enjoyment as a Political Factor*. New York: Verso, 1991: 229–77.

—"Camp Comedy." *Sight and Sound* vol. 10, no. 4 (April 2000): 26–9.

Zryd, Michael. "Found Footage Film as Discursive Metahistory: Craig Baldwin's *Tribulation 99*." *The Moving Image* vol. 3, no. 2 (Fall 2003): 40–61.

Index

CPSIA information can be obtained
at www.ICGtesting.com
Printed in the USA
LVOW10s0346231217
560542LV00023B/441/P